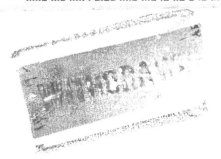

Elements of Mathematical Linguistics

JANUA
LINGUARUM Series Maior 110

Studia Memoriae
Nicolai van Wijk Dedicata

edenda curat

C. H. van Schooneveld
Indiana University

Elements
of Mathematical
Linguistics

Aleksej V. Gladkij
and
Igor A. Mel'čuk

edited by
John Lehrberger

Mouton Publishers
Berlin · New York · Amsterdam

Originally published under the title:
Èlementy matematičeskoj lingvistiki (Moscow: Nauka, 1969)

Library of Congress Cataloging in Publication Data

Gladkij, A. V. (Aleksej Vsevolodovič), 1928–
  Elements of mathematical linguistics.

  (Janua linguarum. Series maior; 110)
  Bibliography: p.
  1. Mathematical linguistics. I. Mel'čuk, I. A.
(Igor' Aleksandrovič), 1932–   II. Lehrberger,
John. III. Title. IV. Series.
P138.G513   410'.72   81-38391
ISBN 90-279-3118-6   AACR2

ISBN 90 279 3118 6

Editor's Preface

Mathematical linguistics enjoys considerable popularity these days – even if there is a good deal of uncertainty about just what it is. Prospective linguists are anxious to find out how much mathematics will be required of them and some would no doubt like to know which areas within linguistics might safely be considered non-mathematical. The increasing use of the formalisms of mathematics and logic in describing the structure of human language has given rise to a large field of study called *formal linguistics* and, as expected in the age of the computer, there is now a very active field called *computational linguistics*. These developments were part of the 'revolution' in linguistics generally associated with the advent of transformational generative grammar. Of course, mathematics had been used before that revolution, but its role changed radically in the 1960's and 1970's. The emphasis on formal rules and derivations in syntax brought mathematics of a certain type into the fore-ground, and the attempt to formalize semantic representation in grammars of natural languages sent linguists scurrying to books on mathematical logic.

Now, one might take mathematical linguistics to include any mathematical study of human language or of formal languages that have some of the properties of human language: for example, statistical studies of texts (word frequency counts, etc.), studies of the algebraic properties of generative grammars and the languages they generate, use of computers in automatic translation, applications of probability theory in glottochronology and in the construction of probabilistic grammars, use of recursive function theory in the study of generative grammars, representation of linguistic structure by directed graphs, mathematical analysis of speech sounds in acoustic phonetics, etc. It is difficult to say where this list would end since mathematics can be applied in some way to nearly any topic in linguistics.

But the notion that mathematical linguistics is the collection of ALL mathematical studies of linguistic phenomena is rejected at the outset in this book. The authors take a point of view which may seem rather narrow to some readers: (1) that mathematical linguistics is a particular mathematical discipline, (2) that it is essentially non-quantitative, and (3) that it is situated within the theory of algorithms. Their starting point is the concept of language as an effective function which maps meanings onto texts, or vice versa. The study of this function constitutes the discipline of mathematical linguistics. It follows that this book is not simply a review of possible uses of mathematics in linguistics, but an account of how a particular branch of mathematics is involved in the meaning-text relation.

The question of just what constitutes mathematical linguistics is to some extent a terminological one. Bar-Hillel wrote (1964: 185): 'the adjective "mathematical" is quite all right if "mathematics" is understood in the sense of "theory of formal systems" ', and he suggested that this discipline might better be called 'algebraic linguistics'. It may be of interest to see how this topic is treated by other writers in the field, so let us compare just a few.

Solomon Marcus (1967) introduces the reader to the use of mathematical modeling for investigating language structure. In his book, which assumes a considerable degree of mathematical sophistication on the part of the reader, Marcus is concerned with analytic rather than generative grammar: analytic grammar takes a language as given in the form of a certain subset of strings over some vocabulary and provides a structural description of these strings (sentences). The description referred to is made from the point of view of classical structural linguistics, with the emphasis on distributional relations of words and substrings within sentences.

In Harris (1968) the author formulates an abstract system to characterize natural language, starting from the data of language and 'finding within the data such relations as can be organized into a suitable model'. That model is developed within the framework of Harris's theory of transformations, which is outlined in the same book. The abstract system he finds adequate to characterize the actual sentences of natural language is expressed in terms of a set of primitive arguments and five sets of operators whose operands are either primitive arguments or resultants of operations. Recursivity follows from the application of operators to resultants.

In contrast with the approach of Marcus or Harris, Baron Brainerd (1971) and Robert Wall (1972) introduce a variety of mathematical topics, as such, to the linguist. They include material from logic, sets, functions, relations, Boolean algebra and the mathematical theory of generative grammars. Brainerd relegates to an appendix a brief discussion of algorithms – a topic which is of central importance to Gladkij and Mel'čuk. Wall takes a definite stand on the use of the term 'mathematical linguistics': for him it means 'the study of formal models of generative grammars and closely allied devices called abstract automata' (p. xiii).

The relation between automata theory and mathematical linguistics had been pointed out by Bar-Hillel in a 1962 lecture *The Role of Grammatical*

Models in Machine Translation (included in Bar-Hillel 1964): 'just as
mathematical logic had its special offspring to deal with digital computers,
i.e., the *theory of automata*, so structural linguistics had its special offspring
to deal with mechanical structure determination, i.e., *algebraic linguistics*,
also called, when this application is particularly stressed, *computational
linguistics* or *mechano-linguistics*. As a final surprise, it has recently turned out
that these two disciplines, automata theory and algebraic linguistics, exhibit
extremely close relationships which at times amount to practical identity'
(pp. 186–7).

Automata theory has certainly played a key role in the study of formal
grammars, as can be seen for example in the early work of Noam Chomsky. In
particular, Chomsky established important results on the equivalence of
classes of automata and generative grammars in 'Formal Properties of Grammars'
(Chomsky 1963). The relation between formal grammars and automata has
been examined in detail by various authors (e.g., Hopcroft and Ullman 1969,
Gladkij 1973) and many investigations have been carried out on the generative
power of grammars proposed for natural languages, culminating in the proof
by Peters and Ritchie (1971, 1973) that transformational grammars of the
kind proposed by Chomsky (1965) have the weak generative capacity of type-0
grammars, i.e. that they are equivalent to Turing machines and can generate all
recursively enumerable sets. Gladkij and Mel'čuk examine the properties
of different classes of grammars in some detail, but they do not discuss the
work of Peters and Ritchie.

Gladkij and Mel'čuk open their book with an explanation of their view of
mathematical linguistics in Chapter 1. After presenting the general concept
of formal grammar in Chapter 2, they discuss the hierarchy of generative
grammars (weak generative capacity) in Chapter 3 and examine the possibility
of describing natural languages by means of generative grammars in Chapter
4. Chapter 5 deals with internal properties of generative grammars, including
estimates of derivational complexity. Chapter 6 includes a discussion of
categorial grammars and predictive analyzers, logical analysis of language,
semantic languages, and the modeling of linguistic research. Reprints of three
articles by the authors form a supplement at the end of the book. In one
of these articles, 'Tree Grammars: A Formalism for Syntactic Transformations
in Natural Languages,' they stress the importance of separating relationships
of linear arrangement and relationships of 'syntactic contingency' (e.g.,
dependency): 'we consider it desirable to include two different mechanisms
in the apparatus for describing the syntax of natural language: one should
deal with syntactic structures which are devoid of linear order, and the other
should map appropriately developed structures into word strings'. Syntactic
structure, including 'surface structure', is represented by dependency trees and

does not specify the order of the terminal elements. If in a given language a particular syntactic relation is manifested by a specific word order, the final mapping carries the corresponding surface structure into a string of words in the proper order.

The main body of this book does not require more than a rudimentary knowledge of mathematics on the part of the reader. There are a number of books available, in addition to those already referred to, whose purpose is to provide general mathematical background considered essential for the study of formal linguistics (e.g., Barbara Hall Partee, 1978), but the present book does not offer a background course in mathematics for linguists. The authors, a mathematician and a linguist, develop the theory of formal grammars at a leisurely pace, backing up the formal presentation with well motivated informal discussions. They have included numerous applications of the theory to various subsystems of Russian, with English glosses provided for the examples. Important theorems are listed in an appendix along with references to the pages on which they occur in the book and to proofs, which are found elsewhere.

This book provides a welcome addition to the literature on mathematical linguistics. Some familiar ground is covered in a refreshingly distinct manner and, as well, the authors present some ideas of their own which may not be so familiar to many generative grammarians. But whatever the reader's theoretical persuasion may be, he should find this a stimulating approach to the subject of mathematical linguistics based on the authors' view of language as an effective function relating meanings and texts.

J. Lehrberger
University of Montreal

Authors' Preface

Many believe there is only one thing more pleasant than finishing a book: to finish revising the translation of your book into a foreign language. One of the authors at least (I.A. Mel'čuk), fully shares this opinion, while the other (A.V. Gladkij) is prone to join in, although he harbors some reservations (as he seems to know still more pleasant things). It so happens that at this moment we have just finished the revision job and, being in high spirits, are tackling the next most pleasant duty: writing the preface.

Three remarks would seem appropriate in view of the fact that more than a decade separates the completion of this book from its appearance in English:

1. During the time elapsed we have come to realize, first, that the book has more lacunae than we had supposed, including some essential ones; and, second, that the wording of several paragraphs should have been radically altered. We do not intend to enumerate here all such deficiences but it seems that at least one deserves mention. Given the present composition of our material and the manner in which it is presented, a special section dealing with f o r m a l   r e p r e s e n t a t i o n   o f   s e n t e n c e   s t r u c t u r e   in natural languages would have been of great help; we have in mind, in particular, i m m e d i a t e   c o n s t i t u e n t   (or   p h r a s e - s t r u c t u r e) vs. d e p e n d e n c y   t r e e s   — two important concepts which are used throughout the book without definition or even explanation. (For a systematic description of both concepts, though somewhat more formal than accepted in the present book, see Gladkij 1973: App. I.)

2. The period 1967–1976 has witnessed a genuinely beneficial expansion of mathematical linguistics in the most diverse directions. A mere enumeration of corresponding achievements would clearly go beyond the limits of a normal preface, so we shall content ourselves with simply mentioning only five of the most salient points.

— New promising results in classical trends of the theory of Chomsky grammars (*Syntactic Structures* through *Aspects*, inclusive), e.g., those concerning measures of derivational complexity (cf. below, pp. 83–85).

— New dimensions in the study of generative grammars, primarily the investigation of g u i d e d   d e r i v a t i o n s in grammars (i.e., restrictions on the order in which rules of the given grammar may be applied; see references on p. 111).

— The emergence of a completely new kind of formal grammar: devices for processing trees rather than strings, which one is tempted to call d e n d r o g r a m m a r s. Here also belong some works suggesting a formal apparatus for Chomsky transformations. (On dendrogrammars see Gladkij — Mel'čuk 1975, with further references; also included in this volume, pp. 151–187.)

— Active investigation of so-called a b s t r a c t   f a m i l i e s   o f l a n g u a g e s (AFL's), concentrating on algebraic properties of different classes of formal languages.

— The publication of a great number of papers exploring the possibilities of applying the expressive means of the language of mathematical logic (such as predicate notation, etc.) to the description of natural-language semantics. This is perhaps one of the most promising trends of today's mathematical linguistics, considering the eminent role of semantic studies in modern linguistics. However, a detailed discussion of relevant problems would lead us too far.

Needless to say, an attempt to cover all the above topics, even in the form of a concise outline, would call for another, altogether different book.

3. Numerous books have been published since 1970 on the subject of mathematical linguistics and, more generally, on mathematical means and methods of studying natural languages. The vast majority of these books, especially those of an introductory nature, are in English. We shall name but five of them: Brainerd 1971, Gross 1972, Wall 1972, Kimball 1973, and Hall-Partee 1978. Yet, curiously enough, there is little intersection between our book and its American counterparts, due to the fact that the latter tend to concentrate on initiating linguists into the field of discrete mathematics and are therefore more mathematical than ours.

This in part can be seen in that existing manuals of mathematical linguistics offer, predominantly, a basic literacy course in set theory, relations and functions, automata theory, propositional and predicate calculi, etc. As for formal grammars and languages, these are as a rule discussed as purely mathematical theories strictly following the manner of presentation adopted, e.g., in Chomsky 1963, with a strong emphasis on algebraic properties and decision problems characteristic of different kinds of grammars. The present book, on the contrary, includes no introductory mathematical course: the authors' main object is formal grammars as such, and these are introduced on the basis of genuine linguistic examples accentuating the linguistic aspects of every formal device; algebraic and algorithmic properties of grammars are paid relatively less attention.

Other differences also can be pointed out which distinguish our book from other extant manuals. Thus, in the case of formal grammars the so-called transformational component (in the sense of Chomsky) is usually given a detailed description. But we give no account of Chomsky transformations at all, since no serious formalization thereof was available at the time when this manuscript was finished. In addition, we touch on mathematical means of describing natural language other than formal grammars: namely, algebraic models theory, which deals primarily with substitutability of linguistic items (see below, p. 120–125). These questions, to the best of our knowledge, are absent from other mathematical linguistics books in English – with the sole exception of Marcus 1967, which is dedicated completely to algebraic models (but is in no way a manual for beginners).

It appears, therefore, that *Elements of Mathematical Linguistics*, in its present form, has its *raison d'être*.

It would be only fair to admit that English readers of this book will be definitely handicapped since almost all of our examples are Russian and it was not feasible to replace them with English equivalents. The examples are so closely interwoven with the main body of the book that an attempt to supply new, English examples would require a radical amendment, if not an overhaul, of the manuscript.

Spring 1976
Pominovo, near Tver' (= Kalinin)

Acknowledgements

In working on this book we frequently availed ourselves of the kind assistance and advice of a number of people. The most important remarks and suggestions were offered by F.A. Dreizin, A.I. Fet, L.N. Iordanskaja, and B.A. Traxtenbrot. In addition, the manuscript was read by Ju. D. Apresjan, A.Ja. Dikovskij, O.S. Kulagina, Z.K. Litvinceva, E.V. Paduceva, V.A. Uspenskij, Ju.A. Šreider, the late A.A. Xolodovič, A.A. Zaliznjak, and some others, from whom we received many valuable comments. To all these people we express our sincere gratitude; their advice has always been taken into consideration, even if not always followed. The responsibility for the shortcomings of the book rests, of course, entirely with the authors.

We are also happy to acknowledge the friendly assistance of Kathleen Parthé (Cornell University, USA) who has generously helped us with many difficulties of style in the English version of the book, and of our editor, John Lehrberger.

Contents

Introduction

The purpose of this book is to characterize in brief the area of research, which arose recently and is known by the name of mathematical linguistics. However, it is not easy to do this. When, for example, it is necessary to answer the question 'What is differential calculus?' or 'What is topology?', what is needed is merely to find the most easily grasped and effective form of wording things which are well-known to specialists and are understood by all of them in the same way, that is to say, things which are canonized. The mathematician who takes it upon himself to explain to the unprepared reader what differential calculus is, will not, of course, initially have to solve this question for himself: he knows the answer well beforehand and should worry only about the pedagogical side of the exposition (which, of course, is in itself a quite difficult task). In our case the situation is different. Mathematical linguistics is a very young discipline which is still in the making and has not yet succeeded in acquiring traditions. There is no generally accepted point of view on its aims, methods, and boundaries. Therefore we have had to elaborate anew, to a certain extent, a point of view on this area as a whole, to ascertain its general structure, and to outline its status. Yet this book is not original research, it is rather a popularization, though not a typical one: at its basis there are no more or less traditional conceptions, but a general picture of mathematical linguistics proposed by the authors themselves. (We in no way lay claim to the definitiveness or the uniqueness of this picture. Other approaches are, of course, also possible: for example, Plath 1961; the authors, however, have chosen not to discuss them.)

From the very name 'mathematical linguistics' one can already see the connection with both mathematics and linguistics (i.e., with the study of natural languages). Therefore, the authors have tried to make this book **NB** [1] readable for mathematicians and linguists alike. However, the reader to whom the authors have principally addressed themselves is the linguist. And this is not by chance. First of all, mathematical linguistics, as it is understood in this book, is a m a t h e m a t i c a l discipline; thus, if we want both linguists and mathematicians to be able to acquaint themselves with it, we must gear the exposition to the linguists, as those in the worse position:

all that the linguists will understand here will be understood in most cases by the mathematicians, but not vice versa. Second, it is the linguist who in the first place is interested in interpretations and linguistic applications of formal structures provided by mathematical linguistics.

In connection with what has been said the authors have presented the material in such a way that no special mathematical knowledge is FORMALLY required of the reader — all the concepts used here, including even the simplest ones, are explained in the text. However, it should honestly be admitted that for a REAL understanding of this book, a good control of certain simple, but at the same time quite fundamental mathematical reasoning, is extremely desirable. In particular, it would be helpful to be acquainted with notions such as set, function, necessary condition, sufficient condition, proof by induction, etc. Let us repeat: all this is not, strictly speaking, absolutely necessary; however, actually it is difficult, although possible, to manage without this — at the price of wasting much greater efforts (since while reading this book the reader will all the same have to master all the indicated concepts).

In general it should be emphasized that the linguist who wants in some way to apply mathematics in his research, needs first of all a general mathematical background and the habit of mathematical thinking, rather than the technical apparatus of mathematics.

It will also be helpful in reading this book to be acquainted with what is known as structural linguistics, which includes works of L. Hjelmslev, L. Bloomfield, Z. Harris, N. Trubetzkoy, R. Jakobson, and others.[2] These works have no direct relation to mathematical linguistics but, in many respects, they prepared the groundwork for its emergence, having advanced a number of concepts and notions (cf., for example, the idea of immediate constituents), which form a substantial basis for the formal models of mathematical linguistics.

The works of Noam Chomsky and his school have a special place here. As opposed to the above-mentioned works, the latter are either directly related to mathematical linguistics, or are closely connected with it. Moreover, they gave the initial impetus to its development, which makes it possible to consider Noam Chomsky the founder of this new discipline. It is therefore natural that a significant part of this book (Chapters 2, 3, 4, and, in part, 5) is devoted basically to the exposition of Chomsky's theory of formal (generative) grammars. Consequently, an aquaintance with the relevant works will be extremely helpful. We recommend, first of all, Chomsky's book *Syntactic Structures* (Chomsky 1957); see also Chomsky 1961, Chomsky 1962, and Chomsky and Miller 1963; for mathematicians we also recommend Chomsky 1963.[3]

NB

However, what has been said above about mathematical knowledge applies also to special linguistic training: strictly speaking, it is not necessary either — all the concepts and facts essential for our exposition which go beyond the framework of high school grammar are explained.

Well then, what DO the authors require of the reader? FORMALLY they require nothing, i.e., no previous mathematical or linguistic knowledge; but IN ESSENCE, some mathematical and linguistic competence is presumed. (This situation is quite normal in books on mathematics: frequently, complex monographs whose reading requires great efforts even for a well-trained specialist begin with a formally correct assertion that no preliminary knowledge is assumed on the part of the reader.)

Now let us describe more precisely what we are offering the reader. In this book he will find an outline of the ideas and concepts of mathematical linguistics, which cannot provide more than a quite preliminary and most general acquaintance with it. If the desire arises for him to expand his knowledge of mathematical linguistics, for example, with the aim of working in this area himself, then he will have to turn to the specialized literature, some of which is indicated at the end of the book, on pages 140–148.

It remains for us yet to explain here our view on the considerable use of mathematics in such an especially humanitarian area as the study of human languages. It seems necessary since this view has a strong impact on the whole of our exposition. If the book were intended only for mathematicians, such an explanation would, apparently, be unnecessary; however, for many linguists (and others, perhaps) it may be useful. The point is that in linguistics this question has been discussed frequently with some vigor, even quite recently. A number of linguists find that 'mathematical linguistics' is a *contradictio in adjecto*, that language and mathematics are incompatible and have nothing in common, and that the attempts to inculcate mathematics in linguistics lead to the 'dehumanization' of the latter and thereby to its death as an independent discipline. The adherents of these views consider mathematical linguistics 'a hybrid of pseudolinguistics and pseudomathematics' (Abaev 1965: 32).

The authors of this book hold exactly the opposite position. There are, of course, many poor works about which it is wittingly said that they are an attempt to apply what little the author knows about mathematics to what little he knows about linguistics (Ju. K. Ščeglov, private communication). But mathematical linguistics must not bear the responsibility for these works — they have no relation to it (just as physics is by no means responsible for numerous projects of *perpetuum mobile*). As to the essence of the matter, we are completely convinced not only of the possibility, but also of the necessity for the mathematical description of linguistic phenomena. We will not give

here specific explanations concerning this description: such explanations
constitute the content of this book. However, we will insist that any
scientific description (including the description of language) should be
LOGICALLY COHERENT (the omission of essential[4] links of the argument is
excluded), NON-AMBIGUOUS (statements allowing more than one understanding are excluded) and quite EXPLICIT (the smuggling in of information which is
not an explicit part of the description is excluded). But such a description is a
formal, i.e. essentially a mathematical, description; this will be the case when
a sufficiently high level of formalization is attained. The word *formal* means
nothing except 'logically coherent + non-ambiguous + absolutely explicit',
so that a formal description in no way excludes an appeal to content, to
meaning (a formal description of meaning is, in particular, quite feasible,
see below, p. 112 and following). Thus, if formalization is identified with
dehumanization, seeing in the latter the greatest possible exclusion of
the human factor from the description (i.e., the subjective element, the
implicit appeal to the intuition and wit of the reader), then we are FOR
such dehumanization. Such an exclusion of the human factor from
descriptions is part and parcel of any scientific method: without this
'dehumanization' no science is possible.

This calls for two elucidations:

1. Of course, IN THE PROCESS OF CONSTRUCTION of a description (in the
process of scientific creation) intuition, wit, etc. play a leading role, and
no one will deny this. It is a question of removing the human factor from the
RESULTS of the study, from the descriptions themselves.

2. What we said above in no way means that we recognize only formalized
('mathematicized') linguistic works, denying value to all others. Nothing
of the sort! It is unquestionable that a study insufficiently clear logically, but
containing new important facts or ideas, is sometimes much more valuable
than an irreproachable formalization of a triviality. However, it is just as
unquestionable that of two works describing the same range of facts with the
same completeness, the one with greater value will be that in which the higher
degree of formalization is achieved.

Thus we proceed from the thesis that the 'dehumanization' of linguistics
(in the above-indicated sense of the word) is highly desirable, and thereby the
question of the feasibility of mathematical linguistics is answered in the
affirmitive.

In connection with recognizing the need to formalize linguistic descriptions,
it is advisable to note the following.

The formal description of any object inevitably entails the schematization
and rounding off of the observed picture.[5] To the person educated in the
classical humanitarian traditions, such an approach may seem faulty. However,

this is the only possible means of acquiring scientific knowledge. Indeed, to study a complex object means nothing other than to establish the laws of its structure, i.e., to isolate its simple components and to formulate the rules by which these components are combined. And what is obtained in this way is precisely the SCHEME of the object in question.

Moreover, different aspects of the examination of our object usually must be separated. In reality all such aspects can be closely connected and interact in a complicated manner. Nevertheless, in order to describe their interdependence accurately, it is first of all necessary to study them separately. In general, the success of scientific research depends mainly on the ability of the researcher to break the complex problem down into simpler problems (i.e., to schematize it) and to separate the appropriate aspects of those simpler problems. Of course, it is necessary that such simplifications preserve all the properties and peculiarities of the object which are essential from the viewpoint of the task before the researcher. The formalization will be useful and productive only to the extent that this condition is observed.

As to the specific formal descriptions offered by mathematical linguistics and cited in this book, the question about their linguistic value is a valid one, but in each concrete instance it should be answered in a specific way. The linguistically oriented reader will find, perhaps, that in certain formal structures some important aspects of the linguistic phenomena being modelled are overlooked. Many such critical remarks can, in fact, be made about mathematical linguistics. However, in our opinion, this means only that particular models require improvement or correction, and in no way affects the very principle of formalization, which is the basic slogan of mathematical linguistics (like any other exact science).

The concept 'formal' is not absolute: different stages, or levels, of formalization, between which there are no sharp boundaries, are possible. It seems reasonable, however, to distinguish two types of formalization: the pre-mathematical type, when the concepts being used preserve to a greater extent the individual, substantive properties of actual objects, and the mathematical type, which operates only with abstract entities given by rigorous definitions (in this case a special interpretation is needed for establishing the connections between abstract units and actual objects).

Mathematical linguistics deals with formalizations of the second type. However, since formalization never is a goal in itself, but a means of studying specific phenomena, then for every science, including mathematical linguistics, not only its formal concepts and propositions are important, but also their interpretations, i.e., how these concepts and propositions are applied to actual objects.

In accordance with this the authors have attempted to saturate the exposition with linguistic examples which show how the introduced formal concepts 'work' with respect to natural language. But the complexity of a natural language is such that a complete description of even a sufficiently simple fragment of it proves too cumbersome for this book. Furthermore, the construction of complete (formal) descriptions for particular fragments of a natural language does not pertain to the proper goals of mathematical linguistics as such: it should only elaborate the means and methods for such descriptions, while their application to language belongs to the competence of linguistics proper (on the relation of mathematical linguistics to 'simply' linguistics see the Conclusion, pp. 131–132). Therefore, our examples, as a rule, are fragmentary and have for the most part a purely illustrative nature.

Finally, we would like to emphasize that this book is not a systematic exposition of mathematical linguistics, nor a survey of the basic works and results in the area. Several important trends are referred to only casually, while many interesting problems (and the results pertaining to them) are not mentioned at all. THE AUTHORS SEE THEIR TASK ONLY AS GIVING THE **NB** READER A GENERAL IDEA ABOUT MATHEMATICAL LINGUISTICS. Therefore the authors have tried to reduce to a minimum the number of references to literature on the subject. The list of references at the end of the book in no way pretends to completeness and should not be viewed as an independent bibliography on mathematical linguistics; in addition, it includes a number of works which have no direct relation to mathematical linguistics, but which proved necessary for our exposition.

Since this book, as noted above, is intended not only (or even primarily) for mathematicians, it was considered expedient to simplify in every way possible the formulations of mathematical assertions. The definitions and theorems in many cases are stated in a free style, alternately with informal explanations, etc., i.e., in a form unusual for a mathematician (although quite rigorous in essence). Proofs, as a rule, are not cited. However, for the sake of readers with mathematical background the book is supplied with an Appendix (pp. 133–139), which lists all the mathematical propositions formulated in a quite canonical manner and provides references to the sources in which it is possible to find corresponding proofs.

There are no exercises in the book, but in order to compensate for their absence, in a number of instances we have deliberately omitted some steps of reasoning (those not too important for the main line of the exposition), have not cited some calculations in full, or have not completed the analysis of individual examples, relying on the reader to fill in these gaps himself. All such instances are indicated in the text and marked by a special symbol in the margins (see below). Doing all these 'quasi-exercises' is not strictly necessary for an understanding of our book, although, of course, the more of them that are done, the better the mastery of the material. It should also be kept in mind that the problems left for the reader are very diverse in difficulty, from the extremely simple to the quite nontrivial.

With the aim of directing the reader's attention we use special markers in the margins:

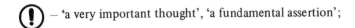 **NB** — 'pay particular attention';

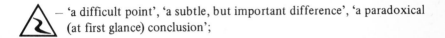 — 'a very important thought', 'a fundamental assertion';

— 'a difficult point', 'a subtle, but important difference', 'a paradoxical (at first glance) conclusion';

$\mathbf{T}_i$ — 'a proposition which is in essence a mathematical theorem' (the subscript i identifies the number of the corresponding theorem in the Appendix);

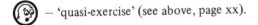 — 'quasi-exercise' (see above, page xx).

NOTES

1. On the markers in the margins see p. xxi.
2. Ju. D. Apresjan's book (Apresjan 1975) can serve as a good introduction to the problems and methodology of structural linguistics.
3. It should be emphasized that no further developments of Chomsky's theory – above all, those presented in his now-classic *Aspects of the Theory of Syntax*, 1965, and many others – are reflected in this book, mainly because they stress the transformational component of Chomsky grammars and at the time our manuscript was being completed there existed no rigorous formalization of this component known to the authors.
4. For example, such that the writer cannot depend on the reader to automatically reconstruct them.
5. It is evident that in accordance with the degree of perfection of our knowledge about the object, the description becomes ever less an approximate one and ever closer to reality. The process of such approximation is, apparently, infinite.

1. The Concept 'Mathematical Linguistics' (Preliminary Remarks)

The term 'mathematical linguistics' became current in the middle of the 1950's and has since achieved wide distribution. However, up until now it has been understood by different people in largely different ways.

The phrase *mathematical linguistics* is most frequently used in a very broad and quite diffuse sense; namely, it is applied to the most diverse linguistic studies if mathematics is used in them to any extent, however little, or even if it only SEEMS to the inexperienced reader that it is being used. Thus the term covers: mathematical models of language using the apparatus of algebra, mathematical logic, or the theory of algorithms; works connected with statistics; and papers in which rather simple concepts and notations are borrowed from mathematics in order to better formulate specific linguistic statements. Also included here by some are all linguistic studies involving computers, in particular works on automatic translation, even if mathematics is not used in them either in essence or in form.

HOW THIS TERM SHOULD BE USED

The use of the term 'mathematical linguistics' to depict A PART of linguistics, seems unfortunate to the present authors. It creates the erroneous impression that there are two different linguistics – one that in principle is not mathematical, and one that is specifically 'mathematical'. In reality linguistics is a single science with its own problems and its own object, which uses mathematical methods where they are needed, and does not use them where they are not. **NB**

In this book, we understand by 'mathematical linguistics' something completely different from what has been outlined in the last section, namely a definite class of essentially mathematical studies which arose from the attempts to describe rigorously the facts of natural language and which contain results that can prove useful for linguistics. This class does not include those

trends of research for which language is only one of the possible applications
(in particular, works of a purely quantitative nature, i.e., linguistic statistics,
etc.): mathematical linguistics thus understood is characterized by the
use of only those mathematical methods which are, in a sense described below,
specific for language as such. Thus, MATHEMATICAL LINGUISTICS IS A
MATHEMATICAL DISCIPLINE GEARED TO NATURAL LANGUAGES AND
LINGUISTICS.

The goal of the present book consists in attempting to characterize the
object and methods of mathematical linguistics, and also its relation to
linguistics proper, using when possible the notions familiar to linguists.

LANGUAGE AS A MAPPING (A FUNCTION)

Since mathematical linguistics is, as we have said, a mathematical discipline, it
will be opportune to begin by examining the following imaginary situation.
A mathematician totally unacquainted with linguistics observes the verbal
behavior of people, i.e., the functioning of language, and tries to describe it;
the description obtained is likely to reflect his inherent mathematical way
of thinking and will be constructed by drawing on at least the simplest
concepts of mathematics. This description could be, for example, as follows.
On the one hand, our mathematician sees that the verbal activity consists
in conveying various desires, feelings, notions, ideas, etc. For short he calls all
this 'the plane of content' (without trying to give a definition to this term).
On the other hand, he sees that the sequences of physical signals (sound
or graphic), which he calls 'the plane of expression', serve as a means of
conveying, or expressing, speech content. For him, as a mathematician, it is
natural to conceive of both the plane of content and the plane of expression
as aggregates, or – using mathematical terminology – s e t s of several
e l e m e n t s, which he calls, let us say, 'meanings' and 'texts' respectively.
Meanings and texts need not be simple units: thus, a text under examination
might be a word-form, a sentence, a very long utterance, etc., up to a whole
book; the situation is analogous with meanings. Furthermore, our
mathematician notes that there is a correspondence between meanings and
texts: each meaning has a more or less definite set of texts associated with it,
and with each text there is associated a more or less definite set of meanings.
The rules determining which texts correspond to which meanings, and vice
versa, form what in current usage is customarily called l a n g u a g e. Our
mathematician will discover in this system of rules (i.e., in the Language!)
a special case of the most important concept of his science – a m a p p i n g,
or a f u n c t i o n. This function associates with each meaning some set
of texts (which he will most likely assume to be finite), namely, the set of

synonymous texts which all have just this meaning (generally speaking, one text may correspond to various meanings — homonymy). Moreover, our mathematician will notice that the function under consideration is, apparently, e f f e c t i v e l y   c o m p u t a b l e (for short: c o m p u t a b l e , or e f f e c t i v e);[1] indeed, language is some regular means of effectively obtaining texts for given meanings and vice versa. Our mathematically minded observer is unaware, for the moment, just how this is done, but the study of the human verbal behavior leads him to the hypothesis that such a means, in some way recorded in the brains of speakers, does exist. He knows that properties of effective functions are studied by a special mathematical discipline — the theory of algorithms, which is in its turn a branch of mathematical logic. If now our mathematician wants to study human language, for him this will mean the study of the corresponding function. He will attempt to represent it in an explicit form as a system of rules and at the same time he will begin to describe its properties. It is only natural that he will turn to the theory of algorithms as the source of information concerning functions of that type and the methods of studying them.

But natural languages form a very specific subclass of effective functions. And our mathematician will immediately find that the information about the effective functions which he can obtain from the theory of algorithms is insufficient for the study of natural languages. Consequently, he will have to study especially the particular effective functions describing natural language, thereby developing the theory of algorithms in a new direction. He may also face the need to investigate properties of the function he studies which are not connected with its effectiveness (and therefore, generally speaking, are not studied by the theory of algorithms) and are very general and quite abstract.

Such properties, i.e., the properties of mappings which do not depend at all on their specific nature (for example, associativity, commutativity, etc.) are studied in algebra. Thus the mathematician-linguist will also have to use algebraic facts and methods.

This is approximately the course of action taken, in all probability, by the mathematicians who actually undertook a systematic study of natural language in the 1950's (which was stimulated, in particular, by the appearance of a number of applied tasks: the automatic processing of linguistic information, etc.). As a result of their efforts there emerged a specific mathematical discipline with its particular topics, studied actively in a number of countries and featuring a large number of works which have since been published. It is this discipline that we propose to call mathematical linguistics.

To sum up: mathematical linguistics is an area which can be viewed, on the one hand, as a special branch of the theory of algorithms, and

on the other, as a special branch of algebra, which explains why this
area is sometimes called algebraic linguistics. In some works on mathematical
linguistics a predominant role is played by the theory of algorithms, in others
by algebra, and in still others the methods of both disciplines are closely
interwoven. In addition, it is frequently necessary to use combinatorial
methods. The proper object of mathematical linguistics is functions (mappings)
of a specific type and various abstract formations arising in connection with
them, which in a number of respects are similar to natural languages.

It needs to be emphasized that, as follows from what has been said,
mathematical linguistics is BASICALLY A NONQUANTITATIVE
DISCIPLINE. Here an explanation seems to be necessary. In a number
of sciences the basic method of describing the properties of the
objects being studied is the establishment of correlations between
the quantities characterizing these objects. For example, in physics
the basic results are quantitative formulas; the experimental verification of
physical assertions reduces, as a rule, to a number of measurements. Of
course, quantitative assertions of physics reflect the deep qualitative
properties of the physical world; however, it is just the quantitative correlations that are the basic form of the description of these properties.

The situation seems to be different in linguistics. The most important
characteristics of language do not have a quantitative nature, i.e., they
are not quantities; the linguistic experiment usually does not entail
measurements. It is not at all by chance that the main achievements of
linguistics, obtained over the entire period of its existence, have not been
formulated as quantitative statements; in general, fundamental
'nonquantitativeness' is typical for the overwhelming majority of linguistic
works. Such a situation is connected, in our opinion, with the very nature
of the object of linguistics – with the properties of natural languages –
and therefore appears quite normal. However, the detailed substantiation of
these considerations should be the topic of a separate study.[2]

The thesis concerning the essentially nonquantitative nature of
mathematical linguistics is in no way contradicted by the fact that in it (just
as in 'ordinary' linguistics) in a number of instances certain calculations
prove necessary: cf. the use of calculations for proving the existence of an
algorithm (pp. 29–30), the estimates of the complexity of derivations
in grammars (pp. 83–85), the algorithm for the classification of letters (pp.
126–127). Such appeals to quantity, no matter how important they are,
always play a subordinate, auxiliary role, in the sense that their final goal is to
obtain purely qualitative results, which cannot be represented in the form
of quantitative dependencies. Thus, although the just mentioned algorithm for
the classification of letters is based on calculations, it produces as a result

of its application a division of letters into those representing vowels and those representing consonants, which in itself is in no way connected with quantity. The estimates of algorithmic and derivational complexity which have great significance in mathematical linguistics (and, probably, will later have an even more important significance[3]), are needed only for judgments about the adequacy or inadequacy of particular models — again, for clearly nonquantitative statements.

The important feature of the calculations used when studying and describing natural language consists, in our opinion, in the fact that such calculations should in many ways be related not to speech, but rather to language itself, i.e., TO THE SYSTEM underlying speech. In other words, the most productive calculations are not calculations of the type 'How many times are the given word, the given construction, words of the given class, etc., encountered in the given texts?' The quantity of linguistic objects in the majority of interesting cases is not determined experimentally (i.e., by a direct counting of these objects, for example, in a real text), but in a purely deductive way (by reasonings which proceed from the abstract properties of the objects in question).[4]

Mathematical linguistics is a nonquantitative discipline to the same extent that modern algebra or the theory of algorithms are recognized as nonquantitative. In these areas quantitative considerations are also frequently referred to which nevertheless remain as such in the background.

We have dwelled on the nonquantitative nature of mathematical linguistics in detail just because among philologists there is a widespread conviction that mathematical linguistics is identical with the statistics of speech. In spite of its general acceptance, such a view seems in fact highly erroneous and methodologically harmful.

NOTES

1. The function $F(x)$ is called e f f e c t i v e l y   c o m p u t a b l e, if for it there can be indicated a quite definite ('mechanical') procedure making it possible, for any value of x, to find in a finite number of steps the value of $F(x)$; i.e., if, roughly speaking, the function can be computed on a computer.
2. Generally speaking, quantitative statements about language are possible (most often these statements concern the distribution of particular quantities, such as the length of sentences or words, the frequency of words of a particular type, etc.; cf. the well-known Zipf's law). However, we suggest that in the description of a language such statements are always only marginal.
3. Presently, in 1975, one can say that this forecast came true; in particular, some important results were obtained in derivational complexity theory by S. Ginsburg and E.H. Spanier, B. Brainerd, M.-K. Yntema, E.D. Stockij, A.Ja. Dikovskij, and others.

We should mention in particular the study of Dikovskij, who has established a connection between derivational complexity in CF grammars and complexity of syntactic structures assigned to the strings generated by these grammars. (For corresponding results and reference see Gladkij 1973: Chapter VII.)

4. What is said here does not cover such fields as sociolinguistics and psycholinguistics, which study the functioning and development of a language in a community rather than its internal structure independently of its use. For this kind of exploration, statistical data prove to be of a primordial importance. However, mathematical linguistics so far does not concern itself with the problems raised in those two domains.

2. Formal Grammars

THE CONCEPT OF FORMAL GRAMMAR

In order to give the reader a more specific idea of mathematical linguistics, we will dwell on one of its divisions, which at present is the most developed, namely, the t h e o r y o f f o r m a l g r a m m a r s . By g r a m m a r s mathematical linguistics understands some special systems of rules, which **NB** specify (or characterize) sets of s t r i n g s (finite sequences of symbols).[1] These strings can be interpreted as linguistic objects of various levels : for example, word-forms (strings of morphs),[2] phrases, clauses and sentences (strings of word-forms), etc.

Thus grammars in mathematical linguistics — f o r m a l g r a m m a r s — deal with abstractions arising by way of generalization of such ordinary linguistic concepts as word-form, word (= lexeme), phrase, clause, and sentence.

Let us explain what is meant when we say 'Formal grammars specify sets of strings'. From a given set of symbols (which represent, for example, all the word-forms of Russian) one can construct any arbitrary strings; some of these strings should be considered correct, or admissible (cf., for example, the grammatically correct Russian sentences *Sosny šumjat na vetru* 'The pine trees rustle in the wind' or *Radosti svistjat na mexu* 'Joys whistle in the fur'), while others are incorrect, or inadmissible (**Vetru na šumjat mexu* 'The wind in rustle fur'). We say that a formal grammar s p e c i f i e s (c h a r a c t e r i z e s) t h e c o r r e c t s t r i n g s, if one of two things occurs:

(1) for any string the grammar can determine whether or not the string is correct, and if it is, then the grammar can specify the structure of this string; or

(2) the grammar can construct any correct string, specifying, moreover, its structure, and does not construct a single incorrect string.

In the first case the formal grammar is called a r e c o g n i t i o n grammar, and in the second, g e n e r a t i v e grammar.[3]

It was indicated above that from the mathematical point of view language may be thought of as an effective function. This function has an extremely complex structure, and therefore it is advisable to study it 'piecemeal': by singling out simpler functions which correspond to the different levels of natural language; for example:

— functions which map meaning representations onto syntactic structures;[4]
— functions which map syntactic structures onto strings of word-forms;
— functions which map abstract structural descriptions of word-forms onto actual word-forms; etc.[5]

Formal grammars are a means of studying and describing such simpler functions, in terms of which the effective function 'LANGUAGE' can be represented. Namely, formal grammars permit us to specify ranges, i.e., sets of values, of these functions. As opposed to the function itself, which associates with any indicated value of an argument a quite definite result, existing grammars describe only s e t s of possible results, without giving direct indications as to how one should proceed to obtain the result corresponding to a particular preselected input.

This feature is characteristic of the formal grammars examined in this book as well as ordinary grammars (i.e., grammars in the current meaning of the word).

However, there is an important difference between ordinary and formal grammars. In formal grammars all statements are made exclusively in terms of a small number of rigorously defined and quite elementary entities (symbols and operations). This makes formal grammars very simple from the viewpoint of their logical structure[6] and *eo ipso* facilitates the study of their properties by deductive methods. However, because of this very fact, formal grammars prove quite cumbersome: if we want the different types of basic components to be as few as possible, and the components themselves to be as simple as possible, then for the description of sufficiently complex phenomena of natural language an enormous number of such components are required (more precisely, INSTANCES of such components). Therefore, formal grammars do not increase the transparency and surveyability of grammatical descriptions and are not satisfactory for direct use by humans (for example, it is hardly advisable to study a foreign language by using its formal grammar). Formal grammars are intended especially for the scientific, theoretical study of the most general properties of language. However, their practical use is not excluded, especially in connection with the application of computers — for example, in automatic translation.

We will not expound on the theory of grammars in its entirety, but will limit ourselves to the basic information about generative grammars (Chapters 2 through 5); in addition, Chapter 6 gives a short characterization of some concepts which pertain to other areas of the theory of grammars (categorial grammars and push-down store machines).

The next section begins the exposition of concrete material – the theory of generative grammars.

A PRELIMINARY EXAMPLE: THE RULES FOR FORMING RUSSIAN PARTICIPLES

Let us assume that we want the set of all forms of participles in written Russian to be specified in some way: for example, by writing down a system of rules which would produce every correct form of every participle and no incorrect forms. (It should be emphasized that this problem is but a special case of the general problem facing formal grammars: their goal consists, as has been said, in specifying sets of strings.)

Below we give an example of such rules – not for all Russian verbs, but only for several selected in a quite random manner; for simplicity the rules are stated as if there were in Russian no verbs of other types and with different properties. Therefore, our examples do not claim any significance for the scientific description of Russian and have a purely illustrative nature. (For a detailed analysis of Russian verb inflexion, including participles, see Jakobson 1948.)

We will conceive of a participle word-form as being a string of from three to five morphs: for example, *ved + š + ij* '(one) that led', *razdel' + a + jušč + ij* '(one) that divides', *razdel' + a + jušč + ij + sja* '(one) that is divided'.[7]

The word-forms and morphs are represented basically in the conventional spelling (transliterated here from Cyrillic into Roman type) with a slight mixing of phonemic transcription – where this is convenient for the formulation of the rules. Thus in a number of cases the softness, or palatalization, of consonants is marked by the symbol ' – but only in paired soft consonants (i.e., in those soft consonants for which there exist in Russian hard, or non-palatalized, counterparts).

Six classes of morphs are distinguished:

1. stems – *razdel'*-'divide', *stroj*- 'build', *ljub'*-'love', etc.;
2. thematic element (stem exponent) – *-i-/-a-/-ova-/-u-*;
3. imperfectivizing suffix (a suffix marking the forms of the imperfective aspect) – *-iva-/-yva-/-a-*;
4. participle suffixes – *-ašč-/-ušč-* (pres, act), *-vš-/-š-* (past, act), etc.;
5. gender-number-case endings (inflexions) of participles – *-aja* (fem, sg, nom), *-uju* (fem, sg, acc), *-ij/-yj* (masc, sg, nom/acc), etc.;
6. the reflexive particle – *-sja*.

In the rules which combine the morphs to form a participle particular cooccurrence features of morphs are used in an important way,[8] namely:

For stems:
(1) transitivity/intransitivity of the verb in question (*t*/*i*);
(2) aspect (perf/imperf/perf-imperf);
(3) conjugation (I/II);
(4) possibility or necessity of a thematic element (a/ova/$\tilde{a}$/$\tilde{i}$/athem);
(5) possibility of an imperfectivizing suffix ($\overline{YVA}$/A/$\emptyset$);
(6) possibility or necessity of *sja* (sja/$\overline{sja}$/sja-$\overline{sja}$).

For participle suffixes:
(1) conjugation (I/II/I-II);
(2) voice (active/passive = act/pass);
(3) tense (present/past = pres/past).

For participle inflexions:
form (long/short = lf/sf).

Lists of morphs of all the named classes with indications of their respective features follow.

Class 1.

Stems

avtomatizir- 'automatize' (*t*, perf-imperf, I, ova, $\emptyset$, sja - $\overline{sja}$)
issled- 'study' (*t*, perf-imperf, I, ova, $\emptyset$, sja-$\overline{sja}$)
kras'- 'color, paint' (*t*, imperf, II,$\tilde{i}$, $\emptyset$, sja-$\overline{sja}$)
kras'- 'make up (one's face)' (*i*, imperf, II,$\tilde{i}$, $\emptyset$, sja)
ljub'- 'love' (*t*, imperf, II,$\tilde{i}$, $\emptyset$, $\overline{sja}$)
nakras'- 'make up (one's face)' (*i*, perf, II, $\tilde{i}$, $\emptyset$, sja)
nes- 'carry' (*t*, imperf, I, athem, $\emptyset$, sja-$\overline{sja}$)
opozd- 'be late' (*i*, perf, I, a, YVA, $\overline{sja}$)
pokras'- 'color, paint' (*t*, perf, II,$\tilde{i}$, $\emptyset$, $\overline{sja}$)
postroj- 'build' (*t*, perf,II,$\tilde{i}$, $\emptyset$, $\overline{sja}$)
poter'- 'lose' (*t*, perf, I, a,$\emptyset$, $\overline{sja}$)
prived-'bring [a person]' (*t*, perf, I, athem, $\emptyset$, $\overline{sja}$)
prines- 'bring [an object]' (*t*, perf, I, athem, $\emptyset$, $\overline{sja}$)
razdel'- 'divide' (*t*, perf, II,$\tilde{i}$, A, sja-$\overline{sja}$)
smej- 'laugh' (*i*, imperf, I, $\tilde{a}$, $\emptyset$, sja)
spros'- 'ask' (*t*, perf, II,$\tilde{i}$, YVA, $\overline{sja}$)
ston- 'groan' (*i*, imperf, I, $\tilde{a}$, $\emptyset$, $\overline{sja}$)
stroj- 'build' (*t*, imperf, II,$\tilde{i}$, $\emptyset$, sja-$\overline{sja}$)
ter'- 'lose' (*t*, imperf, I, a, $\emptyset$, sja-$\overline{sja}$)
ved- 'lead' (*t,* imperf,1, athem, $\emptyset$, sja-$\overline{sja}$)

Class 2.

Thematic Elements

-a-	*-ova-*
-i-	*-u-*

Class 3.

Imperfectivizing Suffixes

-a-
-yva-

Class 4.

Participle-Forming Suffixes

-ašč- (II, act, pres)	*-im-* (II, pass, pres)
-ušč- (I, act, pres)	*-om-* (I, pass, pres)
-vš- (I-II, act, past)	*-nn-* (I, pass, past)
-š- (I-II, act, past)	*-onn-* (II, pass, past)

Class 5.

Gender-Number-Case Participle Inflexions

-aja	*-uju*	
-ogo	*-ye*	
-oe	*-yj*	long forms (lf)
-oj	*-ym*	
-om	*-ymi*	
-omu	*-yx*	

Λ	
-a	
-o	short forms (sf)
-y	

(Λ is zero ending, as in *poterjan* '(one is) lost', which is sg, masc, *vs. poterjan-a* [sg, fem], *poterjan-o* [sg, neut], *poterjan-y* [pl])

Class 6.

Reflexive Particle

-sja

Now we will cite the rules which construct the forms of Russian participles from the above listed morphs.

PARTICIPLE STRUCTURE

I. GENERAL RULES OF PARTICIPLE STRUCTURE

1. The participle word-form should include no more than one morph from each class.
2. The morphs must follow each other in the order of the respective class numbers.
3. The morphs of classes 1, 4, 5 (stem + participle suffix + inflexion) must be present.

II. RULES OF INCOMPATIBILITY (= MUTUAL EXCLUSION)

The participle word-form cannot contain at the same time:
1. Morphs of classes 2 and 3 (a thematic element and an imperfectivizing suffix).[9]
2. A stem with the feature '*i*' and a participle suffix with the feature 'pass' (passive participles cannot be formed from intransitive verbs).
3. A stem with the feature 'sja' and the particle -*sja*.
4. A stem with the feature 'perf' in the absence of an imperfectivizing suffix and a suffix with the feature 'pres' (present participles cannot be formed from perfective verbs).
5. A stem with the features '*t*' and 'perf' in the absence of an imperfectivizing suffix and the particle -*sja* (a transitive perfective verb has no reflexive forms).
6. A stem with the feature '∅' and an imperfectivizing suffix.
7. A stem with the feature 'I' and without the feature 'athem' and a participle suffix with the feature 'II' (thematic verbs of conjugation I do not allow suffixes of conjugation II).
8. A stem with the feature 'athem' and a participle suffix having the feature 'II' and different from -*onn*- (athematic verbs do not allow suffixes of conjugation II, with the exception of -*onn*-).
9. An imperfectivizing suffix and a participle suffix with the feature 'II' (the imperfectivizing suffix transposes any verb into conjugation I).
10. A stem with the feature 'II' in the absence of an imperfectivizing suffix and participle suffix with the feature 'I'.
11. A participle suffix with the feature 'act' and an inflexion with the feature 'sf' (active participles have no short forms).[10]
12. A stem with the feature 'athem' (respectively, without the feature 'athem') and the suffix -*vš*- (respectively, -*š*-); cf. *vedšij* '(one) that was leading', but *opozdavšij* '(one) that was late'.

13. A stem with the feature 'ĩ' or 'ã', a thematic element and participle suffix which begins with a vowel (if in the given stem the thematic element is not necessary, it is not used before the participle suffix which begins with a vowel).

14. A stem with the feature 'ĩ' or 'ã' and a thematic element different from -*i*- or -*a*-, respectively.

15. An imperfectivizing suffix and a participle suffix with the features 'pass', 'past'; cf. **spraš-iva-nn-yj, *razdel'-a-nn-yj.*

16. A participle suffix with the feature 'pass' and the particle -*sja* (passive participles cannot be reflexive).

III. RULES OF INSEPARABILITY (= OBLIGATORY COOCCURRENCE)

The participle word-form must necessarily contain:

1. In the presence of a stem with the feature 'a' either the thematic element -*a*- or an imperfectivizing suffix.

2. In the presence of a stem with the feature 'ova' either the thematic element -*ova*- (if there is a participle suffix with the feature 'past') or the thematic element -*u*- (if there is a participle suffix with the feature 'pres').

3. In the presence of a stem without the feature 'athem' and of a participle suffix beginning with a consonant, either a thematic element or an imperfectivizing suffix.

4. In the presence of a stem with the feature 'sja' the particle -*sja.*

IV. MORPHONOLOGICAL AND PHONOLOGICAL[11] RULES

1. Between two contiguous vowels belonging to different morphs there appears a *j*. (Here are meant cases of the type *razdel' + a + ušč + → razdel' + a + jušč +.*)

2. In the participle word-form containing the suffix -*yva*-, the root vowel *o* (the last *o* of the stem) changes into *a*.[12]

3. Before the suffixes -*onn*- and -*yva*- the final stem consonant -*s'*- changes into -*š'*-, and the final stem consonant -*b'*- into -*bl'*- (analogously, *d' → ž, t' → č, v' → vl'*, etc.; but in our list there are no stems ending in -*d'*-, -*t'*-, or -*v'*-).

4. Before the suffix -*onn*- hard final consonants of athematic stems are softened: *d→d', s→s'*, etc.; e.g., *prines + u / prines' + onn + yj.*

5. Before an inflexion with the feature 'sf' the suffixes -*onn*- and -*nn*- are transformed into -*on*- and -*n*- respectively.

6. The cluster *ji* changes into *i.*

V. SPELLING RULES

1. The clusters *ja, ju, jo* are spelled (in Cyrillic) by the letters я, ю, е . [13]
2. The combinations *X'a, X'u, X'o, X'i, X'y* are spelled as *Xя, Xю, Xё, Xи, Xи* respectively (*X'* is any paired soft consonant).
3. After the letters ж, ч, ш and щ the letters и and е are written instead of ы and о.

These spelling rules (also those on p. 21, Group *X*) are for the Cyrillic script. (For general Roman-to-Cyrillic transliteration rules, see p. 27.)

NOTE. Of special difficulty is the formation of past passive participles from stems of the imperfective aspect without an imperfectivizing suffix. In some cases they are obviously possible – *pisannyj* 'written', *krašennyj* 'colored', in others, as obviously impossible – **vedennyj* 'led', **ljublennyj* 'loved'; there are also many intermediate, not entirely clear instances: ?*terjannyj* 'lost', ?*stroennyj* 'built'. As it seems, it is the usage which has a decisive significance here. But we have not accounted for the usage in our rules; therefore such formations, which formally are always possible, are all admitted by the rules (and are generated by the grammar constructed on the basis of these, pp. 15–21).

Perhaps, the reader will be surprised by the great number and the staggering diversity of the rules which proved necessary for describing the participles of several Russian verbs. It must be admitted that this fact no less surprised the authors themselves, who strove to find an example as simple as possible, but at the same time instructive. However, it is necessary to face the facts: Russian morphology is deservedly considered very complex. In the proposed rules this complexity is much more noticeable than in ordinary descriptions for the reason that here everything is stated in an explicit form, while in the available descriptive grammars of Russian this is never done. However, it should be kept in mind that we had to include among our rules such rules which are not at all specific for participles only (in particular, all the spelling rules). Therefore – and this is especially important – even if we considerably increase our list of stems (i.e., if we consider many more verbs), this would not require any significant increase in the number and complexity of the rules.

THE DEFINITION AND AN EXAMPLE OF GENERATIVE GRAMMAR

Thus we have constructed explicit and exact rules which describe the set of word-forms we want – the forms of the participles of several Russian verbs – and have thus solved the problem formulated on p. 9. However, our description is not satisfactory in at least one respect, namely: it is NOT itself constructed according to some definite rules, i.e., the rules forming it DO NOT consist of previously distinguished and fixed elementary components. (Of course, such components can be distinguished; however, this requires a special study, and we would be left with a completely different description.) If we want not only to describe actual languages, but also to examine in a most general form THE MEANS OF DESCRIBING LANGUAGES, then it is necessary to construct all our descriptions UNIFORMLY, composing them from the elementary components which are themselves combined and put together according to some strict preformulated rules. Only in this case will we be able to apply rigorous (mathematical) reasoning to linguistic descriptions.

NB

Formal grammar is a description of just this type. The entire arsenal of means used by it is fixed in its definition, while all of its statements have a precisely defined form, which is also fixed by definition.

As was already said, we will examine in this chapter only g e n e r a t i v e formal grammars. (R e c o g n i t i o n formal grammars, mentioned on p. 7, and the general problem of classifying formal grammars will be discussed later on: see Chapter 6.) Let us proceed to a definition of the corresponding concept. At the same time, we will construct as an illustration a formal grammar G_0, which generates the same forms of participles as in the above example.

It should be borne in mind that we will in fact examine not any conceivable generative grammars, but only a definite class of such grammars, which was introduced by Noam Chomsky (Chomsky 1957, 1962). It is with grammars of this class that the study of generative formal grammars has begun; moreover, even now Chomsky grammars remain the most studied in all respects: 90%, if not more, of the general theory of generative formal grammars reduces to the theory of Chomsky grammars. This allows us to use instead of the full name 'generative formal grammars in the sense of Chomsky' the term 'generative grammars', or even simply 'grammars' (of course, only in those cases when the context precludes a misunderstanding).

Generative grammar is a system with four components:
— a basic, or terminal, vocabulary;
— an auxiliary, or nonterminal, vocabulary;
— an initial, or starting, symbol;
— a set of rewriting rules, or productions.

1. A BASIC (TERMINAL) VOCABULARY is a finite non-empty set of elements from which the strings generated by the grammar are constructed.

In grammar G_0 this is the set of all Russian letters (here, Roman transliteration equivalents thereof), which are printed in italics as distinct from the other uses of these letters (for example, as symbols used for phonetic transcription or for representing syntactic features of nonterminal symbols). Thus actual Russian morphs and word-forms will be printed in italics. In addition, the terminal vocabulary of G_0 includes the boundary symbol # (which is represented in written or printed texts by spaces between words).

The elements of the terminal vocabulary are called b a s i c (t e r m i n a l) s y m b o l s.

Morphs as such are not considered independent symbols and are therefore not a part either of the terminal or nonterminal (see item 2 below) vocabulary: they are regarded as strings of terminal symbols — letters. The role of the vocabulary of stems (cf. the 1st class of morphs in the example just examined, p. 10) is in essence played here by the rules of Group VIII (see below, p. 20).

NOTE. From the linguistic point of view it would be more correct (and more natural) to describe the forms of the Russian participles with the help of TWO DIFFERENT grammars: one of them would represent the participle in the form of a string of morph symbols, and the other would transform these strings into actual letter strings; i.e., it would construct forms of the Russian participles in conventional spelling. In that manner, the different levels of the language would be described by different grammars. (The second grammar, to be true, would not fully satisfy the above definition of generative grammar,[14] although formally it could easily be made to do so.) The terminal vocabulary of the first grammar would, then, consist of symbols of morphs (a list of stems and affixes), while the nonterminal vocabulary would contain only symbols of morph categories. The second grammar would have in its terminal vocabulary the Russian letters, while in the nonterminal vocabulary there would be symbols of morphs, transcription symbols, a boundary symbol, and, perhaps, categories of letters (vowels/consonants, etc.). It should be emphasized that the second grammar would not be connected by structure or purpose especially with the generation of just participles: it would represent the morphological, phonological, and graphic-orthographic levels of the Russian language and would be needed for the generation of any word-forms (cf. the note at the end of the preceding section, p. 14). In such a division the terminal and nonterminal vocabularies of both grammars would appear more natural. We, however, preferred — for the sake of unity of our example — to construct a single grammar.

2. AN AUXILIARY (NONTERMINAL) VOCABULARY is a finite non-empty set of symbols which designate the classes consisting of basic elements and/or strings of basic elements, as well as, in individual cases, some special elements. These symbols are called a u x i l i a r y, or n o n t e r m i n a l.

In grammar G_O we will introduce the following nonterminal symbols:

PART — participle;

PART (v, t, rf) — a participle of a given voice, tense and reflexivity (the possible values of v, t, and rf are indicated below, rule I);

O' ($a_1, a_2, a_3, a_4, a_5, a_6, a_7$) — the stem of the participle including the imperfectivizing suffix or the thematic element, if they exist, provided with its syntactic features: a_1 — transitivity (t/i); a_2 — aspect (perf/imperf); a_3 — conjugation (I/II); a_4 — thematic element (a/ova/$\tilde{a}$/$\tilde{i}$/athem); a_5 — the possibility of an imperfectivizing suffix (YVA/A/$\emptyset$); a_6 — the possibility of a reflexive form (sja/$\overline{sja}$); a_7 — the possibility of a nonreflexive form ($\neg$sja/$\overline{\neg sja}$[15]);

O ($a_1, a_2, a_3, a_4, a_5, a_6, a_7$) — the bare stem of the participle (without a thematic element and without an imperfectivizing suffix) with the same syntactic features as above;

S(v, t, a_3) — the participle suffix with its syntactic features (v — voice, t — tense, a_3 — conjugation, see above);

F(f) — participle inflexion with its syntactic feature f representing the form of the participle (short/long — sf/lf);

O, S, F — the above-mentioned morphs with no syntactic features;

I — imperfectivizing suffix;

T — the thematic element;

+ — the boundary between morphs (it automatically appears after any morph which cannot be the last one in a word-form);

X' — a soft consonant; here X stands for an arbitrary consonant.

3. AN INITIAL SYMBOL is a distinguished nonterminal symbol sometimes referred to as 'the axiom' or 'starting symbol'. We may think of it as designating the set of all the linguistic objects whose descriptions the grammar is to provide.

In grammar G_O this is the symbol PART, since our goal is to describe the set of all participles. (In a grammar which generates sentences, the initial symbol will be SENTENCE; in a grammar generating admissible syllables the initial symbol designates SYLLABLE; etc.)

4. A SET OF REWRITING RULES, or productions, is an expression of the form $X \rightarrow Y$, which means 'replace X with Y' or 'substitute Y in place of X', where X and Y are arbitrary strings containing any terminal or nonterminal symbols. In grammar G_O the rewriting rules are as follows:

I. GENERATION OF THE GRAMMATICAL MEANINGS OF THE PARTICIPLE[16]

PART → # PART (v, t, rf) #
Here v = act, pass;

t = pres, past;
rf = refl, nonrefl.

If **v** = pass, then **rf** = nonrefl.

NB   The notation PART → PART (**v, t, rf**) is an abbreviation: it represents, indeed, not one, but six different rules, which correspond to the admissible sets of values of the variables **v, t, rf**. For example: PART → PART(act, pres, refl); PART → PART (pass, pres, nonrefl); etc. In all other cases the variables **v, t, rf** are used in the same manner.

II. MANIFESTATION OF THE GRAMMATICAL MEANINGS BY THE CORRESPONDING MORPHS

1. PART(act, pres, refl)→
   O' (imperf, a_3, sja)S(act, pres, a_3) F*sja*[17]
2. PART(act, past, refl) →
   O' (a_3, sja)S(act, past, a_3) F*sja*
3. PART(act, pres, nonrefl) →
   O' (imperf, a_3, ⌐sja)S(act, pres, a_3) F
4. PART(act, past, nonrefl) →
   O' (a_3, ⌐sja)S(act, past, a_3) F
5. PART(pass, pres, nonrefl) →
   O' (**t**, imperf, a_3, ⌐sja)S(pass, pres, a_3) F
6. PART(pass, past, nonrefl) →
   O' (**t**, a_3, ⌐sja)S(pass, past, a_3) F

In writing down the syntactic features of morphs (in parentheses) we omit, for brevity's sake, those features which in the given rule can assume ANY value. Thus, for example, the notation O(imperf, sja) is an abbreviation for many expressions of the form O (a_1, imperf, a_3, a_4, a_5, sja, a_7), where a_1, a_3, a_4, a_5, a_7 assume any admissible values; correspondingly, the notation S (act, pres) is also an abbreviation for two expressions of the form S (act, pres, a_3). Therefore, for example, line II.1 represents in fact not one rule, but 120 different rules; it is a   r u l e   s c h e m a.

III. BREAKING DOWN THE 'COMPLEX' STEM (the isolation of the root proper and the thematic element or the imperfectivizing suffix, if any)

1. O' (a_1, a_2, **not** athem) → O(a_1, a_2, **not** athem) T[18]
2. O' (**t**, perf, **not** athem) SF # → O (**t**, perf, **not** athem) TSF #
3. O' (imperf, **not** ∅)S(**v, t**) → O (perf, **not** ∅) IS (**v, t,** l)

In this rule the variables **v** and **t** must satisfy the following condition: if **v** = pass, then **t** = pres.

4. $O'(a_1, a_2, \text{athem}) \rightarrow O(a_1, a_2, \text{athem})$
5. $O'(t, \text{perf}, \text{athem})$ **SF** # $\rightarrow O(t, \text{perf}, \text{athem})$ **SF** #

In rules III.1 and III.4, $a_1 = i$ or $a_2 = \text{imperf}$ (clearly, $a_1 = i$ and $a_2 = \text{imperf}$ is also possible).

IV. REALIZATION OF THE THEMATIC ELEMENT BY THE CORRESPONDING MORPH

1. $O(\tilde{a})T\alpha \rightarrow O(\tilde{a})\alpha$
2. $O(\tilde{a}, I)T\beta \rightarrow O(\tilde{a}, I)a + \beta$
3. $O(\tilde{i})T\alpha \rightarrow O(\tilde{i})\alpha$
4. $O(\tilde{i}, II)T\beta \rightarrow O(\tilde{i}, II)i + \beta$
5. $O(a)T \rightarrow O(a)a +$
6. $O(\text{ova})TS(\text{pres}) \rightarrow O(\text{ova})u + S(\text{pres})$
7. $O(\text{ova})TS(\text{past}) \rightarrow O(\text{ova})ova + S(\text{past})$

Here α and β are an arbitrary vowel and an arbitrary consonant, respectively.

V. REALIZATION OF THE IMPERFECTIVIZING SUFFIX BY THE CORRESPONDING MORPH

1. $O(A)I \rightarrow O(A)a +$
2. $O(YVA)I \rightarrow O(YVA)yva +$

VI. REALIZATION OF THE PARTICIPLE SUFFIX BY THE CORRESPONDING MORPH

1. $S(\text{act}, \text{pres}, I) \rightarrow u\check{s}\check{c} +$
2. $S(\text{act}, \text{pres}, II) \rightarrow a\check{s}\check{c}$
3. $S(\text{pass}, \text{pres}, I) \rightarrow om +$
4. $S(\text{pass}, \text{pres}, II) \rightarrow im +$
5. $O(\text{not athem})XS(\text{act}, \text{past}) \rightarrow O(\text{not athem}) Xv\check{s} +$
6. $O(\text{athem})S(\text{act}, \text{past}) \rightarrow O(\text{athem}) \check{s} +$
7. $O(\text{not athem})XS(\text{pass}, \text{past}, I) \rightarrow O(\text{not athem}) Xnn +$
8. $O(\text{athem})S(\text{pass}, \text{past}) \rightarrow O(\text{athem}) onn +$
9. $S(\text{pass}, \text{past}, II) \rightarrow onn +$

Here X stands for any imperfectivizing suffix or thematic element, for example, $u +$, $yva +$, etc.

VII. SELECTION OF THE FORM OF THE PARTICIPLE (SHORT OR LONG) AND THE REALIZATION OF THE INFLEXION BY THE CORRESPONDING MORPH

1. $F \rightarrow F(lf)$

2. **S**(pass)**F** → **S**(pass)**F**(sf)

3–15. **F**(lf) → *yj, oe, ogo, omu, ym, om, aja, oj, uju, ye, yx, ym, ymi*

16–19. **F**(sf) → Λ, *o, a, y*

Λ is the empty string, i.e., a string not containing any symbols. The rule **F**(sf) → Λ means 'it is possible to delete the symbol **F** (sf)'.

VIII. REALIZATION OF THE STEM BY THE CORRESPONDING MORPH[19]

O(*t*, imperf, I, athem, ∅, sja, ⌐lsja) → *ved+* 'lead', *nes+* 'carry', . . .

O(*t*, imperf, I, ova, ∅, sja, ⌐sja) → *issled+* 'study', *avtomatizir+* 'automatize', . . .

O(*t*, imperf, **I**, a, ∅, sja, ⌐sja) → *ter'+*'lose', . . .

O(*t*, perf, I, athem, ∅, s̄ja, ⌐sja) → *prived+* 'bring [a person]', *prines+* 'bring [an object]', . . .

O(*t*, perf, I, ova, ∅, sja, ⌐sja) → *issled+* 'study', *avtomatizir+* 'automatize', . . .

O(*t*, perf, I, a, ∅, s̄ja, ⌐sja) → *poter'+* 'lose' . . .

O(*t*, imperf, II,ĩ, ∅, sja, ⌐sja) → *stroj+* 'build', *kras'+* 'color', *ljub'+* 'love', . . .

O(*t*, perf, II,ĩ, A, sja, ⌐sja) → *razdel'+* 'divide', . . .

O(*t*, perf, II,ĩ, YVA, s̄ja, ⌐sja) → *spros'+* 'ask', . . .

O(*t*, perf, II,ĩ, ∅, s̄ja, ⌐sja) → *pokras'+* 'color', . . .

O(*i*, imperf, I, ã, ∅, sja, ⌐sja) → *ston+* 'groan', . . .

O(*i*, imperf, I, ã, ∅, sja, ⌐sja) → *smej+* 'laugh' . . .

O(*i*, imperf, II,ĩ, ∅, sja, ⌐sja) → *kras'+* 'make up', . . .

O(*i*, perf, I, a, YVA, s̄ja, ⌐sja) → *opozd+* 'be late', . . .

O(*i*, perf, II,ĩ, ∅, sja, ⌐sja) → *nakras'+* 'make up [one's face]', . . .

IX. MORPHONOLOGICAL RULES

1. $\alpha_1 + \alpha_2 \rightarrow \alpha_1 + j\alpha_2$ (where α_1 and α_2 are arbitrary vowels)
2. $j + i \rightarrow i$
3. $oX + yva \rightarrow aX + yva$

Here X is an arbitrary string no longer than three symbols. What is meant is the alternation *o/a* in verbal roots of the type *opozd-at'/opazd-yvat'* 'to be late'. As it seems, the consonant cluster which follows in the root the alternating *o* (i.e., separates it from *-yva-*) cannot contain more than three letters.

4. $s' + X \rightarrow š + X$ ⎫
   $b' + X \rightarrow bl' + X$ ⎬ Here, $X = onn, yva$

. . . .

5. $d + onn \rightarrow d' + onn$
   $s + onn \rightarrow s' + onn$
. . . .
6. $nn + \mathbf{F}(\text{sf}) \rightarrow n + \mathbf{F}(\text{sf})$

X. SPELLING RULES

1. $j + a \rightarrow$ я
   $j + u \rightarrow$ ю
   $j + e \rightarrow$ e
. . . .

$ja \rightarrow$ я
$jy \rightarrow$ ю
$jo \rightarrow$ e
. . . .

2. $X' + a \rightarrow X +$ я
   $X' + u \rightarrow X +$ ю
   $X' + o \rightarrow X +$ e $\left.\right\}$ Here, X is any consonant
   $X' + i \rightarrow X +$ и
   $X' + y \rightarrow X +$ и

3. $X +$ ы $\rightarrow X +$ и $\left.\right\}$ Here, $X =$ ж, ч, ш, щ
   $X +$ o $\rightarrow X +$ e   20

Cf. the indication under the spelling rules on p. 14.

XI. DELETION OF BOUNDARY SYMBOLS BETWEEN MORPHS

$X + Y \rightarrow XY$

Here X and Y are any morphs such that there is no rule of Groups IX-X which is still applicable to $X + Y$.

This restriction on X and Y prevents the boundary between morphs from being deleted too early, before the application of all the morphonological rules. Otherwise, some morphonological rules would not be applied, and this could lead to incorrect results (for example, it would be possible to obtain *opozdyvavšij, *sprosennyj, instead of *opazdyvavšij, sprošennyj*): the point is that if a morphonological rule CAN be applied, then it MUST BE applied. In other words, all morphonological rules are obligatory.

DERIVABILITY AND DERIVATION; LANGUAGE GENERATED BY A GRAMMAR

The example of G_0 was used to describe the structure of a generative formal grammar. Now we will introduce the following three concepts necessary for describing how the grammar is applied, i.e., for describing the process of string generation.

1. DIRECT DERIVABILITY. If there are two strings X and Y, with $X = Z_1 A Z_2$ and $Y = Z_1 B Z_2$ (Z_1 and/or Z_2 can be empty) and in grammar G there is the

rule $A \to B$, then Y is   d i r e c t l y   d e r i v a b l e   in G from X. In other
words, X can be transformed into Y in ONE step — by the application of just
one production: Y is obtained from X by the substitution of B in the place
of some occurrence of the string A. For example, from the string
     $O(t, \text{perf, II}, \tilde{\text{i}}, \text{A, sja}, \neg\text{sja})\, i + S(\text{act, past, II})\text{F}$
     the string
     $O(t, \text{perf, II}, \tilde{\text{i}}, \text{A, sja}, \neg\text{sja})\, i + v\check{s} + \text{F}$
is directly derivable by rule VI.5.

2. DERIVABILITY AND DERIVATION. If there is a sequence of strings X_0,
$X_1, \ldots, X_n$, such that each   s u b s e q u e n t   string is directly derivable
from the preceding one, then X_n is   d e r i v a b l e   from X_0; the sequence
$X_0, X_1, \ldots, X_n$ is called the   d e r i v a t i o n   of X_n from X_0. This means
that X_0 is transformed into X_n not necessarily in one step, but by the
successive application of several rewriting rules (= productions). It is evident
that direct derivability is a special case of derivability.
     Let us cite an EXAMPLE OF DERIVATION in the grammar G_O.[21]

	PART
(I)	# PART (pass, past, nonrefl) #
(II.6)	# O' $(t, \text{perf, II}, \tilde{\text{i}}, \emptyset, \overline{\text{sja}}, \neg\text{sja})$S(pass, past, II) F #
(III.1)	# O $(t, \text{perf, II}, \tilde{\text{i}}, \emptyset, \overline{\text{sja}}, \neg\text{sja})$ TS (pass, past, II) F #
(VI.9)	# O $(t, \text{perf, II}, \tilde{\text{i}}, \emptyset, \overline{\text{sja}}, \neg\text{sja})$ Tonn + F #
(IV.3)	# O $(t, \text{perf, II}, \tilde{\text{i}}, \emptyset, \overline{\text{sja}}, \neg\text{sja})$ onn + F #
(VII.1)	# O $(t, \text{perf, II}, \tilde{\text{i}}, \emptyset, \overline{\text{sja}}, \neg\text{sja})onn$ + F (lf) #
(VII.15)	# O $(t, \text{perf, II}, \tilde{\text{i}}, \emptyset, \overline{\text{sja}}, \neg\text{sja})onn$ + ymi #
(VIII. . .)	#$pokras'$ + onn + ymi #
(IX.4)	#$pokra\check{s}$ + onn + ymi #
(X.3)	#$pokra\check{s}$ + enn + ymi #
(XI)	#$pokra\check{s}enn$ + ymi #
(XI)	#$pokra\check{s}ennymi$ # 'by the painted ones'.

Such a derivation (which begins with the initial symbol and ends with a
string consisting only of terminal symbols) is called a   c o m p l e t e
derivation. Of course, not every derivation beginning with the initial symbol
is complete; there are, in fact, derivations beginning with the initial symbol
which cannot be carried out to obtain a complete derivation; these are
called   d e a d - e n d   d e r i v a t i o n s .
     Let us cite an EXAMPLE OF A DEAD-END DERIVATION in G_O.

	PART
(I)	# PART (act, pres, refl) #
(II.1)	# O' $(t, \text{imperf, II, athem}, \emptyset, \text{sja}, \neg\text{sja})$S(act, pres, II)F sja #

(III.4)   # **O** (*t*, imperf, II, athem, ∅, sja, ⌐sja)**S**(act, pres, II)**F** *sja* #

(VI.2)   # **O** (*t*, imperf, II, athem, ∅, sja, ⌐sja)*ašč* + **F** *sja* #

(VII.1)   # **O** (*t*, imperf, II, athem, ∅, sja, ⌐sja)*ašč* + **F** (lf) *sja* #

(VII.11)   # **O** (*t*, imperf, II, athem, ∅, sja, ⌐sja)*ašč* + *ujusja* #

(XI)   # **O** (*t*, imperf, II, athem, ∅, sja, ⌐sja) *aščujusja* #

   This derivation cannot be continued, although it is not complete, i.e., does not end with a string of terminal symbols (Russian letters in transliteration). In grammar G_0 there is no rule such that the left-hand part of the rule is contained in the last string of the above derivation. This is explained by the fact that in Russian there are no athematic verbs which are conjugated according to conjugation II. Thus the features 'athem' and 'II', which when constructing grammar G_0 were treated as independent, are in reality related. Their correlation could have been accounted for, but this would have lead to a noticeable complication of our grammar. We preferred not to do so, since the existence in the grammar of dead-end derivations is not a shortcoming. It is not at all required of a 'good' grammar that any derivation in it end with a correct terminal string: it suffices that ANY COMPLETE derivation would give a correct string (in our case, the form of a Russian participle).

   It should be stressed that a generative grammar is NOT an algorithm.[22] The rewriting rules do not form a sequence of instructions, but rather a set of permissions. This means that, first of all, a rule of the type $A \rightarrow B$ is understood in a grammar as '*A* MAY be replaced by *B*', while in an algorithm $A \rightarrow B$ would mean '*A* MUST be replaced by *B*'; second, the order of applying the rules in a Chomsky grammar is arbitrary (any rule is allowed to be applied after any other one), while in an algorithm a strict order of applying the individual instructions would be given. However, it must be remembered that the permission to apply a rule is one thing, while the possibility of doing this is another: a rule can be actually applied only to such a string which contains an occurrence of its left-hand part (thus the rule $AB \rightarrow CD$ can be applied to the string *AAEABC*, but not to the string *AAAEBC*). Therefore, the order in which the rules are actually applied in a grammar can in fact be dictated by the rules themselves. For example, in grammar G_0 the rules can be applied in the process of derivation only in a definite, almost strict order, although for G_0, as for any grammar in general, there are no external restrictions on the order of rule application. Thus in no complete derivation can a rule of Group III be applied before the rules of Group II, since the left-hand parts of the rules of Group III contain the symbol O' which can appear in the string derived only as a result of applying one of the rules of Group II; analogously, Rule IV.1 or IV.6 cannot apply before a rule of Group VI, etc.

In order to become better acquainted with the concepts of grammar and derivation, it will be to the reader's benefit to construct several complete derivations in grammar G_0, i.e., acting purely mechanically, to generate a number of word-forms of Russian participles. For this it is necessary to do the following: take the initial symbol PART, select any rewriting rule which has this symbol in its left-hand part, and apply that rule; then select any rule which is applicable to the obtained result and apply it; etc. As a model it is possible to use the example of the derivation on p. 22.

3. LANGUAGE GENERATED BY A GRAMMAR. The set of all terminal strings[23] derivable from the initial symbol in grammar G is called the l a n g u a g e g e n e r a t e d   b y   g r a m m a r G and is designated by $L(G)$. It should be emphasized that such a use of the term 'language', which was introduced by Noam Chomsky, does not coincide with the interpretation of it that is more generally accepted in linguistics (and also in mathematics). Chomsky, in distinguishing a linguistic SYSTEM and an infinite (generally speaking) SET OF ITS PRODUCTS, calls the former 'grammar', and the latter 'language'. Yet in linguistics, beginning with F. de Saussure, l a n g u a g e ('langue') is the name usually given to the system, while its products are ordinarily called s p e e c h ('parole'). However, when speaking about generative grammars, it is not convenient to use these terms for a number of reasons (basically of a stylistic nature); cf., for example, *various speeches generated by languages*, etc. Moreover, Chomsky's terminology became generally accepted and customary in the area of mathematical linguistics. Therefore, we will use it in our exposition of the theory of generative grammars. On other occasions we use the term 'language' in the conventional linguistic sense; however, the context always shows clearly which sense is meant.

In our example the language generated by grammar G_0 is the set of all participles of the above-indicated verbs. It is evident that this language is finite. However, grammars can also generate infinite languages — cf., in particular, grammar G_1, pp. 31—33.

Thus the application of a grammar is the construction of complete derivations in it; the terminal strings of these derivations form the language generated by the grammar.

Note that it is possible for two different grammars to generate the same language, i.e., the same set of terminal strings; in this case the grammars are said to be w e a k l y e q u i v a l e n t (hereafter we will refer to weakly equivalent grammars simply as equivalent).

Now, summing up, we can formulate the definition of generative formal grammar (henceforth, for brevity, we will simply say 'grammar').

NB GRAMMAR is an ordered quadruple $\langle V, W, I, R \rangle$, where:

(1–2) *V* and *W* are disjoint finite non-empty sets of symbols ($V \cap W = \emptyset$), which are called the terminal and nonterminal vocabularies respectively,

(3) *I* is a distinguished element of *W* called the i n i t i a l   s y m b o l,

(4) *R* is a finite non-empty set of expressions of the form $A \rightarrow B$, where *A* and *B* are strings consisting of terminal and nonterminal symbols (s t r i n g s o v e r $V \cup W$), and $\rightarrow$ is a symbol belonging neither to *V* nor *W*; these expressions are called r u l e s   o f   t h e   g r a m m a r, and the set *R* t h e s c h e m e   o f   t h e   g r a m m a r.

NOTES

1. The basic operation on strings is *concatenation*, sometimes referred to as 'juxtaposition' of strings. The concatenation operator is binary and is usually symbolized by $\frown$. The operator symbol is normally suppressed; e.g., $a \frown b$ may be written simply *ab*, and $a \frown (a \frown b)$ may be written *aab*. A special string called the *empty* (or *null*) string contains no elements (length zero). A set of strings X, including the empty string, closed under concatenation, forms a monoid:
(i) For all strings a, b, c in X, $a \frown (b \frown c) = (a \frown b) \frown c$. [$\frown$ is associative.] (ii) There is an identity element *e* such that for any string *a* in X, $a \, e = e \, a = a$. [*e* is the empty string.] (Concatenation is not commutative: $a \frown b \neq b \frown a$ if $a \neq b$ and neither *a* nor *b* is the empty string.)   [editor]
2. The meaning of the term 'morph' can approximately be explained for the nonlinguist in the following manner: morphs are the minimal parts of word-forms which are meaningful or have an independent function; for example, Russ. *pere + dokaz + yva + juŠč + emu* 're' + 'prove' + imperfectivizing suffix + present active participle marker + inflexional ending of masc/neut, sg, dative (the plus sign designates the boundary between morphs), i.e. 'to that which tries to prove again'.
3. Cf., however, the remarks on p. 110 and following.
4. Here and below what is meant is 'filled' structures; for example, syntactic trees whose nodes are labeled with symbols of specific lexemes.
5. As can be seen from the preceding exposition, we suggest that the most adequate model of language would not be a mechanism generating (producing or enumerating) its correct sentences, but rather a mechanism establishing correspondences between any given meaning and the texts which carry this meaning or, vice versa, between any given text and its possible meanings (cf. Žolkovskij – Mel'čuk 1967). Thus our approach differs from N. Chomsky's general conception. It would be quite interesting to examine this difference in essence; however, we will not do this, since the corresponding problem goes beyond the aims of this book, while its solution has practically no effect on the exposition of our basic material, in particular the theory of formal grammars.
6. The word *simple* should not be understood here in the current sense as 'obvious', 'easily surveyable', etc. What is meant is the logical simplicity (= noncompoundness, elementariness) of the components and the logical simplicity (= uniformity) of the means for combining the components into a whole – a local simplicity, so to speak. The whole itself can be very big in volume and quite complex and sophisticated in structure, and therefore poorly surveyable, i.e., not at all simple in the literal meaning of the word.

7. Within the framework of this example the combination of root and prefix is regarded as one unanalyzable morph ('stem'). The apostrophe designates the softness of consonants, i.e., *l'a = lja, n'o = nè,* etc.

8. Notations for cooccurrence, or syntactic, features of morphs:

   'perf-imperf' means that the verb is homonymous with respect to aspect (*avtomatizirovat'* 'to automatize' – both imperf. and perf. aspects, *issledovat'* 'to study' – also imperf. and perf. aspects);

   'a' means the obligatoriness of the thematic element -*a*- (*opozd + a +*); 'ova' means the obligatoriness of the thematic element -*ova*-/-*u*- (*issled + ova +, issled + u +ju*); 'ã' means that the thematic element -*a*- is possible, but not always necessary (*ston + a + vš + ij*, but *ston + ušč + ij*); 'ĩ' means that the thematic element -*i*- is possible, but not always necessary (*kras + i + vš + ij*, but *kras +jašč + ij*); 'athem' means the impossibility of a thematic element (*ved + š + ij*);

   'YVA' means the possibility of the imperfectivizing suffix -*yva*-/-*iva*- (*opazdyvat'*), 'A' means the possibility of the imperfectivizing suffix -*a*- (cf. *rešit'* – *resat'*), '∅' means the impossibility of an imperfectivizing suffix (*postroit'*);

   'sja' means the obligatoriness of the -*sja* particle (*smejat'sja*, but not **smejat'*), 'sja' means the impossibility of -*sja* (*stonat'*, but not **stonat'sja*), 'sja–sja' means the possibility of forms both with and without -*sja* (*terjat'* – *terjat'sja*). Note that the possibility/impossibility of -*sja* or its absence with a given verb strongly depends on the sense in which this verb is taken. E.g. *krasit'* 'to paint' admits -*sja* to form the passive (*krasit'sja* 'to be painted'), and thus exhibits two different formations: with or without -*sja*, while *krasit'sja* 'to make (one's face) up' cannot drop its -*sja*; likewise, *pit'* 'to drink' also admits a passive -*sja* (*pit'sja* 'to be drunk', as of liquids), while *pit'* 'to be a drunkard' does not admit -*sja*; etc. However, we do not take this circumstance into consideration.

   'I–II' means that the given suffix can be joined to stems of both conjugations I and II (*terjavšij* – *krasivšij*).

9. For purposes of simplifying the example this rule does not consider the numerous forms of the type *arestovyvavšij* '(one) that was arresting', *vykovyvajuščij* '(one) that is forging', *organizovyvavšij* '(one) that was organizing'.

10. This is but an approximation: in poetic speech short active participles are occasionally encountered. Cf., for example, ... *ix vozduxom* **pojušč** *trostnik i skvažist* 'their reed sings with air and is perforated' (O. Mandel'štam).

11. Morphonological rules are rules dealing with the strings of phonemes (in our case the phonemes, for simplicity, are designated by letters), but necessarily taking into consideration the morphological role of these strings. Phonological rules deal simply with the strings of phonemes, irrespective of their morphological status. In this group of rules only rule IV.6 is phonological.

12. In order to describe such cases as *osnov + at'* – *osnov + yvat'* 'to found', perfective – imperfective aspect (*o/a* alternation does not occur in this verb), or *udosto + it'* – *udosto + ivat'*/*udosta + ivat'* 'to confer, award', perfective–imperfective aspect (*o/a* alternation may, but need not occur), it would be necessary to introduce an additional feature of stems: *o/a* alternation before the -*yva*- suffix is possible/impossible/obligatory.

13. This *e* (like *e* in rules 2–3 below) can correspond both to *e* and *ë*, which in Russian printed texts are usually not differentiated: when stressed, this *e = ë* (*prinesénnyj* or *prinesënnyj* '(one) that has been brought'), without stress *e = e* (*terjaemyj* '(one) that is being lost').

14. Namely, it would generate strings by proceeding not from an initial symbol (see p. 17, item 3), but from the output strings of the first grammar.

15. Here 'sja' means the possibility of the reflexive form, 's͞ja' means the impossibility of the reflexive form, '⌐sja' – the possibility of the nonreflexive form, '⌐s͞ja' – the impossibility of the nonreflexive form. Note that the symbols 'sja' and 's͞ja' do not have the same meaning as on p. 10: the reflexiveness and nonreflexiveness were described there by one feature, which assumed three values, and here by two binary features a_6 and a_7, which allows us to reduce the number of rules.

16. To be better grasped, the rewriting rules are broken down into groups (numbered with Roman numerals), each of which corresponds to a particular linguistic task; this task is indicated along with the number of the group. The numbers of the groups and rules should not be understood as indications about the order of their application: the order of applying the rules of a generative grammar is arbitrary (see p. 23).

17. As indicated above, the real Russian morphs and word-forms are italicized.

18. Here '**not** athem' is used as abbreviation and means any value of the feature a_4 different from 'athem', i.e., 'a', 'ova', 'ã', or 'i̇'. The notation '**not** Ø' has an analogous meaning.

19. The rules of Group VIII are not numbered, since each row here represents a whole set of rules, the number of which is determined by the number of stems being used.

20. This rule as it stands is valid only for o in verbal suffixes (i.e., in suffixes that can be joined to verbal stems).

21. In parentheses (to the left of each line of the derivation) we indicate the number of the rule whose application to the preceding line yields the given line.

22. We cannot explain here what an algorithm is, but it is necessary to know this to understand the book. To the reader who is not certain that he is sufficiently familiar with the concept of algorithm, we could recommend to turn at least to the following three references (in the order of increasing difficulty): Hermes 1965 : Chapter 1; Rogers 1967: §1.1, §1.6; Chomsky 1963: 354–357.

23. A t e r m i n a l s t r i n g is a string consisting only of terminal symbols, see p. 16.

Roman-to-Cyrillic transliteration rules adopted in this book

a →	а	g →	г	n →	н	u →	у
b →	б	i →	и	o →	о	v →	в
c →	ц	j →	й	p →	п	x →	х
$č$ →	ч	ja →	я	r →	р	y →	ы
d →	д	ju →	ю	s →	с	z →	з
e →	е	k →	к	$š$ →	ш	$ž$ →	ж
$è$ →	э	l →	л	$šč$ →	щ	$'$ →	ь
f →	ф	m →	м	t →	т	$''$ →	ъ

3. Classes of Generative Grammars

T

1.1.1

NB

Grammars which satisfy the cited definition are generative devices of a very general nature: they are capable of generating ANY (!) sets of strings which can be generated by an automatic device.[1] However, the set of sentences of a natural language has a number of very specific properties. (An important note: when studying sentences of a natural language from the viewpoint of the theory of formal grammars, they are usually regarded as strings of word-forms or morphs which appear as terminal symbols.) In particular, it is natural to suppose that for the set of sentences of a language there exists a r e c o g n i z i n g   a l g o r i t h m − a means to find out, for any string, whether it is a sentence of the given language or not; the strict division of all sentences into correct and incorrect ones is not necessarily presupposed − it is possible to permit a class or classes of inter-mediate cases. This opinion follows from observing reactions of native speakers: a speaker of a language can always evaluate the correctness of a sentence presented to him, even if he has never heard it before; *ergo*, he must use some recognizing device, or algorithm, whose structure, however, he does not know. Moreover, this algorithm must have certain specific properties: in particular, it always gives an answer quite rapidly. The sets for which recognizing algorithms exist are called   r e c u r s i v e,[2] while those for which such algorithms are rather simple, i.e., can be carried out in 'a not very large' number of steps, form an even narrower class and will be called e a s i l y   r e c o g n i z a b l e   s e t s. If we want a grammar to generate all and only sentences of a natural language, then the grammars defined on p. 25 should be restricted in such a way that the sets generated by them would be recursive and, moreover, easily recognizable. It seems natural that these restrictions would be placed on the rules, i.e., on the substitutions: limiting just what to substitute and for what.

NONSHORTENING GRAMMARS

We will start with the requirement that in a rule of the form $A \rightarrow B$ the string B be no shorter than the string A; then in the process of derivation the strings will never be shortened.[3] It turns out that this (at first glance, insignificant) restriction is sufficient for our purpose: languages generated by 'nonshortening' grammars are easily recognizable! This important fact can be rigorously proven; the proof being quite simple, we will cite it here in order to acquaint the reader to some extent with the inner workings of mathematical linguistics.

T

1.2.13

Consider a nonshortening grammar G which contains p symbols (terminal and nonterminal together). Take an arbitrary string x of length n which consists of terminal symbols of grammar G. In order to prove that $L(G)$ is an easily recognizable set, it suffices to indicate such an algorithm that for each string of length n it would determine in 'a not very large' number of steps whether this string is derivable from the initial symbol of grammar G or not. Such an algorithm exists; its basic idea is as follows. The algorithm constructs one after the other all derivations in grammar G starting with the initial symbol I. The construction of each derivation consists in first applying to I an arbitrary rule of grammar G (such that it is applicable to I), and then applying some rule to the result, etc. The number of the applications of rules in a given derivation is called its length (note that the length of a derivation is equal to the number of strings it contains, not counting the initial symbol). Having completed the construction of each successive derivation, the algorithm verifies whether it ends with the examined string x. If so, the process stops, since the answer is thereby obtained: string x is derivable from I. If not, then the process continues. For this process not to be infinite, the algorithm should 'know' where to stop, i.e., when to cease the construction of new derivations. This can be achieved by providing the algorithm with such a finite set **M** of derivations that if none of the derivations in **M** ends with string x, then no derivation starting with I ends with this string. Then, after checking all the derivations from **M** and not finding among them a single one ending with x, the algorithm should stop and give a negative answer: x is not derivable from I. But it is not sufficient that the set **M** simply should exist; it is also necessary that we can effectively find **M** for any given string x.

Let us indicate a means of forming the set **M** for an arbitrary string x. If string x of length n is derivable from the initial symbol I of grammar G, then there exists a derivation — a sequence of strings that runs from I to x. We may suppose that in this derivation no string is repeated: otherwise the 'loop' that would have been formed (between two occurrences of the same string repeated) could be discarded with no harm done. Since our grammar is

nonshortening, none of the strings of the sequence can be longer than the
string x, i.e., have a length greater than n. (It is just here that we
capitalize in an essential manner on the fact that grammar G is nonshortening.) The number of different strings of a length not exceeding
n, which can be composed from p symbols, is obviously no greater than

$$p^n + p^{n-1} + \ldots + p^2 + p^1 + p^0 = \frac{p^{n-1} - 1}{p-1}^4 \quad \text{(the sum of a geometric}$$

progression) $< p^{n+1}$.

Therefore, the derivation of the string x from I, if it exists, must necessarily
be contained among all possible repetitionless sequences which are composed
from $p^n {}^{+1} = P$ different strings. And of these sequences there are obviously
no more than

$$P! + C_p^1 \cdot (P-1)! + C_p^2 \cdot (P-2)! + \ldots + C_p^{p-2} \cdot 2! + C_p^{p-1} . 1!^{\;5}$$

This sum has P terms; its kth term is equal to

$$C_P^k \cdot (P-k)! = \frac{P!}{k!\,(P-k)!} \cdot (P-k)! = \frac{P!}{k!} \le P!^{\;6}$$

Therefore, the sum cannot be greater than

$$P! \cdot P < (P+1)! = (p^{n+1} + 1)! < (p^{n+2})!$$

Those of the $(p^{n+2})!$ sequences obtained which are derivations in grammar
G form the set **M** that we want. In examining them in turn, we will either
find the needed derivation, or we will convince ourselves that it does not exist.

By presenting an algorithm for recognizing the derivability of an arbitrary
string in grammar G, we thereby proved that $L(G)$ is a recursive set; since for
any string of length n our algorithm gives an answer in no more than $(p^{n+2})!$
steps[7] $L(G)$ is an easily recognizable set. It should be noted that the concept
'not very large' (number of steps) is rather relative; actually, the number
$(p^{n+2})!$ is so large that the proposed algorithm is practically unrealizable
even with the aid of the most powerful digital computers. However, in
the theory of algorithms one frequently encounters recursive sets for whose
recognition an incomparably larger number of steps is required, and even
some recursive sets for which the number of steps of the recognizing algorithm
cannot at all be estimated beforehand.

Thus, having selected sets where the number of steps for recognition depends as indicated on the length of the string being processed, we immediately single out a rather narrow subclass in the class of recursive sets.

PHRASE STRUCTURE GRAMMARS (PS GRAMMARS, OR PSG'S)

For the convenience of studying nonshortening grammars it is expedient to introduce another restriction, which does not change the class of languages generated, but makes the rules of grammar simpler and more uniform in structure, and therefore ensures the elementary nature of each step in the derivation. Namely, let us require that in rule $X \to Y$ the left-hand part (X) have the form $Z_1 C Z_2$, where C is exactly one symbol (it is convenient to agree that this symbol always be nonterminal) and Z_1, Z_2 are some strings (possibly empty), and that the right-hand part (Y) have the form $Z_1 T Z_2$, where T is a nonempty string (the nonemptiness of the string T follows from the fact that the grammar is nonshortening). In this way, at each step of the derivation it is permitted to replace (= rewrite) only one symbol. The grammars satisfying the formulated restriction are called p h r a s e   s t r u c t u r e   g r a m m a r s, or for short, PS g r a m m a r s. It is clear that in any nonshortening grammar a step of derivation which consists in the simultaneous replacement of several symbols can be broken down into several steps, each consisting in replacing, or rewriting, only one symbol at a time. It follows from this that for any nonshortening grammar there can be constructed a **PS** grammar equivalent to it.[8]

T
1.1.2

   PS grammars have the following linguistically important property.

   Let us interpret the terminal symbols of a PS grammar as word-forms (of some natural language), the nonterminal symbols as syntactic categories — classes of words and phrases (for example, V – verb, N – noun, A – adjective, $\tilde{V}$ – verb phrase, $\tilde{N}$ – nominal phrase); the initial symbol will be SENTENCE, and the derivable terminal strings will represent correct sentences of the given language. Then the derivation of a sentence can be naturally interpreted as its syntactic structure, represented in terms of immediate constituents, i.e., in a way long known to linguistics. What has been said is better explained with an example. We will construct grammar G_1, which generates a very simple type of Russian sentence. We will write down only the scheme of the grammar; its terminal symbols are Russian word-forms, while its nonterminal vocabulary contains the above-named syntactic categories. The symbols of these categories are provided with subscripts corresponding to their morphological markers, for example $N_{f,sg,gen}$, which means 'a feminine noun in the genitive singular'. The initial symbol is SENT (Sentence).

THE SCHEME OF GRAMMAR G_1[9]

It should be kept in mind that each line in the given scheme is not one rule, but an abbreviated notation of several rules (see above, p. 18). Thus, line II.1 represents 648 rules:

$$\widetilde{N}_{m,\text{ sg, nom},3} \rightarrow \widetilde{N}_{m,\text{ sg, nom},3} \widetilde{N}_{m,\text{ sg, gen},1}$$
$$N_{m,\text{ sg, gen},3} \rightarrow N_{m,\text{ sg, gen},3}\, N_{m,\text{ sg, gen},1}$$
$$\cdots\cdots\cdots\cdots\cdots\cdots\cdots\cdots\cdots$$
$$\widetilde{N}_{n,\text{ pl, prep},3} \rightarrow \widetilde{N}_{n,\text{ pl, prep},3}\, \widetilde{N}_{n,\text{ pl, gen},3}$$

This abbreviation is applied in subsequent examples as well. Nevertheless, for simplicity of our statements we will call the lines of such abbreviated notations 'rules'.

I. SELECTION OF THE OVER-ALL STRUCTURE OF THE SENTENCE

$$\text{SENT} \rightarrow \#\, \widetilde{N}_{g,\, n,\, \text{nom},\, p}\ \widetilde{V}_{\text{pres},\, n,\, p}\ \#$$

II. EXPANSION OF THE NOMINAL PHRASE

1. $\widetilde{N}_{g,\, n,\, c,3} \rightarrow \widetilde{N}_{g,\, n,\, c,3}\ \widetilde{N}_{g',\, n',\, \text{gen},\, p}$
2. $\widetilde{N}_{g,\, n,\, c,3} \rightarrow \widetilde{A}_{g,\, n,\, c}\ \widetilde{N}_{g,\, n,\, c,3}$
3. $K_1\, \widetilde{N}_{g,\, n,\, c,\, p}\, K_2 \rightarrow K_1\, N^{\text{pron}}_{g,\, n,\, c,\, p}\, K_2\,,$

where K_1 is a symbol distinct from the symbol $A_{g,\, n,\, c}$, while K_2 is a symbol distinct from the symbol with the subscript c' = gen. Here K_1 and K_2 are c o n t e x t   r e s t r i c t i o n s, or   c o n t e x t s. The rationale of their introduction into rule II.3 is that the head of a nominal phrase should not be realized by a personal pronoun if preceded by an adjective modifier or followed by a genitive nominal phrase; cf. the impossibility of *novyj ja 'new I'[10] or *on nežnosti 'he of tenderness'.

4. $\widetilde{N}_{g,\, n,\, c,3} \rightarrow N_{g,\, n,\, c}$

III. EXPANSION OF THE VERB PHRASE

1. $\widetilde{V}_{\text{pres},\, n,\, p} \rightarrow V_{\text{pres},\, n,\, p}\ \widetilde{N}_{g',\, n',\, \text{dat},\, p'}\ \widetilde{N}_{g'',\, n'',\, \text{inst},\, p''}$
2. $\widetilde{V}_{\text{pres},\, n,\, p} \rightarrow V_{\text{pres},\, n,\, p}\ \widetilde{N}_{g',\, n',\, \text{inst},\, p'}\ \widetilde{N}_{g'',\, n'',\, \text{dat},\, p''}$
3. $\widetilde{V}_{\text{pres},\, n,\, p} \rightarrow V_{\text{pres},\, n,\, p}\ \widetilde{N}_{g',\, n',\, \text{dat},\, p'}$
4. $\widetilde{V}_{\text{pres},\, n,\, p} \rightarrow V_{\text{pres},\, n,\, p}\ \widetilde{N}_{g',\, n',\, \text{inst},\, p'}$

IV. REALIZATION OF SYNTACTIC CATEGORIES BY WORD-FORMS

1. $N_{m, n, c} \rightarrow vzgljad_{n, c}$ '(a) look', . . .

2. $N_{f, n, c} \rightarrow nežnost'$ 'tenderness', . . .

3. $N_{n, n, c} \rightarrow predatel'stvo_{n, c}$ 'betrayal', . . .

4. $N^{pron}_{g, sg, c, 1} \rightarrow ja_c$ 'I'

5. $N^{pron}_{g, sg, c, 2} \rightarrow ty_c$ 'you' [sg]

6. $A_{g, n, c} \rightarrow sladkij_{g,n,c}$ 'sweet', $novyj_{g, n, c}$ 'new', $moj_{g,n,c}$ 'my',
$$tvoj_{g, n, c} \text{ 'your', . . .}$$

7. $V_{pres, n, p} \rightarrow grozit'_{pres, n, p}$ 'to threaten', . . .

(In the rules of IV we have not accounted for the agreement of A with animate N in the accusative case.)

Notations: # is the boundary symbol for sentences and is considered terminal (in the text the left sentence boundary is realized by the capital letter of its first word, and the right boundary by a period); **g, n, c, p** are variables corresponding to gender, number, case, and person (in the rules of IV they are used for specifying word-forms, for example, $sladkij_{f,sg,nom}$ = *sladkaja* 'sweet').

See an example of derivation in grammar G_1 on p. 34–35.

Grammar G_1 is capable of generating other sentences as well (which need not be meaningful), for example: *#ja grožu tvoej nežnosti #* 'I threaten your tenderness', *# sladkoe novoe moë predatel'stvo grozit toboj tvoemu vzgljadu predatel'stva tvoego vzgljada predatel'stva #* 'sweet new my betrayal theatens with-you your look of-betrayal of your look of-betrayal', etc. Moreover, grammar G_1 generates INFINITELY MANY different sentences (as distinct from grammar G_0). The point is that it contains so-called r e c u r s i v e rules: II.1 and II.2. The characteristic of a recursive rule is that the result of its application contains an occurrence of its left-hand part, so that such a rule can always be applied to its own output, which leads to an infinite number of sentences; thus along with the phrase *sladkaja nežnost'* 'sweet tenderness' it is possible to obtain *sladkaja sladkaja nežnost'* 'sweet sweet tenderness', *sladkaja sladkaja sladkaja nežnost'*, etc., i.e., the adjective *sladkaja* 'sweet' can be repeated as many times as desired. In connection with this there arises the exceptionally important and far from simple question about the non-finiteness of the number of sentences in a natural language, with respect to which we would like to remark here the following.

NB

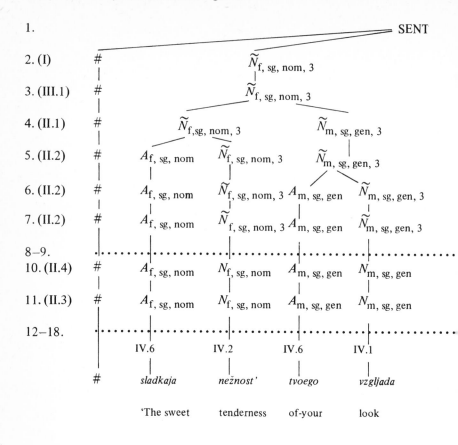

1.   SENT

2. (I)   # $\tilde{N}$f, sg, nom, 3

3. (III.1) # $\tilde{N}$f, sg, nom, 3

4. (II.1)   # $\tilde{N}$f,sg, nom, 3 $\tilde{N}$m, sg, gen, 3

5. (II.2)   # Af, sg, nom $\tilde{N}$f, sg, nom, 3 $\tilde{N}$m, sg, gen, 3

6. (II.2)   # Af, sg, nom $\tilde{N}$f, sg, nom, 3 Am, sg, gen $\tilde{N}$m, sg, gen, 3

7. (II.2)   # Af, sg, nom $\tilde{N}$f, sg, nom, 3 Am, sg, gen $\tilde{N}$m, sg, gen, 3

8–9.   ....

10. (II.4) # Af, sg, nom Nf, sg, nom Am, sg, gen Nm, sg, gen

11. (II.3) # Af, sg, nom Nf, sg, nom Am, sg, gen Nm, sg, gen

12–18.   ....

                   IV.6   IV.2   IV.6   IV.1

            #   sladkaja   nežnost'   tvoego   vzgljada

                   'The sweet   tenderness   of-your   look

It is evident that at any given moment the number of words of any natural language is finite. In addition, the maximum length of the sentences encountered in any language is in practice limited: people hardly ever use sentences of more than, let us say, 1000 words (if this number seems insufficient, it is possible to take any larger one). Hence it follows that the actual number of sentences in a natural language should be finite.

 Nevertheless, it is also evident that IT IS IMPOSSIBLE TO INDICATE THE LONGEST SENTENCE IN A LANGUAGE: no matter what sentence we are offered, we can in principle always lengthen it, having added to it, for example, another conjunct with *i* 'and' or a relative clause with *kotoryj* 'which'. This means that in principle a natural language has at its disposal possibilities for constructing sentences as long as one wants, i.e., sentences of ANY length are potentially realizable, although in actual speech excessively long sentences are not used.

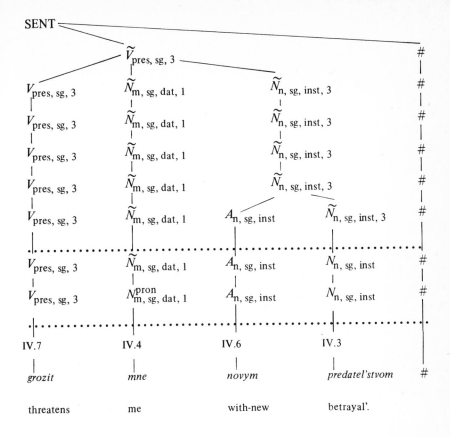

SENT

$\tilde{V}_{pres, sg, 3}$

$V_{pres, sg, 3}$	$\tilde{N}_{m, sg, dat, 1}$	$\tilde{N}_{n, sg, inst, 3}$	#
$V_{pres, sg, 3}$	$\tilde{N}_{m, sg, dat, 1}$	$\tilde{N}_{n, sg, inst, 3}$	#
$V_{pres, sg, 3}$	$\tilde{N}_{m, sg, dat, 1}$	$\tilde{N}_{n, sg, inst, 3}$	#
$V_{pres, sg, 3}$	$\tilde{N}_{m, sg, dat, 1}$		$\tilde{N}_{n, sg, inst, 3}$	#
$V_{pres, sg, 3}$	$\tilde{N}_{m, sg, dat, 1}$	$A_{n, sg, inst}$	$\tilde{N}_{n, sg, inst, 3}$	#
$V_{pres, sg, 3}$	$\tilde{N}_{m, sg, dat, 1}$	$A_{n, sg, inst}$	$N_{n, sg, inst}$	#
$V_{pres, sg, 3}$	$N^{pron}_{m, sg, dat, 1}$	$A_{n, sg, inst}$	$N_{n, sg, inst}$	#

IV.7   IV.4   IV.6   IV.3

grozit   *mne*   *novym*   *predatel'stvom*   #

threatens   me   with-new   betrayal'.

This potential unlimitedness of sentence length cannot be neglected by formal grammars, since their aim is exactly the modelling of the THEORETICAL possibilities of natural languages. But if the lengths of sentences generated by a grammar are u n l i m i t e d (= u n b o u n d e d), then the set of all these sentences is infinite.

In addition, when we regard the set of sentences as infinite, rules for dealing with them become more uniform, while the description as a whole – no matter how paradoxical this may seem at first glance – becomes simpler and more insightful, i.e., it leads to the disclosure of more important regularities. An analogous situation obtains, for example, in arithmetic: natural numbers with which people must deal in any practical problems whatsoever are not 'too big', thus a number bigger than 10^{10} is hardly ever used. Nevertheless, arithmetic proceeds from the unlimitedness of the set of natural numbers (for in principle it is indeed unlimited), and it is

NB exactly this assumption that makes the laws of arithmetic so general and simple, and thus also suitable for use in those problems in which 'too big' numbers are never encountered.

As to the practical (= factual) limitation of sentence length, this circumstance is in itself very important, and a complete theory of language, undoubtedly, should take it into consideration. However, the nature of this phenomenon pertains to a different aspect of language — not to the (syntactic) aspect formal grammars are called upon to model; therefore, it is not reflected within the framework of the latter.

Of course, as a result our picture of language becomes considerably more approximate. However, there is nothing unexpected in this: the reader will recall that in the Introduction (pp. xviii–xix) the inevitability of rather rough approximations in mathematical modelling was specially noted. This is precisely the situation with formal grammars of the type discussed in this book: the approximateness of language description appears here not only because of not considering the empirical limitation of sentence length, but also, and to a much greater extent, because of completely ignoring the semantic aspect — in particular, the semantic combinability of linguistic items. In order to reflect these as well as other essential aspects of natural languages, it is necessary to construct, along with formal grammars, models of another type, which would be more suitable for describing such aspects. (On some attempts to model semantics see below, p. 112 and following.)

Let us return now to our example of derivation on pp. 34–35. Each step of this derivation consists either in expanding one of the symbols of the preceding string (thus, in the transition from string 2 to string 3 the symbol $\tilde{V}_{\text{pres, sg, }3}$ is expanded into three symbols — $V_{\text{pres, sg, }3}\tilde{N}_{\text{m, sg, dat, }1}\tilde{N}_{\text{n, sg, inst, }3}$), or in its replacement by another (for example, in the transition from string 10 to string 11 the symbol $\tilde{N}_{\text{m, sg, dat, }1}$ is replaced by $N^{\text{pron}}_{\text{m, sg, dat, }1}$); the other symbols are copied without change. Let us call the expanded, replaced or copied symbols   p r e d e c e s s o r s,   and the symbols that arise as a result of expansion, replacement or copying, their   d e s c e n d a n t s   (descendants of descendants are also descendants). Let us join the predecessors by lines with the immediate descendants. Then we will obtain nothing other than the   t r e e   o f   (i m m e d i a t e)   c o n s t i t u e n t s   well known to linguists, or the   s y n t a c t i c   s t r u c t u r e   of our sentence in terms of immediate constituents (an IC structure) — or, using another terminology, a   p h r a s e   m a r k e r   (a P-marker).[11] In order to show this more explicitly, we'll eliminate from the diagram on pp. 34–35 all the predecessor symbols which are copied without change (for example, $\tilde{N}_{\text{m, sg, dat, }1}$ in strings 4–10) and collapse the uniform steps 4–5, 5–6, and 6–7, representing them on the same level. The tree depicted on p. 37 will be obtained.

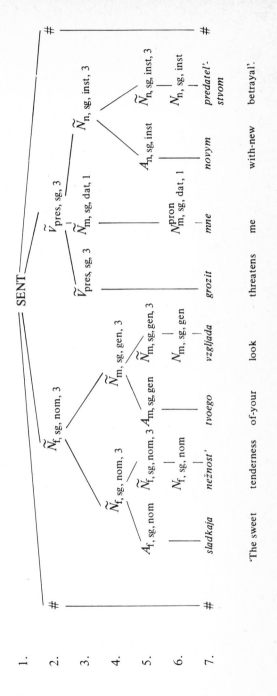

The representation of syntactic structure in terms of IC is widely accepted in linguistics. It has been studied many times in the most diverse aspects and, undoubtedly, has won citizenship both on the purely theoretical plane and in works of an experimental or applied nature (automatic translation, etc.). Therefore, the fact that the grammars defined on p. 31, when generating terminal strings — for example, sentences of a natural language — SIMULTANEOUSLY SPECIFY THEIR IC STRUCTURE (their P-markers) makes them especially interesting from the linguistic point of view. (Note that the derivation of a sentence IS in fact its IC structure.)

 The arbitrary nonshortening grammar (without the requirement of replacing only one symbol at a time) no longer has the property of associating with sentences their IC structures (P-markers). In such a grammar, each time a string consisting of more than one symbol is replaced (i.e. rewritten), in the derivation it is impossible to indicate in a unique way the predecessor of each replacing symbol, and therefore the derivation cannot be transformed into a P-marker.

CONTEXT-FREE GRAMMARS (CF GRAMMARS, OR CFG'S)

The following interesting fact should be brought to the reader's attention: although in the rules of PS grammar only a single symbol is rewritten (C, p. 31), the left-hand part of a rule (i.e. X) does not necessarily consist only of this symbol: in the left-hand part on the right and left of C there can be other symbols specifying the context; i.e., X can have the form $Z_1 C Z_2$ with nonempty Z_1 and/or Z_2. Then the rule of the form $Z_1 C Z_2 \rightarrow Z_1 T Z_2$ means permission to rewrite C as T only in the context $Z_1 \ldots Z_2$. The context itself is copied without change. An example of such a rule is II.3 in grammar G_1. Rules of this kind are called c o n t e x t - b o u n d, o r c o n t e x t - s e n s i t i v e, and the rules using no context (i.e., rules of the form $X \rightarrow Y$, where X is a single symbol), c o n t e x t - f r e e. Grammars containing only context-free rules are called c o n t e x t - f r e e (or CF) g r a m m a r s, abbreviated cfg's.[12] Languages generated by CF grammars are, naturally, called CF l a n g u a g e s, or cfl's.

CF grammars are an important special case of PS grammars. Their value is explained by the following two circumstances. First, the rejection of context, i.e., the requirement that there be exactly one symbol in the left-hand part of any rule, makes the structure of grammars even more simple, which facilitates their study. Second, although in natural languages the replacement of some expressions by others is often permissible only in certain contexts, it is expedient to study the possibility of describing languages by disregarding this fact. This allows a strict differentiation of cases in which the use of context is actually necessary, and cases in which it is possible in principle to do without context. In particular, of special interest is the study of situations in which the context seems necessary from a linguistic viewpoint, but where formally it can be accounted for with the help of context-free rules, i.e., the context ceases to be regarded as such; this can be achieved by introducing new non-terminal symbols (i.e., categories) into the grammar. Thus in grammar G_1 the context-sensitive rule II.3 can be eliminated if the grammar is transformed in the following manner:

(1) there are introduced into the nonterminal vocabulary the new symbols $\tilde{N}'_{g,n,c}$, which are interpreted as NONPRONOMINAL noun phrases, as distinct from the symbols $\tilde{N}_{g,n,c}$ standing for arbitrary nominal phrases;

(2) rule II.3 is replaced by two new rules: $\tilde{N}_{g,n,c,p} \rightarrow N^{pron}_{g,n,c,p}$ and $\tilde{N}_{g,n,c,3} \rightarrow \tilde{N}'_{n,g,c}$;

(3) in rules II.1, II.2 and II.4 all occurrences of the symbols $\tilde{N}_{g,n,c,3}$ are replaced by the symbols $\tilde{N}'_{g,n,c,p}$.

Linguistically all this has the following meaning: when expanding an arbitrary nominal phrase $\tilde{N}_{g,n,c,p}$ into the construction $A + N$ or $N + N_{gen}$ it is necessary to make sure that in the position of the head of this construction there does not appear a personal pronoun such as *ja* 'I', *vy* 'you[pl]', *on* 'he', which cannot take adjective modifiers or genitive attributes (A or N_{gen}: **novyj ja* 'new I' or **my vzgljada* 'we of the look'). This can be achieved in various ways:

(i) In grammar G_1 we do it as follows: The personal pronouns are considered nouns (although of a special class — N^{pron}) and are treated as noun phrases ($\tilde{N}$) on a level with 'ordinary' nouns. However, it is permitted to rewrite a nominal phrase $\tilde{N}$ as N^{pron} only under the condition that this $\tilde{N}$ did not earlier 'detach from itself' an A to the left or a N_{gen} to the right (see rules II.1 and II.2), i.e., if on the left of the rewritten symbol there is no adjective, and on the right of it there is no noun phrase in the genitive. This condition is covered by rule II.3.

(ii) When proceeding in another fashion (see above), the pronouns are also considered a special subclass of nouns, but along with the category 'arbitrary noun phrase' $\tilde{N}$ there is introduced the category 'nonpronominal noun phrase' $\tilde{N}'$, and the symbol $\tilde{N}$ in the course of derivation — prior to its expansion — is necessarily rewritten either as N^{pron} (which cannot be further expanded) or as $\tilde{N}'$ (which is expanded in the usual manner). A and N_{gen} have as their source only $\tilde{N}'$, but $\tilde{N}'$ cannot be transformed into a pronoun.

(iii) A third way is also feasible: pronouns are not considered a subclass of nouns and from the very beginning a special symbol P is used for them. Then many rules of grammar G_1 will have to be repeated twice; for example, along with rule I we'll have to introduce an extra rule I':

SENT $\to P_{\text{sg, nom, p}}\ \widetilde{V}_{\text{pres, sg, p}}$,

along with rule III.3 the rule III.3':

$V_{\text{pres, n, p}} \to V_{\text{pres, n, p}}\ P_{\text{g}', \text{n}', \text{dat}, \text{p}'},$ etc.

With this third approach the resulting grammar will also be context-free.

This example shows that in natural languages it is possible to have situations in which the phenomena that seem essentially dependent on context, can apparently be described also as not dependent on context, i.e., in terms of CF grammars. Here, of course, the description can become more complicated in other respects; for example, many new categories and/or rules may be needed. In each individual case it is necessary to decide what is preferable, proceeding from the specific aim of the description.

It should not, however, be thought that EVERY context-sensitive PS grammar can be assigned an equivalent CF grammar. It is well known that there are PS languages which are NOT CF languages; for example, an infinite language consisting exactly of all possible strings of the form $a^n b^n a^n$ (i.e., *aba,*

T
1.1.3   *aabbaa,* . . .) or of all possible strings of the form $a^n b^n c^n$ cannot be generated by any CF grammar.

Almost all existing examples of PS languages that are not CF languages are of an algebraic nature and have no interpretation in natural languages. Cf., however, the examples on p. 65 and following.

So far we have been occupied with introducing additional restrictions on the classes of grammars under discussion. First we required that the number of symbols in the right-hand part of any rule be no less than that in the left-hand part, and we obtained nonshortening grammars. Then we required that only one symbol be rewritten, and we obtained PS grammars. Finally, we required that the left-hand part of any rule should contain exactly one symbol, and we obtained CF grammars. It is clear that no further natural restrictions can be imposed upon the left-hand parts of the rules. Therefore, if we want to specify still narrower classes of grammars (the expediency of such an approach will be discussed below, p. 46), it will be necessary to impose new restrictions on the right-hand parts of the rules.

BINARY CF GRAMMARS

Let us begin with the number of symbols. We will require that the right-hand part of any rule contain no more than two symbols. (Obviously, two is the minimum number: if the right-hand parts are allowed to have only one symbol each, then the generated language will consist only of one-element strings, which is not interesting.) As a result there will be obtained a special subclass of CF grammars (let us called them b i n a r y), with the property that in their corresponding constituent trees (i.e., in the syntactic structures, or PS-markers, of the sentences obtained from their derivations) no more than two branches originate from each node. This means that any complex constituent always consists of exactly two immediate constituents, i.e., that a sentence is always divided into two halves (for example, 'the subject phrase' + 'the predicate phrase'), each of these halves is again divided in two, etc. PS grammars (in particular, CF grammars) without such a restriction do not specify a binary structure. We direct the reader's attention to this fact because there is a tendency to understand IC structure necessarily as binary. But such a view is clearly wrong. Thus grammar G_1 does not specify a binary structure. This occurs owing to rules III.1 and III.2, which reflect such an intuitive understanding of the structure of a sentence, in which the predicate phrase is considered to consist of a finite (or tensed) verb and some complement or object phrases, each of which lies on the same level as the verb.

However, for every CF grammar it is possible to construct a binary CF grammar equivalent to it. For example, the CF grammar described on p. 39 can be transformed into a binary one by replacing rules III.1 and III.2 (p. 32) with the following new rules:

T
1.1.4

III.1′. $\widetilde{V}_{\text{pres, n, p}} \rightarrow \widetilde{V}^1_{\text{pres, n, p}} \, \widetilde{N}_{\text{g}'',\text{n}'', \text{inst, p}''}$

III.2′. $\widetilde{V}_{\text{pres, n, p}} \rightarrow \widetilde{V}^2_{\text{pres, n, p}} \, \widetilde{N}_{\text{g}'',\text{n}'', \text{dat, p}''}$

III.1″. $\widetilde{V}^1_{\text{pres, n, p}} \rightarrow \widetilde{V}_{\text{pres, n, p}} \, \widetilde{N}_{\text{g}',\text{n}', \text{dat, p}'}$

III.2″. $\widetilde{V}^2_{\text{pres, n, p}} \rightarrow V_{\text{pres, n, p}} \, \widetilde{N}_{\text{g}',\text{n}', \text{inst, p}'}$

In addition, it is also necessary to replace rule I, which has in its right-hand part four symbols, with rule I′:

SENT $\rightarrow \widetilde{N}_{\text{g, n, nom, p}} \, \widetilde{V}_{\text{pres, n, p}}$;

thereby we eliminate the boundary symbols. (In general, in a CF grammar the boundary symbols are formally not necessary, while in a PS grammar which has context-sensitive rules boundary symbols may be necessary as context; cf. rule II.3 in G_1. If the existence of boundary symbols is considered desirable from some linguistic considerations, they can be preserved also in the binary CF grammar, but for simplicity of exposition we will not do this.)

The derivation of a sentence with the help of the grammar transformed in the above indicated way will give just the binary P-marker represented on p. 42.

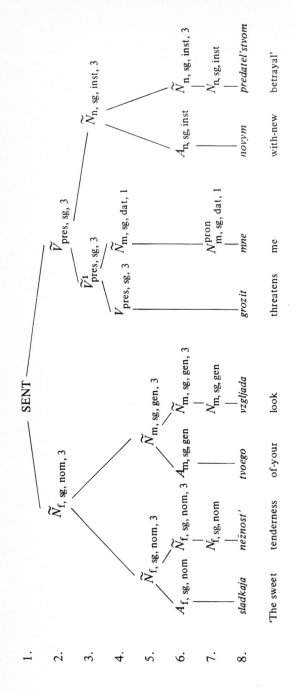

The restriction just introduced (no more than two symbols in the right-hand part of a rule) can also be imposed upon an arbitrary PS grammar, formulating it, however, in a somewhat different manner. Namely, we will require that each rule have the form $Z_1CZ_2 \rightarrow Z_1TZ_2$, where T consists of one or two symbols. Such a PS grammar is naturally also called b i n a r y. It is not difficult to show that for each PS grammar it is possible to construct a binary PS grammar equivalent to it.

Thus any sentence described by a PS grammar (in particular, by a CF grammar) and assigned in accordance with this grammar an IC structure (= a P-marker), can always be described by a binary PS (CF) grammar; i.e., its IC structure can always be represented in terms of strictly binary constituents. This can be done 'uniformly', in an identical manner for all sentences of the language. What has been said is a proven fact; however, from this it in no way follows that the binary representation of sentences of a natural language is always satisfactory and natural from the viewpoint of linguistic interpretation. The theory asserts only that the same phenomena can be described in different ways: binarily and not binarily (a similar situation was noted above — the context-bound and context-free descriptions of the same sentences, p. 40). The criteria for the selection of the appropriate description lie outside the theory: this selection should be made on the basis of the considerations pertaining to specific goals and the nature of the task we are facing.

FINITE STATE GRAMMARS (FS GRAMMARS)

Now we will return to our course — the introduction of further restrictions on the grammars being examined. Since the number of symbols in the right-hand part of a rule has already been made minimal, it remains to impose restrictions on the NATURE of the replacing symbols. Let us require, for example, that the right-hand part of each rule either consist of one symbol, or have the form bB, where b is a terminal symbol and B is a nonterminal symbol (i.e., a symbol representing a syntactic category). As a result we obtain a special class of CF grammars; the grammars of this class are called f i n i t e   s t a t e   (FS) g r a m m a r s.[13] The languages generated by FS grammars are also called f i n i t e   s t a t e, or FS, l a n g u a g e s.

The most important feature of FS grammars is the specific form of derivation. Let us construct as an example the FS grammar G_2, keeping in mind the generation of sentences of the type *Sladkaja nežnost' grozit novym predatel'stvom* 'Sweet tenderness threatens with-new betrayal' (a simplified variant of the sentence on p. 42).

THE SCHEME OF GRAMMAR G_2

1. $\text{SENT} \rightarrow N_{g,\,n,\,nom}$

2. $N_{g,\,n,\,c} \rightarrow sladkij_{g,\,n,\,c}\, N_{g,\,n,\,c}$

3. $N_{g,\,n,\,c} \rightarrow novyj_{g,\,n,\,c}\, N_{g,\,n,\,c}$

4. $N_{f,\,n,\,nom} \rightarrow nežnost'_{f,\,n,\,nom}\, V_{n,3}$

5. $N_{n,\,n,\,nom} \rightarrow predatel'stvo_{n,\,n,\,nom}\, V_{n,3}$

6. $N_{f,\,n,\,inst} \rightarrow nežnost'_{f,\,n,\,inst}$

7. $N_{n,\,n,\,inst} \rightarrow predatel'stvo_{n,\,n,\,inst}$

8. $V_{n,3} \rightarrow grozit'_{n,3}\, N_{g,\,n',\,inst}$

The indicated sentence will have in this grammar the following derivation:

SENT

(1) $N_{f,\,sg,\,nom}$

(2) $sladkaja\, N_{f,\,sg,\,nom}$

(4) $sladkaja\, nežnost'\, V_{sg,\,3}$

(8) $sladkaja\, nežnost'\, grozit\, N_{n,\,sg,\,inst}$

(3) $sladkaja\, nežnost'\, grozit\, novym\, N_{n,\,sg,\,inst}$

(7) $sladkaja\, nežnost'\, grozit\, novym\, predatel'stvom$ 'sweet tenderness threatens with-new betrayal'

As we see, each intermediate string contains exactly one nonterminal symbol, which occupies in it the rightmost position.

This means that the sentence is being generated from left to right: at each step the grammar outputs an actual word-form and after it a nonterminal symbol which indicates what construction (in other words, phrase type) may follow this word-form; then (at the next step) a word-form which begins or constitutes this construction is produced, after which there again follows a nonterminal symbol of the next construction; etc. The FS grammar predicts, so to speak, what can follow the output word-form, with the depth of the prediction being one symbol; each selection is conditioned entirely by only one preceding selection.

It is important to note that the derivation of a sentence in an FS grammar **NB** does not specify a natural representation of the IC structure of the sentence (as was the case for PS and CF grammars). Strictly speaking, FS grammars also produce some constituent structure, as do all PS grammars, but these constituents usually have a purely formal nature and do not lend themselves to natural linguistic interpretation. Thus the above cited derivation gives for our sentence the following analysis into 'constituents':

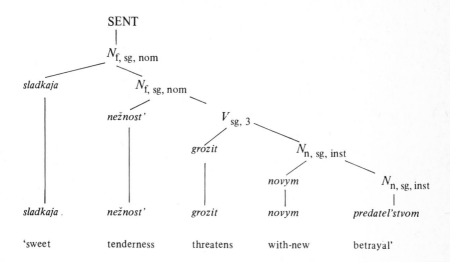

sladkaja	neznost'	grozit	novym	predatel'stvom
'sweet	tenderness	threatens	with-new	betrayal'

One can hardly agree with breaking the sentence down into two constituents — *sladkaja* 'sweet' and everything else, or with the categories ascribed to the constituents obtained. In the sentence *Neznost' grozit mne predatel'stvom* 'Tenderness threatens me with-betrayal' the result would be even worse: the string *mne predatel'stvom* 'me with-betrayal' would be considered a constituent![14] Therefore, the interpretation of the derivation in a FS grammar as an IC structure, generally speaking, makes no sense; usually the FS derivation is interpreted in another manner, as a sequence of syntactic predictions and their realizations. **NB**

Note that the class of FS languages is narrower than the class of CF languages: there are CF languages which are not generated by FS grammars (for example, the language consisting of all possible strings of the form $a^n b^n$).[15] **T**
1.1.5

CONCLUDING REMARKS

In the foregoing exposition we were far from exhausting all the possibilities for restricting the classes of grammars (not even those that seem natural from the viewpoint of linguistic interpretation). However, we will not examine other restrictions here but instead indicate the hierarchy of the established classes of grammars:

arbitrary grammars ⊃ nonshortening grammars ⊃ PS grammars ⊃ CF grammars ⊃ binary CF grammars ⊃ FS grammars.

These six classes of grammars generate only four different classes of languages:

recursively enumerable languages ⊃ PS languages ⊃ CF languages ⊃ FS languages

(since nonshortening and PS grammars generate the same languages, as is also the case with CF grammars and binary CF grammars).

Note that N. Chomsky and some other authors often employ a different terminology, see below:

Terms used in this book	Chomsky's terms
arbitrary grammars	type 0 grammars
PS grammars	type 1 grammars
CF grammars	type 2 grammars
FS grammars	type 3 grammars

Arbitrary grammars are sometimes called also unrestricted rewriting systems (URS's).

Since recursively enumerable languages form too broad a class, seemingly devoid of linguistic interest, we will consider below only three subsequent classes, i.e., PS languages, CF languages, and FS languages, along with the corresponding grammars.

The reader might well ask the following question: why does it prove useful to introduce ever more restrictions on the examined grammars, thus establishing their ever narrower classes? This is nothing other than the methodological device that is widely used in most sciences: in describing a complex domain, one deliberately limits the set of one's descriptive means, **NB** examining also such means which seem in the general case to be obviously insufficient. The study may begin with the minimum available means; each time these prove insufficient, new means are gradually introduced; thus one can determine by what means it is possible or impossible to manage to describe a particular phenomenon and thereby to better understand its nature. Until the appearance of mathematical models of language such an approach was, in general, alien to linguistics. Linguistics owes its subsequent inculcation first of all to mathematical linguistics, especially the theory of grammars.

NOTES

1. Sets generated by automatic devices of an arbitrary form are called in the theory of algorithms r e c u r s i v e l y   e n u m e r a b l e. The fact that any recursively enumerable set is generated by some grammar has been rigorously proven (Davies 1958: Chapter 6, § 2; Gladkij 1973: § 1.4; see also the sketch of the proof in Chomsky 1963: 338).
2. Every recursive set is recursively enumerable, but the converse is not true: there exist recursively enumerable sets for which there is no recognizing algorithm (decision procedure).
3. The length of a string is the number of symbols in it: for example, the length of the string $AABC_+D$ is equal to 5 (C_+ is a SINGLE symbol). Note that grammar G_0 does not satisfy the above requirement: it contains 'shortening' rules, namely IV.1, IV.2, IX.2, IX.6, X.1 and XI (see pp. 19–21). However, language $L(G_0)$ is recursive, simply because it is finite.
4. The number of strings of length n which can be composed of p symbols is equal to p^n, the number of strings of length $(n-1)$ of p symbols is equal to p^{n-1}, etc.; the number of strings of 0 symbols is equal to $p^0 = 1$ (the string of length 0 – the empty string – is unique). Note also that we always have $p > 1$, since the terminal and nonterminal vocabularies are assumed to be nonempty.
5. Let us explain how this expression is obtained. If there are P different elements and we construct from them sequences without repetitions, then the length of each such sequence does not exceed P: it is equal to P if the sequence includes all the elements, otherwise it is less than P. The number of sequences of length P composed of P elements is $P!$ (the number of permutations of P elements taken P at a time). The number of sequences of length $P-1$ composed of the given P elements is $(P-1)! \cdot P$ (from the given $P-1$ elements it is possible to compose $(P-1)!$ sequences, while it is possible to select $P-1$ elements from P elements in $P = C_P^1$ ways).

Analogously, the number of sequences of length $P-2$ of the given P elements is $(P-2)! \cdot C_P^2$ (since $P-2$ elements can be selected from the given P elements precisely in C_P^2 ways), etc.

6. Here we have used the well-known formula for the number of combinations:

$$C_P^k = \frac{P!}{k!\,(P-k)!}$$

7. By 'a step' we understand here constructing the next derivation along with verification of whether it ends in x.
8. Without citing here a complete proof of this statement, we'll explain its basic idea using as illustration a special case: the rule of the form $AB \rightarrow BA$, where A and B are nonterminal symbols. Such a rule can be replaced by four PS rules:

   (1) $AB \rightarrow 1B$
   (2) $1B \rightarrow 12$
   (3) $12 \rightarrow B2$
   (4) $B2 \rightarrow BA$

(here 1 and 2 are NEW nonterminal symbols which are not encountered in any of the old rules). It is clear that the sequential application of these rules is equivalent to the application of the rule $AB \rightarrow BA$, while the fact that we have replaced the latter by rules (1)–(4) cannot lead to the appearance of 'superfluous' derivations, since the symbols 1 and 2 are new.

9. Our notations are explained below, after the scheme of the grammar.

10. Yet in poetic speech such combinations are allowed: *v četyrexletnjuju menja* 'in the four-year-old me' (M. Cvetaeva).

11. On constituents also see below, p. 120 and following.

12. PS grammars containing context-sensitive rules are correspondingly called c o n t e x t - s e n s i t i v e   g r a m m a r s (CS grammars, or csg's).

13. Usually FS grammars are defined somewhat differently: it is required that in any rule containing only one symbol in its right-hand part, this symbol be terminal. However, the classes of languages generated by FS grammars in the sense of both definitions coincide; therefore, we allow ourselves to use the same term.

14. The latter sentence is not generated by grammar G_2, but it will not be difficult for the reader to complete the grammar in such a way that it would be generated (it is sufficient to add two rules).

15. Let us recall that languages $\left\{a^n b^n a^n\right\}$ and $\left\{a^n b^n c^n\right\}$ are not CF languages; cf. p. 40.

4. Generative Grammars and Natural Languages

We will now make some remarks concerning the following problem: what is the possibility of describing natural languages by means of generative formal grammars?

Following the principle just indicated, we will begin with their narrowest class, finite state grammars.

The relation between generative formal grammars and natural languages is unquestionably extremely important and interesting from the linguist's viewpoint; the mathematician studying the theory of formal grammars is no less excited by the problem — for just in natural languages he should see the main interpretation of his own theory, while a convincing interpretation not only increases the 'external' value of the theory, but also serves as a source for new ideas and methods within the theory itself.

However, this problem is very complex and has so far been little studied. Therefore, we are not in a position to offer the reader a coherent exposition of clear-cut results obtained in the descriptions of actual languages with the help of the generative grammars of one or another particular class. We will have to satisfy ourselves with some considerations of a general nature and with a few well-known facts.

FS GRAMMARS AND NATURAL LANGUAGES

Two primary properties of an FS grammar are, first, that it generates sentences strictly in one direction (under our definition, from left to right), expanding them word by word, and second, that it has a 'short memory' — it can 'remember' exactly one step, and no more. This means the following. In a natural sentence it frequently happens that words b and c, which are not contiguous, agree (in the broad sense of the term); i.e., between them there is a certain grammatical correspondence. In PS grammars and even in CF grammars this can be accounted for in a simple and natural manner: it is sufficient for words b and c (or their predecessors) to appear together at the same step of the derivation as direct descendants of the same symbol. It is at this moment that they are assigned information about the grammatical correspondence between them; after this they can be separated by as many symbols as one wants — the information about their correspondence will all the same be preserved. For example, in grammar G_1 the predecessors of the grammatical subject and the finite verb (the symbols $\tilde{N}_{g, n, nom, p}$ and $\tilde{V}_{pres, n, p}$) appear simultaneously as the descendants of the symbol SENT through the application of rule I: their agreement in number and person (n, p) is preserved up to the end of the derivation, no matter what lexical material is placed between them. Thus the information about the agreement of words b and c is 'remembered' with ANY distance between them. In this sense it can be said that CF grammars have an unlimited memory. As to FS grammars, they have in the same sense a limited memory. The point is that an FS grammar is capable of conveying information about the correspondence only from the immediately preceding symbol to the immediately following one: for example, in rules 4 and 5 of grammar G_2 (p. 44) the information about number (the subscript n) is conveyed from the grammatical subject to the predicate (= main verb) immediately following it. Therefore, if the information about a correspondence between b and c is to be conveyed across some intermediate symbols, then in an FS grammar this can be done only by ascribing the indications about this correspondence to ALL the intermediate symbols, for which these indications are in essence unnecessary. Thus, if we want an FS grammar to generate Russian sentences in which the grammatical subject is separated from the main verb by some words, for example, by a noun in the genitive case modifying the subject (*Nežnost' vzgljadov grozit predatel'stvom* 'The-tenderness of-glances threatens with-betrayal'), we will have to introduce special rules in which the verb will be formally made to agree in number, person, or gender with the immediately preceding genitive noun. However, such agreement has to be accomplished not on the basis of the proper features of this noun, but rather on the basis of artificial 'nonproper' features which would reflect the grammatical number, person and gender of the subject — for in fact the verb should agree precisely with the latter. This means that along with each symbol $N_{g, n, gen}$ we would have to introduce six new symbols: $N_{g,n,gen} \|_{m, \, \text{sg}}$, $N_{g, n, gen} \|_{m, pl}$, $\cdot \cdot \cdot$, etc., i.e., 'a noun of gender g, in number n, in the genitive case, which depends on a grammatical subject of masculine gender in the singular', 'a noun of gender g, in number n, in the genitive case, which depends on a grammatical subject of masculine gender in the plural', etc. It is necessary to act in the same fashion also in case the subject and the predicate are separated by adverbs, for example, *Nežnost' vzgljada surovo grozit mne* 'The-tenderness of-a-glance severely threatens me': here it will be necessary to introduce special categories of adverbs, namely: (1) adverbs depending on a verb that agrees with a masculine subject in the singular, (2) adverbs depending on a verb that agrees with a masculine subject in the plural, etc.

Moreover, if the subject and the predicate are separated by one or several subordinate clauses, then each of the categories encountered in these clauses should be split into at least six categories, and, consequently, all the rules for generating subordinate clauses should in fact be repeated six times. Of course, all that has been said remains valid even for those cases when the subject and the predicate are separated by arbitrarily many words, for example, by a string of genitive cases of any length whatsoever or by any number of subordinate clauses. Thus, although an FS grammar, like a CF grammar, is capable of ensuring agreement between words standing arbitrarily far apart — $a \ldots a'$ — this is achieved in a cumbersome and, what is most important, a quite unnatural way: it is necessary to introduce many additional lexical categories (word classes) which clearly contradict linguistic intuition.

But this is not all. If it is necessary to deal not with one, but with many word pairs linked by agreement, with each following one 'nested' in the preceding one and the number of such nested pairs theoretically unlimited —

$a'\,b\,c\,d \ldots d'c'b'a'$,

then an FS grammar proves in principle incapable of ensuring agreement. This fact can be rigorously proven (see, for example, Gladkij 1973, the corollary from theorem 5.7, and exercise 5.16); we will not give the proof here, but try instead to explain, with the aid of some informal remarks, why this is so.

As we have already seen, to ensure the agreement of a single word pair (in an FS grammar) it is necessary to split all the categories capable of separating the words of this pair; in our example with the subject and predicate the number of categories is multiplied by six. If between words linked by agreement there is nested another pair with agreement — $a\,b \ldots b'a'$ — then each of the already split intermediate categories will have to be split once more, which again increases the number of categories (each category encountered between b and b' will have to bear indications of the agreement both of a with a' and b with b'). Consequently, if the number of nested pairs is potentially unlimited, then for ensuring agreement it would be necessary to have in our FS grammar infinitely many categories (hence infinitely many nonterminal symbols), while the number of symbols in any grammar is finite. Therefore, the above situation cannot be described by an FS grammar.

However, this situation is typical enough in natural languages. For example, it occurs in complex sentences of the following type:

$$
\begin{array}{cccc}
a & b & c & d
\end{array}
$$

(1) Russ. *Čelovek, kotoromu gostja, kotoraja, kogda xozjain, kotoryj . . . ,*

$$
\begin{array}{ccc}
d' & c' & b'
\end{array}
$$

vstal, sobralas' tancevat' v sosednej komnate, isportila kostjum,

$$
\begin{array}{cccc}
a' & a & b & c
\end{array}
$$

ušël domoj 'The man, whose suit the female guest, who, when

$$
\begin{array}{ccc}
d & d' & c'
\end{array}
$$

the host, who . . . , stood up, had gotten ready to dance in the

$$
\begin{array}{cc}
b' & a'
\end{array}
$$

next room, ruined, went home'.

In (1), all the verbs a'–d' agree with their subjects in number and gender. The slot marked by three dots may be filled with any clauses, including ones containing many further subordinate clauses, also with a sequential nesting. Such sentences are regularly encountered in very different languages.

Examples of a potentially unlimited nesting of word-pairs with agreement can be cited for simple sentences as well. Such, for example, are Russian constructions with the sequential nesting of preposed participial phrases:

$$
\begin{array}{cccc}
a & b & c & d
\end{array}
$$

(2) *. . . dlja rasstavšejsja s razyskivajuščim vljublënnogo v ètu čarujuščuju*

$$
\begin{array}{cccccc}
d' & c' & b' & a' & a' & a
\end{array}
$$

vsex devušku čeloveka pisatelem ženy 'for the wife who separated with

$$
\begin{array}{ccccc}
b' & b & c' & c & d'
\end{array}
$$

the writer who was seeking the man who was in love with this girl

$$
\begin{array}{c}
d
\end{array}
$$

who charmed everyone',

where all the participles a–d agree in gender, number and case with their nominal heads a'–d' Cf. also the sequential nesting of pairs of conjoined nouns which agree in case:

$$
\begin{array}{cccc}
a & b & c & d
\end{array}
$$

(3) *Ot lemmy trebuetsja èkvivalentnost' teoreme o kompaktnosti otrezkov*

$$
\begin{array}{ccc}
d' & c' & b'
\end{array}
$$

i kvadratov, ili o Δ-kompaktnosti, no ne utverždeniju 4377, a takže

$$
\begin{array}{ccc}
a' & a & b
\end{array}
$$

prostota 'From the lemma we require equivalence to the theorem about

$$\overset{c}{} \qquad \overset{d}{} \qquad \overset{d'}{} \qquad\qquad\qquad \overset{c'}{}$$

the compactness of segments and squares, or about the Δ-compactness,

$$\overset{b'}{} \qquad\qquad\qquad\qquad \overset{a'}{}$$

but not to assertion 4377, as well as simplicity'.[1]

A further example is provided by the French construction

N′*de* N″*de* N‴ . . . A‴ A″ A′,

which is current in all Romance languages (even if stylistically somewhat awkward):

$$\overset{a}{} \qquad\qquad\qquad\qquad \overset{b}{} \quad \overset{c}{} \quad \overset{c'}{}$$

(4) . . . *les qualités extraordinaires de cet homme de taille moyenne,*

$$\overset{b'}{} \qquad\qquad \overset{a'}{}$$

intelligent et courageux, décrites à maintes reprises dans le fameux ouvrage de M. Clas. . .

Also well known are two more examples of the inapplicability of FS grammars (in these cases CF grammars are also inapplicable, see below, p. 65 and following), which pertain, however, to rather marginal phenomena.

As for the just mentioned examples (1)–(4), although the number of languages in which such constructions are permissible is probably limited, they nevertheless appear quite typical, and therefore it seems impossible to disregard them entirely. Consequently, it must be admitted that it is impossible to construct a COMPLETE description of an arbitrary natural language on the basis of ONLY FS grammars. Strictly speaking, this means the following: either the FS grammar we have constructed for a language will not generate certain correct sentences (in particular, sentences of the type *abcd . . . d′c′b′a′*, see above), or, if we make it capable of generating any correct sentences (and this is always possible), then it will necessarily generate certain incorrect sentences as well: for example, along with the sentence *abcd . . . d′c′b′a′* it will generate the sentence *abcd . . . c′a′b′d′*, with agreement violated.

Below, when speaking about the impossibility of describing a language with a particular class of grammars, we have always in mind just this — either the grammar does not generate certain correct sentences of a rather ordinary and widespread type (i.e., our grammar is incomplete), or necessarily generates, in addition to all correct sentences, certain incorrect ones (i.e., our grammar is inadequate).

However, the fact that FS grammars are insufficient for describing a natural language in its entirety still does not exclude the possibility of describing particular FRAGMENTS of a natural language in terms of FS grammars. It seems likely enough that in natural languages the 'FS fragments', as a rule, cover the main part. In fact, constructions which exhibit an unlimited nesting of word-pairs with agreement are few, while constructions of the type indicated on p. 65 are, moreover, marginal. FS grammars are thereby capable in principle of describing a rather substantial subset of the set of sentences (simple, compound and complex) of a natural language. In addition, FS grammars can describe other linguistic objects: for example, phrases (see below, pp. 55–57, the description of Russian elementary noun phrases), word-forms, and syllables. Of course, from what has been said it does not at all follow that in all those instances where FS grammars are applicable, they describe their object in a natural manner, i.e., that they are always illuminating. On the contrary, from the exposition on pp. 49–51 it is evident that this is not the case. However, any grammar which is specially suited for the natural description of some FS fragment of a language (e.g., for describing simple sentences not containing constructions like (1)–(4) above), will be equivalent to some FS grammar. But since grammars equivalent to FS grammars (while not being such) are usually characterized in some respect – either with respect to their rules, or with respect to their derivations – by approximately the same degree of simplicity as FS grammars, we thereby obtain something like a standard of simplicity. In constructing a grammar that describes simple sentences, we should seek that in at least one of the indicated respects it be not much more complex than the corresponding FS grammar. (Let us recall that 'simplicity' should be understood in the logical and not in the everyday sense – Chapter 2, fn. 6.) Cf. below, pp. 70 and 73, the examples of grammars with bounded memory and of 'left-to-right' grammars.

NB

As to the question of exactly where FS grammars prove not only applicable, but also natural, generally it has so far remained little studied, though its clarification is of great interest. On the preliminary level it seems possible to suppose that FS grammars are rather convenient in describing elementary noun phrases[2] of the type

(5) Russ. *ili ne tol'ko iz vsex ètix trëx našix pervyx ogromnyx trëxaročnyx metalličeskix železnodorožnyx mostov* 'or not only of all these three (of) our first great three-arched metal railroad bridges'

(this is an example of the maximal pattern of the elementary noun phrase – ENP – in Modern Standard Russian; in fact such phrases usually appear in some simpler form since particular positions might not be filled).

We will now cite an example of an FS grammar, namely grammar G_3, which generates any Russian ENP's of the indicated type (with inanimate N only).

THE SCHEME OF GRAMMAR G_3

I.

$$\text{ENP} \rightarrow \left\{ \begin{array}{l} \textit{ili} \text{ 'or'} \\ \textit{i} \text{ 'and'} \\ \textit{libo} \text{ 'either'} \\ \cdots\cdots\cdots \\ \Lambda \end{array} \right\} \text{ENP}^1$$

As above (p. 20). Λ is the empty string; the presence of Λ means that the corresponding position in ENP may remain unfilled.

II.

$$\text{ENP}^1 \rightarrow \left\{ \begin{array}{l} \textit{ni} \text{ 'neither'} \\ \textit{ne} \text{ 'not'} \\ \textit{ne tol'ko} \text{ 'not only'} \\ \textit{otnjud' ne} \text{ 'in no way'} \\ \textit{liš'} \text{ 'only'} \\ \textit{tol'ko} \text{ 'only'} \\ \textit{xotja by} \text{ 'at least'} \\ \cdots\cdots\cdots\cdots\cdots \\ \Lambda \end{array} \right\} \text{ENP}^2$$

III.

1.
$$\text{ENP}^2 \rightarrow \left\{ \begin{array}{l} \textit{iz} \text{ 'out of'} \\ \textit{s} \text{ 'from'} \\ \textit{bez} \text{ 'without'} \end{array} \right\} \text{ENP}^3{}_{\text{g, n, gen}}$$

2.
$$\text{ENP}^2 \rightarrow \left\{ \begin{array}{l} \textit{k} \text{ 'to'} \\ \textit{po} \text{ 'along'} \end{array} \right\} \text{ENP}^3{}_{\text{g, n, dat}}$$

$\cdots\cdots\cdots\cdots\cdots\cdots\cdots\cdots\cdots\cdots\cdots$

6. $\text{ENP}^2 \rightarrow \text{ENP}^3{}_{\text{g, n, c}}$

IV.

$$\text{ENP}^3{}_{\text{g, n, c}} \rightarrow \left\{ \begin{array}{l} \textit{ves'}_{\text{g, n, c}} \text{ 'all'} \\ \textit{každyj}_{\text{g, n, c}} \text{ 'each'} \\ \textit{kakoj-libo}_{\text{g, n, c}} \text{ 'some'} \\ \cdots\cdots\cdots\cdots\cdots \\ \Lambda \end{array} \right\} \text{ENP}^4{}_{\text{g, n, c}}$$

V.

$$\text{ENP}^4{}_{\text{g, n, c}} \rightarrow \left\{ \begin{array}{l} \textit{ètot}_{\text{g, n, c}} \text{ 'this'} \\ \textit{tot}_{\text{g, n, c}} \text{ 'that'} \\ \textit{ètot že samyj}_{\text{g, n, c}} \text{ 'this very'} \\ \cdots\cdots\cdots\cdots\cdots \\ \Lambda \end{array} \right\} \text{ENP}^5{}_{\text{g, n, c}}$$

VI.

1.

$$ENP^5_{g,n,c} \rightarrow \left\{ \begin{array}{l} odin_{g,n,c} \text{ 'one'} \\ \Lambda \end{array} \right\} \qquad ENP^6_{g,n,c}$$

2.

$$ENP^5_{g,n,c} \rightarrow \left\{ \begin{array}{l} dva_{g,c} \text{ 'two'} \\ tri_c \text{ 'three'} \\ četyre_c \text{ 'four'} \end{array} \right\} \qquad ENP^6_{g,\,sg,\,gen}$$

Here c = nom, acc

3.

$$ENP^5_{g,n,c} \rightarrow \left\{ \begin{array}{l} pjat'_c \text{ 'five'} \\ šest'_c \text{ 'six'} \\ \cdots\cdots\cdots\cdots\cdots \\ tysjača\ devjat'sot \\ šest'desjat\ šest'_c \text{ '1966'} \end{array} \right\} \qquad ENP^6_{g,\,pl,\,gen}$$

Here c = nom, acc

4.

$$ENP^5_{g,n,c} \rightarrow \left\{ \begin{array}{l} dva_{g,c} \text{ 'two'} \\ \cdots\cdots\cdots\cdots\cdots \\ pjat'_c \text{ 'five'} \\ šest'_c \text{ 'six'} \\ \cdots\cdots\cdots\cdots\cdots \\ tysjača\ devjat'sot \\ šest'desjat\ šest'_c \text{ '1966'} \end{array} \right\} \qquad ENP^6_{g,\,pl,\,c}$$

Here c ≠ nom, acc

VII.

$$ENP^6_{g,n,c} \rightarrow \left\{ \begin{array}{l} moj_{g,n,c} \text{ 'my'} \\ tvoj_{g,n,c} \text{ 'your'} \\ \cdots\cdots\cdots\cdots \\ ix \text{ 'their'} \\ \Lambda \end{array} \right\} \qquad ENP^7_{g,n,c}$$

VIII.

$$ENP^7_{g,n,c} \rightarrow \left\{ \begin{array}{l} pervyj_{g,n,c} \text{ 'first'} \\ vtoroj_{g,n,c} \text{ 'second'} \\ \cdots\cdots\cdots\cdots\cdots\cdots \\ tysjača\ devjat'sot \\ šest'desjat\ šestoj_{g,n,c} \text{ '1966th'} \\ \cdots\cdots\cdots\cdots\cdots \\ \Lambda \end{array} \right\} \qquad \begin{array}{l} ENP^{8i}_{g,n,c} \\ (1 \leq i \leq p) \end{array}$$

IX. $\text{ENP}^{8i} \rightarrow a^i_{g,n,c} \quad \text{ENP}^{8j}_{g,n,c} \quad (1 \leq j \leq i \leq p)$

The notation $a^i_{g,n,c}$ is explained in a note following the grammar (Note to rule IX).

X. $\text{ENP}^{8i}_{g,n,c} \rightarrow N_{g,n,c}$

XI.

1.
$$N_{m,n,c} \rightarrow \left\{ \begin{array}{l} most_{n,c}\,\text{'bridge'} \\ nos_{n,c}\,\text{'nose'} \\ sakvojaž_{n,c}\,\text{'travelling bag'} \\ \cdots \cdots \cdots \cdots \cdots \end{array} \right\}$$

2.
$$N_{f,n,c} \rightarrow \left\{ \begin{array}{l} reka_{n,c}\,\text{'river'} \\ guba_{n,c}\,\text{'lip'} \\ sumka_{n,c}\,\text{'hand bag'} \\ \cdots \cdots \cdots \cdots \cdots \end{array} \right\}$$

3.
$$N_{n,n,c} \rightarrow \left\{ \begin{array}{l} ozero_{n,c}\,\text{'lake'} \\ uxo_{n,c}\,\text{'ear'} \\ vedro_{n,c}\,\text{'bucket'} \\ \cdots \cdots \cdots \cdots \cdots \end{array} \right\}$$

Note to rule IX. The symbol a^i stands for a specific adjective of the ith class; to one class belong adjectives capable of occupying the same linear position with respect to the modified noun, while the inequality $i > j$ means that an adjective of the ith class should stand farther away (i.e., more to the left) from the noun than an adjective of the jth class. For example, the adjective *francuzskij* 'French' (*anglijskij* 'English', *sovetskij* 'Soviet', . . .) has a smaller class index than the adjective *interesnyj* 'interesting' (*novyj* 'new', *cennyj* 'valuable', . . .), since the expression *interesnye francuzskie žurnaly* 'interesting French magazines' is more usual than *francuzskie interesnye žurnaly* 'French interesting magazines'. The total number of such adjective classes is designated by p. (For interesting details on a similar classification of adjectives in English see Vendler 1967: 174–191.)

Grammar G_3 should therefore be supplemented with a list of adjectives furnished with class indices. For our example we take a small list which contains five classes of adjectives (see p. 58).

1st class	2nd class	3rd class	4th class	5th class
političeskij 'political'	*stal'noj* 'steel-'	*nemeckij* 'German'	*belyj* 'white'	*xorošij* 'good'
muzykal'nyj 'musical'	*bumažnyj* 'paper-'	*somalijskij* 'Somali'	*sinij* 'blue'	*negodnyj* 'worthless'
literaturnyj 'literary'	*derevjannyj* 'wood-'	*češskij* 'Czech'	*žëltyj* 'yellow'	*zamečatel'nyj* 'remarkable'
matematičeskij 'mathematical'	*kostjanoj* 'bone-'	*gruzinskij* 'Georgian'	*rozovyj* 'rose'	*interesnyj* 'interesting'
ximičeskij 'chemical'	*vinogradnyj* 'grape-'	*norvežskij* 'Norwegian'	*čërnyj* 'black'	*otličnyj* 'outstanding'
. . . .	. . . .	. . . .	. . . .	. . . .

This partition of adjectives is undertaken exclusively for illustrative purposes and reflects the real picture quite roughly: the rules of mutual ordering of Russian adjectives cannot in reality be confined to the framework of linear ordering; in addition, the order of adjectives depends also on the so-called logical accent (or the 'functional perspective' of the respective phrase). Thus, *interesnaja matematičeskaja kniga* ≈ 'there is a book on mathematics, it is interesting,' while *matematičeskaja interesnaja kniga* ≈ 'there is an interesting book, it is on mathematics'. Accordingly, in a linguistic paper devoted to NOMINAL constructions of a language, there can be a discussion of 'attributive nominal constructions', 'subject nominal constructions', etc., while in papers on ATTRIBUTIVE constructions we will more likely encounter 'nominal attributive constructions', 'verbal attributive constructions', etc. In describing such cases here we have in mind the most neutral, most ordinary word order.

Let us cite AN EXAMPLE OF A DERIVATION in grammar G_3:

ENP

(I) i ENP^1 'and'
(II) i *xotja by* ENP^2 'and at least'
(III.4) i *xotja by s* ENP$^3_{f, pl, inst}$ 'and at least with'
(IV) i *xotja by s* ENP$^4_{f, pl, inst}$ 'and at least with'
(V) i *xotja by s* ENP$^5_{f, pl, inst}$ 'and at least with'
(VI.4) i *xotja by s devjat'ju* ENP$^6_{f, pl, inst}$ 'and at least with nine'

(VII) *i xotja by s devjat'ju našimi* $\text{ENP}^7_{\text{f, pl, inst}}$ 'and at least with nine (of) our'

(VIII) *i xotja by s devjat'ju našimi* $\text{ENP}^{85}_{\text{f, pl, inst}}$ 'and at least with nine (of) our'

(IX) *i xotja by s devjat'ju našimi otličnymi* $\text{ENP}^{82}_{\text{f, pl, inst}}$ 'and at least with nine (of) our outstanding'

(IX) *i xotja by s devjat'ju našimi otličnymi bumažnymi* $\text{ENP}^{82}_{\text{f, pl, inst}}$ 'and at least with nine (of) our outstanding paper'

(X) *i xotja by s devjat'ju našimi otličnymi bumažnymi* $N_{\text{f, pl, inst}}$ 'and at least with nine (of) our outstanding paper'

(XI.2) *i xotja by s devjat'ju našimi otličnymi bumažnymi sumkami* 'and at least with nine (of) our outstanding paper bags'.

We emphasize again that it will be quite helpful for the reader to practice the independent construction of derivations. This is also true, of course, of all the preceding and subsequent examples of grammars.

Now let us focus attention on the fact that the constituents which are obtained from the just cited derivation by the method described on p. 36, prove in this case to be quite natural (unlike those obtained by using Grammar G_2), see p. 60. This is explained by the peculiarities of the syntactic structure of elementary noun phrases in Russian — the Russian ENP's happen to be constructed according to the pattern

$$\ldots (h(g(f(e(d(c(b(a))))))))\ldots$$

I.e., all the elements related to the main element *a* stand to the left of it, and each of them is immediately related to (either modifies or subordinates) the whole phrase that follows it; any element, except for the main one (i.e., the last one), can be absent. The nonterminal symbols encountered in the derivation — ENP^1, ENP^2, ... — are naturally interpreted as symbols for incomplete ENP's, i.e., as types of constituents: ENP^1 is a noun phrase with no conjunction, ENP^2 is a noun phrase with no conjunction and no restrictive (negative) particle, ENP^3 is a noun phrase with no conjunction, no restrictive particle, and no preposition, etc.

In general, FS grammars are in some respect suitable for describing precisely those linguistic objects which have the type of structure indicated above, i.e., which are increased only from one side. As an example we may cite agglutinatively constructed word-forms such as

(6) Russ.$((((((posled)ova)tel')n)ost)n)yj)$, roughly '$((((($sequent$)ial)$-i$)ty)$ness$)$', or $(((((predskaz)u)em)ost)n)ost')$'$((((($predict$)a)bil)$-

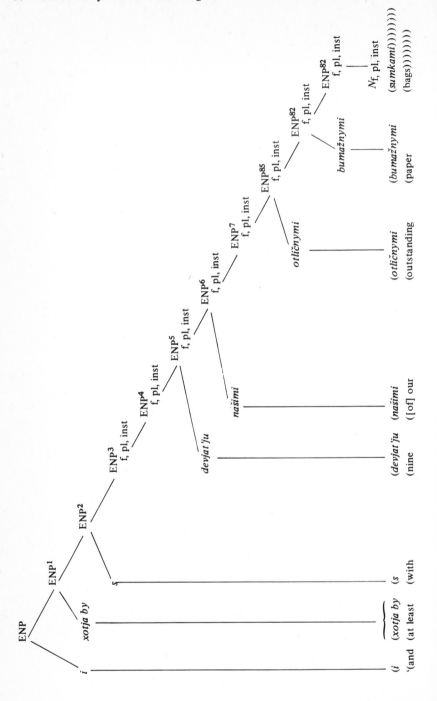

i)ty)'; cf. also (((((*cel)u*)*jušč*)*ego*)*sja*) '(of-one who is) kissing with somebody', etc.

(In languages such as Turkish or Hungarian such forms have an incomparably more regular nature.)

Of course, for describing objects expanding to the right, FS grammars not entirely like those defined on p. 43 are more natural, and namely: in this definition rules of the type $A \rightarrow bB$ should be replaced with rules of the type $A \rightarrow Bb$; i.e., it is advisable to shift from right-linear FS grammars to left-linear ones. (The term 'right-linear FS grammar' is sometimes used for FS grammar in the sense of definition on p. 43; a left-linear FS grammar is a grammar with the rules of the form $A \rightarrow Bb, A \rightarrow B, A \rightarrow b$ where A, B are nonterminals and b terminal.)

In conclusion we will explain what exactly is understood when it is said that FS grammars offer an illuminating description of linguistic objects of the type $((((a)b)c)d) \ldots$ — 'laminated' objects, so to speak. FS grammars are good here precisely because the lamination is revealed explicitly by FS derivations of the corresponding objects (this is the very 'some respect' mentioned just above). However, in other respects FS grammars might not be convenient in describing even such objects — for example, in the description of all the morphonological processes accompanying the generation of word-forms. In such cases it may prove advisable to split the corresponding phenomena into different levels and to describe them with the help of several different grammars, one of which will be finite state (for example, the FS grammar can be charged with generating word-forms on the morphemic level and, perhaps, on the 'morphic' level, too, while the subsequent morphonemic, phonemic and phonetic realization of the string obtained should be accomplished by grammars of other types).

Now we move on to the examination of context-free (CF) grammars.

CF GRAMMARS AND NATURAL LANGUAGES

The main characteristic of CF grammars is the following: at each stage of the derivation EXACTLY ONE symbol is 'processed', i.e., in no way can the presence/absence or the properties of different contiguous symbols be taken into consideration. This might create the impression that CF grammars are not well suited for describing natural languages: for in ordinary ('non-formal') grammars most assertions about the selection of particular forms, about the variation or expansion of particular elements of an utterance are, as a rule, formulated precisely with consideration for contextual conditions. Thus in describing inflected forms the linguist normally indicates which inflexion should be chosen depending on the type of stem (the stem type thus serves as context); in describing the use of Russian cases we should indicate that the accusative case of a direct object is replaced by the genitive case if the main verb is negated (and, in addition, if some other, more sophisticated conditions are met); an agentive phrase in the instrumental is possible in Russian with a deverbal noun only if this noun also has an object in the genitive case (*rassmotrenie voprosa sovetom* 'examination of the question by the council', but not **rassmotrenie sovetom* 'examination by the council'), etc. However, even an FS grammar (a quite special case of CF grammar) is, as we have seen, capable of generating the overwhelming majority of simple, compound and complex sentences of a natural language. This should be all the more valid for arbitrary CF grammars. It turns out, indeed, that in almost all cases in which the use of the context seems at first glance inevitable, it is possible, at least in principle, to get rid of it. Roughly speaking, this is done as follows: let there be a class X of linguistic elements such that in the neighborhood of the elements of some other class Y the elements of X behave differently than in the neighborhood of the elements of a third class Z, so that we have, for example, the rules:

1. $YX \rightarrow YAB$
2. $ZX \rightarrow ZCD$

These rules make use of context: Y in 1, Z in 2.

It is possible, however, to introduce two new symbols X_1 and X_2, designating by X_1 the element X in the position after Y, and by X_2 the element X in the position after Z. Then it would be possible to replace rules 1, 2 by rules 1′, 2′ using no context:

1′. $X_1 \rightarrow AB$
2′. $X_2 \rightarrow CD$

What we have done is to introduce more detailed categories of elements to account for the different behavior of elements of X in different contexts.

We will now illustrate the shift to context-free statements in the above-cited examples of reference to context. On the left we place the corresponding fragment of the context-sensitive grammar and on the right the equivalent fragment consisting of context-free rules only.

(a) Selection of case inflexion in Russian depending on the type of stem:

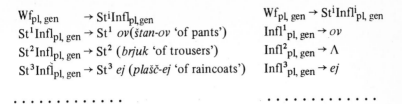

$$\text{Wf}_{\text{pl, gen}} \rightarrow \text{St}^i \text{Infl}_{\text{pl, gen}}$$
$$\text{St}^1 \text{Infl}_{\text{pl, gen}} \rightarrow \text{St}^1 \ ov(\check{s}tan\text{-}ov \text{ 'of pants'})$$
$$\text{St}^2 \text{Infl}_{\text{pl, gen}} \rightarrow \text{St}^2 \ (brjuk \text{ 'of trousers'})$$
$$\text{St}^3 \text{Infl}_{\text{pl, gen}} \rightarrow \text{St}^3 \ ej \ (pla\check{s}\check{c}\text{-}ej \text{ 'of raincoats'})$$

$$\text{Wf}_{\text{pl, gen}} \rightarrow \text{St}^i \text{Infl}^i_{\text{pl, gen}}$$
$$\text{Infl}^1_{\text{pl, gen}} \rightarrow ov$$
$$\text{Infl}^2_{\text{pl, gen}} \rightarrow \Lambda$$
$$\text{Infl}^3_{\text{pl, gen}} \rightarrow ej$$

. . . .

where Wf is a word-form, St^i a stem of type i ($i = 1, 2, 3, \ldots$), and $\text{Infl}_{\text{pl,gen}}$ is the inflexion of the genitive plural.

(b) Selection of the case of a direct object depending on the presence of negation (also in Russian):

$$\widetilde{V} \rightarrow V^{\text{tr}} \ Obj_{\text{dir}} \qquad\qquad \widetilde{V} \rightarrow V^{\text{tr}} \ Obj^1_{\text{dir}}$$
$$\widetilde{V} \rightarrow Neg \ V^{\text{tr}} \ Obj_{\text{dir}} \qquad \widetilde{V} \rightarrow Neg \ V^{\text{tr}} \ Obj^2_{\text{dir}}$$
$$X V^{\text{tr}} Obj_{\text{dir}} \rightarrow X V^{\text{tr}} \ \widetilde{N}_{\text{acc}} \ \Big| \ X \neq Neg \qquad Obj^1_{\text{dir}} \rightarrow \widetilde{N}_{\text{acc}}$$

(*Mal'čik čitaet žurnal* 'The boy is reading a magazine')
$$Neg \ V^{\text{tr}} \ Obj_{\text{dir}} \rightarrow Neg \ V^{\text{tr}} \ \widetilde{N}_{\text{gen}} \qquad Obj^2_{\text{dir}} \rightarrow \widetilde{N}_{\text{gen}}$$

(*Mal'čik ne čitaet žurnala* 'The boy is not reading a magazine')

where $\widetilde{V}$ stands for a verb phrase, V^{tr} a transitive verb, Obj_{dir} a direct object, $\widetilde{N}$ a noun phrase, and *Neg* a negation.

(c) Selection of the case of an agentive phrase which modifies a deverbal noun depending on the presence of an object in the genitive:

$$\widetilde{N} \rightarrow \widetilde{N}'Obj \ Ag \qquad \widetilde{N} \rightarrow \widetilde{N}'Obj \ Ag^1$$
$$\widetilde{N} \rightarrow \widetilde{N}'Ag \qquad\quad \widetilde{N} \rightarrow \widetilde{N}'Ag^2$$
$$Obj \ Ag \rightarrow Obj \ \widetilde{N}_{\text{inst}} \qquad Ag^1 \rightarrow \widetilde{N}_{\text{inst}}$$

(*rassmotrenie voprosa sovetom* 'examination of the question by the council')

$$X \ Ag \rightarrow X \widetilde{N}_{\text{gen}} \ \Big| \ X \neq Obj \quad Ag^2 \rightarrow \widetilde{N}_{\text{gen}}$$

(*zasedanie soveta* 'the meeting of the council')

(*Obj* – object, *Ag* – agent)

In these three examples (linguistically quite different) the very same formal device is used: the necessary information about the context is 'driven' into new categories. Thus, the less we want to use the context, the more categories we will have to introduce, and vice versa. The attractiveness of using exclusively context-free rules results from the difficulty in estimating the degree of complexity of the diverse and linguistically heterogeneous references to context, while in CF grammars the 'measure' of complexity is easily available; it is simply the number of categories being used. As to the linguistic value of such an approach, in a number of cases the introduction of new categories along with a rejection of references to context proves justified, while in other cases it may seem too artificial a device — a simple fudge. However, even there the shift to context-free rules can be helpful: at least it forces the researcher to state clearly the question about the linguistic expedience of using or not using context in specific situations.

Thus, as was already noted, in ALMOST all instances the context can be eliminated from the rules of a grammar. Nevertheless, there are cases in which this is not so. In particular, it is impossible to get rid of the context, i.e., to manage with a single symbol in the left-hand part of a rule, if the rule should permute symbols: for permutation, by its very nature, is not a unary operation. Consequently, a CF grammar cannot generate a language consisting of strings for which the only method of construction is the use of permutations.

Consider, for example, a language which contains all possible strings of the type $a_1 a_2 a_3 q a'_1 a'_2 a'_3$, $a_2 a_1 a_2 a_3 q a'_2 a'_1 a'_2 a'_3$, $a_1 a_3 a_2 a_1 q a'_1 a'_3 a'_2 a'_1$, etc. and no other strings. (In general we may represent such strings in the form xqx', where the symbols a_1 and a'_1, a_2 and a'_2, etc. can be interpreted as elements which agree with, or match, each other in some special way.[3]) This language can easily be generated by a grammar containing rules of permutation, for example, by the following one:[4]

$$
\left.
\begin{array}{ll}
1. & I \rightarrow IA_i a'_i \\
2. & a'_i A_j \rightarrow A_j a'_i \\
3. & IA_i \rightarrow a_i I \\
4. & I \rightarrow q
\end{array}
\right\} \quad i, j = 1, 2, 3
$$

(a_i, a'_i, q are terminal symbols, I, A_i — nonterminal symbols, and I is the initial symbol).

Let us show as an example how the string $a_2 a_1 a_1 a_3 q a'_2 a'_1 a'_1 a'_3$ can be derived in this grammar:

	I
(1)	$IA_3 a'_3$
(1)	$IA_1 a'_1 A_3 a'_3$
(1)	$IA_1 a'_1 A_1 a'_1 A_3 a'_3$
(1)	$IA_2 a'_2 A_1 a'_1 A_1 a'_1 A_3 a'_3$
(2)	$IA_2 A_1 a'_2 a'_1 A_1 a'_1 A_3 a'_3$

· ·

$(2; 5 \text{ times}) \quad IA_2A_1A_1A_3a'_2a'_1a'_1a'_3$

$(3) \qquad\qquad\quad a_2IA_1A_1A_3a'_2a'_1a'_1a'_3$

· ·

$(3; 3 \text{ times}) \quad a_2a_1a_1a_3Ia'_2a'_1a'_1a'_3$

$(4) \qquad\qquad\quad a_2a_1a_1a_3qa'_2a'_1a'_1a'_3$

However, it is known that the language $\{xqx'\}$ cannot be generated by any CF grammar. (For a rigorous proof of this fact see, for example, Gladkij 1973: §4.3, example 2.)

It turns out that this phenomenon, i.e., fragments consisting of strings of the type xqx', is encountered in natural languages as well.

In the literature two examples of this type are described:

(1)   Constructions of the type:

$$a \qquad b \qquad c \qquad d \qquad a' \quad b' \quad c' \quad d'$$

Russ. *Miša, Perepetuja, Griša, Fëkla,* ... *ušël, prišla, vstal, sela,* ...,

$$a \qquad\qquad b \qquad\qquad c \qquad\qquad d \qquad\qquad a' \qquad b'$$

sootvetstvenno 'Michael, Perepetue, Gregory, Thekla, ... went, came,

$$c' \qquad\quad d'$$

stood up, sat down, ..., respectively'.

Here the role of x (= *abcd*. ..) is played by the string of proper nouns, and the role of x (= $a'b'c'd'$...) by the string of verbs in the past tense which in Russian obligatorily agree with these nouns in gender[5]; q is here empty.

(2)   In the American Indian language Mohawk, as P. Postal (1964) shows, there are numerous sentences in which the object of the main verb is duplicated by incorporating the corresponding stem into the main verb: 'The girl book-reads books'. In addition, any verb (including those already containing incorporated objects) is easily nominalized to produce a *nomen actionis* and so acquires the ability to function as an object — in particular, to be incorporated into the main verb: 'I book-reading-like book-reading' (i.e., 'I like reading books'). Theoretically this process can be repeated an unlimited number of times: 'You book-reading-like-discuss book-reading-liking' ('You

$$a \qquad b \qquad c$$

discuss liking (= the pleasure of) reading books'), 'They book-reading-like-

$$d \qquad q \qquad a' \qquad b' \qquad c' \qquad d'$$

discuss-see book-reading-like-discussion' ('They see a discussion of the liking of reading books'), etc. Here x'(= $a'b'c'd'$) is the object, x (= *abcd*) is its duplicate incorporated into the main verb, and q is the main verb stem proper (i.e., the main verb minus all the incorporated objects). Note that such a construction is correct in Mohawk only when the incorporated duplicate of the object corresponds exactly to the object itself in composition and the order of noun stems.

If we try to account for these examples, then it must be admitted that, generally speaking, CF grammars are insufficient for describing EVERY natural language IN ITS ENTIRETY. However, it is immediately evident that both examples are of a rather marginal nature: the first construction, although probably possible in any language, is extremely specific and does not belong to those generally used, while the second, which has a very general meaning and, apparently, may be widely used, is known so far in just one exotic language. Therefore, with all the theoretical value of these examples, they might, for certain purposes, be safely ignored. If they are disregarded, then CF grammars can be considered IN PRINCIPLE a sufficient means for describing natural languages. This assertion, of course, cannot be strictly proven; our belief that it is true is based on a number of empirical observations, in particular, the following:

NB

1.   There are so-called c a t e g o r i a l   g r a m m a r s, which belong to the class of r e c o g n i t i o n   g r a m m a r s (see p. 88 and following). These grammars were elaborated and applied to natural languages quite independently of CF grammars, and no examples of their inadequacy (except for the two indicated above) have so far been cited. However, it has been proven (see below, p. 96) that the class of languages described by categorial grammars is exactly the class of CF languages.

2.   P u s h d o w n   s t o r e   a u t o m a t a[6], which are capable both of recognition and generation of strings, have been proposed for describing natural languages. It was proven by Chomsky (see p. 109) that all languages which can be processed by nondeterministic pushdown store automata are CF languages, and vice versa. Thus it turns out that another formal model of natural language, which was introduced from independent considerations and did not encounter important theoretical difficulties, is equivalent to CF grammar.

3.   Within the framework of that branch of mathematical linguistics which, concerns the modelling of linguistic research (see below, p. 119 and following), there is readily distinguished the class of so-called   f i n i t e l y c h a r a c t e r i z a b l e   l a n g u a g e s (see p. 125), which intuitively are very close to natural languages. It turns out that all finitely characterizable languages are CF languages (the converse is not true!). This again implies that CF grammars should be capable of generating natural languages in a more or less perspicuous manner.

4.   Finally, there are a large number of algorithms for automatic analysis (= parsing) and generation of texts in natural language which use as a means of describing the corresponding languages just CF grammars or some systems

equivalent to CF grammars. Many of these algorithms have been programmed for electronic computers and have been tested in quite extensive experiments; based on CF grammars, for example, are the algorithms of syntactic analysis, or parsers, for English, German, French and other languages, which were elaborated at the University of Texas (Tosh 1965), a number of parsers which use the so-called Cock method (Hays 1962: 412–414), and several other parsers mentioned in Bobrow 1963, Kuno 1968, Montgomery 1969, Kay – Sparck-Jones 1971; cf. also systems for random generation of natural sentences described in Yngve 1961 and Arsent'eva 1965.

All this suggests CF grammars as being sufficient for natural languages. **NB**

In particular, it is worth noting that constructions of the type $abcd \ldots d'c'b'a'$ (p. 51), which cannot be described by FS grammars, are easily generated with the aid of CF grammars. Thus it is easy to show that a language consisting exactly of strings of the indicated type (composed of the symbols $a_1, a_2, a_3, a'_1, a'_2, a'_3$) is generated by a CF grammar containing the following six rules:

$$\left.\begin{array}{l} I \to a_i I a'_i \\ I \to a_i a'_i \end{array}\right\} \quad i = 1, 2, 3$$

Now it seems necessary to make two important remarks.

First, what has been said so far in no way means that CF grammars generate only natural languages or languages close to them: among CF languages there are many which are not at all similar in their structure to natural languages.

Second, from the fact that CF grammars are practically sufficient for describing natural languages, it does not follow that they are always **NB** CONVENIENT for this purpose, i.e., that they allow one to describe any constructions of any natural languages in a natural manner. Moreover, it is well known that this is not so (cf. the similar remark concerning FS grammars, p. 54). CF grammars do not ensure, for example, a natural description (natural in Chomsky's terms, i.e., 'achieving the level of explanatory adequacy') for so-called n o n p r o j e c t i v e c o n s t r u c t i o n s.[7] (We mean constructions with discontinuous constituents – or, which is the same thing, with intersection (, , etc.) or framing (,) of the arrows of syntactic dependency.) But nonprojective constructions abound in the most diverse languages:

Russ. *K étoj poezdke možet probudit' interes tol'ko vystuplenie direktora,*
   lit. 'To this trip (it) may awaken interest only a speech by the director'.

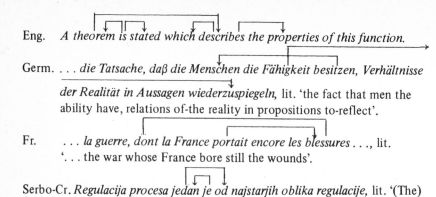

Eng.   *A theorem is stated which describes the properties of this function.*

Germ.   . . . *die Tatsache, daß die Menschen die Fähigkeit besitzen, Verhältnisse der Realität in Aussagen wiederzuspiegeln,* lit. 'the fact that men the ability have, relations of-the reality in propositions to-reflect'.

Fr.   . . . *la guerre, dont la France portait encore les blessures* . . ., lit. '. . . the war whose France bore still the wounds'.

Serbo-Cr. *Regulacija procesa jedan je od najstarjih oblika regulacije,* lit. '(The) regulation of-a-process one is of the-oldest types of-regulation'.

Hung.   *Azt hisszem, hogy késedelemmel sikerült bebizonyítani, hogy. . . ,* lit. 'That (I) believe that by-coming-late it-was-possible to-demonstrate that'. . .

If we want to describe the structure of such sentences in terms of phrase-structure, or constituents (and Chomsky grammars, in particular CF grammars, describe syntactic structure just this way), then for our description to be natural it is necessary to use discontinuous constituents: all words depending on the same word should form (along with it) one constituent, which in the absence of projectivity necessarily leads to discontinuous constituents (*k ètoj poezdke* . . . *interes, a theorem* . . . *which describes the properties of this function,* etc.). However, systems of constituents (IC structures), which are associated with sentences by the CF grammar and, moreover, by any PS grammar, cannot contain discontinuous constituents.

We will return to this difficulty below, on p. 74. In the meantime let us examine two special cases of CF grammars that are equivalent to FS grammars (as was promised on p. 54).

FIRST CASE. Natural languages place dependent words either to the right or left of the governing word ('right subordination': Russ. *list bumagi* 'a sheet of paper', Fr. *une règle stricte* 'a strict rule', Eng. *give him*; 'left subordination': Russ. *belyj list* 'a white sheet', Fr. *cette règle* 'this rule', Eng. *good advice*).

Both right and left subordination can be sequential: Russ. *žena syna zamestitelja predsedatelja vtoroj sekcii èklektiki soveta po prikladnoj mistike pri prezidiume Akademii nauk korolevstva Murak* 'the wife of the son of the deputy of the chairman of the second section of eclectics of the council on applied mysticism of the presidium of the Academy of Sciences of the kingdom of Muraq'; and Russ. *očen' bystro beguščij olen'* 'a very swiftly running deer'.

Depending on the language, a particular construction with sequential subordination to the right or left is theoretically unlimited: such, for example, is the construction with sequential subordination of genitive cases in Russian (unlimited right subordination) or the analogous construction in Lithuanian (where N_{gen} always stands before the word it modifies, which leads to unlimited left subordination). The fact that the languages of the world are differentiated and can be classified according to the predominance in them of right or left subordination — and, in particular, depending on the possibility of unlimited sequential subordination to one side or the other — was already noted and studied by L. Tesnière (1959: 32–33). Yngve (1960, 1961) devoted some attention to this problem in connection with the use of CF grammars for describing natural languages. He noted that there are a great number of languages (for example, English, Russian, French, etc.) in which sequential right subordination is in principle unlimited, while in left subordination the length of the string is always limited owing to the structural features of these languages.[8] It turns out that the CF grammar generating such a language (i.e., a language with limited left subordination) has the following interesting property: for any derivable terminal string there is a derivation such that in each line of it all the nonterminal symbols are clustered at the right end, occupying no more than K final positions (K is a constant fixed for a given grammar, i.e., the same for all derivations in it).[9]

In other words, let each line of the derivation be divided into two parts: a left-hand part including only terminal symbols up to the first nonterminal symbol X and a right-hand part — from X to the end inclusive (in the right-hand part there can also be terminal symbols), then the right-hand part will always contain no more than K symbols. The left-hand part is interpreted as the already generated substring of the derived string (in the subsequent steps of the derivation this substring is not subject to further processing), while the right-hand part is interpreted as the working area which the grammar should, so to speak, hold in its memory. Thus the number K is nothing other than the maximum capacity of the memory necessary for generating any string in the given grammar (i.e., a string can be found that will not be generated if the capacity of the memory is less than K). This number coincides with the maximum length of the chain of sequential left subordinations which is admissible in the language under examination. If in some language there are admissible no more than three sequential subordinations to the left, then in generating this language we can, for any string, construct a derivation in which the need does not arise to memorize more than three symbols at one time. This correlation between the permissible depth of the left subordination and the capacity of the memory was established by V. Yngve (1960, 1961).

Now we will illustrate what has been said with an example; namely, we will consider grammar G_4, which generates some of the noun phrases of Russian in which the right subordination is not limited and the depth of the left subordination does not exceed two.

THE SCHEME OF GRAMMAR G_4

$$\widetilde{N}_{g,n,c} \rightarrow N_{g,n,c}\, \widetilde{N}_{g',n',gen}$$
$$\widetilde{N}_{g,n,c} \rightarrow \widetilde{A}_{g,n,c}\, \widetilde{N}_{g,n,c}$$
$$\widetilde{A}_{g,n,c} \rightarrow \left| \begin{array}{l} o\check{c}en'\ \text{'very'}, sover\check{s}enno \\ \text{'quite'}, ves'ma\ \text{'entirely'}, \ldots \end{array} \right| A_{g,n,c}$$
$$\widetilde{N}_{g,n,c} \rightarrow N_{g,n,c}$$
$$\widetilde{A}_{g,n,c} \rightarrow A_{g,n,c}$$
$$\widetilde{N}_{m,n,c} \rightarrow syn_{n,c}\ \text{'son'},\ zamestitel'_{n,c}\ \text{'deputy'},\ predsedatel'_{n,c}\ \text{'chairman'},$$
$$\qquad komitet_{n,c}\ \text{'committee'}, \ldots$$
$$N_{f,n,c} \rightarrow \check{z}ena_{n,c}\text{'wife'},\ sekcija_{n,c}\ \text{'section'}, \ldots$$
$$A_{g,n,c} \rightarrow krasivyj_{g,n,c}\ \text{'beautiful'},\ tolstyj_{g,n,c}\ \text{'thick, stout'},\ va\check{z}nyj_{g,n,c}$$
$$\qquad \text{'important'}, \ldots$$

(Notations: see pp. 31–33; the last three lines are an abbreviation whose meaning is obvious. As in G_1 and G_3, the particularities of the agreement of A with animate N_{acc} are not considered here.) The following is an example of a derivation in grammar G_4:

$$\widetilde{N}_{f,sg,acc}$$
$$\widetilde{A}_{f,sg,acc}\, \widetilde{N}_{f,sg,acc}$$

očen' 'very' $A_{f,sg,acc}\, \widetilde{N}_{f,sg,acc}$

očen' krasivuju 'very beautiful' $\widetilde{N}_{f,sg,acc}$

očen' krasivuju $N_{f,sg,acc}\, \widetilde{N}_{m,sg,gen}$

očen' krasivuju ženu 'very beautiful wife' $\widetilde{N}_{m,sg,gen}$

očen' krasivuju ženu $N_{m,sg,gen}\, \widetilde{N}_{m,sg,gen}$

očen' krasivuju ženu syna 'the very beautiful wife of the son' $\widetilde{N}_{m,sg,gen}$

. . . .

očen' krasivuju ženu syna zamestitelja predsedatelja 'the very beautiful wife
  of the son of the deputy of the chairman' $N_{\text{f, sg, gen}}$

očen' krasivuju ženu syna zamestitelja predsedatelja sekcii 'the very
  beautiful wife of the son of the deputy of the chairman of the section'

In this derivation the memory capacity equals two: no intermediate string
contains more than two auxiliary symbols. The same string could also be
derived in another way, using a greater memory capacity: for example,
we could begin by obtaining from $\widetilde{N}_{\text{f,sg,acc}}$ the string
očen' 'very' $A_{\text{f,sg,acc}}\, N_{\text{f,sg,acc}}\, N_{\text{m,sg,gen}}\, N_{\text{m,sg,gen}}\, N_{\text{m, sg, gen}}\, N_{\text{f,sg,gen}}$
and then deriving from it our terminal string. Important for us, however,
is the NECESSARY capacity of the memory, i.e., a capacity such that with
a smaller one it would be impossible to derive the given string. It is just
this capacity that is equal here to two.

It can be proven that any terminal string derivable in G_4 can be derived
with a memory capacity ≤ 2. The proof (omitted here) proceeds from a
very simple observation: a 'good' derivation needs to be carried out in
such a way that for each noun, first all its left dependents should be
generated in terminal form, and only then the right expansion of the noun
phrase should take place.

A CF grammar of the type described ('a CF grammar with bounded
memory') is always equivalent to some FS grammar. This is not difficult
to prove (the idea of the proof, which we are not citing here, is that the
right part of a line of a derivation which consists of K symbols is coded by
a new nonterminal symbol). Thus we see that in the cases of languages with
a limited 'depth' of left subordination, CF grammars with bounded memory,
which are equivalent to FS grammars and close to them in the structure of
derivations (i.e., which are much simpler than arbitrary CF grammars), turn out
to be not only sufficient in principle but also quite convenient – they provide
a rather natural description.

T
1.1.6

SECOND CASE. There are, however, languages in which not only the right,
but also the left sequential subordination has an unlimited depth. Such, for
example, is Hungarian, in which unlimited left subordination is possible,
due to preposed expanded modifiers,[10] and unlimited right subordination as
well – due, for example, to relative clauses with *ami/aki* 'which' (cf. *The house
that Jack built* from 'Nursery Rhymes'). For generating languages with such a
property it is possible to suggest another special type of CF grammar, which in
some sense is more general than the CF grammars with bounded memory that
were examined above.

First of all let us formulate more precisely what languages we mean here.

These are languages in which there is possible an unlimited number of constructions $X_1 X_2 \ldots X_i \ldots$ sequentially subordinated from left to right (unlimited right subordination), and in each of the constructions X_i there is possible an unlimited left sequential subordination — the sequence of constructions $\ldots X_{ij} \ldots X_{i2} X_{i1}$; however, within the constructions X_{ij} further unlimited expansion is impossible. As applied to Hungarian, an X_i (except the first) can be understood as a relative clause modifying some noun in the preceding clause, while an X_{ij} is understood as a preposed participal phrase (cf. the example in fn. 10).

Consider the grammar

$$G^* = \langle V^*, W^*, I^*, R^* \rangle,$$

whose terminal vocabulary V^* consists of the n symbols $A_1, A_2, \ldots, A_n$ and whose rules have the form

$$X \rightarrow YA_i \ \text{or} \ X \rightarrow A_i,$$

where X and Y belong to W^*. Let us associate with each of the symbols A_i some FS grammar

$$G_i^* = \langle V, W^i, A_i, R_i \rangle,$$

where V is the terminal vocabulary common for all G_i^*, W^i is the nonterminal vocabulary which does not contain any symbols from V^* and W^*, except A_i; A_i is the initial symbol; the rules of scheme R_i have the form $C \rightarrow dD$ or $C \rightarrow c$ (here, as in the other examples, the nonterminal symbols are designated by capital letters and the terminal symbols by small letters). We will suppose that the nonterminal vocabularies of grammars G_i^* are pairwise disjoint.

Grammar G^* is very close to a finite state grammar, differing from it only by the direction of the expansion[11] of the generated string; in essence it is a finite state grammar up to a mirror symmetry. Thus we are dealing with one 'right-expanding' (i.e., left-linear) grammar and with n 'left-expanding' FS grammars.

We will now consider the union of all these grammars, more precisely, grammar G, whose terminal vocabulary is V (the same as for all G_i^*), whose nonterminal vocabulary is $W = V \cup W^* \cup W^1 \cup W^2 \cup \ldots \cup W^n$ (i.e., the union of the nonterminal vocabularies of all the grammars $G^*, G_1^*, \ldots, G_n^*$, and of the terminal vocabulary of grammar G^*), whose initial symbol is I^*, (the same as for G^*), and whose scheme R is the union of the schemes of all the grammars $G^*, G_1^*, G_2^*, \ldots, G_n^*$. This grammar G is a special CF grammar

which can be called a C F g r a m m a r w i t h i n d e p e n d e n t
b i l a t e r a l e x p a n s i o n.[12]

An example (of the scheme) of such a grammar might be as follows:

THE SCHEME OF GRAMMAR G

$$
R^* = \begin{cases} I^* \to BA_1 \\ B \to CA_1 \\ C \to BA_2 \\ C \to DA_3 \\ D \to DA_4 \\ D \to A_2 \end{cases}
\qquad
R_3 = \begin{cases} A_3 \to aP_3 \\ A_3 \to bQ_3 \\ A_3 \to cR_3 \\ P_3 \to a \\ Q_3 \to b \\ R_3 \to dR_3 \\ R_3 \to eR_3 \\ R_3 \to d \end{cases}
$$

$$
R_1 = \begin{cases} A_1 \to bP_1 \\ P_1 \to aQ_1 \\ Q_1 \to aQ_1 \\ Q_1 \to c \end{cases}
\qquad
R_4 = \begin{cases} A_4 \to cP_4 \\ P_4 \to b \end{cases}
$$

$$
R_2 = \begin{cases} A_2 \to d \end{cases}
$$

A grammar of this type works in the following manner. At first the generated string expands without limit from right to left by adding symbols A_i on the left (A_i can be interpreted, for example, as phrases or clauses); this is done by rules of R^*. Then any of the A_i can (by the rules of R_i) be expanded without limit from left to right and at the same time be transformed into a string of terminal symbols (which can be interpreted as words). Such a process of generation is convenient in such instances, for example, as Hungarian sentences of the above type.

Each CF grammar with independent bilateral expansion is equivalent to some FS grammar. We will not cite here the proof of this fact.

T
1.1.7

PS AND NONSHORTENING GRAMMARS AND NATURAL LANGUAGES

As was noted above, PS grammars (and nonshortening grammars, equal to them in generative capacity, cf. p. 31) are only a special case of generative formal grammars. Nevertheless, PS grammars are unquestionably sufficient (although not necessarily convenient) for describing any natural language in its entirety. This results from the following practically obvious assumption: any natural language (more precisely, the set of all its correct sentences) is an easily recognizable set. Remember that this means (see p. 28) the existence of a rather simple algorithm for recognizing (= a decision procedure for) the correctness of sentences; it is beyond doubt that the speakers have at their disposal such an algorithm. It seems reasonable to suppose that the algorithm for recognizing the correctness of natural sentences should ensure a process of recognition, in which the required capacity of the operative memory would be comparable to the length of the sentence — for example, it would not exceed the number Mn, where n is the length of the sentence and M is a sufficiently large number not dependent on n (i.e., M is some constant). This assumption is all the more natural since, as is known from psychological experiments, the capacity of human operative memory is limited and moreover quite small.[13]

If the language is recognizable by an algorithm with the indicated limitation on the capacity of the memory used ('an algorithm with bounded extension'), then it can be generated by a grammar in which for any derivable terminal string of length n there exists a derivation such that no intermediate string in it exceeds the number Kn in length (K is some constant).[14] Such a grammar may be called a grammar with bounded extension; more precisely,   a g r a m m a r   w i t h   b o u n d e d   e x t e n s i o n   is a grammar for which the capacity function (p. 85) is not greater than a linear function.

T
1.3.4   It has been proven that for any grammar with bounded extension a PS grammar can be constructed which is equivalent to it. Thus, if both of our assumptions are accepted (and they should evidently be accepted), then it must be admitted that PS grammars are in principle capable of describing the set of all and only correct sentences of any natural language, i.e., of generating all correct sentences of the given language, without generating any incorrect ones. (In particular, both constructions cited above as examples of the unsuitability of CF grammars are easily described by PS grammars. Indeed the grammar on p. 64, which generates the language $\{xqx'\}$, as was noted in fn. 4 on page 78, can be replaced by an equivalent PS grammar.)

But this is only one aspect of the situation. The other aspect, as in the preceding instances, is the convenience and naturalness of the description. It is well known that the problem of the acceptability and limitations of immediate constituent analysis has been discussed many times in linguistics. Without treating this complex and interesting problem in all its details, we will try to briefly summarize its basic content. The usually noted

NB   SHORTCOMINGS OF THE IC METHOD, i.e., of PS grammars, reduce to three points.

(1) PS grammars DO NOT ALLOW FOR A NATURAL DESCRIPTION OF SENTENCES CONTAINING DISCONTINUOUS CONSTITUENTS. This fact was discussed above, with respect to CF grammars (p. 67). Since PS grammars associate a system of constituents with a sentence in the same manner as

do CF grammars, everything said above about nonprojective sentences applies as well to PS grammars.

Points (2) and (3) concern not only PS grammars, but also ALL generative grammars in the strict sense of the definition on p. 25.

(2)   A PS grammar, like any generative grammar, contains only f o r m a t i o n   r u l e s   (for linguistic expressions), for example, for word-forms, phrases, clauses, or sentences. This means that the grammar defines correct expressions as opposed to incorrect ones. The very notion (and term) 'formation rules' is borrowed from mathematical logic, where it designates the rules for constructing correct (= well-formed) formulas.[15]

However, in logic another type of rule is also considered: t r a n s f o r m a t i o n   r u l e s.   The latter define specific correlations between correct formulas, these being in essense SEMANTIC relations. Thus in elementary algebra these are (as is known to everyone from high school) rules of identity transformations: with their aid, from one expression we can obtain another with the same numerical value, which plays the role of meaning here; in the propositional calculus these are rules of inference, which allow us to derive from some true expressions other true expressions: in the role of meaning we have here the truth values ('true' vs. 'false'). The introduction of transformation rules always means a shift to a higher level of language study, in this case to the semantic level.

It is quite evident that transformation rules are necessary in the description of natural languages as well (cf. p. 112). The mastery of a language necessarily presupposes the ability not only to construct any correct sentence in it, but also to shift from one sentence to another, which is either entirely synonymous to it or differs from it in meaning by a certain 'quantity'. Thus the speaker easily makes from an affirmative sentence an interrogative or negative sentence, from an active construction a passive one; he changes without difficulty the stylistic coloring of a text, expresses the same idea by different linguistic means, etc. These possibilities, which should necessarily be accounted for in any good description of a language, cannot be stated in terms of generative grammars, and therefore there arises the question concerning the elaboration of a new formal apparatus for transformation rules as applied to natural languages.

The corresponding task was for the first time clearly stated by Chomsky (1957). His linguistic doctrine quickly acquired great popularity under the name of 'transformational grammar'. The inspiration of this doctrine, in our opinion, consists in introducing another higher – semantic – level of linguistic description.[16] In fact, the invariant in all linguistic transformations is usually meaning; in other words, Chomsky's transformations are transformations which preserve (or almost preserve) meaning. Thus the theory of transformations proves in essence to be a theory of linguistic synonymy.[17] (We mean synonymy in the broadest sense of the word, primarily synonymy of sentences as well as of greater segments of texts.) In recent times it has become more and more evident that the description of synonymy should occupy one of the central positions in linguistics. Hence follows the paramount role of transformations (in the sense of Chomsky).

However, Chomsky's transformations do not pertain to the same linguistic level as PS grammars: the latter pertain to the syntactic (in the broad sense of the word, see below, p. 112) level, while transformations pertain to the semantic level. Therefore, when speaking about the inadequacy of PS grammars for describing natural language, it should be remembered that this is true only in the sense that PS grammars do not cover the semantic level; but on their own, i.e., purely syntactic, level PS grammars prove in principle to be quite sufficient.

Generative grammars (in the sense of the definition on p. 25) are considered within the framework of a strictly formal theory. As for transformations, such a level of formalization has not yet been attained: the transformational rules suggested so far have not been stated in terms of one (or several) simple operation(s), as have the rules of formal grammars (with their rewriting operation, or substitution). The problem of the formalization of transformations is quite pressing.[18]

In conclusion we would like to make the following remark, of a terminological nature. In the works of Noam Chomsky and several other authors the term 'generative grammar' is used in two senses: in a broad sense, for designating any system of formal rules describing language, including transformational and morphonological components; and in a narrow sense, for designating formal grammars in the sense of the definition on p. 25. In our exposition this term is always used only in the narrow sense, and with such usage transformational rules turn out to be beyond the framework of generative grammar.

(3)   A PS grammar, as any generative grammar, CONSTRUCTS SENTENCES ALONG WITH A PRECISELY DEFINED WORD ORDER, namely, with the word order which these sentences should have in their final form. The generated sentence is provided with its syntactic structure in the form of AN ORDERED TREE, i.e., a tree in which, in addition to the relation of subordination (between the nodes) given by the tree itself, there is also the relation of linear order (right – left). Thus the syntactic structure generated by PS grammars does not differentiate two relations, which although interconnected are quite different in nature: syntactic (hierarchic) subordination and mutual linear arrangement. Meanwhile linguistic tradition always thought, and with good reasons, that to characterize a syntactic structure means to indicate the

relations of syntactic subordination (no matter how the latter concept be interpreted). As for the relation of linear order, it should characterize not the syntactic structure of a sentence, but the sentence itself. Word order, of course, is dependent on the syntactic structure; it is determined necessarily with consideration for the latter and is thereby something derived and secondary with respect to it.

Since this is so, it seems expedient to modify the concept of generative grammar in such a way that the left- and right-hand parts of the rewriting rules would be — instead of linearly ordered strings — more complicated graphs. These could be, for example, trees (without linear ordering of nodes) which represent syntactic structures. Then the rules could presumably have, say, the following form:

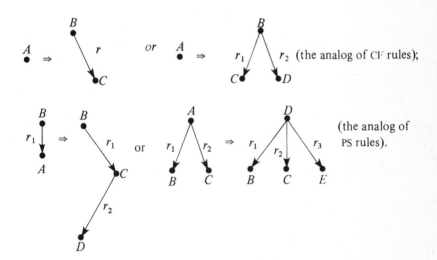

Labeled arrows represent syntactic relations (= dependencies) of different types; the letters *A, B, C,* ... stand for syntactic categories. **NB**: the mutual linear arrangement of symbols of one level of subordination is irrelevant so that

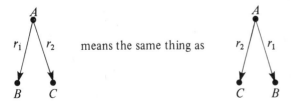

As a result we would obtain a calculus of syntactic structures (but not sentences!) of the language. This calculus would not be a generative grammar in the narrow sense of the term, but it can well be regarded as a component of a generative grammar in the broad sense; it is necessary, however, to construct a corresponding formal definition.[19] The other component of this grammar would be a calculus which would associate with any given syntactic structure all the linear word sequences possible for it (possibly taking into consideration some other factors; for example, in Russian it must account for logical accents, emphasis, etc.). In such an approach the problem of discontinuous constituents, in particular, is eliminated; see above, p. 74. An example of the calculus which generates syntactic structures and then carries out the linear ordering of their terminal symbols is given in Lomkovskaja 1965–1966; a tentative system of rules for ordering words in Russian (proceeding from the syntactic structure, the properties of the words themselves and the information about the communicative structure of the sentence) is contained in Mel'čuk 1965; a calculus of Russian synonymous sentences ('paraphrasing system') in which the formation of the sentence structures is separated from the construction of corresponding word strings is described in Žolkovskij – Mel'čuk 1967; cf. also Mel'čuk – Žolkovskij 1970, and Mel'čuk 1974: 268–299.

NOTES

1. The constructions of both types were brought to our attention by F.A. Dreizin.
2. By an elementary noun phrase we understand a noun with all its agreeing modifiers, as well as with a preposition, (restrictive) particles and the coordinate conjunction introducing the entire phrase.
3. Strictly speaking, we mean here OCCURRENCES of the symbols a_1, a'_1, etc. in the strings, rather than the symbols themselves.
4. According to theorem $T_{1.1.2}$ (p. 134), for this grammar there exists an equivalent PS grammar (which the reader can construct without difficulty by himself, using the modelling of permutation by means of PS rules, as is shown in Chapter 3, fn. 8).
5. An analogous example was first indicated by Y. Bar-Hillel and E. Shamir (1960).
6. They will be discussed on p. 98 and following.
7. On the concept of projectivity see Padučeva 1964b, and Gladkij 1973: Appendix 1, §2.
8. We will not dwell here on the so-called 'Yngve hypothesis' (Yngve 1961), which attempts to explain this empirical observation by some general laws of human psychology.
9. Strictly speaking, in order for a CF grammar to have the indicated property, limiting sequential left subordination is not sufficient. A number of stronger and more sophisticated requirements must be met (see Padučeva 1967), from which follows, for example, the limitation of right parallel subordination (⟨⟨⟨ . . .) and of subsequent subordination of the type ⟨⟨⟨⟩⟩ . On this question see also Šrejder 1966.

10. Cf. the following Hungarian example from a short story by G. Fehér; it is a jocular toast (cited in Varga 1964: 70):

Kivánom, hogy valamint aż agyag[23] ölelő karjai[22] közül kibontakozni[21] akaró[20] kocsikerék[19] rettentő nyikorgásától[18] megriadt[17] juhászkutya[16] bundájába[15] kapaszkodó[14] kullancs[13] kidülledt félszeméből[12] alácseppent[11] könnycseppben[10] visszatükröződő[9] holdvilág fényétől[8] illuminált[7] rablólovagvár[6] felvonóhidjából[5] kiálló[4] vasszegek[3] kohéziós erejének[2] hatása[1] évszázadokra összetartja annak materiáját, aképpen tartsa össze ezt a társaságot az igaz szeretet 'I wish that true love would bind this company in the same manner as for centuries the material of the bridge is bound by the action[1] of the binding force[2] of the nails[3] protruding[4] from the drawbridge[5] of the brigand feudal castle[6] illuminated[7] by the moon light[8] being reflected[9] in the tear[10] that dropped[11] from the protruding eye[12] of the tick[13] that clung[14] in the hair[15] of the sheep-dog[16] excited[17] by the terrifying scraping[18] of the cart-wheels[19] striving[20] to break[21] from the embraces[22] of the mud[23].'

This sentence is not concocted on purpose, but is taken from an actual artistic text and yet it has a depth of 22 being absolutely correct from the grammatical point of view (to the same extent as is its translation). Moreover, nothing hinders the continuation of the chain of modifiers to the left *ad libitum*.

11. By the direction of expansion we understand here the direction in which the terminal symbols are put out; for example, $C \rightarrow dD$ shows left expansion.

12. The fact that this grammar is not finite state is evident because some of its rules (the rules of scheme R) contain in their right-hand parts two nonterminal symbols. In fact, the terminal symbols of G* (i.e., $A_1, A_2 \ldots, A_n$) are nonterminal in G, so that in G rules of the type $X \rightarrow YA_i$ turn out not to be finite state. However, G is equivalent to an FS grammar, see below.

13. The capacity limitations of human operative memory underlie also those linguistic considerations which led to the concept of 'a grammar with bounded memory', see above, pp. 69–71.

14. This assertion can be rigorously formulated and proven if the concept of algorithm is specified in an appropriate manner – for example, in terms of Turing machines.

15. For example, the algebraic formula $(a + b)c$ is correct, while the formula $(a +)$ is incorrect.

16. For more detail on the description of the semantic level of language see below, p. 112 and following.

17. Note that in the works of Z. Harris (for example, Harris 1957) the term 'transformation' has quite a different meaning.

18. Even now (in 1975) there is no unanimity of opinion about the LINGUISTIC status of Chomsky's transformations. The place of transformational rules in general linguistic theory and, in particular, their interrelations with semantics are still at issue. The purely FORMAL aspects of transformations, which by right also warrant inclusion here, are too complex to be discussed in this introductory exposition. The more advanced reader can consult such works as Ginsburg – Partee 1969; Brainerd 1971: Chapter 5; Barbault – Desclés 1972; and Chauché 1972.

19. Such a definition was suggested by the present writers in Gladkij – Mel'čuk 1969; for a full exposition see Gladkij – Mel'čuk 1975 (in this volume, pp. 151–187).

5. On Some Formal Properties of Generative Grammars

In the preceding chapter we dealt with a number of questions connected with the use of generative formal grammars for describing natural languages. There we examined mostly those properties of grammars which are of immediate interest precisely in linguistic applications, i.e., we studied grammars from the viewpoint of linguistic interpretation. Now we will dwell on some 'internal', purely formal properties of grammars, introducing here some interesting facts from the mathematical theory of generative grammars. Grammars are genuine mathematical objects and as such can be studied by purely mathematical methods. By no means all the results of such a study have an immediate linguistic interpretation; many of them are, as such, hardly necessary for the study of natural languages. Nevertheless, all facts pertaining to grammars — we have in mind their formal properties — occupy in the unified mathematical theory of grammars a definite place and are necessary within the framework of this theory. The point is that any theory develops according to its internal laws and can exist only as a whole. It is impossible to distinguish in a theory some special fragments that are interesting for applications and to develop them autonomously. Therefore, if the very theory of grammars is recognized as useful and important for linguistics, its purely mathematical results also prove, in the final analysis (i.e., even if indirectly), equally necessary.

The mathematical theory of grammars is at present quite well developed. We will dwell here on only two of its branches — decision problems and estimates of derivational complexity.

DECISION PROBLEMS

In the theory of grammars questions about the existence or non-existence of certain decision procedures (i.e., algorithms) often arise. For example:

(1) Is there a decision procedure which allows us, for any given CF

grammar G, to find out whether the language generated by G is finite (i.e., whether the set of terminal strings generated by G is finite)?

(2) The analogous question can be asked about PS grammars.

(3) Is there for any given grammar G a decision procedure which allows us, for any pair of (terminal) strings x and y which are derivable in G, to determine whether x is substitutable[1] by y in language $L(G)$?

(4) Is there a decision procedure which allows us, for any CF grammar G, to find out whether G provides for each terminal string generated only one syntactic structure, i.e., whether there are terminal strings which can be derived in G in more than one way?

It is just such questions that are subsumed under the heading of decision problems in the theory of grammars.

Following are some results pertaining to this area.

1.   In the class of all grammars no nontrivial property of the languages generated by grammars is decidable. (We call a property of languages n o n t r i v i a l in the given class of languages if this class includes both languages which have the property and languages which do not have it. For example, the property 'to be generated by a grammar' in the class of languages generated by grammars is trivial, while the property 'to be finite' is not.) The undecidability of nontrivial properties in the class of all grammars means that if we are dealing with arbitrary grammars (= unrestricted rewriting systems), then there is no nontrivial property of languages such that a decision procedure exists which would allow us, for any grammar, to find out whether the language generated by it has this property. **T** 1.2.1

2.   In the class of PS grammars:

(a) The property of generating a language that contains a given string is decidable, i.e., for any string there is a decision procedure allowing one, for any PS grammar G, to find out whether this string belongs to the language generated by G. The proof of this fact is found on pp. 29–30, where we have given a procedure allowing one, for any nonshortening grammar G and any string x, to find out whether x is derivable in G (i.e., whether x belongs to $L(G)$). Note that this procedure is the same for every G and every x and, thus, is not dependent on G or on x. Consequently, the decidability of the property of containing a given string is proven for the class of nonshortening grammars and for its subclass – PS grammars. **T** 1.2.2

Hence the decidability of certain similar properties also follows – such as containing simultaneously 2, 3, . . . , n given strings, containing at least one of n given strings, containing a given string x under the condition that another given string y belongs to the language, etc.

(b) Practically all other 'good' (i.e., naturally arising) nontrivial properties of languages are undecidable in the class of PS grammars: **T** 1.2.3

for example, the properties of generating a given (arbitrary) PS language, of generating a finite language, of generating a CF language, of generating a language with substitutability of x by y (where x and y are arbitrary fixed strings), etc.

3.   In the class of CF grammars some of the properties prove to be decidable which are undecidable in the class of PS grammars. (Of course, the properties decidable for PS grammars [cf. 2(a)], are also decidable for CF grammars.) Thus the following properties are decidable in CF grammars:

T
1.2.4
(a)   The property of generating the empty language (there is a decision procedure which, for any CF grammar, allows us to find out whether it generates at least one terminal string).

(b)   The property of generating a finite language.

(c)   The property of generating at least one string which contains an occurrence of a given string x. In the linguistic interpretation this can mean, for example, the following: any CF grammar of the language allows us, for any phrase, to determine whether it is a part of at least one sentence of the language. Thus, as opposed to PS grammars, where the correctness of whole sentences only, but not of parts thereof, is decidable, for CF grammars both are decidable.

T
1.2.5
Nevertheless, many important properties are undecidable for CF grammars, too. In particular, the following properties are undecidable: the property of generating an FS language; of generating the full language (the language which contains all possible nonempty strings of terminal symbols); of having an equivalent CF grammar which gives for any string only one syntactic structure; etc.

T
1.2.7
Note also that the problem of recognizing the equivalence of two arbitrary CF grammars is unsolvable; i.e., there is no decision procedure which allows one, for any pair of CF grammars, to determine whether they are equivalent.

T
1.2.6
T
1.2.8
4.   In the class of FS grammars practically all 'interesting' properties are decidable, including the ones enumerated in the preceding paragraphs; the problem of recognizing the equivalence of any two FS grammars is also solvable.

T
1.2.10
T
1.2.9
Among the problems concerning decision procedures for specific (fixed) grammars — rather than for classes of grammars — we will mention only one: the so-called problem of recognizing substitutability. It consists in finding for any given grammar G a decision procedure which would allow us, for any pair of strings x, y, to determine whether x can be substituted by y in the language $L(G)$. Such procedures exist for some grammars — in particular, for all FS grammars. However, there are examples of CF grammars for which there is no such procedure.

ESTIMATES OF DERIVATIONAL COMPLEXITY

In the mathematical theory of grammars, along with decision problems there are also problems of estimating the complexity of derivations in grammars. It seems natural to measure the complexity of a derivation either by the number of steps in it, i.e., by the number of intermediate strings, or by the necessary capacity of the 'memory' — for example, by the length of the intermediate strings.[2]

For estimating derivational complexity by the number of steps the following measure is suggested:

$$(1) \quad \tau_G(n) = \max_{l(x) \leq n} \tau_{G,x}$$

where G is the given grammar, x is an arbitrary string derivable in G, $l(x)$ is the length of the string x (that is, the number of occurrences of symbols in x — e.g., the string *keen* has length 4), $\tau_{G,x}$ is the number of steps ('time') of the shortest derivation of the string x in G, and n is an arbitrary positive integer.

In order to compute $\tau_G(n)$, it is necessary, as is evident from (1), to find for each derivable string not exceeding n in length the shortest 'time' (number of steps) sufficient for the derivation of this string in G (the point is that the string x can have in G many different derivations of different lengths); then among all these 'times' the maximum one is chosen. This will be the value of the function $\tau_G(n)$ — the so-called t i m e   f u n c t i o n. In other words, $\tau_G(n)$ is the number of steps which, on the one hand, is sufficient for the derivation of any string not longer than n, and, on the other hand, is necessary; among the derivable strings not longer than n there is at least one string which cannot be derived in less than $\tau_G(n)$ steps.

Using time functions it is possible to estimate the complexity of derivations in different grammars. Thus on pp. 29–30 it was shown that for any nonshortening grammar G the inequality $\tau_G(n) < p^{n+1}$ holds, where p is the total number of terminal and nonterminal symbols of G. It is evident that this inequality is valid, in particular, for PS and CF grammars. However, for the latter this bound can be significantly improved (i.e., lowered): for any CF grammar G_1 the inequality $\tau_G(n) \leq 2Cn$ holds, where C is the number of nonterminal symbols of G_1. This bound is obtained from the following simple considerations: any CF derivation can be carried out so that at each step the leftmost nonterminal symbol is replaced; at each step the length of the string either does not change, or increases, with steps of the three following types being possible:

T 1.3.1

T 1.3.2

1. $A \to B$ (a 'nonlengthening nonterminal' step, A and B being nonterminal symbols);

2. $A \to a$ (a 'nonlengthening terminal' step, A being a nonterminal symbol, a a terminal symbol);

3. $A \to d_1 d_2 \ldots d_m$, $m > 1$ (a 'lengthening' step).

If the derivation does not contain loops (repetitions of intermediate strings; cf. p. 29), then it can nowhere have more than C 'nonlengthening nonterminal' steps in sequence.

Indeed, had k such steps been carried out one after another, where $k > C$, then the corresponding strings of the derivation would have the form:

$$
\begin{array}{ll}
xA_0 Y & \text{1st step} \\
xA_1 Y & \text{2nd step} \\
xA_2 Y & \text{3rd step} \\
\cdots & \\
& C\text{th step} \\
xA_C Y & (C+1)\text{th step} \\
\cdots & \\
xA_k Y & k\text{th step}
\end{array}
$$

Here x is a string of terminal symbols; $A_0, A_1, \ldots, A_k$ are nonterminal symbols; Y is some string of an arbitrary form.

Now, C steps give $(C+1)$ strings; since these strings differ only by the symbols $A_0, A_1, \ldots, A_C$, and among these strings there are no more than C different ones, two of these strings necessarily coincide, i.e., a loop arises.

Thus an arbitrary CF derivation without loops (and, clearly, the shortest derivation) cannot contain more than $(C-1)$ nonlengthening nonterminal steps in sequence. Between two series of such steps, at least one step of type 2 or 3 must occur and these steps are, in all, no more than $2n$ (no more than n terminal steps, since the entire string consists of n terminal symbols, and no more than n lengthening steps, since each lengthening step increases the length of the string, while this length cannot be increased by more than n). Consequently, we have no more than $2n$ series of steps of type 1 (no more than $(C-1)$ steps per series) and no more than $2n$ steps of type 2 and 3; the total number of steps does not exceed $2n(C-1) + 2n = 2Cn$; q.e.d.

We have shown how to obtain the upper bounds for the time function. To obtain the lower bounds proves more difficult. Let us cite without proof a result concerning one such bound.

A language consisting of all possible strings of the form xqx' (see p. 64) cannot be generated by any PS grammar G for which the order of time function $\tau_G(n)$ is less[3] than n^2. At the same time, a PS grammar for which the order of τ is equal[4] to n^2 does generate such a language: the time function of the grammar given on p. 64 has just such an order.

T
1.3.3

A grammar for which the time function is not greater than a linear function, is called a g r a m m a r   w i t h   b o u n d e d   r e t a r d a t i o n. In particular, every CF grammar is a grammar with bounded retardation – this follows from the inequality proven on pp. 83–84. But a PS grammar need not be a grammar with bounded retardation.

It is possible to introduce in an analogous manner the c a p a c i t y f u n c t i o n $\sigma_G(n)$, which characterizes the capacity of memory necessary for deriving a string of length $\leq n$:

$$(2) \quad \sigma_G(n) = \max_{l(x) \leq n} \sigma_{G,x}$$

where G, x and n have the same meaning as in (1) (p. 83), while $\sigma_{G,x}$ is the capacity of (= 'the capacity of the memory necessary for') a derivation of the string x in G which requires the minimal capacity. (The c a p a c i t y   o f a   d e r i v a t i o n is the length of the longest string in this derivation.)

The mathematical theory of grammars has other directions of study as well; however, we will not pursue these further at this time.

NOTES

1. For the definition of substitutability, see p. 122.
2. The capacity of the memory can be measured in another way, too: by the number of nonterminal symbols in the intermediate strings, by the distance from the first nonterminal symbol to the end of the string (cf. p. 69), etc.
3. The words 'the order of . . . is less' mean approximately 'much less', 'grows considerably slower'. The rigorous definition is as follows: the order of the function $f(n)$ is less than the order of the function $g(n)$ if $\lim \frac{f(n)}{g(n)} = 0$ as $n \to \infty$.
4. This means that $\lim \frac{\tau(n)}{n^2}$ as $n \to \infty$ exists and is not equal to 0.

6. Some Other Notions and Problems of Mathematical Linguistics

Having surveyed, in a more or less coherent fashion, one of the branches of mathematical linguistics – the theory of generative grammars, we will now try to give a brief outline of a number of other branches so that the reader might obtain a more complete idea of the entire discipline. This outline is in no way meant to serve as a synopsis of even the basic achievements of mathematical linguistics and in no manner lays claim to completeness or consistency. We will simply touch upon – with a different degree of detail – several individual, quite important questions, without particularly worrying about the unity of our exposition.

In recent years within linguistics the following conception of the main trends in the study of natural language and of their interrelations has developed.[1] There are distinguished first of all:

    A.   Linguistic studies proper

and, so to speak,

    B.   Linguistic studies of second order.

The content of the former is the description of language as such – in particular, the modelling of human linguistic behaviour; the latter are aimed rather at studying the METHODS OF STUDYING LANGUAGE – in particular, the modelling of the linguists' activities. The difference between **A** and **B** does not coincide with the difference between descriptive and theoretical linguistics: **A** includes not only descriptions of specific languages, but also the general theory of describing language, the construction of universal schemes for specific descriptions, etc. Within the second trend (= **B**) it is possible to distinguish

    I.   Problems connected with refining the linguistic concepts themselves (the study of the foundations of linguistics); and **II.** Problems connected with refining the procedures of linguistic research.

The latter, in turn, can be subdivided into
(1) procedures for working exclusively with texts — the purely 'deciphering' approach,
and (2) procedures for working with an informant — the 'experimental' approach.
(Our classification of linguistic trends is similar to that suggested in Apresjan 1975.)
For greater clarity, the situation outlined above can be represented in the following manner:

Linguistics
  A. Linguistics proper (= the modelling of languages).
  B. The modelling of linguistic research.
    I.   Foundations of linguistics.
    II. Procedures of linguistic research.

(It should be emphasized once more that all of these divisions are only approximate; there are, of course, no sharp and clear boundaries between the branches!)
It turns out that in mathematical linguistics, too, analogous trends are naturally distinguished. Therefore we will make use of the same headings in our survey of the latter.
Well, then, mathematical linguistics can also be subdivided into:

  A. The modelling of languages, and
  B. The modelling of the study of languages (cf. the 'A and B devices' in N. Chomsky's conception — Chomsky 1964: 922–923).

A. THE MODELLING OF LANGUAGES

This part of mathematical linguistics includes, first of all, the theory of formal grammars. A part of this theory, involving generative formal grammars, was presented in Chapters 2–5; the other part of the theory covers recognition formal grammars (p. 7). We will characterize here two classes of recognition grammars: categorial grammars and push-down store automata.
It seems reasonable to include in this section as well works which are usually subsumed under the heading of 'logical analysis of language' (see below, p. 112 ff).

CATEGORIAL GRAMMARS (C GRAMMARS)

Suppose we are faced with the task of constructing a mechanical procedure for the syntactic analysis (= parsing) of sentences. The usual idea of how this should be done is approximately as follows. First of all, it is necessary to break all word-forms down into classes and to compile a dictionary in which each word-form will be assigned its syntactic class (for example, Russ. *dlinnaja* 'long' $- A_{f, sg, nom}$; *kriča* '(while) shouting' $- V_{adv. part}$; etc). Then rules are formulated for combining syntactic classes; that is, it is indicated which classes can combine with which and what the classes of the resulting phrases (= word combinations) will be. These rules may have the form of the PS, or IC, rules well known to linguistics; i.e., they may be something like the following:

$$A + N = \tilde{N}$$
$$N_c + N_{gen} = \tilde{N}_c$$
$$V^{tr} + N_{acc} = \tilde{V}^{itr}$$
$$\cdots \cdots \cdots \cdots$$

Note that these rules are, essentially, 'inverted' CF rules; for greater detail see also below, p. 110.

However, it seems tempting to do without a list of rules of the indicated type. We could, e.g., proceed as follows: construct a system of coding for syntactic classes (i.e., classes of word-forms and phrases) such that the possibility of combining two classes C_1 and C_2, as well as the class of the resulting combination could be perceived directly from the codes of C_1 and C_2. In other words, each code should have a certain internal form — should be, as it were, 'speaking' — and, what is especially important, the codes of different classes should be in accordance and form an algebraic system so that with the aid of some simple operations it would be possible to automatically compute from the codes of the combining classes the code of the class of the combination obtained. Thus all the information about syntactic combinability would be stored here not in a list of rules (as is usually done in linguistics and as it was in all the grammars examined above), but rather in the word syntactic codes themselves.

Capitalizing on the idea of storing all information concerning word combinability in the syntactic codes of these words, it is possible to construct, generally speaking, different classes of grammars. However, so far there is only one such class, namely C grammars, which are being discussed here.

The essence of C grammars is that in order to implement the idea of a 'speaking' syntactic code the following fundamental consideration is

NB

evoked. All syntactic classes can be divided into two types: some classes are **NB** considered basic, or elementary, while others are viewed as u n a r y o p e r a t o r s,[2] each of which, when applied to some syntactic class (of any type), gives again a syntactic class.[3] For those operators a special notation is used, which can be illustrated by the following example: let there be two elementary syntactic classes – N_{nom} (a noun in the nominative) and SENT (a sentence); then the syntactic class adjoined to N_{nom} on the right and giving a sentence (i.e., an intransitive verb like Russ. *spit* 'sleeps', *xodit* 'walks', *plačet* 'cries', . . . : *More spit* 'The sea is sleeping', etc.) is an operator acting upon N_{nom} from the right and converting N_{nom} into SENT; such an operator is notated $[N_{nom} \backslash \text{SENT}]$. The effect of applying this operator to N_{nom} can be interpreted as the cancellation of a fraction: $N_{nom} [N_{nom} \backslash \text{SENT}] = \text{SENT}$. The class of verbs of the type *suščestvuet* 'there exists', *imeetsja* 'there is', *pojavljaetsja* 'there appears', . . . should be regarded as an operator acting upon N_{nom} from the left and giving again SENT (*Suščestvuet zakon* 'There exists a law', etc.); such an operator is notated $[\text{SENT} / N_{nom}]$ and is also 'canceled' with N_{nom}: $[\text{SENT} / N_{nom}] N_{nom} = \text{SENT}$. An adjective can be notated either $[N/N]$ (preposed adjective or $[N \backslash N]$ (postposed adjective); the corresponding cancellations have the form: $[N/N] \ N = N$ and $N \backslash N] = N$.

It is already evident from these simplified examples how the analysis of a sentence should be carried out: all word-forms are assigned syntactic codes of the above type with the help of a dictionary (in the case of syntactic ambiguity of a word-form it is assigned several codes); then all the possible cancellations are effected, and if as a result we obtain the symbol SENT, then this means that the sentence being analyzed is grammatically correct, while the way of cancellation which resulted in the symbol SENT specifies the syntactic analysis of this sentence.

The concept of C grammar was introduced by Y. Bar-Hillel (Bar-Hillel, Gaifman and Shamir 1960), who relied considerably on the works of K. Ajdukiewicz. An informal statement of the corresponding ideas can be found in Bar-Hillel 1953; see also Bar-Hillel 1959, and Gladkij 1973: § 6.1.

Now we can proceed with the definition of C grammar. For this it is necessary to introduce the following concepts:

1. Let there be a finite set V of symbols, the t e r m i n a l v o c a b u l a r y ; its role and interpretation are the same as for generative grammars.

2. Furthermore, there is a finite set W of p r i m i t i v e (syntactic) c a t e g o r i e s – PC's; formally a PC is simply a symbol of W which can be interpreted as a word class (more precisely, a word-form or morpheme class)

or a phrase class. From PC's we will construct c a t e g o r i e s according to the following rules:

1) Every PC is a category.
2) If Φ and Ψ are categories, then $[\Phi/\Psi]$ and $[\Phi\backslash\Psi]$ are also categories.
3) There are no other categories (on the interpretation of the expressions $[\Phi/\Psi]$ and $[\Phi\backslash\Psi]$ see above).

3.   There is also a many-valued function f, which assigns to each terminal symbol one or several (but a finite number of !) categories. This a s s i g n m e n t   f u n c t i o n   can be interpreted as the assigning of syntactic categories to the words in the terminal vocabulary (several in the case of syntactic ambiguity or homonymy: Russ. *teč'* is a noun 'a leak' or a verb 'to flow'/'to leak').

4.   Among PC's there is distinguished the m a i n   c a t e g o r y F; this is, so to speak, a 'final' symbol whose role is in a sense the converse of the role of the initial symbol I of a generative grammar (the string under generation expands from I; the string under recognition reduces to F).

A C grammar is a system of the four described objects; i.e., formally speaking, the ordered quadruple $\langle V, W, f, F \rangle$.

To show how such a grammar works we have to introduce another concept: c a n c e l l a t i o n   o f   s t r i n g s   o f   c a t e g o r i e s .   We will define d i r e c t   c a n c e l l a t i o n   as follows:

−   either an occurrence of the string $[\Phi/\Psi] \Psi$ is replaced by Φ (r i g h t c a n c e l l a t i o n),
−   or an occurrence of the string $\Phi [\Phi\backslash\Psi]$ is replaced by Ψ (l e f t c a n c e l l a t i o n).

The notation $[\Phi/\Psi]$ is read as 'Φ over Ψ', while $[\Phi\backslash\Psi]$ is read as 'Φ under Ψ', and it is convenient to conceive of direct cancellation as cancellation of arithmetical fractions, with the important difference that here − in contradistinction to fractions − the mutual arrangement of 'factors' is relevant. The category $[\Phi/\Psi]$ is assigned to such a string X that, occurring to the immediate left of a string Y with the category Ψ, X forms together with Y a new string XY having as a whole the category Φ:

$$\underbrace{\;\Phi\;}_{\displaystyle \cdots\quad\underbrace{}_{[\Phi/\Psi]}\;\underbrace{}_{\Psi}\quad\cdots}$$

In other words, $[\Phi/\Psi]$, as already indicated, is an operator which, acting on Ψ from the left, transforms it into Φ.

The category $[\Phi \backslash \Psi]$ is interpreted in much the same way, but here we have, first, adjoining to Φ rather than to Ψ, and second, from the right rather than from the left.

Let us now define c a n c e l l a t i o n (not necessarily direct): the string of categories α is c a n c e l e d to the string of categories β if β can be obtained from α by a sequence of direct cancellations.

For example, the string

$$\alpha = [[[X \backslash Y]/X]/Z]Z \ [Y/Y] \ [[Y/Y] \backslash X] \ [Z/X] \ X$$

is canceled to the string $\beta = [X \backslash Y]Z$ by four direct cancellations:

$$\alpha = [[[\underbrace{X \backslash Y]/X}_{\gamma}]/Z]Z \ [Y/Y] \ [[Y/Y] \backslash X] \ [Z/X]X$$

1. $[\gamma/Z]Z \to \gamma$

$$[[\underbrace{X \backslash Y]/X}_{\gamma}] \ \underbrace{[Y/Y]}_{\delta} \ [\underbrace{[Y/Y]}_{\delta} \backslash X] \ [Z/X]X$$

2. $\delta[\delta \backslash X] \to X$

$$[\underbrace{[X \backslash Y]/X}_{\epsilon}] \ X \ [Z/X]X$$

3. $[\epsilon/X]X \to \epsilon$

$$\underbrace{[X \backslash Y]}_{\epsilon} \ [Z/X]X$$

4. $[Z/X]X \to Z$

$$\beta = [X \backslash Y]Z$$

Note that the same string of categories can, generally speaking, be canceled in different ways — by applying direct cancellations in a different order. A corresponding example will be examined below, on p. 95.

Now we will proceed to the description of the working of C grammars. For greater clarity, we will first of all construct an example of such a grammar: G_1.

The terminal vocabulary V of this grammar (G_1) consists of Russian word-forms; as the primitive categories we select the following:

SENT is the category of sentences;

$V^{itr}_{g,n,p,t}$, where V^{itr} is the category of intransitive verbs, and g, n, p, and t are variables denoting respectively: g — gender, n — number, p — person, and t — tense, cf. p. 33. Thus, $V^{itr}_{g,n,p,t}$ is not one PC, but an abbreviated notation of 54 PC's: 54 = 3 (genders) x 2 (numbers) x 3 (persons) x 3 (tenses);

$V^{tr}_{g,n,p,t}$ is the category of transitive verbs, and g, n, p, and t the same variables as above;

Pr_i, where Pr denotes a preposition in general, and i is a variable ranging over the set of specific Russian prepositions: *bez* 'without', v 'in', *na* 'on', *ot* 'from', ... Pr_i is also an abbreviated notation for several tens of PC's.

We will consider SENT as the main category.

Of course, we will be dealing not with all Russian word-forms, but only with a few: *lepila* 'fashioned', *na* 'on', *metel'* 'snow storm', *kružki* 'circles', *strely* 'arrows', *stekle* 'glass', *i* 'and'. Only for them will we specify the values of the assignment function f, indicating not all its possible values,[4] but only those which are necessary for our example:

(1) $f(lepila) = V^{tr}_{f, sg, 3, past}$,

(2) $f(na) = Pr_{na}$,

(3) $f(metel') = [\text{SENT} / V^{itr}_{f, sg, 3, t}]$,

(4,5) $f(kružki) = f(strely) = [V^{tr}_{g,n,p,t} \backslash V^{itr}_{g,n,p,t}]$,

(6) $f(stekle) = [Pr_{na} \backslash [V^{tr}_{g,n,p,t} \backslash V^{tr}_{g,n,p,t}]]$,

(7) $f(i) = [[[V^{tr}_{g,n,p,t} \backslash V^{itr}_{g,n,p,t}] \backslash [V^{tr}_{g,n,p,t} \backslash V^{itr}_{g,n,p,t}]] \backslash [V^{tr}_{g,n,p,t} \backslash V^{itr}_{g,n,p,t}]]$.

The category assigned to the word-form *metel'* 'snowstorm' is an operator which, acting from the left on an intransitive verb of the corresponding gender, number and person, forms out of it a sentence; in other words, this is the category 'grammatical subject standing before the main verb' (i.e. 'left subject'). In order to account for the possibility of placing the subject in Russian after the main verb, we would have to assign to the word-form *metel'* another category: $[V^{itr}_{f,sg,3,t} \backslash \text{SENT}]$.[5] And if we wanted also to account for the homonymy of cases — the form *metel'* can also be a direct object (in accusative), right or left — we would have to assign to this word-form two more groups of categories:

$[V^{tr}_{g,n,p,t} \backslash V^{itr}_{g,n,p,t}]$ and $[V^{itr}_{g,n,p,t} / V^{tr}_{g,n,p,t}]$

However, even this is not all: in order to reflect the ability of the form *metel'* to combine with different prepositions (*v metel'* 'into the snowstorm', *za metel'* 'behind the snowstorm', etc.), it should be assigned a large number of further categories.

What has been said here is true also of items (4) – (7): these word-forms are assigned only a few of all the categories they actually have in Russian — only those that are needed for our example. Namely, the word-form *kružki* 'circles' and *strely* 'arrows' are assigned the category 'right direct object',[6] and the form *stekle* 'glass' the category 'object of the preposition *na*' (an operator which acting on *na* 'on' from the right yields an adverbial

modifying transitive[7] verbs), while the word-form *i* 'and' is assigned
the category 'conjunction linking two right direct objects' (the operator
which, appearing between two right direct objects, forms again a right direct
object).

Grammar G_1 has, then, been constructed. Using it as an example we can
describe now the working of C grammars in general.

Let there be a string $x = a_1 a_2 a_3 \ldots a_k$ of symbols belonging to the terminal
vocabulary of some C grammar G_1. The function f of this grammar allows us
to associate with the string x a string ξ of categories, $\xi = f(a_1) f(a_3) \ldots f(a_k)$;
generally speaking, there can be several such strings – owing to the many-
valuedness of the function f, i.e., to the homonymy of some a_i. If this
string (in the general case, at least one such string) can be canceled to one
category Φ, then we say that grammar G_1 assigns the string x the category Φ.

Consider, for example, the following string of Russian word-forms: *Metel'
lepila na stekle kružki i strely* 'The snowstorm fashioned on the glass circles
and arrows' (it happens to be a famous line from a well-known poem by
B. Pasternak). Grammar G_1 associates with this string the string of categories
presented in Fig. 1 below.

Metel'	*lepila*	*na*	*stekle*	*kružki*
'The snowstorm'	'fashioned'	'on'	'the glass'	'circles'
$[\text{SENT}/V^{itr}]$	V^{tr}	Pr_{na}	$[Pr_{na}\backslash[V^{tr}\backslash V^{tr}]]$	$[V^{tr}\backslash V^{itr}]$
$\underbrace{\quad}_{\alpha}$	$\underbrace{\quad}_{\beta}$	$\underbrace{\quad}_{\gamma}$	$\underbrace{\quad}_{\lambda}$	$\underbrace{\quad}_{\epsilon}$

$$\underbrace{\qquad\qquad\qquad}_{\delta}$$

i	*strely*
'and'	'arrows'
$[[[V^{tr}\backslash V^{itr}]\backslash[V^{tr}\backslash V^{itr}]]/[V^{tr}\backslash V^{itr}]]$	$[V^{tr}\backslash V^{itr}]$,
$\underbrace{\qquad}_{\kappa}$	$\underbrace{\quad}_{\epsilon}$

$$\underbrace{\qquad\qquad\qquad}_{\zeta}$$

with every V being in the feminine, 3rd person singular, past tense.
Figure 1.

This category string can be canceled in the following manner:

(1) $\zeta\epsilon \to \kappa$ (2) $\epsilon\kappa \to \epsilon$ (3) $\gamma\delta \to \lambda$ (4) $\beta\lambda \to V^{tr}_{\text{f,sg,3,past}}$

(5) $V^{tr}_{\text{f,sg,3,past}}\, \epsilon \to V^{itr}_{\text{f,sg,3,past}}$ (6) $\alpha\, V^{itr}_{\text{f,sg,3,past}} \to \text{SENT}$

This means that G_1 assigns to the string *Metel' lepila na stekle kružki i strely*
the category SENT; i.e., G_1 'recognizes' this string as a Russian sentence.

Correspondingly, the string *kružki i strely* 'circles and arrows' is assigned the category $\epsilon = [V^{tr}_{f,sg,3,past} \setminus V^{itr}_{f,sg,3,past}]$ ('right direct object'), the string *lepila na stekle* 'fashioned on the glass' the category $V^{tr}_{f,sg,3,past}$, and the string *lepila na stekle kružki i strely* the category $V^{itr}_{f,sg,3,past}$. At the same time it is easy to see that grammar G_1 does not assign any categories to such strings as *metel' lepila na* 'the snowstorm fashioned on', *stekle kružki i* '[on] glass circles and', or *na i* 'on and', *na lepila* 'on fashioned', *lepila stekle* 'fashioned [on] glass' (prepositional case), etc.

Thus for an arbitrary string of symbols from vocabulary V a C grammar allows one to find out which categories characterize this string and whether it is at all characterized by any categories whatsoever. In particular, for any string, a C grammar allows one to find out whether this string is a correct sentence of the language; i.e., it allows one to recognize the grammaticality of sentences. In addition, if the string turns out to be a grammatical sentence, then the C grammar distinguishes in it grammatical phrases, i.e., its constituents (in the usual sense of this word). The way of constructing the PS (or IC) tree from the representation of the process of canceling the initial string of categories is extremely simple: a substring will be a constituent of the given string if the string of categories corresponding to this substring is, at some step in the process of cancellation, canceled to one category; this category can be taken to be the syntactic class of the given constituent. In our example there are six constituents (not counting one-element constituents), which correspond to the six steps of the cancellation process:

1) *i strely* 'and arrows' (type κ),
2) *kružki i strely* 'circles and arrows' (type ϵ),
3) *na stekle* 'on the glass' (type λ),
4) *lepila na stekle* 'fashioned on the glass' (type $V^{tr}_{f,sg,3,past}$),
5) *lepila na stekle kružki i strely* 'fashioned on the glass circles and arrows' (type $V^{itr}_{f,sg,3,past}$),
6) the entire sentence as a whole (type SENT).

This system of constituents can be represented by an ordinary IC tree (= PS marker):

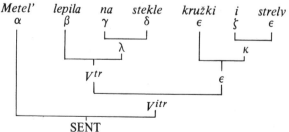

In the case of a syntactically ambiguous sentence a C grammar can specify for it DIFFERENT systems of constituents, i.e., yield different parsings. First of all, this happens because the string of categories that corresponds to the sentence can be canceled in different ways; for example:

... *medlennye*	*protony*	*i*	*nejtrony*
'slow'	'protons'	'and'	'neutrons'
$[N/N]$	N	$[[N\backslash N]/N]$	N

$$\underbrace{\quad\quad}_{\alpha} \quad\quad\quad \underbrace{\quad\quad\quad\quad\quad\quad}_{\beta}$$
$$\underbrace{\quad\quad\quad\quad\quad\quad\quad\quad\quad\quad}_{\gamma}$$

The first way of performing the cancellation is: $\alpha N \to N$, $\gamma N \to \beta$, $N\beta \to N$, which gives the parsing
... (*medlennye protony*) *i nejtrony.*
The second way of performing the cancellation is: $\gamma N \to \beta$, $N\beta \to N$, $\alpha N \to N$, which gives
... *medlennye* (*protony i nejtrony*).
Second, a sentence can be assigned several strings of categories, and this can also lead to different systems of constituents, see Figure 2 below.

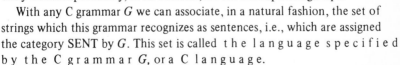

	On	*vynul*	*trubku*	*iz*	*gliny*
	'He'	'took out'	'a pipe'	'of'	'clay'
1.	$[SENT/V^{itr}]$	V^{tr}	$[V^{tr}\backslash V^{itr}]$	Pr_{iz}	$[Pr_{iz}\backslash[[V^{tr}\backslash V^{itr}]\backslash[V^{tr}\backslash V^{itr}]]]$
2.	$[SENT/V^{itr}]$	V^{tr}	$[V^{tr}\backslash V^{itr}]$	Pr_{iz}	$[Pr_{iz}\backslash[V^{itr}\backslash V^{itr}]]$

Figure 2.

For the first string of categories we obtain the parsing
(*On*(*vynul*(*trubku*(*iz gliny*)))) '(He(took out(a pipe(of clay))))',
i.e., the pipe was made of clay and it was taken out of, say, a drawer, while for the second string the parsing is
(*On*((*vynul trubku*)(*iz gliny*))) '(He((took out a pipe)(out of clay)))',
i.e., the pipe was extracted out of clay. We recommend that the reader carry out independently, as an exercise, all the corresponding steps.[8]

With any C grammar G we can associate, in a natural fashion, the set of strings which this grammar recognizes as sentences, i.e., which are assigned the category SENT by G. This set is called t h e   l a n g u a g e   s p e c i f i e d   b y   t h e   C   g r a m m a r G, or a   C   l a n g u a g e.
The question arises: what is the relation between languages specified by categorial grammars and languages generated by generative grammars?

T
2.1
It is easy to see that every C language is a CF language and, moreover, that for every C grammar G it is possible to construct a CF grammar G' equivalent to G (i.e., G' generates precisely that language which is specified by G). The proof of this fact (which we only outline here) is very simple:

If $G = \langle V, W, f, \text{SENT} \rangle$ is a C grammar, then the corresponding CF grammar G' is constructed as follows:

1) The terminal vocabulary of G' will be V.

2) The nonterminal vocabulary of G' will be the set of all categories that are values of the assignment function f or their parts.[9]

3) The initial symbol will be SENT.

4) The rules of grammar G' will be of two types:

First, rules of the type $\Psi \rightarrow \Phi \, [\Phi\backslash\Psi]$ and $\Phi \rightarrow [\Phi/\Psi] \, \Psi$, where $[\Phi\backslash\Psi]$ and $[\Phi/\Psi]$ are arbitrary derived categories from the nonterminal vocabulary of grammar G (there are clearly only a finite number of such categories, see p. 89).

Second, rules of the type $f(a) \rightarrow a$, where a is a terminal symbol, and $f(a)$ is an arbitrary value of the assignment function corresponding to a.

The equivalence of the thus constructed CF grammar G' and the C grammar G is almost obvious; we will omit the formal proof.

T
2.2
It turns out that the converse is also true: every CF language is a C language, and for every CF grammar it is possible to construct a C grammar equivalent to it.

NB
From what has been said it follows directly that the class of C languages coincides exactly with the class of CF languages. Therefore, the question concerning the theoretical suitability of C grammars for describing natural languages is resolved in the same way as for CF grammars (see p. 66 and following). As for practical convenience, C grammars are clearly inconvenient in two very important respects.

1. Their application to natural languages, especially to languages with a rich morphology (for example, to Russian), requires the introduction of a large number of derived categories, which may turn out to be extremely cumbersome — cf. the categories for i 'and' in the example on p. 92. What is even worse, these categories are used rather uneconomically: almost every word, even if it is not ambiguous (i.e., it is not of the type *peč*' 'to bake' — 'stove', or of the type Eng. [*to*] *work* — [*the*] *work*), is assigned a great number of different categories. We have already discussed this in connection with the Russian word-form *metel*' 'snowstorm' (p. 92); let us turn our attention again to the conjunction i 'and': on p. 93 it was assigned 54 categories, but this set of categories is sufficient only for the case when i 'and' links two right direct objects! For all the other numerous cases (joining of left direct objects, of right prepositional phrases with the preposition v

'in', and also with the prepositions *bez* 'without', *na* 'on', etc., of transitive verbs, of left modifiers of a verb, . . . , of entire clauses and/or sentences) the conjunction *i* 'and' should be assigned new special sets of categories, generally speaking, of the same complexity. As a result, the conjunction *i* will be assigned several thousand categories.

It is obvious that if the majority of words are assigned so many categories, then the number of strings of categories for each string of words becomes astronomically large.

Note that there are no adjectives in our example. This is by no means accidental; if, following the above principle of introducing primitive categories, we had to assign categories to adjectives as well, this would entail an even greater increase in the number of categories per word. Too much space is needed to fully explain this; the reader may try to assign adjectives the necessary categories within the suggested grammar by himself (this will require several changes in the categories already introduced; the main difficulty here is to ensure agreement in gender between adjective and modified noun). Similar difficulties connected with specifying categories for English gerunds — for example, in *Playing cards is fun* — were noted by Y. Bar-Hillel (1960).

2. In C grammars the syntactic categories are too closely related to the word order: the left and right grammatical subject, the left and right object, etc. are, from the viewpoint of C grammars, totally different categories, which seems to sharply contradict linguistic intuition.

At the same time C grammars have three unquestionable merits:

(a) C grammars have no rules at all (with the exception of the cancellation rules, of which there are only two and which are common to all C grammars). All the necessary information about the syntactic properties of words is contained only in 'dictionary entries'; i.e., it is specified exclusively by the assignment function, cf. p. 90.

(b) C grammars presuppose a very close analysis of the syntactic properties of individual word-forms, i.e., a detailed differentiation of their syntactic functions. Each 'microfunction' has in C grammars its individual explicit expression — its category.

The reverse side of both merits is precisely the cumbersomeness and multiplicity of categories.

(c) C grammars allow us to obtain for a sentence not only a system (and tree) of constituents, but also a system (tree) of dependencies.[10] (It should be emphasized that a CF grammar, generally speaking, does not give the unique tree of dependencies even for syntactically non-ambiguous sentences.) This property makes C grammars interesting from the viewpoint of automatic analysis and translation of texts, where it seems expedient to have the possibility of simultaneously representing the structure of sentences both in terms of IC and in terms of dependencies.[11]

However, along with all this, C grammars in pure form — due just to the above-mentioned shortcomings — are apparently little suited for similar practical goals.

PUSH-DOWN STORE AUTOMATA (PDS AUTOMATA)

First of all we will try to give an informal presentation of push-down store automata with the aid of an example. The use of push-down store underlies an interesting class of automatic syntactic analysis algorithms[12] — we mean the so-called p r e d i c t i v e   a n a l y z e r s, introduced by A. Oettinger (P analyzers: Kuno 1963; Kuno — Oettinger 1963; Plath 1963).

We describe below a P analyzer not exactly of the same type as those in the above works. Since, unlike authors of these works, we are not bound by the requirements of practical convenience for the processing of actual texts, but are rather concerned about the maximum simplicity and generality of the exposition, it proved expedient to give the P analyzer a somewhat different form.

The main difference between the version of the P analyzer proposed below and the 'traditional' versions lies in the fact that P analyzers are usually treated as syntactic analysis ALGORITHMS, while we regard them here as CALCULI (grammars). In other words, in the ordinary P analyzer each step is uniquely determined by the preceding step, while in our version there are, generally speaking, MANY continuations ('permissible variants') for each step, from which it is possible to select any one (cf. the remark about the relation between grammars and algorithms on p. 23).

The central idea of predictive analysis consists, roughly speaking, in the following. A sentence is processed (= scanned) word by word in one direction only — from left to right. For each word considered a s y n t a c t i c   p r e d i c t i o n (SP) is formulated which states just what construction (i.e. constituent) can follow that word in the sentence. If the next word satisfies, or fulfills, this SP, the analysis continues; otherwise it is blocked. Since a word can predict many different constituents, many 'paths' of analysis may be started off; but if the sentence analysed is syntactically non-ambiguous the analysis is completed (i.e., the sentence is processed up to the end) only along one path.

As a result of the analysis the sentence is assigned a system of constituents (an IC analysis). The boundaries of a constituent are represented by brackets labeled with the class symbol of this constituent.

We will describe the work of a P analyzer using as an example the analysis of the Russian sentence *Malen'kij mal'čik na dalëkom ot goroda polustanke ždal priezda roditelej* 'A little boy at a small station far from the city awaited the arrival of his parents'. For processing this sentence the analyzing device needs information about Russian syntax; this information is stored in the following two components of the P analyzer:

1) The dictionary (or the dictionary + the algorithm for morphological analysis), which assigns each textual word-form its syntactic code: part of speech, case, gender, person, animateness, etc.; for example, for *malen'kij* 'little' — $A_{\mathrm{m,sg,nom\,-acc}}$, for *na* 'at' — $Pr_{\mathrm{acc/prep}}$, etc. This component — an analog of the assignment function of categorial grammar — is characteristic not just of the P analyzer alone: such a dictionary is necessary in some form for any recognition grammar (and, in fact, also for any generative grammar; cf. the example on p. 33, where the role of the dictionary is played by Group IV rules).

2) A specific feature of the P analyzer is that it makes use of two SYNTACTIC TABLES: A and Ω (see pp. 100, 103), which contain all the necessary information about the syntax of the language considered.

Table A, which describes the possible beginnings of different constituents, has three columns.

Column I lists all the types of constituents[13] that are admitted in the given description of this language, for example, 'noun phrase', 'verb phrase', 'prepositional phrase', etc.

Column II lists for each type C of constituent all the classes w_1, w_2, w_3, . . ., w_n of word-forms with which the C type constituent can begin; for example, for the Russian nominative noun phrase we have in Column II:

(1) an adverb (*očen' xorošaja kniga* '(a) very good book'),
(2) A_{nom} (*malen'kij mal'čik* 'little boy'),
(3) N_{nom} (*tablica* 'table'), etc.

And finally, column III holds the syntactic predictions (SP) themselves. Namely, for each pair $< C,\ w_i >$ column III specifies which constituents (one or several) can follow w_i within the constituent C. For example, one of the syntactic predictions for a word-form of the type *priezd* 'arrival', *pryžok* 'jump', etc. which begins a noun phrase would be 'genitive noun phrase'. It means that in Russian such a word-form is capable of having a complement in the genitive case as distinct, for example, from such forms as *on* 'he' or *nas* 'us', after which a genitive noun phrase belonging to the same constituent

Syntactic Table A

Number of line	I Constituent	II Class of the beginning word-form	III Syntactic Prediction	Examples
1.	$NP_{g,n,c}$	Adv	$AP_{g,n,c} + + NP_{g,n,c}$	*Očen' malen'kij mal'čik* 'A very little boy'
2.	$NP_{g,n,c}$	$A_{g,n,c}$	$NP_{g,n,c}$	*Malen'kij mal'čik* 'Little boy'
3.	$NP_{g,n,c}$	$A_{g,n,c}$	$PP + NP_{g,n,c}$	*Blednoe ot ustalosti lico* 'A face pale from fatigue'
4.	$NP_{g,n,c}$	$N_{g,n,c}$	PP	*Dom s mezoninom* 'A house with a mezzanine'
5.	$NP_{g,n,c}$	$N_{g,n,c}$	$NP_{g',n',\text{gen}}$	*Syn našix staryx sosedej* 'The son of our old neighbors'
6.	$AP_{g,n,c}$	$A_{g,n,c}$	PP	*Blizkij k okončaniju* 'Close to the end'
7.	PP	Pr_c	$NP_{g,n,c}$	*Na zelënom lugu* 'In the green meadow'
8.	$VP_{g,n,p}$	Adv	$VP_{g,n,p}$	*Davno mečtaet* '(He) has dreamt long since'
9.	$VP_{g,n,p}$	Pr_c	$NP_{g',n'c} + + VP_{g,n,p}$	*Na goloj veršine stoit* 'On the bare summit (there) stands'
10.	$VP_{g,n,p}$	$V_{g,n,p}$	PP	*Stoit za uglom* 'Stands behind the corner'
11.	$VP_{g,n,p}$	$V_{g,n,p,c'}$	$NP_{c'}$	*Ždët biletov* 'Awaits tickets'
12.	$VP_{g,n,p}$	$V_{g,n,p,c',c''}$	$NP_{c'} + NP_{c''}$	*Daët bilet podruge* 'Gives a ticket to his girlfriend'

NOTATIONS (in tables A and Ω):

NP – noun phrase Pr_c – preposition governing case c
PP – prepositional phrase $V_{c'}$ – verb requiring an object in case c'
VP – verbal phrase $V_{c'c''}$ – verb requiring two objects: in case c' and in
AP – adjective phrase   case c''

The other notations have the same meaning as above, p. 33.

is excluded. Among SP's for adjectives beginning a noun phrase there is 'prepositional phrase + noun phrase' (see table A, line 3); it means that a noun phrase in Russian may have the following structure: 'adjective + prepositional phrase + noun phrase' — for example *trudnaja + dlja nas + algebraičeskaja zadača* 'difficult + for us + algebra problem' (i.e., 'an algebra problem difficult for us').

For each pair $< C, w_i >$ there are, generally speaking, several alternative predictions: for example, after the word-form *priezda* 'of the arrival' we can immediately find — within a noun phrase — a prepositional phrase (*priezda v Moskvu* 'of the arrival in Moscow'), a genitive noun phrase (*priezda alžirskix studentov* 'of the arrival of Algerian students'), a relative clause with *kotoryj* 'which', or nothing at all (*priezda* may constitute a whole noun phrase by itself).

Syntactic table A (like syntactic table Ω) is no more than an illustration and does not at all claim to be an adequate representation of (a fragment of) Russian syntax; a rather complete table A would be many times greater (the syntactic table for Russian, contained in Plath 1963, has 2344 lines and a much more complex structure; the syntactic table for English, according to Kuno 1963, has more than 2100 lines).

It should be kept in mind that, just as before (cf. pp. 31–32), we use here abbreviations by means of variables as subscripts. Each line of table A (and table Ω) is then in fact a condensed representation of many lines.

Table Ω describes the possible 'endings' of different constituents and has two columns.

Column I, as in table A, lists all the types of constituents, except the atomic (or point) ones.

Column II lists for each type C of constituent all the classes of word-forms (in our example not all of them are cited!) with which the constituent of the type C can end. For example, for the noun phrase such a word class is N, etc.

In our example, table Ω has the form shown on page 102.

In addition to both of the components described, which provide all the necessary information about the syntax of the language in question, the **NB** P analyzer has a further, most important component — a working area, structured in a special way, called (s y n t a c t i c) p r e d i c t i o n p o o l (PP). As opposed to the dictionary and both syntactic tables, which are used as passive reference books (their content does not change in the process of the analysis), PP is precisely that storage zone where processing of all intermediate results takes place. The PP consists of an unlimited number of p u s h - d o w n s t o r e s,[14] each of which is a device very much like a rifle magazine or a vending machine serving sandwiches (or those devices for stacking plates in cafeterias): it is possible to enter (record) in each push-down store only one symbol at a time and only from one end — say the upper; and only from that end is it possible to 'extract' symbols from the push-down store (to delete them), so that the symbol entered into the push-down store last, is extracted from it first (last-in-first-out principle). The push-down store (PDS) is like a box with a spring in the bottom: when a new symbol is entered into it, all the symbols that were there previously are pushed down, and when the upper symbol is deleted (extracted from the PDS), the remaining symbols automatically pop upward (see the diagram on p. 103).

Now we can move on to the exposition of the very process of analyzing sentences by a P analyzer.

First of all, it should be stressed that owing both to the grammatical ambiguity of many word-forms (Russ. *peč'* – $V_{\text{inf}}/N_{\text{sg.nom-acc}}$ 'to bake/an oven', *linii* – $N_{\text{pl,nom-acc}}$, $N_{\text{sg,gen}}/N_{\text{sg,dat}}/N_{\text{sg,prep}}$ 'line', etc.) and to the existence in most cases of several SP's for a word-form, each step of the analysis permits, generally speaking, more than one continuation. This results in many variants, or 'paths', of analysis.

Syntactic Table Ω

Number of line	I Constituent	II Class of the closing word-form	Examples
1.	$NP_{g,n,c}$	$N_{g',n',c'}$	*bereg s nebol'šim lesočkom* 'a shore with a small wood'
2.	$AP_{g,n,c}$	$N_{g',n',c'}$	*važnye dlja čitatelja* 'important for the reader'
3.	$AP_{g,n,c}$	$A_{g,n,c}$	*davno zabytyj* 'long forgotten'
4.	PP	$N_{g,n,c}$	*na zelënom lugu* 'in the green meadow'
5.	$VP_{g,n}$	$V_{g,n}$	*userdno rabotaet* 'works diligently'
6.	$VP_{g,n}$	$N_{g',n',c'}$	*rabotaet nad knigoj* 'works on a book'
7.	SENT	$N_{g,n,c}$	*Lodka kolotitsja v sonnoj grudi* 'The boat is knocking in the sleepy chest' (B. Pasternak)
8.	SENT	$V_{g,n}$	*Serdce s domom razlučaetsja* 'The heart bids farewell to the house' (Yu. Daniel)

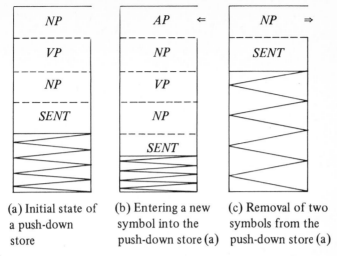

(a) Initial state of a push-down store

(b) Entering a new symbol into the push-down store (a)

(c) Removal of two symbols from the push-down store (a)

However, in some analysis variants a situation can arise in which at some step no permissible continuation is available even though the processing of the sentence is still not completed. This means that either the sentence analyzed is syntactically incorrect, or (if it is correct) in one of the preceding steps a wrong continuation was selected, which led the analysis into a blind alley. Thus the correctness of a path (i.e., of an analysis variant) is signalled by the attainment of the end of the sentence, and its incorrectness by the impossibility of reaching the end of the sentence.

Each path is assigned a push-down store which plays the role of a memory preserving the syntactic predictions corresponding to the given path.

In examining the example we will follow only one path of analysis, which corresponds to the correct syntactic interpretation of the sentence given on p. 99 (this sentence also has another correct interpretation; see below, p. 107).

Before the start of the analysis the analyzer puts a left bracket labeled SENT in front of the first word to be processed and enters into its push-down store predictions $NP_{m,sg,nom}$ + $VP_{m,sg,3}$ + SENT (see state 0 of the PDS on p. 106), since it is possible to suppose a priori that the segment being analyzed is a sentence (SENT) and consists of a subject noun phrase (NP_{nom}) and a verb phrase (VP), with NP_{nom} standing to the left of VP and being masculine singular. This supposition, of course, is not the only one; the other push-down stores may contain other sets of a priori predictions — for instance, predictions of the subject (and, correspondingly, of the main verb) of feminine or neuter gender or in the plural — which, however, for our sentence will not give correct analyses.

Each analysis step consists in the processing of one word. This processing includes the following operations (let it be recalled — cf. p. 98 — that what we describe here is not an analysis algorithm, but rather a set of PERMISSIBLE operations, so that at each step it is possible to perform any one of the actions permitted in this case):

1. Compare the syntactic code of the current word with the current (topmost) prediction in the push-down store; i.e., seek a correspondence pair in table A and thereby ascertain whether the current word can begin the predicted constituent. If not, continuation of the analysis is impossible.

2. If yes, the beginning of this constituent is marked by a left bracket, and then we can do one of two things:

2a. Under the assumption that the constituent just begun continues, select any of the SP's of the current word, place it in the push-down store (on top of the predictions already stored there)[15] and proceed to the next step, i.e., to the next word of the sentence under analysis.

2b. Under the assumption that the constituent just begun ends with the current word, seek in table Ω the pair

< current SP, syntactic code of the current word >

and thereby ascertain whether the current word can end this constituent. If not, continuation of the analysis is impossible. If yes, the end of the constituent is marked by a right bracket, and the corresponding (current) SP is removed from the push-down store. Operation 2b can be repeated any number of times (since the current word can end not only the given constituent, but also a larger one which was begun earlier and includes the given one); then the analyzer should proceed to the next step of the analysis.

The analysis is considered complete and its result correct if after the last word of the sentence is processed the push-down store proves to be empty. With all this in mind, let us begin the description of the analysis of our sentence.

1st step. We examine the word *malen'kij* 'little'; the current (i.e., the top one in the push-down store) SP = $NP_{m,sg,nom}$. Since the pair $<NP_{m,sg,nom}$, $A_{m,sg,nom}>$ is present in table A (lines 2 and 3), we conclude that the word-form of the type *malen'kij* can begin the predicted constituent. We place before *malen'kij* a left bracket labeled $NP_{m,sg,nom}$, and select path 2a — i.e., we select from column III one of the SP's of the given pair, namely $NP_{m,sg,nom}$, and place it in the push-down store; now the push-down store will contain the predictions $NP_{m,sg,nom} + NP_{m,sg,nom} + VP_{m,sg,3} + SENT$ (see state 1 of the PDS, p. 106).

2nd step. The current word is *mal'čik* 'boy' and the current pair is $<NP_{m,sg,nom}$, $N_{m,sg,nom}>$. This pair is also contained in table A (lines 4 and 5), and, having placed before *mal'čik* the corresponding bracket, we select path 2b: we look up the current pair in table Ω, and finding it there (line 1), we place after *mal'čik* a right bracket ($NP_{m,sg,nom}$), whereupon we remove the current prediction from the push-down store. Then we repeat operation 2b: again we find in Ω the current pair $<NP_{m,sg,nom}, N_{m,sg,nom}>$, place after *mal'čik* another bracket with the label $NP_{m,sg,nom}$, remove from the push-down store the topmost prediction and proceed to the next word.

After the 2nd step our sentence has the form:

(1)
	0	1	2	2	2	
	(	(*Malen'kij*	(*mal'čik*	)	)	*na dalëkom ot goroda . . .*
	SENT	$NP_{m,sg,nom}$	$NP_{m,sg,nom}$	$NP_{m,sg,nom}$	$NP_{m,sg,nom}$	

(the number above the bracket being the number of the step at which this bracket appeared), while the push-down store has the form 2b on p. 106.

3rd step. The current word is *na* 'at' and the current pair is $<VP_{m,sg,3}, Pr_{prep}>$; it is found in table A (line 9). We open the left bracket of the verb phrase (i.e., the bracket labeled with *VP*) and take one of the SP's of the pair that are found in table A: e.g., $NP_{m,sg,prep} + VP_{m,sg,3}$, which is placed in the push-down store (state 3).

4th step. The current word is *dalëkom* 'far', and the current pair is $<NP_{m,sg,prep}, A_{m,sg,prep}>$. Having found the current pair in table A, we open before *dalëkom* a bracket labeled $NP_{m,sg,prep}$, and as the next SP we select $PP + NP_{m,sg,prep}$ (line 3); the push-down store assumes the form of 4, p. 106.

5th step. The current word is *ot* 'from', and the current pair is $<PP, Pr_{gen}>$. Since this pair is contained in table A, we place before *ot* a left bracket (*PP*) and place into the push-down store the SP of the given pair (line 7); now the push-down store contains the predictions (from top to bottom): $NP_{m,sg,gen} + PP + NP_{m,sg,prep} + NP_{m,sg,prep} + VP_{m,sg,3} + VP_{m,sg,3} + \text{SENT}$ (state 5).

6th step. The current word is *goroda* 'city', and the current pair is $<NP_{m,sg,gen}, N_{m,sg,gen}>$. This pair is found in table A; we open before *goroda* a bracket ($NP_{m,sg,gen}$), but instead of path 2a, as in steps 3–5, we now choose 2b. Having found the current pair in table Ω, we close the bracket after *goroda* and remove the current prediction $NP_{m,sg,gen}$·from the push-down store (state 6a). Then we repeat operation 2b once more: the new current pair $<PP, N_{m,sg,gen}>$ is found in table Ω (the prepositional phrase can end with a noun), therefore we place after *goroda* another right bracket, now with the label *VP*, and we remove the current SP from the push-down store (state 6b), after which we proceed to the next word.

As for the remaining steps (7–10), the reader can carry them out by

himself; but in order to make his task easier, we will show the states
of the push-down store after each of steps 7–10 (states 7a–10e, p. 107)
and the sentence in the form which it should have after completing the
analysis (the number ABOVE a bracket is the number of the step at which this
bracket appeared; the number BELOW a bracket is an abbreviated designation
of the phrase type):

(2) 0 1   2   2 2 3   4   5   6   6 6 7   7
    (*(Malen'kij* *(mal'čik)*) *(na* *(dalëkom* *(ot* *(goroda)*) *(polustanke)*
    1 2   2   2 2 3   4   5   6   6 5 4   4

    7 8   9   9   10   10 10 10 10
) *(ždal* *(priezda* *(roditelej)*   )   )   )   ) . 'A little boy at a small
    4 3   6   7   7   6   3 3   1

station far from the city awaited the arrival of his parents'.

Phrase types in (2) are:

1 – SENT   4 – $NP_{m,sg,prep}$ 6 – $NP_{m,sg,gen}$
2 – $NP_{m,sg,nom}$ 5 – PP 7 – $NP_{m,pl,gen}$
3 – $VP_{m,sg,3}$

The states of the push-down store in the course of our analysis are:

0	1	2a
$NP_{m,sg,nom}$ $VP_{m,sg,3}$ SENT	$NP_{m,sg,nom}$ $NP_{m,sg,nom}$ $VP_{m,sg,3}$ SENT	$NP_{m,sg,nom}$ $VP_{m,sg,3}$ SENT

2b	3	4
$VP_{m,sg,3}$ SENT	$NP_{m,sg,prep}$ $VP_{m,sg,3}$ $VP_{m,sg,3}$ SENT	PP $NP_{m,sg,prep}$ $NP_{m,sg,prep}$ $VP_{m,sg,3}$ $VP_{m,sg,3}$ SENT

5	6a	6b
$NP_{m,sg,gen}$ PP $NP_{m,sg,prep}$ $NP_{m,sg,prep}$ $VP_{m,sg,3}$ $VP_{m,sg,3}$ SENT	PP $NP_{m,sg,prep}$ $NP_{m,sg,prep}$ $VP_{m,sg,3}$ $VP_{m,sg,3}$ SENT	$NP_{m,sg,prep}$ $NP_{m,sg,prep}$ $VP_{m,sg,3}$ $VP_{m,sg,3}$ SENT

7a	7b	8
$NP_{m,sg,prep}$ $VP_{m,sg,3}$ $VP_{m,sg,3}$ SENT	$VP_{m,sg,3}$ $VP_{m,sg,3}$ SENT	$NP_{m,sg,gen}$ $VP_{m,sg,3}$ $VP_{m,sg,3}$ SENT

9	10a	10b
$NP_{m,sg,gen}$ $NP_{m,sg,gen}$ $VP_{m,sg,3}$ $VP_{m,sg,3}$ SENT	$NP_{m,sg,gen}$ $VP_{m,sg,3}$ $VP_{m,sg,3}$ SENT	$VP_{m,sg,3}$ $VP_{m,sg,3}$ SENT

10c	10d	10e
$VP_{m,sg,3}$ SENT	SENT	

Thus we have obtained a quite conventional representation of IC structure. However, one not very significant peculiarity may be noted: atomic constructions (i.e., individual word-forms) which begin bigger constituents are not bracketed. This is connected with a technicality of the P analyzer, namely the fact that it processes a sentence from left to right in only one scan.

Note that our sentence has another syntactically correct interpretation:

(3)((*Malen'kij* (*mal'čik* (*na* (*dalëkom* (*ot* (*goroda*)) (*polustanke*))))) (*ždal* (*priezda* (*roditelej*)))), i.e., the phrase *na. . .polustanke* does not belong to the verb phrase, but rather enters into the subject noun phrase (*mal'čik na polustanke* 'a boy at a small station', and not *ždal na polustanke* 'awaited at a small station'). Although such an interpretation is semantically hardly acceptable, syntactically it is absolutely normal and should be produced by the P analyzer. In our example we could have obtained this interpretation if at the 2nd step we had chosen operation 2a instead of 2b, and had taken from table A the prediction *PP* (line 4). We recommend that the reader independently conduct the analysis along that path.

Formally, the P analyzer is a special case of the p u s h - d o w n   s t o r e a u t o m a t o n   (P D S   a u t o m a t o n).[16] A rigorous definition of a PDS automaton is hard to formulate within the framework of the present exposition (which is intended for readers not acquainted with the theory of algorithms) since, in order to understand it, familiarity with Turing machines is necessary. For the prepared reader this definition is cited below in small print.

In the literature, two subclasses of PDS automata are considered: nondeterministic and deterministic ones. In this book, we always understand PDS automata as nondeterministic PDS automata and therefore the adjective *nondeterministic* is omitted in what follows.

A nondeterministic Turing machine[17] is called a P D S   a u t o m a t o n if it satisfies the following three conditions.

1. The machine has three t a p e s (called respectively an i n p u t tape, a s c r a t c h (= storage, or working) tape and an o u t p u t tape), and three h e a d s , one head on each tape. A tape consists of a sequence of s q u a r e s . All three tapes are limited on the left and unlimited on the right.

2. The machine has three external alphabets: an i n p u t   a l p h a b e t for the input tape (interpreted as the terminal vocabulary + the 'empty' symbol), a w o r k i n g   a l p h a b e t for the scratch tape (interpreted as the set of syntactic predictions + the 'empty' symbol), and an o u t p u t   a l p h a b e t (interpreted as the set of left and right brackets labeled with symbols for constituent types + the 'empty' symbol).

3. The machine can perform the following elementary operations:

(a) On the input tape it can only read the symbol recorded in the square being scanned and move the head one square TO THE RIGHT. (Thus the input head is a reading head.)

(b) On the scratch tape the machine can

either write a (nonempty) symbol in the square being scanned and move the head one square TO THE RIGHT,

or it can move the head one square TO THE LEFT and read and erase the symbol recorded in the square the head is now scanning. The scratch tape always has the form shown on p. 109.

From this diagram it is obvious that the scratch tape is nothing other than a push-down store.

(c) On the output tape the machine can only write a symbol and move the head one square TO THE RIGHT. (Thus the output head is a writing head.) In our interpretation, as a result of a PDS computation there should appear on the output tape a labeled bracketing representing the constituent structure of the sentence being analyzed.

4. At each move the machine works on only one tape.

5. At the initial moment all three heads are positioned on the leftmost squares of the corresponding tapes, and the scratch and output tapes are empty. The computation is considered completed (= the machine halts) if the input head has reached the first empty square on its tape (which means that the entire input has been read), while the scratch tape is at this moment empty.

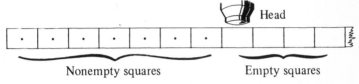

Nonempty squares   Empty squares

The reader acquainted with Turing machines will easily understand that a P analyzer corresponds to a PDS automaton with the following additional restriction: before each writing of a symbol on the scratch tape the automaton should read a symbol on the input tape. (Informally, this restriction is explained by the fact that the storing of a syntactic prediction in the push-down store of the P analyzer should always be directly controlled by the reading of the next word of the sentence analyzed.) Note also that the PDS automaton is allowed to write on the scratch tape at each move only one symbol, while the P analyzer sometimes records several symbols at once; it is obvious that this difference is not too important.

For each PDS automaton it is possible to consider a set consisting of all and only those strings (segments of text) which it is capable of analyzing — the language determined, or accepted, by this PDS automaton — a P D S l a n g u a g e (cf. the concept of C language, p. 95). It has been proven that:

(a) for each PDS automaton it is possible to construct a CF grammar equivalent to it, i.e., a CF grammar generating the same language;   **T**$_{2.3}$

(b) for each CF grammar it is possible to construct a PDS automaton equivalent to it.   **T**$_{2.4}$

Thus the class of PDS languages coincides with the class of CF languages (and thereby, in virtue of theorem $T_{2.2}$, p. 137, with the class of C languages).

The importance of this fact has been discussed above, pp. 66–67.

CLASSIFYING FORMAL GRAMMARS

Having surveyed the basic types of grammars, we can now make the following observation concerning the problem of classifying them. In the literature on mathematical linguistics, grammars are usually subdivided into generative and recognition grammars; the present authors also have held to this widely accepted classification, although it seems to them ill founded.

Indeed, it is easy to see that generative grammars of the most important type, namely nonshortening grammars (and, in particular, PS grammars), can also be used for recognition, i.e., for differentiating grammatically correct (derivable) sentences from incorrect (non-derivable) ones. This was in fact proven on pp. 29–30. For arbitrary grammars this is not true; there are grammars for which there exists no procedure recognizing the derivability of arbitrary strings by means of these grammars. This boils down to an equivalent formulation: the problem of derivability of strings in such grammars is unsolvable (cf. Chapter 3, fn. 2). However, the essence of matter is that IT IS ACCEPTANCE RATHER THAN RECOGNITION THAT IS NATURALLY OPPOSED TO GENERATION. Namely, it is natural to say that some grammar G a c c e p t s language L, if G gives a procedure capable, for any string x belonging to L, of establishing this fact (i.e., of establishing that $x \in L$); if x does not belong to L, then this procedure can either detect that $x \notin L$ or give no result at all; i.e., it can continue endlessly. (Remember that more is required of a recognition procedure: it should give a result in ANY case — a positive result if $x \in L$, and a negative result if $x \notin$ L.)

If instead of recognition we consider acceptance then ALL generative grammars can as well be treated as acceptance grammars. The acceptance procedure consists simply in applying the rules of grammar to the given string 'backwards' — from right to left: an occurrence of the right-hand part of some rule is sought in the string and when found, it is replaced by the left-hand part; the process continues as long as possible. The accepted strings will be precisely those which can be reduced by the indicated process to the initial symbol; it is clear that these are just the same strings which in the normal use of a grammar are derived from its initial symbol.

On the other hand, recognition grammars (which are a particular case of acceptance grammars) can be used for generation as well. For instance, in order for a categorial grammar to be capable of generating strings it is sufficient to reformulate the cancellation rules as the expansion rules (i.e., in fact simply to read them backwards):

1) every category Ψ can be expanded into $\Phi[\Phi \setminus \Psi]$ where Φ is an arbitrary category (left expansion);

2) every category Φ can be expanded into $[\Phi/\Psi]\Psi$, where Ψ is an arbitrary category (right expansion).

It is easy to see how the process of generation will then be realized (the reader should be able to carry this out on his own). Cf. p. 96.

As for PDS automata, we will not describe here the way of using them for generation; what is important for us is that this can unquestionably be done.

To sum up: formal grammars seem to be in essence neutral with respect to generation *vs.* acceptance (or recognition, where the latter is possible). So instead of using the term 'generative grammar' and 'recognition grammar' (or, more generally, 'acceptance grammar') it might be better to speak simply of grammars, considering the aspect 'direction of application' (i.e., application of a grammar for generation or acceptance) autonomously, IN ISOLATION from the definition of grammar as such. Then any actual grammar will be treated as a 'grammar of some class in some aspect'; for example, 'acceptance PS grammar', 'generative PDS automaton', etc.

The common classification of grammars into generative and recognition grammars has a natural historical explanation. Those grammars which are called generative (respectively, recognition) grammars were devised to be used just for generation (recognition). However, as we have just seen, independently of the purpose a grammar has been devised for it can be used 'in both directions'. Therefore, the opposition 'generation *vs.* recognition' seems to reflect the essence of the matter rather poorly.

More profound, so it seems to us, is THE DIFFERENCE IN THE WAY OF REPRESENTING INFORMATION ABOUT SYNTACTIC COMBINABILITY OF LINGUISTIC ITEMS: this information is stored either in the rules (of any type), or in the dictionary, i.e., in the syntactic codes of individual words (in the latter case rules are also necessary, but they are relatively few and contain no information about the specific language; cf. the two cancellation rules in C grammars). This distinction might underlie the subdivision of grammars into two main classes: 'rule' grammars and 'ruleless' grammars. The first class would include Chomsky grammars and PDS automata (for the latter the role of rules is played by syntactic tables A and Ω), and the second, C grammars (cf. p. 88).

NB

Neither class is exhausted by the types of grammars named; however, we will not introduce further types here, but will merely mention two species of grammars which seem most important:

(i)   Grammars which associate with strings d e p e n d e n c y s t r u c t u r e s rather than IC structures (d e p e n d e n c y   g r a m m a r s of D.G. Hays (1967); a generalization of the latter, d o m i n a t i o n a l g r a m m a r s of M.I. Beleckij (1967) and g e n e r a l i z e d d o m i n a t i o n a l Δ - g r a m m a r s of L.S. Modina (1975) .

(ii)   Grammars with c o n t r o l l e d   d e r i v a t i o n s (among numerous types of such grammars, we shall include m a t r i x   g r a m m a r s of S. Abraham (1965), p r o g r a m m e d   g r a m m a r s of D.J. Rosen-krantz (1969) and so-called g e n e r a l i z e d   g r a m m a r s of È.D. Stockij (1967 and 1968)).

To conclude this section, let us note that we are speaking here not simply about a new classification of grammars, but rather ABOUT A NEW ASPECT OF THE STUDY of grammars. In the concept of formal grammar the way of using the grammar is usually implicitly included, although it does not figure in formal definitions of grammars. What we have suggested is the complete separation of this way from the very concept of grammar. At the same time we would like to emphasize the way of storing information about specific languages; this property of grammars should be (and generally is) reflected in their definitions.

LOGICAL ANALYSIS OF LANGUAGE

 All of the linguistic models we have examined so far — we mean formal grammars — concerned in fact only one, although extremely important, aspect of natural language: syntax in the broadest sense of the word, i.e., rules for combining certain elementary units with each other in a text. Syntax in the broad sense includes both syntax in the traditional sense (i.e., laws of constructing phrases from words, clauses from phrases, sentences from clauses, etc.) and morphology (i.e., laws for constructing word-forms from morphs). Of course, the distinction between morphology (it operates within the word) and syntax proper (it operates outside the word) is quite expedient and even necessary. However, from a more general point of view it is convenient to unite them under the common name 'syntax in the broad sense', which is done here.

To put it differently, formal grammars contain, as was indicated above, p. 75, only f o r m a t i o n   r u l e s for linguistic expressions.

However, language has another, not less important aspect: semantics, whose description calls for rules of another kind. These must be rules of transition from certain linguistic expressions to some other expressions bearing the same information (having the same meaning), i.e.,   t r a n s f o r m a t i o n   r u l e s for linguistic expressions, cf. p. 75. The meaning of a linguistic expression is regarded here as something that is common to the given expression and all the other expressions synonymous to it (of the same or some other, not necessarily natural, language). In other words, MEANING IS AN INVARIANT OF SYNONYMY TRANSFORMATIONS (cf. R.O. Jakobson's thesis; *signans*, or signifiant, is perceivable, *signatum*, or signifié, is translatable). Under such an approach, to describe the semantics of some natural language *L* means:

   (i)   to specify another language *L'* into which the expressions of language *L* will be translated, and (ii) to specify the rules for translating any expression from L into L' and vice versa.

For practical purposes (in particular, for teaching the semantics of a foreign language) some other natural language is usually taken as L' – for example, the student's native language. But if we are dealing with the scientific description of the semantics of a language for theoretical purposes, then L' obviously cannot be a natural language. Scientific description presupposes a maximum logical clarity, explicitness and simplicity, while in this respect natural languages seem about equally unsuitable. Therefore, for a scientific description of natural language semantics the language L' should be devised by the researcher and should meet at least the following four requirements:

1.   All elements of L' should be in one-to-one correspondence with the entities signified; i.e., L' should exclude not only obvious homonymy of the type Rus. *luk*$_1$ 'bow' – *luk*$_2$ 'onion' or *glava*$_1$ 'chapter' - *glava*$_2$ 'head (of a family)', but also polysemy, as, for example, in Rus. *dopuskat'*: *dopuskat'*$_1$ 'to admit' – *dopuskat'*$_2$ 'to allow'. In all such cases L' should have different elements. On the other hand, to take an example, the relation 'agent – action', which in natural languages can be implemented in many different ways (cf. *Chomskian analysis – Chomsky's analysis – Chomsky analysis – an analysis of Chomsky – an analysis by Chomsky – Chomsky analyzes [some raw data]*, etc.) should have a unique representation in L'.

2. L' should have sufficient means (be sufficiently rich) for describing the semantic content of any expressions of language L or at least of an important fragment of it. However, L' should have no obligatory semantic categories – those whose use would be imposed by L's own rules, like grammatical number of nouns and tense of verbs in Russian or in English (in these two languages it is impossible to produce a sentence where the nouns would be 'in no number' and the verbs 'in no tense') or the quantifiers in the language of predicate logic (the standard use of this language presupposes the variables in the well-formed formulas to be necessarily bound by quantifiers[18]). The presence in L' of its own obligatory categories would apparently bring distortions into the picture of the semantics of the language being studied. Of course, L' should have proper means for expressing all concepts connected with grammatical number or tense, but the use of these means should not be obligatory, just as in Russian or English it is possible to express the size or color or shape of objects, but it is never necessary to do this.

3. L' should have a sufficient, but not excessive 'resolving power': it should be capable of expressing all the semantic distinctions observed in L, which intuitively seem important. But at the same time L' should differentiate no more than L does, for L' serves not to perfect L,

but to describe it. Note that in studying the semantics of natural language researchers — for the most part philosophers and logicians — usually concentrate their attention on how not to overlook any distinctions, forgetting that it is no less dangerous to introduce superfluous distinctions that proceed from logic and not from linguistic data.

4.   Language L' should be quite formal; i.e., it should be specified by some clear and absolutely explicit apparatus — for example, by a generative grammar.

The language satisfying the above four requirements may be called a s e m a n t i c   l a n g u a g e . Thus a model of a natural language accounting for its semantic aspect is a semantic language plus rules of translation from this semantic language into the natural language and vice versa.

The construction of actual semantic languages and rules of natural-to-semantic and semantic-to-natural translation hardly belongs to mathematical linguistics proper, just as the elaboration of generative grammars for actual languages does not belong to it: mathematical linguistics covers only the GENERAL theory of grammars, concerning their abstract and universal properties. Similarly, only a GENERAL theory of semantic languages should be a part of mathematical linguistics, not the elaboration of actual semantic languages as such.

However, at present there is no such theory so far as we know — at least no full-fledged one and there are no sufficiently complete semantic languages. However, it is possible to indicate a number of partial semantic languages which have been constructed for modelling quite narrow and very special fragments of semantics (see below, pp. 118—119). Since these languages are a basis both for the elaboration of complete semantic languages and for the construction of a theory of the latter, it seems worthwhile to say a few words about them.

The language of predicate logic is a classical example of a partial semantic language. The subsequent remarks are intended for the reader who is already acquainted with this language[19] since it would not be advisable to describe it here. However, owing to the exceptional importance of this language, especially in connection with semantic investigations of natural and artificial languages (it is the language of predicate logic that underlies all of the partial semantic languages known to the authors), we urgently recommend to the reader who has not yet mastered the language of predicate logic that he do so. (He has at his disposal such handbooks as, for example, Mendelson 1964 or Kleene 1967, as well as more elementary introductions like Tarski 1941 or Freudenthal 1966.)

The language of predicate logic — the basic expressive tool of mathematical

logic — is highly formalized and very well studied. It is intended for the
description of a very limited part of semantics, namely, that part which
deals with truth or falsity of propositions. Nevertheless, its elements —
p r o p o s i t i o n a l c o n n e c t i v e s, q u a n t i f i e r s, and, in
particular, the p r e d i c a t e s themselves — allow a much broader use. This
explains the fact that most attempts to describe formally the semantics of
natural languages involve the use of the language of predicate logic or at least
of some of its components.

Such attempts can be subdivided into two types. To the first belong studies
which compare natural languages with the language of predicate logic, aiming
at revealing in the former some items and categories that are similar to the
items and categories of the latter; i.e., they try to explain how logical
categories are expressed in natural languages. These works are usually subsumed
under the common heading 'logical analysis of language'. Unfortunately,
studies in this area, very promising and often insightful, still do not form a
unified formal theory. (This is perhaps explained by the fact that until recently
the logical analysis of natural language has been carried out primarily not by
linguists, but rather by logicians and philosophers, for whom languages are
not so much independent objects of description as illustrative material.)
Therefore we must limit ourselves to simply mentioning several works of this
type without laying the slightest claim to the completeness of the exposition
of even the most important of them.

We will begin with the classic study by G. Frege (1892) developing many
profound ideas which underlie some recent trends in linguistic semantics   **NB**
(in particular, R. Montague's school, see below). This study has foreshadowed
in several respects modern semantic explorations and it is strongly
recommended to anyone about to be initiated into the field. Specifically,
Frege offers a provocative logical analysis of complex sentences and introduces
the notion of presupposition, which plays such an important part in today's
linguistics.

Next we will mention B. Russell who noted many years ago the most
essential fact that in natural languages prepositions and verbs are of the same
semantic nature — namely, both are names of predicates. For example, the
preposition *before* and the verb *(to) precede*, for all the difference of their
grammatical properties, mean the same thing — they express the binary predicate 'A precedes B' (Russell 1940: 124).[20] From this follows, in particular,
the very important idea (which was subsequently developed in a large number
of works) that the identity/difference of meanings of words of a natural
language can be better described by associating with them some precisely
defined predicates.

A special place among works on the logical analysis of language belongs to

H. Reichenbach's 'Analysis of Conversational Language' (Chapter VII of Reichenbach 1960, in particular, pp. 251–354). Reichenbach develops the idea of classifying words on the basis of their logical-semantic nature rather than their formal-grammatical properties, and the resulting word classes differ sharply from the common parts of speech. Examples of logical-semantic classes are:

The class of unary predicates: verbs like (*to*) *die*, (*to*) *sleep*, (*to*) *disappear*; adjectives like *intelligent, stupid, beautiful*; nouns like *fool* or *beauty.*

The class of binary predicates: (*to*) *love*, (*to*) *follow*, (*to*) *read*, . . . ; *similar, superior, pleasant*, . . . ; *wife, murder, performance*, . . . ; *over, before, behind*, . . .

The class of ternary predicates: (*to*) *give*, (*to*) *teach*, (*to*) *tell*, . . . ; *similar* (*in*); *comparison; between*, . . .

The class of individual constants including proper nouns: *tree, moon, cannon*, . . . ; *Dreizin, Haifa*, . . .

The class of quantifiers: *all, one, exist, everywhere, something*, . . .

The class of propositional connectives: *and, or, but, if . . . then*, . . . ; etc.

The logical-semantic classification of words has profound linguistic value; in particular, the membership of a word in a particular logical-semantic class considerably affects its syntactic properties.

Reichenbach also examined a larger number of other important questions in the domain of linguistic semantics. We will mention here only his attempt to analyze the category of the article in terms of such concepts as the ι-operator ($\approx$ 'that . . . which') and the ϵ-operator ($\approx$ 'a . . . such that'), and his insightful outline of a universal scheme of verbal tenses. This study by Reichenbach became a classic, and most subsequent works on the logical analysis of natural language are based on it to a greater or lesser extent.

An interesting formulation of the task of logical analysis of natural language and several instructive examples are found in Quine 1961: we mean Quine's remarks about paired conjunctions as analogs of parentheses, about words of the type *every* – *any*, about personal pronouns as analogs of individual variables, etc. See also Quine 1960.

Further, we would point out a series of works by Elinor K. Charney (for example, Charney 1961, 1962), in which the logical-semantic structure of English conjunctions (of the type *if, unless* etc.) and quantifying words (*all, every, any*, . . .) is studied. Among other questions Mrs. Charney examines, in particular, the synonymy of such sentences as:

and (1) *To invite all women and no men is to make a dull party*
(2) *To invite only women and no men is to make a dull party,*

which mean exactly the same thing on one reading, although the words *all* and *only*, which distinguish them, are not at all synonyms.

The results of Charney's earlier work are summarized in Charney 1966, which also presents some general observations concerning the study of semantics by logical means.

K. Döhmann's paper (1966) surveys linguistic means for expressing all dyadic functions of the algebra of logic: conjunction $A \& B$, disjunction $A \lor B$, strict disjunction $(A \lor B) \& \neg(A \& B)$, implication $A \supset B$, etc. — 16 functions in all, used in the most diverse natural languages. For example, conjunction can be expressed by simple juxtaposition (Chin. *ma lü* 'a horse and an ass', lit. 'horse ass'), by a simple conjunction (Russ. *i*, Eng. *and*, French *et*), by a paired conjunction (Russ. *kak. . .tak i* 'both. . .and', Eng. *either. . .or*), by a preposition (*Petja s Mašej prišli. . .* 'Petya with [= and] Masha came. . .'), by a postpositive particle (Lat. *Senatus populus*que *Romanus* 'the Senate and the Roman people'), etc.

The opposite approach is followed by Padučeva 1964c, where it is claimed that the Russian conjunction *ili* 'or' may express three different logical functions:

— strict disjunction, as in

(3) *Tvoja kniga ležit v škafu ili na stole* 'Your book is lying either in the bookcase or on the table'[21] ;

— nonstrict disjunction (in the context of an explicit or 'covert' implication), as in

(4) *Esli u menja zabolit gorlo ili povysitsja temperatura, to ja ne poedu katat'sja na lyžax* 'If my throat gets sore or my temperature rises, I will not go skiing';

(5) *Studenty, vystupavšie s dokladom ili podavšie pis'mennyj otčët, osvoboždajutsja ot èkzamena* 'The students who have presented a paper or who have handed in a written report are excused from the exam';

— and conjunction:

(6) $x_2 > 0$ *pri* $x > 0$ *ili pri* $x < 0$ '$x_2 > 0$ when $x > 0$ or when $x < 0$'.

The same problem (i.e., the logical analysis of *ili* 'or' in Russian) is dealt with in Gladkij 1979, where the conclusions are, however, different from those of Padučeva.

In connection with the problem of translating predicate logic into Russian, E.V. Padučeva has also examined (Padučeva 1964a, 1964d) the means of expressing in Russian the parentheses which indicate the scope of propositional connectives. It turned out that Russian ensures uniqueness of interpretation from the viewpoint of the arrangement of these parentheses: the role of left parentheses is fulfilled by the first and second components of paired conjunctions, while it proves possible to manage without right parenthesis; cf. *(A & B)* V *C* = *ili A i B, ili C* 'either *A* and *B*, or *C*'; *A* & *(B* V *C)* = *kak A, tak i B ili C* 'both *A*, and *B* or *C*'.

Perhaps the most systematic and general survey of the properties of natural languages from the logical viewpoint can be found in Weinreich 1963; however, even a brief discussion of its content would take us too far from our purpose.

Now we will deal with semantic studies of another type (the reader should be reminded that we are speaking here about two types of attempts to describe linguistic semantics formally, see above, p. 115) — namely, the attempts to construct broader semantic languages on the basis of the language of predicate logic.

Since it is quite impossible to describe briefly enough even a very simple semantic language, we have to abstain from all explanations concerning the works listed here; consequently, what follows should be regarded simply as a reference list.

Best known are the so-called informational, or documentation, languages, which are created for specific areas of science and which are intended for the recording of information from these areas in a clear, explicit and simple form which is convenient for computer processing (automatic information retrieval, automatic logical inference, automatic abstracting, etc.). To illustrate we cite as an example the informational language for elementary geometry which was developed at the All-Union Institute of Scientific and Technological Information of the Academy of Sciences of the USSR (see Kuznecov et al. 1961).

An interesting example of a semantic language (which, owing to its unusual purpose, has acquired wide renown — not in the sense that many **know it**, but in the sense that many **know about it**) is 'LINCOS' (Lingua Cosmica), which was constructed by H. Freudenthal and intended for, as he puts it, cosmic intercourse — i.e., for communication with extraterrestrial civilizations (Freudenthal 1960).

Finally, there are a number of semantic languages devised for the purpose of automatic language translation, where a semantic language functions as an interlingua. Here we may mention the semantic languages of the Cambridge Language Research Unit (Masterman 1961 and Parker-Rhodes 1961) and also the language SM-1 for representing mathematical texts (Gladkij et al. 1961). As distinct from the just mentioned informational language for geometry, SM - 1 is intended to render not the mathematical content itself, but only the sentences which constitute any mathematical text in a natural language; therefore, it is not suitable, for example, for automatic inferencing or theorem proving. A semantic language based on predicate notation using semantic factors

is actually proposed in Žolkovskij, Leont'eva and Martemjanov 1961;
its development and considerable enrichment have led to a new (quasi-
semantic) language described in Žolkovskij—Mel'čuk 1967 ('the language
of deep-syntactic structures and the paraphrasing system'). Note that in the
last two works mentioned there is no explicit grammar specifying the
corresponding languages.

To conclude this section, let us emphasize again (cf. p. 114) that its
content is not a part of mathematical linguistics, so that this section falls
outside the framework of our book. Nevertheless, we considered it helpful
to include it in the book in order to at least 'stake out' the corresponding
topics: first of all, to stress the need for a semantic branch in mathematical
linguistics, and second, to indicate the material which is a likely basis for
eventual creation of such a branch.

A caveat to the reader: The manuscript of the Russian version of this book
was completed in 1967 and we are not in a position to revise it now to
any serious extent, so we are unable to include a number of interesting
studies in the logical analysis of language, semantic representation, documentation languages, etc. which have appeared since then. Even a mere list of
references would be out of the question.

It seems, however, that some further references picked up at random
would not be out of place here. An interested reader can find more recent
insights and ideas concerning the relation between natural language and
(mathematical) logic in at least the three following books: Davidson —
Harman 1973; Hintikka, Moravcsik and Suppes 1973; Hockney, Harper and
Freed 1975. But probably the most important achievements to date are to
be found in the work by R. Montague and his followers. Their research,
using a powerful and sophisticated formal apparatus, represents an actual
breakthrough in modern linguistic semantics, as well as in mathematical logic.
Several major papers of Montague himself are collected in the volume
Montague 1974; a rather popular presentation of his theory, including some
of the basic notions, is found in Lewis 1970.

THE MODELLING OF LINGUISTIC RESEARCH

So far we have concerned ourselves exclusively with the formalization of the
description of natural language as such, i.e., with the modelling of the
system determining speech behavior. In fact, formal grammars of all types are
models of language: their 'behavior' (the generation or recognition of texts)

is similar, in some important aspects, to the behavior of humans
communicating by means of language. In constructing these models, we used
extensively our intuitive notions about the general properties of human
languages, our practical knowledge of specific languages (in our examples,
mostly Russian), and also a large number of concepts and categories which
are generally accepted and quite common in linguistics (and for the
most part in high school grammars as well) such as 'noun', 'verb',
'gender', 'case', 'noun phrase', etc. We have not asked questions such
as: Where did we get particular notions about language? How, exactly, do we
carry out the scientific study of languages? Why were such categories (and
not some other ones) selected and what are they? etc. We were fully entitled
to so act, since we were interested only in the formal grammars themselves
irrespective of how we arrived at them. However, these questions are quite
legitimate and, moreover, extremely interesting. In order to answer them we
have to create formal models of those procedures and means which we in fact
used extensively without explicitly specifying them in any way when
constructing the grammars. This means that it is necessary to develop formal
models of the activity of a linguist (or, more generally, of a person learning
a language). A system of such models should produce, as its terminal result, a
model of the language under investigation; i.e., a formal model of linguistic
research is a model of the process of constructing models of languages.

   We will not try here to survey the existing or possible models of linguistic
research, but will be satisfied with a brief characterization of only two
specific models. The first concerns the formalization of some basic concepts
and categories of linguistics, and the second, the formalization of the very
procedures of linguistic research. Of course, both of these aspects are closely
interrelated since any procedure leading to isolating and specifying a class
of objects can be regarded as a formal definition of this class, i.e., a so-called
constructive definition. Nevertheless, it is expedient to differentiate them:
first, not every formal definition gives an effective procedure, and second,
there is a difference in point of view, in logical emphasis. The first aspect
centers primarily on the very concept under analysis, while the second
deals with possible procedures leading to the discovery of the corresponding
objects.

   Today, mathematical linguistics has at its disposal a number of works which
attempt to formally define some traditional linguistic concepts – part of
speech, case, gender, phoneme, etc.[22] (Zaliznjak 1967; Revzin 1967;
Uspenskij 1974; Marcus 1963). We choose as an illustration those devoted to
the concept of c o n s t i t u e n t . It is clear that this concept is absolutely
necessary for describing natural language. Modern Western (especially,
American) linguistics uses it explicitly. Traditional Soviet linguistics, although

it avoids that term, deals with more or less analogous concepts: word combination, syntagm (in the sense of V.V. Vinogradov), syntactic group (= phrase), sentence part (subject, object, predicate, etc.), and so on.

But these concepts are not defined with sufficient clarity and are frequently understood in different ways even by scholars belonging to the same school. This makes the construction of a formal analog for the concept of constituent an important and interesting task (all the more so in our book, where this concept has already been used several times − cf., for example, p. 36 ff.).

In order to facilitate formal considerations we will cite once more some examples of constituents. In the Russian sentence

(1) *Snaruži v'juga mečetsja i vsë zanosit v losk* 'Outside the blizzard dashes and covers everything completely with snow'

(the first line of a famous poem by B. Pasternak) there are 14 constituents:

1) the entire sentence as a whole;
2) *v'juga mečetsja i vsë zanosit v losk* 'the blizzard. . . with snow';
3) *mečetsja i vsë zanosit v losk* 'dashes and covers. . . with snow';
4) *vsë zanosit v losk* 'covers everything completely with snow';
5) *vsë zanosit* 'covers everything with snow';
6) *v losk* 'completely' (lit. 'to lustre');
7) − 14) each word taken by itself.

Two important remarks:

1. The analysis of a sentence into constituents is not necessarily unique even in a syntactically non-ambiguous sentence. For example,

(2) . . . *na čërnom dne tvoix zelënyx glaz* 'at the black bottom of your green eyes'

(a line from a Nikoloz Baratašvili's poem translated from Georgian by E. Evtušenko) can be divided into constituents in many different ways:

1) ((*na (čërnom dne)*) (*tvoix(zelënyx glaz)*))
   '((at(the black bottom)) (of your (green eyes)))', or
2) (*na((čërnom dne)* (*tvoix(zelënyx glaz)*)))
   '(at((the black bottom)(of your(green eyes))))', or
3) (*na(čërnom(dne(tvoix(zelënyx glaz)))))*'
   '(at(the black(bottom(of your(green eyes)))))', or
4) ((*na(čërnom dne)*)((*tvoix zelënyx)glaz*))
   '((at(the black bottom))((of your green)eyes))',

and these still far from exhaust all possible parses. (Obviously, it would be to the reader's benefit to continue this list.)

2.   The words capable of forming a constituent do not necessarily form it in any sentence containing the string of these words. If what is meant is a 'natural' system of constituents, then, for example, the Russian word string *delo mastera* 'work of a master' is a constituent in the sentence *Èto, bezuslovno, delo mastera* 'This is unquestionably the work of a master', but not in the sentence (a Russian proverb) *Delo mastera boitsja*, lit. 'Work fears a master' (i.e., 'It takes a good man to do the job well'); analogously, the word string *spiski nomerov, kotorye xranjatsja v pamjati* 'lists of numbers which are stored in the memory' is a constituent in the sentence *Rassmotrim spiski nomerov, kotorye xranjatsja v pamjati* 'Let us examine lists of numbers which [= lists of numbers] are stored in the memory', but it is not a constituent in the sentence *Lišim spiski nomerov, kotorye xranjatsja v pamjati* 'Let us deprive the lists of the numbers which [= numbers] are stored in the memory'.

NB   Now we can proceed to the formal definition of constituent. More precisely, we will define the concept of c o n f i g u r a t i o n , or potential constituent. Linguistically, a configuration is a segment of text (a word string) which can be a constituent in at least one sentence of the language under study. Thus the segments *delo mastera* 'work (of) a master' and *spiski nomerov, kotorye xranjatsja v pamjati* 'lists of numbers which are stored in the memory' are configurations, although they are not always constituents (see above).

We define first of all the concepts of s u b s t i t u t a b i l i t y and m u t u a l   s u b s t i t u t a b i l i t y .   Let L be a formal language over vocabulary V (i.e., L is a set of strings composed of symbols belonging to V). Examine two arbitrary strings x and y which consist of symbols of V (**NB**: x and y do not necessarily belong to L). The string x is s u b s t i t u t a b l e   by y in L (notation: $x \Rightarrow y\ (L)$), if for any two strings p and q from $pxq \in L$ it follows that $pyq \in L$ (p and q do not necessarily belong to L; they can also be empty). Informally this means that in any correct sentence the string x can be substituted by y without affecting the correctness; the converse, generally speaking, is not true. For example, the Russian word-form *čaj* 'tea' is substitutable by the word-form *kofe* 'coffee', but not vice versa (*pačka kofe* 'a pack of coffee', but not **pačka čaj* 'a pack of tea', because we have *pačka čaju/čaja*); *napevy* 'tunes' is substitutable by *zabytye napevy* 'forgotten tunes', but not vice versa (*davno zabytye napevy*, lit. 'long ago forgotten tunes', but not **davno napevy* 'long ago tunes').

The string x is m u t u a l l y   s u b s t i t u t a b l e   with y in L (notation: $x \Leftrightarrow y(L)$), if $x \Rightarrow y(L)$ and $y \Rightarrow x(L)$. Examples: *peskom* 'with sand' and *graviem* 'with gravel', *isključitel'no važnyx* 'of exceptionally important' and *važnyx* 'of important', etc.

The concept of configuration is defined inductively: first we define configuration of rank 1 (the induction basis), and then configuration of higher ranks (the induction step).

(a) INDUCTION BASIS. A configuration of rank 1 of language *L* is a string which consists of no less than two symbols and is mutually substitutable with a certain symbol (i.e., with a string consisting of one symbol) called t h e r e s u l t a n t o f t h e g i v e n c o n f i g u r a t i o n .

NB 1. The resultant need not necessarily be one of the symbols belonging to the configuration.

NB 2. The configuration does not necessarily have only one resultant.

Examples: *isključitel'no važnyj* 'exceptionally important' ⟺ *važnyj* 'important', *cennyj* 'valuable', *poleznyj* 'useful', . . . ; *ne očen'* 'not very' ⟺ *sliškom* 'too'.

Note that the detection of configurations in Russian (and probably in other natural languages as well) necessarily presupposes a fairly rough approximation; i.e., we have to evaluate very roughly the grammaticality of sentences we consider. For example, the recognition of the mutual substitutabilities figuring in our examples entails the recognition of grammaticality, on the one hand, of such strings as *isključitel'no isključitel'no isključitel'no . . . važnyj* 'exceptionally exceptionally exceptionally . . . important' (since in *isključitel'no važnyj* 'exceptionally important' the word *važnyj* 'important' can be substituted by *isklučitel'no važnyj* 'exceptionally important', etc., arbitrarily many times), and on the other hand, of such strings as *očen' isključitel'no važnyj* 'very exceptionally important' (from *očen' važnyj* 'very important'). Cf. also **èto uže ne očen'*, lit. 'this is already not very', obtainable from the quite grammatical expression *èto uže sliškom* 'now this is too much', *ne ne očen' vljubčiv* 'not not very amorous' obtainable from *ne sliškom vljubčiv* 'not too amorous', etc.; similarly, *pečal'nye zabytye napevy* 'sad forgotten tunes' from *pečal'nye napevy* 'sad tunes', while *zabytye pečal'nye napevy* 'forgotten sad tunes' would be more correct (see above, pp. 57–58). A similar situation arose earlier: when constructing examples of formal grammars, we had to admit arbitrarily long strings of the type *sladkaja sladkaja sladkaja . . . nežnost'* 'sweet sweet sweet . . . tenderness' (p. 33) or such strings as *sladkaja gor'kaja nežnost'* 'sweet bitter tenderness', *sladkaja sol'* 'sweet salt', etc.

NB

(b) INDUCTION STEP. Assume that we have already defined configurations of all ranks up to *n* inclusively. We then define a configuration of rank *n* + 1. This is the string *x*, which consists of no less than two symbols and satisfies the following two conditions:

1°. In the vocabulary of language *L* there is a symbol *a*, which is substitutable by *x*.

2°. The string x is also substitutable by a, but with certain restrictions. Namely, in the string pxq ($pxq \in L$; p and q are arbitrary strings) x can be substituted by a (i.e., $paq \in L$), if the string pxq does not contain configurations of rank n or of rank less than n which intersect with x without being contained in it. (The meaning of this condition is that in order for the string x to be replaced by a the string x should not have on its left or right modifying words which would remain without a governor in case we substitute x by a; see the examples below.)

The symbol a is called the   r e s u l t a n t   o f   t h e   c o n f i g u r a t i o n x.[23]

From the linguistic standpoint this definition means the following. First, any configuration can be obtained by expanding some symbol, namely its own resultant. Second, any configuration can be reduced to its resultant; however, the reduction of a configuration of rank n is allowed only after all the configurations of lower ranks (from 1 through $n-1$) in the sentence which have a common part with the configuration of rank n are reduced. For example, the configuration of rank 2 *važnyj faktor* 'important factor' in . . . *učityvaet ètot isključitel'no važnyj faktor* '. . . considers this exceptionally important factor' cannot be reduced until the configuration of rank 1 *isključitel'no važnyj* 'exceptionally important', which intersects with it, is reduced, since otherwise we would obtain the incorrect *. . .*učityvaet ètot isključitel'no faktor* 'considers this exceptionally factor'. Furthermore, the configuration of rank 3 *vodu pit'* 'to drink water' (with the resultant *pit'* 'to drink') in the sentence *Grjaznuju vodu pit' ne sleduet* 'One should not drink dirty water' cannot be reduced until the configuration of rank 2 *grjaznuju vodu* 'dirty water' is reduced (we do not consider as correct the elliptical sentence *Grjaznuju pit' ne sleduet* 'One should not drink dirty', which would otherwise be obtained).

It is important to emphasize that the above definition of configuration is not constructive since it does not indicate ways of detecting configurations in strings of the language. Moreover, the definition of substitutability is also not constructive: in fact, if we wanted to find out, by using only our definition, whether a specific string x is substituable by some other string y (in language L), we would have to examine ALL the strings of language L which contain x, and there are in general infinitely many such strings.

T

1.2.11 It turns out that it is possible to assert more: there are CF grammars for which there exists no procedure for recognizing configurations, i.e., no decision procedure capable of determining whether an arbitrary string is a configuration or not (cf. above, p. 82).

The concept of configuration can be naturally associated with a number of other concepts such as   s i m p l e   c o n f i g u r a t i o n   (a configuration

not containing other configurations of the same rank, and thereby
configurations of lower ranks[24] ; simple configuration is an analog of the
minimal non-atomic constituent) and i r r e d u c i b l e   s t r i n g
(a string which belongs to the language, and which does not contain configurations, i.e., does not permit reductions; for example, Russian impersonal
sentences of the type *Morozit* 'It is freezing' or *Smerkalos'* 'It was getting
dark', and any English or French predicative pairs of the type *He reads* or *Il
pleut* are irreducible strings). On the basis of these concepts we can construct
the notion of c o n f i g u r a t i o n a l   c h a r a c t e r i s t i c of a
language. The configurational characteristic is a pair of lists: 1) a list
of simple configurations with an indication, for each configuration, of its
resultant(s); 2) a list of irreducible strings. Generally speaking, both of these
lists can be infinite.

Interestingly, the configurational characteristic fully specifies a language in
the sense that there cannot be two different languages with the same
configurational characteristic. The point is that in essence the
configurational characteristic is nothing other than the set of elementary
strings and rules of their combination into strings of the language. It is clear
that if the sets of elementary strings and rules of their combination are
identical, then the languages obtained should be identical too.

T
3.1

In case the lists of simple configurations and irreducible strings are finite,
the corresponding language is called f i n i t e l y   c h a r a c t e r i z a b l e .
(It seems to us intuitively evident that natural languages are finitely
characterizable.) It has been noted above (p. 66) that all finitely
characterizable languages are CF languages.

T
3.2

We will not expound the theory of configurations in more detail,
since our only goal was to cite an example of a formal concept (in our case,
configuration) which has been developed by mathematical linguistics as
an exact and rigorous model for one of the rather diffuse linguistic concepts
of general interest – i.e., for constituents (or, to be more precise, for a
type of constituent, and not for a specific constituent in a specific sentence).

As for the formalization of research procedures in linguistics, this area
abounds in works of the most diverse trends. Formalization of research
procedures was at the focus of attention of an entire linguistic school – the
American Descriptive School – for more than thirty years (see, for example,
Harris 1963). This area also includes works on the deciphering of texts
written in unknown languages or unknown writing systems. (The activity of
descriptive linguists of Bloomfieldian–Harrisian flavor or of deciphering
specialists for the most part does not pertain directly to mathematical
linguistics, but has prepared the ground for the development of that branch
of mathematical linguistics which we are now discussing.) At present, for

instance, the theory of so-called automatic classification is being actively developed, which sets out the following task: let there be a set of text elements, which are each assigned certain properties; it is required to break this set down automatically into classes such that the elements of one class would be, from the viewpoint of the indicated properties, more similar to each other than would any elements of different classes; such classes are called   c l u m p s .   There are also works of other types.

We will examine here as an illustration an algorithm proposed in Suxotin 1962 which can 'tell' vowels from consonants in any text written in a language unknown for the algorithm (but of course, in an alphabetical script). To do this, the algorithm uses no information about the specific language in which the text is written. The only assumption is that a common property of natural languages is the comparatively even, or uniform, distribution of vowels and consonants in human speech. This means that in texts of any natural language a vowel and a consonant are found to be contiguous (i.e., immediate neighbors) much more often than are a vowel and a vowel, or a consonant and a consonant. (For example, in the preceding sentence – leaving aside the parenthesized phrase – there are 105 combinations of vowels with consonants, 28 combinations of consonants with consonants, and 7 combinations of vowels with vowels. The calculation is made as if the sentence were printed without spaces; letters, not sounds, are counted. Interestingly, in the Russian equivalent of the sentence considered there are 94 VC and CV combinations, 31 CC combinations and 7 VV combinations; that is, the percentage is roughly the same.)

It is just the formulated assumption that underlies Suxotin's algorithm for detecting vowels and consonants in a text. This algorithm partitions the set of all the letters encountered in the text into two classes, V and C, in such a way that the total number of combinations of the type VC and CV would be greater than the total number of the combinations VV and CC. There can be many such partitions, and the algorithm has to choose the best one among them. It seems natural to consider as best the partition which maximizes the difference between the total number of VC and CV combinations on the one hand, and the total number of VV and CC combinations on the other; i.e., the partition which makes the classes V and C maximally polar.

Now we will formulate the same thing more accurately. Let there be n different letters $(a_1, a_2, \ldots, a_n)$ in a text. Assume that all these letters are already somehow partitioned into two classes – X and Y. For each pair of letters $a_i a_j$ $(i, j = 1, 2, \ldots, n)$ we count the number of appearances of this pair in the text (the linear order of a_i and a_j is irrelevant; i.e., $a_i a_j$ is taken to be identical to $a_j a_i$). We designate this number by $F(a_i a_j)$, F standing for 'frequency'. For example, in the sentence for which the calculations were made above ('This means . . . and a consonant'), $F(th) = 5$, $F(an) = 16$, $F(rw) = 1$, $F(dh) = 0$. Let Σ_1 be the sum of all the numbers $F(a_i a_j)$ for such pairs $a_i a_j$ where a_i and a_j belong to different classes ($a_i \in X$, $a_j \in Y$, or $a_i \in Y$, $a_j \in X$). Furthermore, let Σ_2 be the sum of all numbers $F(a_i a_j)$ for such pairs $a_i a_j$ where a_i and a_i belong to the same class (either a_i, $a_j \in X$, or a_i, $a_j \in Y$). The difference $\Sigma_1 - \Sigma_2$ is called the u t i l i t y (o b j e c t , or v a l u e) f u n c t i o n and is designated by $P(X, Y)$. The best partition of all letters into the classes X and Y will be the one in which the value of $P(X, Y)$ is maximum. This may be considered a definition of the best partition.

Since the set of letters is finite, there is a trivial algorithm for finding the maximum of the utility function $P(X, Y)$ – a trial-and-error algorithm providing for an exhaustive screening of all values of P: it is sufficient to partition the set of letters into the classes X and Y in all possible ways, to calculate $P(X, Y)$ for each partition and then to select the best one among the calculated values of P (this is possible since their number is finite). The corresponding partition will be the one sought.[25]

However, such an algorithm cannot be implemented in practice: for example, with an alphabet of 30 letters it would be necessary to examine 2^{30} (more than a billion) different partitions. Therefore, Suxotin has come up with other more economic algorithms (Suxotin 1962, 1963), which are easily programmed for electronic digital computers. These algorithms were tested on a computer for Russian, English, German, French, and Spanish. The results of the experiments turned out quite satisfactory; the few errors are explained basically by spelling conventions – for example, by the fact that one sound can be represented by a letter combination (cf. Germ. *sch* [= š], Engl. *th, wr, sh*, etc.). The algorithms themselves are not described here since their actual design is less important for our purposes than the statement of the problem and some principles for solving it.

The reader may have wondered if there is a contradiction between the above (pp. 4–5) assertions about the nonquantitative nature of mathematical linguistics and the inclusion in it of works of the type just examined, in which quantitative data (in our case, frequencies) are essentially used. In fact, we see no contradiction here. All these works have as their final goal PURELY QUALITATIVE results – classifications, etc., and not quantitative characteristics, or quantitative laws. The calculations are an intermediate stage; for all their importance they remain no more than an auxiliary means.

The use of different utility functions also underlies other algorithms for detecting and classifying linguistic units. For example, Suxotin 1963 suggests an algorithm for dividing texts written without spaces into morphs. The utility function is constructed there proceeding from the observation that the frequency of co-occurrence of the letters belonging to one morph is greater than the frequency of co-occurrence of letters from different morphs. Cf. also Suxotin's algorithm for detecting syntactically connected words in a text in an unknown language (Suxotin 1963). The most interesting results of Suxotin's approach were recently summarized in Suxotin 1975.

Here our exposition comes to an end. It remains for us to bid farewell to the reader who has taken upon himself the task of working with us up to these lines. However, if his patience has not yet been exhausted, he can turn to the Conclusion and then to the Appendix which offers a summary of the most important mathematical results in the theory of grammars. Thank you for your attention!

NOTES

1. For the sake of clarity we present this conception in schematized and simplified form.
2. It is possible to define such a system with operators having any finite number of arguments. Bar-Hillel (1953) used the notation

$$\frac{\gamma}{(\alpha_1), \ldots, (\alpha_m) \, [\beta_1], \ldots, [\beta_n]}$$

for the category of an operator string which forms a string of category γ out of m left arguments belonging to the categories $\alpha_1, \ldots, \alpha_m$ respectively and n right arguments belonging to the categories $\beta_1, \ldots, \beta_n$ respectively. An alternate notation was used by H. Hiż (1960):

$$(\gamma; \alpha_1, \ldots, \alpha_m \longrightarrow \beta_1, \ldots, \beta_n).$$

The latter notation is easily extended to discontinuous operators. For example, *if . . . then . . .* can be assigned to a category (S; ___ S ___ S) which indicates that a sentence may be formed from *if* followed by a sentence followed by *then* followed by another sentence.

[editor]

3. The resulting class can, in a particular case, coincide with the initial class.
4. Let us recall that f is a many-valued function (p. 90). Thus it should assign to the word-form *metel'* 'snow storm' MANY different categories; see below.
5. Strictly speaking, this is not one category, but a group of three categories: the variable t can assume three different values (present, past, future).
6. The 'right direct object' is an operator which acts upon a transitive verb from the right and transforms it into a verb phrase syntactically equivalent to an intransitive verb.

7. An adverbial modifying an intransitive verb should belong to a different category.

8. What is in fact being touched upon here is s y n t a c t i c a m b i g u i t y : its nature, its different types, its correlation with semantic ambiguity, etc. However, in this book we do not have the opportunity to dwell on these questions. See, e.g., Kuno–Oettinger 1963.

9. Parts of a derived category are all categories which are contained in it; for example, the following categories: $[X\backslash[Y/X]]$, $[Y/X]$, $[Y/Z]$, X, Y, and Z – are parts of the category $[[X\backslash[Y/X]]/[Y/Z]]$ (along with this category itself).

10. For exposition and comparison of both methods of representing syntactic structure see Padučeva 1964b; Hays 1961, 1964; Gladkij 1973: Appendix I; Meľčuk 1979: 4–7 ff.

11. A number of algorithms for parsing English scientific texts which are based on particular modifications of C grammars are mentioned in Bobrow 1963; cf. also: Montgomery 1969; Woods 1970; Kay–Spark-Jones 1971.

12. The algorithm for automatic syntactic text analysis is a system (of rules) which is capable of assigning to sentences of a given natural language their syntactic structures. Such algorithms are the most important parts in systems of automatic language translation. For more detail on automatic syntactic analysis see: Meľčuk 1963, 1964; Tosh 1965; Iordanskaja 1967; Kuno 1968; Petrick 1972.

13. With the exception of constituents equal to individual word-forms (atomic, or 'point', constituents) or to whole sentences.

14. This means that any P analyzer has an unlimited set of push-down stores; i.e., the analyzer can have as many push-down stores as prove necessary in the process of analysis. The necessary number of push-down stores depends on the length and syntactic properties of the sentence being analyzed: each push-down store corresponds to one variant of the analysis, and the individual push-down stores are eventually needed not only for the correct variants (the ones reaching the end of the sentence), but also for incorrect ones (those blocked off somewhere along the way).

    The push-down stores themselves are also considered to have an unlimited capacity, which is connected with the fundamental assumption that there is no upper bound on the length of sentences of a natural language (see pp. 34–35).

15. If this SP consists of more than one phrase (see column III of table A, lines 1, 3, 9 and 12), then these phrases are placed in the push-down store from right to left, so that the leftmost phrase ends up on the top.

16. Other terms for the same notion are: p u s h d o w n a u t o m a t o n (PD automaton, PDA), p u s h - d o w n s t o r e m a c h i n e (PDS machine).

17. A nondeterministic Turing machine differs from an ordinary (deterministic) Turing machine only in that its program may contain different commands with identical left-hand parts.

18. In fact, logical formulas are frequently encountered which contain free variables, i.e., variables not bound by a quantifier. However, in such cases a universal quantifier is understood (i.e., we have a 'zero' expression of a quantifier).

19. What is meant here is familiarity only with the language of predicate logic, rather than with the predicate logic itself: no knowledge of any theorems of mathematical logic is required.

20. It is interesting that in a number of natural languages, for example in Vietnamese, the preposition and the verb belong to one grammatical category as well: Vietn. ɑ is the preposition 'in' and the verb 'to be located in'.

21. Cf. *Tvoi knigi ležat v škafu ili na stole* 'Your books lie in the bookcase or on the table',

in which, because of the plural of *knigi* 'books', the conjunction *ili* 'or' can have the meaning of nonstrict disjunction.

22. The majority of such works of Soviet and some Western researchers go back, to a greater or lesser extent, to the pioneering paper of O.S. Kulagina (1958).

23. It should be kept in mind that in the literature of mathematical linguistics other variants of the definition of the concept of configuration are encountered which are not equivalent to the one just formulated (cf. Kulagina 1958, or Novotný 1965). However, these can be considered variants of the same concept — i.e., not radically different from it.

24. A configuration of rank n is at the same time a configuration of any rank higher than n; this follows directly from the definition of configuration.

25. In the general case, the utility function $P(X, Y)$ can have the same maximum value for several different partitions. Linguistically, this implies the existence of several 'equally good' classifications of letters. Such a situation is indeed encountered in actual languages: there are letters (in fact, sounds) whose combinatory properties can classify them both as vowels and consonants (the so-called semi-vowels, in some languages also the sonorants, etc.).

Conclusion

At the very beginning of the book, on p. 2, we said that mathematical
linguistics is a mathematical discipline geared to natural languages and
linguistics. Now that our exposition is completed, we can, and should, make
that formulation more precise. This requires that we examine somewhat closer
the relation between mathematical linguistics and linguistics proper, on the
one hand, and between mathematical linguistics and mathematics, on the other.

Linguistics, or, more precisely, theoretical linguistics (as opposed to
descriptive linguistics), can be roughly characterized as the science concerned
with the construction of formal models for natural languages and the
methodology of constructing such models. It constructs MODELS, since the
theoretical study of any object (in this case, language) cannot be anything
other than the creation of its models, and these models should be FORMAL
since in studying natural language it is useless to consider any other 'models'.

At the same time the reader has probably noticed that mathematical
linguistics is also concerned with formal constructions called upon to serve as
models of natural languages.

However, there is a quite important difference between linguistics and
mathematical linguistics, which consists in the following. Linguistics develops
the theory of language as such, i.e., strives to produce a general model of
language, and also constructs specific models of actual languages or of their
fragments; mathematical linguistics studies on an abstract level the most
general properties of such models, investigating means and methods of their
construction. In other words, mathematical linguistics creates and investigates
abstract (one could say 'speculative') models of specific linguistic models,
i.e., 'models of the second order'. Mathematical linguistics is concerned,
so to speak, with the materials, instruments, and general theory of model
construction; linguistics as such directly erects the buildings. If linguistics is
the theory of specific languages and of Language in general, then
mathematical linguistics is the theory of the construction of this theory — i.e.,
a m e t a t h e o r y , or m e t a l i n g u i s t i c s . In constructing
models of natural languages, linguistics inevitably uses some definite language

of its own (which is a metalanguage with respect to the natural languages being described). Mathematical linguistics is concerned with the elaboration and purely formal study of this language of linguistics.

Of course, it is impossible to draw a perfectly clear borderline between linguistics and mathematical linguistics. A linguist elaborating a specific model of a language can concern himself with studying in general form the means he uses; a mathematical linguist, while studying his purely abstract constructions, may become interested in a possible linguistic interpretation — i.e., in their application to actual languages. As a result, in many works the spheres of linguistics and mathematical linguistics are so closely interwoven that it is sometimes difficult to relegate a paper to one of these areas rather than to the other. Nevertheless, the above-formulated opposition remains, in principle, valid: linguistics is focused first of all on the description of general laws and properties of language, as well as of individual languages, while mathematical linguistics is focused on studying means and methods of this description.

As to the interrelations between mathematical linguistics and mathematics, the former, as should be seen from the preceding text, is a part of the latter. Of all the mathematical disciplines, mathematical linguistics stands closest to mathematical logic; moreover, a significant part of mathematical linguistics (here we mean the theory of grammars) is simply a branch of mathematical logic. But, since mathematical logic is concerned with studying the language of mathematics, mathematical linguistics proves applicable and is actually applied for this purpose, too. In particular, it is interesting to note that categorial grammars were introduced by K. Ajdukiewicz as early as 1935 for studying the structure of certain mathematical systems. In recent times formal grammars have been widely used for specifying (describing) p r o g r a m m i n g   l a n g u a g e s (artificial languages used for the recording of algorithms with the purpose of giving them a standard form which would facilitate their input into a computer).

Appendix: A Synopsis of Mathematical Results

Below are formulated a number of important propositions which pertain to different branches of mathematical linguistics. The majority of them, but not all, are found in the text of this book (cf. the remark on p. xx). For greater clarity we also repeat here some definitions. After each theorem the corresponding pages of our book are indicated, as well as reference(s) where the proof of the theorem can be found.

1. GENERATIVE GRAMMARS

BASIC DEFINITIONS. A generative grammar (GG) is an ordered quadruple $\langle V, W, I, R \rangle$, where V and W are disjoint non-empty finite sets of symbols (V is the terminal vocabulary, W the nonterminal vocabulary), I is a designated element of W (the initial, or starting, symbol), and R is a finite non-empty set of rules of the form $A \rightarrow B$, where A and B are arbitrary strings over the vocabulary $V \cup W$ (the scheme of the grammar). For the definitions of direct derivability, derivability and derivation, see pp. 21–22; for the definition of language generated by grammar, see p. 24.

1.1. HIERARCHY AND SOME PROPERTIES OF DIFFERENT CLASSES OF GENERATIVE GRAMMARS

A nonshortening grammar is a GG in which the right-hand part of each rule is not shorter than the left-hand part: $l(A) \leq l(B)$, where $l(X)$ is the length of the string X; for the definition of length see fn. 3 on p. 47.

A phrase structure grammar (PS grammar) is a GG in which each rule has the form $Z_1 C Z_2 \rightarrow Z_1 T Z_2$, where C is a nonterminal symbol, Z_1 and Z_2 are arbitrary strings (possibly empty), and T is a nonempty string.

A context-free grammar (CF grammar) is a GG in which each rule has the form $C \to T$, where C is a nonterminal symbol, and T is a nonempty string.

A binary CF grammar is a CF grammar in which the right-hand part of each rule contains no more than two symbols.

A finite state grammar (FS grammar) is a CF grammar in which the right-hand part of each rule either consists of one symbol, or has the form bB, where b is a terminal symbol, and B is a nonterminal symbol.

A CF grammar with bounded memory is a CF grammar for which there is a number K such that for any terminal string x derivable in this grammar, a derivation of x from the initial symbol in the grammar can be found such that each intermediate string of the derivation contains nonterminal symbols in no more than K final positions.

For the definition of a CF grammar with an independent bilateral expansion, see pp. 72–73.

THEOREM 1.1.1. The class of languages generated by arbitrary grammars coincides with the class of recursively enumberable languages (p. 28; Davies 1958, Chapter 6, §2; Gladkij 1973: §1.4).

THEOREM 1.1.2. The class of languages generated by nonshortening grammars coincides with the class of PS languages; moreover, for every nonshortening grammar it is possible to effectively construct an equivalent PS grammar (p. 31; Chomsky 1963: 360; Gladkij 1973: theorem 3.1).

THEOREM 1.1.3. There are PS languages which are not CF languages, for example, $\{a^n b^n a^n\}$ (p. 40; Bar-Hillel, Perles and Shamir 1961; Gladkij 1973: §4.3, example 1).

THEOREM 1.1.4. For each CF grammar it is possible to effectively construct an equivalent binary CF grammar (p. 41; Gladkij 1973: lemma 4.3).

THEOREM 1.1.5. There are CF languages which are not FS languages, for example, $\{a^n b^n\}$ (p. 45; Gladkij 1973: the example after the corollary from theorem 5.7).

THEOREM 1.1.6. For each CF grammar with bounded memory it is possible to effectively construct an equivalent FS grammar (p. 71; Gladkij 1973: the corollary from theorem 7.2).

THEOREM 1.1.7. For each CF grammar with an independent bilateral expansion it is possible to effectively construct an equivalent FS grammar (p. 73).

THEOREM 1.1.8. (a) The class of recursively enumerable languages is closed under the operations of set union and intersection, and not closed under complementation.

(b) The class of PS languages is closed under the operations of set union and intersection.[1]

(c) The class of CF languages is closed under the operation of set union and not closed under the operations of set intersection and complementation.

(d) The class of FS languages is closed under the operations of set union, intersection and complementation (see Chomsky 1963 and Gladkij 1973: theorems 1.1, 3.4, 4.8, 5.4, and the note at the end of §1.4).

Table 1.   The closure properties of formal languages

Language type	Closed under the operation of:		
	Union	Intersection	Complementation
recursively enumerable	yes	yes	no
PS	yes	yes	?
CF	yes	no	no
FS	yes	yes	yes

1.2.   DECISION PROBLEMS IN THE THEORY OF GENERATIVE GRAMMARS

THEOREM 1.2.1.   In the class of all grammars no nontrivial property of the languages generated by grammars is decidable (see p. 81; Gladkij 1973: theorem 8.1).[2]

THEOREM 1.2.2.   In the class of PS grammars the property of generating a language containing a given string is decidable (p. 81).

THEOREM 1.2.3.   In the class of PS grammars the following properties are undecidable: generating a given (arbitrary) PS language, generating a finite language, generating a CF language, generating a language with substitutability of x by y, where x and y are arbitrary (fixed) strings (p. 81; Chomsky 1963; Gladkij 1964b; Gladkij 1973: corollary 1 from theorem 8.3).

THEOREM 1.2.4. In the class of CF grammars the following properties are decidable: generating an empty language, generating a finite language, generating at least one string containing an occurrence of a given string x (p. 82; Bar-Hillel, Perles and Shamir 1961; Gladkij 1973: theorems 4.1, 4.2).

THEOREM 1.2.5. In the class of CF grammars the following properties are undecidable: generating an FS language, generating a full language (a language containing all the nonempty strings over the given terminal vocabulary), having an equivalent CF grammar which assigns to each terminal string only one syntactic structure (p. 82; Bar-Hillel, Perles and Shamir 1961; Gladkij 1973: corollary 1 from theorem 8.4, corollary from theorem 8.5).

THEOREM 1.2.6. In the class of FS grammars the following properties are decidable: generating a full language, and generating a language with a finite complement (p. 82); Bar-Hillel, Perles and Shamir 1961).

THEOREM 1.2.7. There is no decision procedure which allows us to determine, for any pair of CF grammars, whether they are equivalent (p. 82; Bar-Hillel, Perles and Shamir 1961; Gladkij 1973: corollary 2 from theorem 8.4).

THEOREM 1.2.8. There is a decision procedure which allows us to determine, for any pair of FS grammars, whether they are equivalent (p. 82; Bar-Hillel, Perles and Shamir 1961; Gladkij 1964a).

THEOREM 1.2.9. There is a CF grammar G for which there is no decision procedure which allows us to determine, for any pair of strings x, y, whether x is substitutable[3] by y in language $L(G)$ (p.82; Gladkij 1965; Gladkij 1973: the end of §8.4).

THEOREM 1.2.10. For any FS grammar G there is a decision procedure which allows us to determine, for any pair of strings x and y, whether x is substitutable by y in language $L(G)$ (p. 82; Gladkij 1964a).

THEOREM 1.2.11. There is a CF grammar G for which there is no decision procedure which allows us to determine, for any string, whether it is a configuration[3] of language $L(G)$ (p. 124; Lučkin 1966).

THEOREM 1.2.12. For any FS grammar G there is a decision procedure which allows us to determine, for an arbitrary string x, a symbol a and a natural number n, whether x is a configuration of rank n of language $L(G)$ with the resultant a (Gladkij 1964a).

THEOREM 1.2.13. For any nonshortening grammar there is a decision procedure which allows us to determine, for any string, whether it is derivable in the given grammar from the initial symbol (p. 29).

1.3. ESTIMATES OF DERIVATIONAL COMPLEXITY

THEOREM 1.3.1. For any nonshortening grammar G the inequality $\tau_G(n) < p^{n+1}$ holds, where τ_G is the time function of grammar G (see p. 83), and p is the total number of terminal and nonterminal symbols of the grammar (p. 83).

THEOREM 1.3.2. For any CF grammar G the inequality $\tau_G(n) \leq 2Cn$ holds, where C is the number of nonterminal symbols of grammar G (p. 83).

THEOREM 1.3.3. The language $\{xqx'\}$ (see p. 64) cannot be generated by any PS grammar which has the time function $\tau_G(n)$ of an order less than n^2 (p. 85; Gladkij 1964c; Gladkij 1973: theorem 3.7).

THEOREM 1.3.4. The class of languages generated by grammars with bounded extension[4] coincides with the class of PS languages; moreover, for each grammar with bounded extension it is possible to effectively construct an equivalent PS grammar (p. 74; Gladkij 1964a; Gladkij 1973: theorem 3.1').

2. OTHER TYPES OF FORMAL GRAMMARS

For the definition of categorial grammar (C grammar) see pp. 89–90; for the definition of a push-down store automaton (PDS automaton) see pp. 108–109.

THEOREM 2.1. Every C language is a CF language; moreover, for any C grammar it is possible to effectively construct an equivalent CF grammar (see p. 96; Bar-Hillel, Gaifman and Shamir 1960; Gladkij 1973: theorem 6.1a).

THEOREM 2.2. (Gaifman). Every CF language is a C language; moreover, for any CF grammar it is possible to effectively construct an equivalent C grammar (see p. 96; Bar-Hillel, Gaifman and Shamir 1960; Gladkij 1973: theorem 6.1b).

THEOREM 2.3. (Chomsky). Every PDS language is a CF language; moreover, for any PDS automaton it is possible to effectively construct an equivalent CF grammar (p. 109; Chomsky 1963; Gladkij 1973: theorem 4.9b).

THEOREM 2.4. Every CF language is a PDS language; moreover, for any CF grammar it is possible to effectively construct an equivalent PDS automaton (p. 109; Chomsky 1966; Gladkij 1973: theorem 4.9a).

3. CONFIGURATIONS

The string x is substitutable by the string y in language L (notation: $x \Rightarrow y(L)$), if for any two strings p and q, from $pxq \in L$ it follows that $pyq \in L$. The string x is mutually substitutable with the string y in language L if $x \Rightarrow y(L)$ and $y \Rightarrow x(L)$ (notation: $x \Leftrightarrow y(L)$).

If x is a string consisting of at least two symbols and a is a symbol, then x is called a configuration of rank 1 (of language L) with the resultant a if $x \Leftrightarrow a(L)$. Let configurations of ranks $\leq n$ be defined, and let x be a string consisting of at least two symbols and a a symbol. Then x is called a configuration of rank $n+1$ (of language L) with the resultant a, if: (1) $a \Leftrightarrow x(L)$, and (2) for any two strings p and q, from the fact that pxq belongs to L and does not contain occurrences of configurations of ranks $\leq n$ which intersect with the distinguished occurrence of x without being fully contained in it, it follows that paq belongs to L (see p. 122).

A simple configuration (of language L) is a configuration not containing occurrences of other configurations of the same rank. An irreducible string of language L is a string belonging to language L and not containing occurrences of configurations of language L.

The configurational characteristic[5] of language L is the ordered pair $\langle B(L), P(L) \rangle$, where $B(L)$ is the set of all irreducible strings of language L, and $P(L)$ is the set of all possible ordered pairs (a, x), where x is a simple configuration of language L and a is its resultant.

If $B(L)$ and $P(L)$ are finite, then L is called a finitely characterizable language.

THEOREM 3.1. If L_1 and L_2 are languages over the same vocabulary and $B(L_1) = B(L_2)$, $P(L_1) = P(L_2)$, then $L_1 = L_2$; in other words, a language over a vocabulary is fully specified by its configurational characteristics (p. 125; Gladkij 1963b; Gladkij 1973: theorem Π II.1, p. 321).

THEOREM 3.2. The class of finitely characterizable languages is contained in the class of CF languages; moreover, given any finitely characterizable language L and its finite configurational characteristic $\langle B(L), P(L) \rangle$, it is possible to effectively construct a CF grammar which generates L (p. 125); Gladkij 1963b; Gladkij 1973: theorem Π II.2, p. 323).

THEOREM 3.3. There are CF languages (and even FS languages) which are not finitely characterizable (Gladkij 1963b; Gladkij 1973: § Π II.2, ex. 3, p. 324).

THEOREM 3.4. Every FS language without homonymy[6] is a finitely characterizable language; the converse is not true (Gladkij 1963b).

THEOREM 3.5. There are CF languages in which for any natural number n there are configurations of rank n which are not configurations of rank $n - 1$ (Lučkin 1966).

NOTES

1. The question about the closure of the class of PS languages under complementation remains open. (What is meant is the complementation up to the set of all nonempty strings over a given terminal vocabulary.)
2. This theorem easily follows from a known theorem of H.G. Rice (Rice 1953; a proof can be found also in Gladkij 1973: theorem 8.2).
3. For the definition of substitutability and configuration see pp. 122–124.
4. Gladkij 1963a uses the term 'a grammar with linear memory' instead of 'a grammar with bounded extension'.
5. Gladkij 1963b and Gladkij 1973 use the term 'reduced configurational characteristic' instead of 'configurational characteristic'.
6. That is, a language generated by an FS grammar such that no two of its rules which have different left-hand parts can contain the same terminal symbol in their right-hand parts.

Bibliography

Abaev, V. I.
1965   'Lingvističeskij modernizm kak degumanizacija nauki o jazyke' [Linguistic
         Modernism as the Dehumanization of the Science of Language], *Voprosy*
         jazykoznanija (3): 22–43.
Abraham, S.
1965   'Some questions of phrase structure grammars. I.' *Computational Linguistics* 4
         (Budapest: Computing Centre of the Hungarian Academy of Sciences),
         61–69.
Apresjan, Ju. D.
1965   'Sovremennye metody izučenija značenij i nekotorye problemy strukturnoj
         lingvistiki' [Modern Methods of Studying Meaning and Some Problems of
         Structural Linguistics]. *Problemy strukturnoj lingvistiki 1963* [Problems
         of Structural Linguistics – 1963] (Moscow: Izd. AN SSSR), 102–150.
1975   *Principles and Methods of Contemporary Structural Linguistics* [= Janua
         Linguarum. Series Minor, 144] (The Hague: Mouton) [First published in
         Russian in 1966].
Arsent'eva, N. G.
1965   'O dvux sposobax poroždenija predloženij russkogo jazyka' [On Two Ways of
         Generating Russian Sentences], *Problemy kibernetiki* [Problems of Cybernetics]
         14: 189–218.
Barbault, Marie-Claire and J.P. Desclés
1972   *Transformations formelles et théories linguistiques (= Documents de*
         linguistique quantitative 11) (Paris: Dunod).
Bar-Hillel, Y.
1953[1] 'A Quasi-Arithmetical Notation for Syntactic Description,' *Language*
         29(1): 47–58.
1959   'Decision Procedures for Structure in Natural Languages,' *Report on the State*
         of Machine Translation in the United States and Great Britain (Jerusalem),
         Appendix III. Simultaneously published also in *Logique et analyse* 2(5):
         19–29.
1960[1] 'Some Linguistic Obstacles to Machine Translation,' In: *Advances in*
         Computers 1: 146–157. (New York, London).
1962   'Some Recent Results in Theoretical Linguistics,' In: Ernest Nagel, Patrick
         Suppes, and Alfred Tarski, eds., *Logic, Methodology and Philosophy of*
         Science. Proceedings of the 1960 International Congress (Stanford, California:
         Stanford University Press), 551–557.
1964   *Language and Information* (Reading, Mass.: Addison–Wesley).

Bar-Hillel, Y., C. Gaifman, and E. Shamir
1960[1] 'On Categorial and Phrase-Structure Grammars,' *Bulletin of the Research Council of Israel*, 9F: 1–16.
Bar-Hillel, Y., M. Perles, and E. Shamir
1961[1] 'On Formal Properties of Simple Phrase Structure Grammars,' *Zeitschrift für Phonetik, Sprachwissenschaft und Kommunikationsforschung* 14(2): 143–172.
Bar-Hillel, Y., and E. Shamir
1960[1] 'Finite State Languages: Formal Representation and Adequacy Problems,' *Bulletin of the Research Council of Israel*, 8F (3): 155–166.
Beleckij, M. I.
1967 'Beskontekstnye i dominacionnye grammatiki i svjazannye s nimi algoritmičeskie problemy' [CF and Dominational Grammars and Decision Problems Connected with Them], *Kibernetika* (4): 90–97.
Bobrow, D. G.
1963 'Syntactic Analysis of English by Computer – A Survey,' *AFIPS Conference Proceedings* 24: 365–387.
Brainerd, B.
1971 *Introduction to the Mathematics of Language Study* (New York: American Elsevier).
Charney, Elinor K.
1961 *On the Semantic Interpretation of Linguistic Entities that Function Structurally* (Teddington:National Physical Laboratory. Paper 8).
1962 'On the Problem of Sentence Synonymy,' *Quarterly Progress Report* 66: 289–293. (Cambridge Mass. : MIT).
1966 *Structural Semantic Foundations for a Theory of Meaning* (Chicago : University of Chicago Press).
Chauché, J.
1972 *Arborescences et transformations* (Grenoble).
Chomsky, N.
1957 *Syntactic Structures* (The Hague : Mouton).
1961 'On the Notion "Rule of Grammar",' In: R. Jacobson, ed., *Structure of Language and Its Mathematical Aspects. Proceedings of the 12th Symposium in Applied Mathematics* (Providence, R.I.: Amer. Math. Soc.), 6–24.
1963 'Formal Properties of Grammars', In: R. D. Luce, R. Bush, and E. Galanter, eds., *Handbook of Mathematical Psychology* 2: 328–418. (New York).
1964 'The Logical Basis of Linguistic Theory', In: *Proceedings of the Ninth International Congress of Linguistics*, 914–978. (The Hague: Mouton).
1965 *Aspects of the Theory of Syntax* (Cambridge, Mass.: M.I.T.).
Chomsky, N., and G. A. Miller
1963 'Introduction to the Formal Analysis of Natural Languages', In: R.D. Luce, R. Bush, and F. Galanter, eds., *Handbook of Mathematical Psycholody* 2: 269–322. (New York).
Davidson, D., and G. Harman, eds.
1973 *The Semantics of Natural Language* (Dordrecht : D. Reidel).
Davies, M.
1958 *Computability and Unsolvability* (New York : McGraw-Hill).
Döhman, K.
1966 'Zur Semantik und Etymologie der sprachlichen Darstellung der dyadischen

Funktoren,' *Studium generale* 19(7): 398–401.

Frege, G.

1892   'Über Sinn und Bedeutung', *Zeitschrift für Philosophie und philos. Kritik,* 10? neue Serie, 25–30 [Reprinted in: Frege G. *Translations from the philosophical writings,* Oxford, 1952].

Freudenthal, H.

1960   *LINCOS. Design of a Language for Cosmic Intercourse,* part 1 (Amsterdam).

1966   *The Language of Logic* (Amsterdam).

Ginsburg, S., and Barbara Partee

1969   'A Mathematical Model of Transformational Grammars', *Information and Control* 15(2): 262–337.

Gladkij, A. V.

1963a   'Grammatiki s linejnoj pamjat'ju' [Grammars with Bounded Memory], *Algebra i logika* 2(5): 43–55.

1963b   'Konfiguracionnye xarakteristikı jazykov' [Configurational Characteristics of Languages], *Problemy kibernetiki* [Problems of Cybernetics] 10: 251–260.

1964a   'Algoritm raspoznavanija konfiguracij dlja klassa avtomatnyx jazykov' [An Algorithm for Recognizing Configurations in the Class of Finite State Languages], *Problemy kibernetiki* [Problems of Cynernetics] 12: 243–245.

1964b   'Algoritmičeskaja priroda invariantnyx svojstv grammatik neposredstvenno sostavljajuščix' [Decision Problems Concerning the Invariant Properties of Phrase Structure Grammars], *Algebra i logika* 3(2): 17–31.

1964c   'O složnosti vyvoda v grammatikax neposredstvenno sostavljajuščix' [Complexity of Derivations in Phrase Structure Grammars], *Algebra i logika* 3(5–6): 29–44.

1965   'Nekotorye algoritmičeskie problemy dlja kontekstno-svobodnyx grammatik' [Some Decision Problems for Context-Free Grammars], *Algebra i logika* 4: (3): 3–13.

1966   *Lekcii po matematičeskoj lingvistike dlja studentov NGU* [Lectures on Mathematical Linguistics for the Students of Novosibirsk State University] (Novosibirsk).

1973   *Formal'nye grammatiki i jazyki* [Formal Grammars and Languages] (Moscow: Nauka).

1979   'O značenii sojuza *ili*' [On the Meaning of the Russian Conjunction *ili*], *Semiotika i informatika* [Semiotics and Informatics] 13: 196–214.

Gladkij, A. V., and I.A. Mel'čuk

1969   'Tree Grammars (Δ-grammars)', *International Conference on Computational Linguistics* (COLING-69) (Stockholm).

1975   'Tree Grammars. I. A Formalism for Syntactic Transformations in Natural Languages', *Linguistics* 150: 47–82. See also this volume, pp. 151 ff.

Gladkij, A, V., Maya V. Rybakova, and Tamara I. Šed'ko

1961   *Sxema semantičeskogo jazyka-posrednika dlja zapisi matematičeskix tekstov* [The Design of a Semantic Interlingua for Representing Mathematics Texts] (= VINITI AN SSSR. Doklady na konferencii, No. 10) (Moscow).

Gleason, H.

1961   *An Introduction to Descriptive Linguistics,* 2nd edition (New York: Holt, Rinehart and Winston).

Gross, M.
  1972   *Mathematical Models in Linguistics* (Englewood Cliffs, N.J. : Prentice-Hall).
Hall-Partee, Barbara.
  1978   *Fundamentals of Mathematics for Linguistics* (Dordrecht, London: D. Reidel)
Harris, Z. S.
  1957   'Co-occurrence and Transformation in Linguistic Structure', *Language*
           33(3, Part 1): 283–340.
  1963   *Structural Linguistics* (Chicago, London: The University of Chicago Press)
           [first published in 1950 under the title *Methods in Structural Linguistics*].
  1968   *Mathematical Structures of Language* (New York: J. Wiley).
Hays, D. H.
  1961   'Grouping and Dependency Theories', In: *Proceedings of the National
           Symposium on Machine Translation*, 258–266, (Englewood Cliffs, N.J.).
  1962   'Automatic Language Data Processing', *Computer Applications in
           Behavioral Sciences*, 394–421, (Englewood Cliffs, N.J.).
  1964   'Dependency Theory: A Formalism and Some Observations', *Language*
           64(4): 511–525.
Hermes, H.
  1965   *Enumerability, Decidability, Computability* (Bonn: Springer-Verlag).
Hintikka, J. J., J. M. E. Moravcsik, and P. C. Suppes, eds.
  1973   *Approaches to Natural Language* (Dordrecht: D. Reidel).
Hiż, H.
  1960   'The Intuitions of Grammatical Categories', *Methodos*, 311–319.
  1968   'Computable and Uncomputable Elements of Syntax', In: Rootselaar and
           Staal, eds., *Logic, Methodology and Philosophy of Sciences III*, 239–254,
           (Amsterdam: North Holland).
Hockney, D. J., W. Harper, and B. Freed, eds.
  1975   *Contemporary Research in Philosophical Logic and Linguistic Semantics*
           (Dordrecht: D. Reidel).
Hopcroft, J.E., and J. D. Ullman
  1969   *Formal Languages and Their Relation to Automata* (Reading, Mass.:
           Addison-Wesley).
Iordanskaja, Lidija N.
  1967   *Avtomatičeskij sintaksičeskij analiz* [Automatic Syntactic Analysis], vol. II
           (Novosibirsk: Nauka).
Jakobson, R. O.
  1948   'Russian Conjugation', *Word* 4(3): 155–167. [Reprinted in Jakobson,
           1971 : 23–71.]
  1971   *Selected Writings. II. Word and Language* (The Hague : Mouton).
Kay, M., and Karen Sparck-Jones
  1971   'Automated Language Processing', *Annual Review of Information Science
           and Technology* 6: 146–166. (Chicago).
Kimball, J. P.
  1973   *The Formal Theory of Grammar* (Englewood Cliffs, N.J. : Prentice-Hall).
Kleene, S. K.
  1967   *Mathematical Logic* (New York, London, Sidney: J. Wiley).
Kulagina, O. S.
  1958   'Ob odnom sposobe opredelenija grammatičeskix ponjatij na baze teorii
           množestv' [On a Way of Defining Grammatical Notions on the Basis of Set

Theory], *Problemy kibernetiki* [Problems of Cybernetics] 1: 203–214.

Kuno, S.
1963 'The Multiple-Path Syntactic Analyzer for English', *Mathematical Linguistics and Automatic Translation* (Computation Laboratory of Harvard University. Report No. NSF–9, vol. I) pp. I/1–I/152 (var. pag.). (Cambridge, Mass.).
1968 'Automatic Syntactic Analysis', *Seminar on Computational Linguistics* (Bethesda, Maryland), 19–41.

Kuno, S., and A. Oettinger
1963 'Syntactic Structure and Ambiguity of English', *AFIPS Proceedings of the Fall Joint Computer Conference* . . . 24: 397–418. (Baltimore, London).

Kuznecov, A. V., E. V. Padučeva, and N. M. Ermolaeva
1961 'Ob informacionnom jazyke dlja geometrii i algoritme perevoda s russkogo jazyka na informacionnyj' [On an Information Language for Geometry and an Algorithm for Translating from Russian into the Information Language], In: *Lingvističeskie issledovanija no mašinnomu perevodu* [Linguistic Studies on Machine Translation] (2): 40–73. (Moscow). See also *Mašinnyj perevod i prikladnaja lingvistika* [Machine Translation and Applied Linguistics] (5): 3–21; (6): 9–18.

Lambek, J.
1958 'The Mathematics of Sentence Structure', *American Mathematical Monthly* 65: 154–170.

Lewis, D.
1970 'General semantics', *Synthese* 22: 18–67.

Lomkovskaja, M.V.
1965–1966 'Isčislenie, poroždajuščee jadernye russkie predloženija' [A Calculus for Generating Russian Kernel Sentences], *Naučno-texničeskaja informacija* [Scientific and Technological Information] (7) (1965): 35–41 (part I); (9) (1965): 37–40 (part II); (11) (1966): 56–65 (part III).

Lučkin, V. D.
1966 'O rangax konfiguracij kontekstno-svobodnyx jazykov' [On the Ranks of Configurations in Context-Free Languages], *Algebra i logika* 5 (3): 59–70.

Marcus, S.
1962 'Le genre grammatical et son modèle logique', *Cahiers de linguistique théorique et appliquée* 1: 103–122.
1963 'Modèles mathématiques pour la catégorie grammaticale du cas', *Revue de mathématiques pures et appliquées* 3(4): 585–610.
1967 'Algebraic Linguistics: Analytical Models', In: *Mathematics in Science and Engineering 29*. (New York: Academic Press).

Masterman, M.
1961 *Semantic Message Detection for Machine Translation, Using an Interlingua* (Teddington: National Physical Laboratory, Paper 36).

Mel'čuk, I. A.
1963 'Avtomatičeskij analiz tekstov (na materiale russkogo jazyka)' [Automatic Analysis of Texts (As Applied to Russian)]. In: *Slavjanskoe jazykoznanie (Doklady sovetskoj delegacii. V Meždunarodnyjs' 'ezd slavistov)* [Slavic Linguistics (Papers of the Soviet Delegation. V International Congress of Slavists)] (Moscow), 477–509.

1964   *Avtomatičeskij sintaksičeskij analiz* [Automatic Syntatic Analysis], vol. I
          (Novosibirsk : Nauka).
1965   'Porjadok slov pri avtomatičeskom sinteze russkogo teksta (Predvaritel'noe
          soobščenie)' [Word Order in the Automatic Synthesis of Russian Texts
          (Preliminary Report)], *Naučno-texničeskaja informacija* [Scientific and
          Technological Information] (12): 36–41.
1974   *Opyt teorii lingvističeskix modelej "Smysl ⟺ Tekst"* (Moscow : Nauka).

Mel'čuk, I. A., and A. K. Žolkovskij
1970   'Towards a Functioning "Meaning-Text" Model of Language', *Linguistics*
          57: 10–47.

Mendelson, E.
1964   *Introduction to Mathematical Logic* (Princeton, Toronto, New York,
          London: Van Nostrand).

Modina, L. S.
1975   'Drevesnye grammatiki i jazyki' [Tree Grammars and Languages], *Kibernetika*
          5: 86–93.

Montague, R.
1974   *Formal philosophy* (New Haven, London: Yale University Press).

Montgomery, Christine A.
1969   'Automated Language Processing', *Annual Review of Information Science
          and Technology* 4: 145–174. (Chicago).

Novotný, M.
1965   'Über endlich charakterisierbaren Sprachen', *Spisy prirodovědecké fakulty
          university v Brne* (10): 495–502.

Padučeva, E. V.
1964a   'Nekotorye voprosy perevoda s informacionno-logičeskogo jazyka na russkij'
          [Some Questions of Translation from an Informational Logical Language
          into Russian], *Naučno-texničeskaja informacija* [Scientific and Technological
          Information] (2): 20–27.
1964b   'O sposobax predstavlenija sintaksičeskoj struktury predloženija' [On Ways of
          Representing the Syntactic Structure of a Sentence]. *Voprosy jazykoznanija*
          (2): 99–113.
1964c   'Opyt logičeskogo analiza značenija sojuza *ili*' [Attempting Logical Analysis of
          the Meaning of the Conjunction *ili* 'or'], *Filosofskie nauki* [Philosophical
          Sciences] (6): 145–148.
1964d   'Sintez složnyx predloženij s odnoznačnoj sintaksičeskoj strukturoj (pri
          perevode s informacionno-logičeskogo jazyka na russkij)' [Synthesis
          of Complex Sentences with a Non-ambiguous Syntactic Structure (Under
          Translation from an Informational Logical Language into Russian)],
          Naučno-texničeskaja informacija [Scientific and Technological Information]
          (6): 43–49.
1967   'O svjazjax glubiny po Ingve so strukturoj dereva podčinenij' [On Correlations
          Between Yngve's Depth and the Structure of Dependency Trees], *Naučno-
          texničeskaja informacija* [Scientific and Technological Information] (6):
          38–43.

Parker-Rhodes, A. F.
1961   'Some Recent Work on Thesauric and Interlingual Methods in Machine
          Translation', In: *Information Retrieval and Machine Translation, Pt. 2*
          923–934. (New York, London).

Peters, P.S. and R.W. Ritchie
    1971   'On Restricting the Base Component of Transformational Grammars',
            Information and Control 18: 483–501.
    1973   'On the Generative Power of Transformational Grammars', *Information
            Sciences* 6: 49–83.
Petrick, S. R.
    1972   'Computer-oriented Grammars and Parsing', In: *Research Trends in
            Computational Linguistics*, 22–37. (Arlington, Virginia).
Plath, W. J.
    1961   'Mathematical Linguistics', In: *Trends in European and American Linguistics,
            1930–1960*, 21–57. (Utrecht, Antwerp).
    1963   *Multiple-Path Syntactic Analysis of Russian* (published as: *Mathematical
            Linguistics and Automatic Translation*, Computation Laboratory of Harvard
            University. Report No. NSF-12) (Cambridge, Mass.).
Postal, P. M.
    1964   'Limitations of Phrase Structure Grammars', In: *The Structure of Language.
            Readings in the Philosophy of Language*, 137–151. (Englewood Cliffs, N.J.:
            Prentice-Hall).
Quine, W. V.
    1960   *Word and Object* (New York, London: J. Wiley).
    1961   'Logic as a Source of Syntactic Insights', In: R. Jakobson, ed., *Structure of
            Language and Its Mathematics Aspects. Proceedings of the 12th Symposium in
            Applied Mathematics*, 1–5. (Providence, R.I.: Amer. Math. Soc.).
Reichenbach, H.
    1960   *Elements of Symbolic Logic* (New York:Macmillan).
Rezvin, I. I.
    1967   *Metod modelirovanija i tipologija slavjanskix jazykov* [The Method of
            Modelling and the Typology of Slavic Languages] (Moscow : Nauka).
Rice, H. G.
    1953   'Classes of Recursively Enumerable Sets and Their Decision Problems', *Trans.
            Amer. Math. Soc.* 74(2): 358–366.
Rogers, H.
    1967   *Theory of Recursive Functions and Effective Computability* (New York :
            McGraw-Hill).
Rosenkrantz, D. J.
    1969   'Programmed Grammars and Classes of Formal Languages', *Journ. Ass.
            Comput. Mach.* 16 (1): 107–131.
Russell, B.
    1940   *An Inquiry into Meaning and Truth* (New York).
Stockij, È.D.
    1967   'O nekotoryx ograničenijax na sposob vyvoda v grammatikax neposredstvenno
            sostavljajuščix' [On Some Restrictions on Derivations in PS Grammars],
            Naučno-texničeskaja informacija [Scientific and Technological Information]
            ser. 2, (7): 35–38.
    1968   'Poroždajuščie grammatiki i upravlenie vyvodom' [Generative Grammars and
            Guided Derivations], *Naučno-texničeskaja informacija* [Scientific and
            Technological Information], ser. 2, (10): 28–31
Šrejder, Ju. A.
    1966   'Xarakteristiki složnosti struktury teksta' [Characteristics for the Complexity

of the Structure of a Text], *Naučno-texničeskaja informacija* (7): 34–41.

Suxotin, B. V.

1962   'Eksperimental'noe vydelenie klassov bukv s pomošč'ju èlektronnoj vyčislitel'-noj mašiny' [An Experiment in Distinguishing Classes of Letters with the Aid of a Computer], In: *Problemy strukturnoj lingvistiki* [Problems of Structural Linguistics], 198–206. (Moscow: Izd. AN SSSR).

1963   'Algoritmy lingvističeskoj dešifrovki' [Algorithms for Linguistic Deciphering], *Problemy strukturnoj lingvistiki 1963* [Problems of Structural Linguistics –1963], 75–101, (Moscow:Izd. AN SSSR).

1975   'Optimizacionnye algoritmy lingvističeskoj dešifrovki' [Optimization Algorithms for Linguistic Deciphering], *Naučno-texničeskaja informacija* [Scientific and Technological Information], serija 2, (5): 36–42.

Tarski, A.

1941   *Introduction to Logic and the Methodology of Deductive Sciences*, translated by Olaf Helmer, enlarged and revised edition (New York: Oxford University Press).

Tesnière, L.

1959   *Eléments de syntaxe structurale* (Paris : Klincksieck).

Tosh, L. W.

1965   *Syntactic Translation* (The Hague : Mouton).

Trakhtenbrot, B. A.

1963   *Algorithms and Automatic Computing Machines* (Boston : Haith).

Uspenskij, V. A.

1964   'Odna model' dlja ponjatija fonemy' [A Model for the Concept of Phoneme], *Voprosy jazykoznanija* (6): 39–53.

Varga, D.

1964   'Yngve's Hypothesis and Some Problems of the Mechanical Analysis', *Computational Linguistics* 3: 47–74. (Budapest : Computing Centre of the Hungarian Academy of Sciences).

Vendler, Z.

1967   *Linguistics in Philosophy* (Ithaca, N.Y. : Cornell University Press).

Wall, R.

1972   *Introduction to Mathematical Linguistics* (Englewood Cliffs, N.J. : Prentice-Hall).

Weinreich, U.

1963   'On the Semantic Structure of Language', In: J.H. Greenberg, ed., *Universals of Language*, 114–171. (Cambridge, Mass.: M.I.T.).

Woods, W. A.

1970   'Transition Network Grammars for Natural Language Analysis', *Communications of ACM* 13(10): 591–606.

Yngve, V. H.

1960   'A Model and a Hypothesis for Language Structure', *Proceedings of the American Philosophical Society* 104(5): 444–466.

1961a   'The Depth Hypothesis', In: R. Jakobson, ed., *Structure of Language and Its Mathematical Aspects, Proceedings of the 12th Symposium in Applied Mathematics*, 130–138. (Providence, R.1: American Mathematical Society).

1961b   *Random Generation of English Sentences* (Teddington. National Physical Laboratory, Paper 6).

Zaliznjak, A. A.

1967   *Russkoe imennoe slovoizmenenie* [Russian Nominal Inflexion] (Moscow :

Nauka).
Žolkovskij, A.K., N.N. Leont'eva, and Ju. S. Maŗtem'janov
1961   'O principial'nom ispol' zovanii smysla pri mašinnom perevode' [On the Basic
        Use of Meaning in Machine Translation], In: *Mašinnyj perevod* [Machine
        Translation] (= Trudy ITM i VT, No. 2), 17–46. (Moscow).
        See also in: V. Ju. Rozencvejg, ed., *Essays on Lexical Semantics*, vol. I, 1974,
        115–141. (Stockholm: STRIPTOR).
Žolkovskij, A. K., and I. A. Mel'čuk
1967   'O semantičeskom sinteze' [On Semantic Synthesis], *Problemy kibernetiki*
        [Problems of Cybernetics], 19: 177–238.
        See also in: V. Ju. Rozencvejg, ed., *Essays on Lexical Semantics*, vol. II, 1974,
        1–52. (Stockholm: STRIPTOR).

NOTE

1. These papers have been reprinted in Bar-Hillel 1964.

Supplement

Tree Grammars: A Formalism for
Syntactic Transformations in Natural Languages

1. INTRODUCTION

There is no doubt that formal generative grammars, such as those of N. Chomsky, are an effective means of describing the syntax[1] of natural (and artificial) languages.

A FORMAL GENERATIVE GRAMMAR (henceforth: GENERATIVE GRAMMAR, or, when it does not create ambiguity, simply GRAMMAR) is an ordered quadruple $\langle V, W, I, R \rangle$ where V is the terminal vocabulary (or alphabet), W the auxiliary (or non-terminal) vocabulary ($V \cap W = \emptyset$), I the initial symbol, and R a finite set of rewriting rules, or productions, of the form $X \to Y$ (X and Y are arbitrary strings of elements of $V \cup W$).

There exists, however, a broader understanding of the term *generative grammar*, according to which the so-called transformational component, consisting of rules of a quite different type, is included in the grammar; Chomsky himself adheres to this latter usage. Nevertheless, we will use the term *generative grammar* only in the narrow sense indicated above, i.e., with the exclusion of transformations (in the technical, 'Chomskian' meaning of the term).

It is well known that generative grammars, while in a number of respects providing a fruitful approach to the study of language, in many (rather essential) cases do not enable one to deal with the facts in an adequate, natural manner. We shall try to formulate two of what, in our opinion, are the most important causes of the inadequacy of generative grammars.

In the first place, a generative grammar, in its classical form, is designed to generate the set of grammatical sentences of a language; more precisely, it enumerates all the grammatical sentences (and only these) and also assigns to each grammatical sentence its syntactic structure. However, from the viewpoint of linguistics, there is obviously a more interesting and natural undertaking: namely, TO CORRELATE A GIVEN MEANING WITH ALL THE GRAMMATICAL SENTENCES WHICH CORRESPOND TO IT. This is the approach which would be in keeping with the generally accepted view of language as an instrument of communication, or as a means of expressing thought.

It would hardly be appropriate here to offer substantiation for the expediency of the meaning ⇔ text approach (although its adoption leads to far-reaching consequences).[2] We will limit ourselves to the following conclusion: if this approach and the conception of linguistics which it implies were to be adopted, then it would be desirable to have, in the capacity of a formal apparatus for linguistic description, a device which would not only enumerate the grammatical sentences (along with their syntactic structures), but which would also (ideally) be capable of assigning to any given meaning all the grammatical sentences which have that meaning, and conversely, of assigning to any given sentence its meaning or meanings.

Remark 1. The word 'meaning' is to be understood here very broadly, as referring to any content of any speech unit (whatever it may be: from the standpoint of logic it could be false, contradictory, or even absurd).

Remark 2. It is assumed that meanings can be represented as constructive objects, composed, in accordance with some fixed rules, from the elements of a finite set – for example, as graphs whose vertices are labeled with symbols of 'elementary meanings' and whose edges are labeled with symbols of 'elementary semantic relations'.

Secondly, generative grammars deal with strings – linearly ordered sets (i.e. sequences) of symbols – which leads to an identical treatment of two totally different types of relationships existing among the elements of a natural text. These two kinds of relationships obtaining among the words of a sentence are RELATIONSHIPS OF SYNTACTIC CONTINGENCY ('A is dependent on B', or 'A and B together form the constituent C', etc.) and RELATIONSHIPS OF LINEAR ARRANGEMENT ('A is adjacent to B', 'A is to the left of B', 'A is between B and C', etc.). In languages with fixed word order, where the second type of relationship is an important syntactice device – for example, English – these two types of relationships are easily confused, since a given syntactic structure is manifested, as a rule, by a single order of elements (by one string only), or at most by a small number of permissible orders. It was probably this very peculiarity of English which caused preferential development to be given to IC analysis, or phrase structure description, in the Anglo-American grammatical tradition; Chomsky grammars are to a great extent a formalization of just this analysis.[3]

However, if word order is (relatively) free in a language, that is, if a syntactic structure may generally speaking be manifested by means of various possible arrangements of words, as, say, in Russian, then the necessity of distinguishing between syntactic relationships proper and linear relationships is immediately apparent. This fact has been discussed extensively in the literature; it is sufficient to cite the well-known book by L. Tesnière (1959) and the article by D. Worth (1964).

In keeping with the above discussion, we consider it desirable to include two different mechanisms in the apparatus for describing the syntax of natural languages: one should deal with syntactic structures which are devoid of linear order, and the other should map appropriately developed structures into word strings (this principle was previously formulated in Worth 1964; an analogous idea underlies Mel'čuk 1965 and Arapov and Borščev 1967).

Thus what is needed is a formal construction which will implement the transformation 'meaning ⇔ text'; this transformation should be carried out in several steps, which are associated with various levels of text representation. In principle, these steps can be distinguished in a number of ways; we shall follow the division of the meaning-to-text process which is adopted in Žolkovskij and Mel'čuk 1966, 1967a, b, 1969; Mel'čuk and Žolkovskij 1970; Mel'čuk 1973, 1974:32-35. We shall briefly summarize these suggestions from the indicated papers which we will need later on.

We use dependency trees as a means of representing (syntactic) structure.[4] It should be noted that two kinds of syntactic structure are distinguished: surface and deep structures. Our surface structure is related, quite naturally, to the surface structure of transformational grammar, with the important distinction that transformationalists' surface structure is a structure of constituents, i.e. a PS-marker, and gives the order of terminal symbols, which is not the case for us. For the purposes of the present paper, it is sufficient to view the surface structure of a sentence as a tree (in the graph-theoretic sense) whose nodes (= vertices) are labeled with the lexemes of the sentence in question and whose branches (= edges) are labeled with types of corresponding syntactic relationships.

In proceeding from meaning to text, the surface structure of a sentence must ultimately be derived from a description of its meaning (in general, not uniquely). We will not undertake any serious discussion concerning the specific form of the semantic representation of a sentence; we may suppose (cf. remark 2 on p. 152) that this is probably a complex graph, not necessarily a tree, but rather a network, such that there will not be any simple correspondence between it and the surface structure(s), either with respect to topology or with respect to elements (i.e., labels on vertices and edges). Inasmuch as a direct transition from a semantic representation to the many corresponding surface trees[5] is too complicated, it will be convenient to posit some intermediate level: underlying, or deep, syntactic structures (DSS).

Each DSS is for us a generalized representation of a number of synonymous surface trees. Specifically, it also is a tree with labels on its nodes and branches; however, these labels must be quite different from those of a surface structure: it is precisely because the former are of a general and abstract nature that a reduction of synonymy is achieved in DSS's. As far as the correspondence between our DSS and the deep structure of transformational grammar is concerned, along with substantial similarities there is also an important difference: in addition to a deep syntax (as in deep structure of transformational grammar), DSS also employs what we call a deep lexicon – in particular, the so-called lexical functions (Žolkovskij and Mel'čuk 1967b, 1969ff; Mel'čuk and Žolkovskij 1970:24-32); on deep lexicon cf. also Section 5, p. 168ff.

The transition from the input semantic representation to the surface structure of a sentence by way of DSS is assumed to consist of at least three steps: (1) from the semantic representation to at least one corresponding DSS; (2) from a DSS to other (ideally, to all) DSS's synonymous with it ('paraphrasing'; for more details see Žolkovskij and Mel'čuk 1967a, b; Mel'čuk and Žolkovskij 1970); (3) from each DSS to all corresponding surface structures. For more details see Mel'čuk 1974 and 1979.

The transition from the meaning representation to the 'primary' DSS is not considered in the present article.[6] Thus our subject matter is drastically restricted. Of the entire sophisticated process of transition from meaning to text, we will discuss only two steps: the transition from an underlying deep syntactic structure to all other synonymous DSS's, and the transition from a DSS to the corresponding surface syntactic structures.

We can now formulate our goal more precisely. It is to give an account of the fundamentals of a formal apparatus which will permit the implementation of certain tree transformations. These transformations must be oriented toward the transition from certain deep trees (DSS's) to others, and from deep trees to surface trees. In other words, we propose to construct formal grammars which deal with trees – TREE GRAMMARS, or DENDROGRAMMARS (a term from Rounds 1970), so to speak. We will call these grammars FORMAL Δ-GRAMMARS, or, more briefly, Δ-GRAMMARS (Δ – from Greek δένδρον 'tree').

It should be pointed out that many of the ideas which are developed here were formulated and elaborated earlier. Above all, the by now classical works of N. Chomsky must be mentioned, for example Chomsky 1965, and also certain closely associated investigations into the formalization of deep syntax and semantics, such as those by Katz and Fodor, Katz and Postal, Weinreich, Lakoff, Bach, and others. We have in mind especially transformations *sensu stricto* which represent operations performed on (constituent) trees, i.e., on PS-markers. Dependency grammars (Hays 1964; Fitialov 1968) and dominance grammars (Beleckij 1967) also make use of a certain type of transformations – those for trees with linear order on the set of nodes (ordered trees). An approach similar to our Meaning ⟺ Text Model is suggested by P. Sgall (see, for example, Sgall 1967). The necessity of separating syntactic relationships and linear order has been emphasized at length by S. K. Šaumjan (see, in particular, Šaumjan 1965: 93-94). A similar idea is discussed in papers of Arapov and Borščev (1967), and Varšavskaja (1968). An example of a grammar which generates non-ordered tree-structures (of Russian sentences) with subsequent linearization has been constructed by M. V. Lomkovskaja (1965).

Graph transformations, which are similar to our operation of tree substitution, are defined in a number of works; see, for example, Kolmogorov and Uspenskij 1958, and Arapov *et al.* 1967. C.F. Hockett (1967) suggests the use of similar operations on graphs in the elaboration of formal grammars for natural languages.

Veillon *et al.* (1967) is particularly concerned with transformations of trees which are interpreted as constituent trees; these tree transformations are aimed at the formalization of certain linguistic transformations. The operations which are introduced in Veillon *et al.* 1967 are rather similar to the ones which we are suggesting, although they differ from ours in that they are carried out on trees with partial order on the set of nodes.

Operations on trees (which, however, differ from ours) are examined also in Gavrilova (1965). A method of generating dependency trees is introduced in Varšavskaja (1968).

Finally, the work by O. S. Kulagina (1969) is concerned with the same area of investigation as is our paper; it is natural that the contents of both articles turn out to be similar in most of the essential aspects, especially since the authors have discussed the relevant issues at length with O. S. Kulagina. She read the first version of the present article, which underwent substantial revision in response to her suggestions.

Perhaps it would not be out of place to stress the fact that in the seventies the problem of tree processing has become very popular. There are at least two kinds of research: for one thing, investigations are being conducted in automata theory and formal grammar theory concerning abstract systems for tree processing; for another, many attempts are known aiming at a better formalization of the concept '(linguistic) transformation' (in the sense of Chomsky). Let us mention here some of the studies published so far (and providing further references): Brainerd 1969; Ginsburg and Partee 1969; Rounds 1970; Thatcher 1970; Barbault and Desclés 1971, 1972; Chauché 1972; Ogden and Rounds 1972; Baker 1973; Peters and Ritchie 1973; Modina 1975.

The authors wish to express their sincere gratitude to O. S. Kulagina. They also thank A. Ja. Dikovskij, who pointed out a number of inaccuracies, S. Ja. Fitialov, Ju. A. Šixanovič, Ju. A. Šrejder, and other colleagues, who read the manuscript and offered valuable comments.

2. SYNTACTIC Δ-GRAMMARS

We now proceed to the basic definitions concerning Δ-grammars. The objects which the latter deal with are to be thought of as finite 'labeled' trees, that is, trees whose nodes and branches are all labeled with symbols of a finite alphabet.

It is convenient to begin with a special class of Δ-grammars. We will call the grammars of this class SYNTACTIC Δ-GRAMMARS. Syntactic Δ-grammars are distinguished from other possible types of Δ-grammars by the fact that they process trees which do not have labels on their nodes (but which do have labels on their branches); in a sense, such trees may be regarded as 'pure' syntactic structures, having no lexical content whatever.

Thus the objects which form the domain of syntactic Δ-grammars are oriented trees with labeled branches (henceforth, for the sake of brevity, they will simply be called trees).

When speaking of trees, we will use terminology which is widely accepted in linguistics and automatic translation, and which differs from the usual terminology of graph theory. Namely, where graph theory uses the terms *vertex*, *edge*, and *root*, we will use the terms *node*, *branch*, and *top node*, respectively.

We will say that trees T_1 and T_2 are ISOMORPHIC if it is possible to establish a one-to-one correspondence between the sets of the nodes of these trees, such that for any pair of nodes a and β in the tree T_1 a branch with some label leads from a to β if and only if a branch with the same label leads from the image of a to the image of β in the tree T_2.

We will further say that a tree is a MINIMAL TREE if all its nodes different from the top node are terminal[7]; a special case of a minimal tree would be a tree which consists of only a top node – a UNIT TREE (notation: &).

We now introduce an operation on trees which we shall call COMPOSITION. It is defined as follows. Let there be a tree t_0, and n trees $t_1, t_2, \ldots, t_n$. Assume that in the tree t_0 there are selected n nodes $a_1, a_2, \ldots, a_n$, not necessarily pairwise distinct. Then the result of the composition of the tree t_0 (with the distinguished nodes $a_1, a_2, \ldots, a_n$) and of the trees $t_1, t_2, \ldots, t_n$ will be, by definition, any tree T which is isomorphic to the tree derived from t_0 by identifying the top nodes of the trees $t_1, t_2, \ldots, t_n$ with the nodes $a_1, a_2, \ldots, a_n$ of t_0, respectively.

It should be emphasized that the result of composition is defined up to an isomorphism: if a tree T is the composition of the tree t_0 (with distinguished nodes $a_1, a_2, \ldots, a_n$) and of the trees $t_1, t_2, \ldots, t_n$, then the tree T' will be the composition of the same t_0 (with the same distinguished nodes) and of the same trees $t_1, t_2, \ldots, t_n$ if and only if T' is isomorphic to T.

We will denote the composition of a tree t_0 (with distinguished nodes a_1, $a_2, ..., a_n$) and of the trees $t_1, t_2, ..., t_n$ by

(1) $C(t_0; a_1, a_2, ..., a_n \mid t_1, t_2, ..., t_n)$.

We will say that the tree t OCCURS in the tree T (or that the tree t IS A SUBTREE of the tree T), if t is a connected subgraph of the tree T up to an isomorphism; that is, if T can be represented in the form

(2) $T = C(T^0; a_0 \mid C(t; a_1, a_2, ..., a_n \mid T^1, T^2, ..., T^n))$,

where a_0 is a terminal node in the tree T^0, and $a_1, a_2, ..., a_n$ is a repetition-free enumeration of all the nodes of the tree t.[8]

It is clear that this concept is also defined up to an isomorphism: if a tree t occurs in the tree T, then any tree which is isomorphic to t occurs in any tree which is isomorphic to T.

Example.

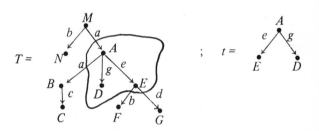

The tree t occurs in the tree T (this occurrence is circled in the diagram), since $T = C(T^0; A \mid C(t; A, E, D \mid T^1, T^2, T^3))$ where

$$T^0 = \quad , T^1 = \quad A \xrightarrow{a} B \xrightarrow{c} C, \quad T^2 = \quad , \text{ and } T^3 = \mathcal{E}.$$

The tree t can occur in T, so to speak, several times, that is, at different places. We can then speak of the various OCCURRENCES of t in T.

Now we will define elementary tree transformation. Under an elementary transformation, a tree t_2 is substituted for (= replaces) some occurrence of another tree t_1 in the tree T which undergoes the transformation (t_1 is a subtree of T). To specify such a substitution, it is necessary to indicate: (1) both the replaced and the replacing trees – t_1 and t_2; and (2) the way in which the new nodes (i.e., the nodes of the replacing tree t_2) are to be connected with the remaining old nodes of the tree T.

Formally speaking, an ELEMENTARY TRANSFORMATION is an ordered triple

$$\langle t_1, t_2, f \rangle$$

where t_1 and t_2 are trees, and f is a one-valued mapping of the set of nodes of t_1 into the set of nodes of t_2. Thus, if a node a of t_1 is transformed into the node β of t_2, i.e., if $\beta = f(a)$, then all the remaining nodes of T which hung from a are to hang from β, with the preservation of the relationships (labels on branches).

Instead of $\langle t_1, t_2, f \rangle$, for greater clarity we will use the notation

$$t_1 \Rightarrow t_2 \mid f.$$

We will say that the tree T' is derived from the tree T by the elementary transformation $t_1 \Rightarrow t_2 \mid f$ if T and T' can be represented respectively as:

(3) $T = C(T^0; a_0 \mid C(t_1; a_1, a_2, ..., a_n \mid T^1, T^2, ..., T^n))$

and

(4) $T' = C(T^0; a_0 \mid C(t_2; f(a_1), f(a_2), ..., f(a_n) \mid T^1, T^2, ..., T^n)),$

where a_0 is a terminal node in the tree T^0, and $a_1, a_2, ..., a_n$ is a repetition-free enumeration of the nodes of t_1.[9]

From the preceding it is clear that the concept of the application of an elementary transformation is also defined up to an isomorphism: if T' is derived from T by some elementary transformation, then any tree which is isomorphic to T' is derived from any tree which is isomorphic to T by the same transformation.

Example.
Let $t_1 \Rightarrow t_2 \mid f$ be an elementary transformation where

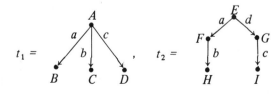

and f is given by the table:

$$f(A) = E \qquad f(C) = H$$
$$f(B) = G \qquad f(D) = F$$

We apply this transformation to the tree T:

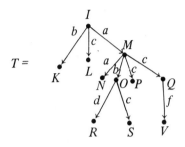

There are three occurrences of t_1 in T: one having the top node I, and two with the top mode M. We apply our transformation to the occurrence of t_1 which consists of the nodes M, N, O, Q; the tree T' is then derived:

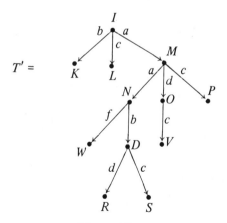

Here, representations (3) and (4) appear as:

$$T = C(T^0; M \mid C(t_1; M, N, O, Q \mid T^1, T^2, T^3, T^4))$$

and

$$T' = C(T^0; M \mid C(t_2; M, O, D, N \mid T^1, T^2, T^3, T^4)),$$

where

$$T^0 = \quad , \quad T^1 = \quad , \quad T^2 = N = \&,$$

$$T^3 = \quad , \quad T^4 = $$

Now, we can proceed directly to syntactic Δ-grammars.

A syntactic Δ-grammar consists of a vocabulary and a finite set of rules (productions).

The vocabulary is a finite set of symbols – labels on the branches of trees. More specifically, these are types of syntactic relationships, or dependency connections.

Each rule is an elementary transformation (in the sense of the above definition), in which the branches of the left-hand and the right-hand parts are labeled with symbols from the vocabulary.

In accordance with what was said in Section 1 concerning the goals of Δ-grammars, a syntactic Δ-grammar must provide for the conversions of certain trees into other trees. Now we are in a position to give a rigorous definition of such conversions, which we call DERIVATIONS.

A DERIVATION in a syntactic Δ-grammar is a finite sequence of trees such that each tree in it is derived from the preceding one by one of the rules (= elementary transformations) of the grammar.

The tree T' is said to BE DERIVED from the tree T in a syntactic Δ-grammar G if there exists a derivation in G which begins with T and terminates with T'.

Syntactic Δ-grammars are calculi of a quite general type, and it is their various special classes that are obviously of interest for possible linguistic applications.

The specialization of classes of grammars may be achieved, in particular, by imposing restrictions on their rules.

Let us start with the requirement that the tree t_2 on the right-hand part of the rule $t_1 \Rightarrow t_2 \mid f$ must not have fewer nodes than the tree t_1 on its left-hand part. We will call rules which satisfy such a requirement EXPANSIONS, and we will call grammars which contain only this type of rule EXPANSIVE SYNTACTIC Δ-GRAMMARS.

The elementary transformation presented earlier (on page 158) could serve as an example of an expansion rule.

Let us further require that an expansion rule replace exactly one elementary 'fragment' of the input tree. It is natural to consider a single node to be the most elementary fragment of a tree. However, we must take care that when a node is replaced its relationships are preserved; that is, exactly those branches which go down, or issue, from the node being replaced should go down from the tree which will replace that node. Since we cannot consider a branch without also considering both of its end points, it becomes necessary to speak of the replacement of a minimal tree rather than of a node (see discussion at the beginning of Section 2). Thus all the terminal nodes of the minimal tree being replaced must become terminal nodes of the tree which replaces it, and the branches which enter the terminal nodes of the replaced tree and the branches which enter the corresponding nodes of the replacing tree must be labeled in the same way.

Furthermore, we must take into account the fact that although only one minimal tree is replaced, the possibility of replacement may be conditioned by the context (the environment both 'above' and 'below') of the replaced minimal tree in the tree undergoing transformation.

We can thus derive from these considerations a form of rule, whose right-hand part t_2 differs from its left-hand part t_1 only in that some minimal tree μ which occurs in t_1 is replaced in the right-hand part by another tree which is not necessarily minimal but which contains no fewer terminal branches than the replaced tree; and for every branch in the replaced minimal tree μ, there should be a corresponding terminal branch with the same label in the replacing tree. Everything else in t_1 remains unchanged and functions as the context which states the conditions on the replacement of μ. We will call such rules MINIMAL EXPANSION rules, and correspondingly, we will call grammars which contain only such rules MINIMAL EXPANSIVE Δ-GRAMMARS.

Let us now formulate a definition.

Rule $t_1 \Rightarrow t_2 \mid f$ is called a minimal expansion rule if t_1 and t_2 can be represented, respectively, as

(5) $t_1 = C(\tau^0; a_0 \mid C(\mu; a_1, a_2, ..., a_n \mid \tau^1, \tau^2, ..., \tau^n))$

and

(6) $t_2 = C(\tau^0; a_0 \mid C(\nu; f(a_1), f(a_2), ..., f(a_n) \mid \tau^1, \tau^2, ..., \tau^n)),$

where: (1) μ is a minimal tree; (2) $a_1, a_2, ..., a_n$ is a repetition-free enumeration of the nodes of the tree μ; (3) a_1 is the top node of μ; (4) $f(a_1), f(a_2), ..., f(a_n)$ are pairwise distinct; (5) $f(a_2), f(a_3), ..., f(a_n)$ are terminal nodes of the tree ν; (6) for every $i = 2, 3, ..., n$, the label on the branch of the tree μ which enters a_i coincides with the label on the branch of the tree ν which enters $f(a_i)$; (7) for all nodes of the tree t_1 which are different from $a_1, a_2, \ldots, a_n$, the mapping f is the identity.

The next step is to require that the left-hand side of a minimal expansion rule consist only of a minimal tree (i.e., that the context be empty); in other words, we will require that trees $\tau^0, \tau^1, \tau^2, \ldots, \tau^n$, which enter into representations (5) and (6), be unit trees. It is natural to call such rules CONTEXT-FREE (minimal expansion) rules; grammars which contain only such rules will be called CONTEXT-FREE Δ-GRAMMARS.

Thus, we have defined four classes of syntactic Δ-grammars, which form the following hierarchy: arbitrary syntactic Δ-grammars $\supset$ expansive syntactic Δ-grammars $\supset$ minimal syntactic Δ-grammars $\supset$ context-free syntactic Δ-grammars.

3. SPECIAL ELEMENTARY TRANSFORMATIONS.
A UNIVERSAL SYNTACTIC Δ-GRAMMAR

From the substantive description of the transition from certain deep syntactic structures to others (in the system of paraphrasing; see Žolkovskij and Mel'čuk 1966, 1967a, b; Mel'čuk and Žolkovskij 1970) and from deep structures to surface structures, it can be seen that among the elementary transformations, as defined above, certain highly special elementary transformations are of particular interest from the standpoint of linguistic applications.

These transformations can be subdivided into the following three types:

(1) Splitting a node (growing a new branch): a transformation of the form

$$\begin{array}{ccc} & A & B_a\,C \\ \bullet & \Rightarrow & \bullet \overset{}{\to} \bullet \end{array};$$

here obviously either (a) $f(A) = B$, or (b) $f(A) = C$. Such transformations will be written: (a) $A \Rightarrow a\,(B, C) \mid f(A) = B$; (b) $A \Rightarrow a\,(B, C) \mid f(A) = C$.

(2) Transposing a node (a branch): a transformation of the form

either $\overset{A}{\bullet}\overset{a}{\longrightarrow}\overset{B}{\bullet}\overset{b}{\longrightarrow}\overset{C}{\bullet} \Rightarrow$ (tree with root D, branch a to E, branch b to F)

or (tree with root A, branches a to B and b to C) $\Rightarrow \overset{D}{\bullet}\overset{a}{\to}\overset{E}{\bullet}\overset{b}{\to}\overset{F}{\bullet}$, where, in both cases, $f(A) = D$, $f(B) = E$, $f(C) = F$. These transformations will be written: (a) $a(A, B) \cdot b(B, C) \Rightarrow a(D, E) \cdot b(D, F)$; (b) $a(A, B) \cdot b(A, C) \Rightarrow a(D, E) \cdot b(E, F)$.

(3) Merging nodes (contracting a branch): a transformation of the form

$$\overset{B}{\bullet} \overset{a}{\rightarrow} \overset{C}{\bullet} \overset{A}{\Rightarrow} \overset{}{\bullet};$$

in this case $f(B) = f(C) = A$. This transformation will be written $a(B, C) \Rightarrow A$.

Transformations of types 1-3 will be called SPECIAL.

It turns out that ARBITRARY ELEMENTARY TRANSFORMATIONS, IN A CERTAIN SENSE, ARE FULLY.REDUCIBLE TO SPECIAL TRANSFORMATIONS.

In order to make this statement precise, it is necessary to introduce the concept of the SIMULATION of elementary transformations. Let there be an elementary transformation $t_1 \Rightarrow t_2 \mid f$ and a set M of elementary transformations. Then the expression 'the transformation $t_1 \Rightarrow t_2 \mid f$ can BE SIMULATED by the transformations of M' has the following meaning: there exists a finite sequence of transformations $m_1, m_2, \ldots, m_n$ belonging to M, such that for any trees T and T', if T' can be derived from T by a (single) application of the transformation $t_1 \Rightarrow t_2 \mid f$, then T' can also be derived from T by sequential applications of transformations $m_1, m_2, \ldots, m_n$.

The following theorem holds:

THEOREM 1. Any elementary transformation can be simulated by special elementary transformations.

The proof of Theorem 1, as well as the proofs of Theorems 1' and 2, which will be formulated below, are given in the Appendix, p. 172 ff.

Example. The elementary transformation $\overset{A}{\bullet}\overset{a}{\longrightarrow}\overset{B}{\bullet} \Rightarrow \overset{A}{\bullet}\overset{b}{\longrightarrow}\overset{B}{\bullet}$

where $f(A) = A$ and $f(B) = B$ (i.e., the branch a relabeling), can be replaced by two sequentially applied special transformations:

(1) $A \Rightarrow b (A, C) \mid f(A) = C$ and (2) $a (C, B) \Rightarrow B$.

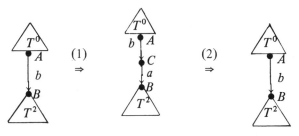

It should be emphasized that the possibility of simulating elementary transformations by other elementary transformations by no means implies that the corresponding grammars are equivalent.[10] It does not follow from Theorem 1 that for any Δ-grammar there exists an equivalent Δ-grammar with only splitting, transposition, and merger rules.[11] This theorem implies only that all the rules of any Δ-grammar can be represented, so to speak, in terms of elementary operations of the three types indicated; however, these operations are not themselves rules of the grammar. They can be carried out only in blocks (each block corresponding to ONE rule of the grammar), and strict order is observed within each block; moreover, the point at which each special transformation applies depends upon the point at which its predecessor applied (it will be recalled that, in particular, a transformation can be applied at several points in the same tree).

From a substantive (i.e., linguistic) point of view, Theorem 1 seems highly significant. It means, in fact, that any transformations of syntactic structures WITHIN A SINGLE SENTENCE which are possible in natural languages, i.e., any purely syntactic transformations of the type 'sentence ⇒ sentence'[12], can be reduced to three simple operations: splitting a node, transposing a node, and merging two nodes (= contracting a branch).

This makes it possible to have a calculus of all conceivable purely syntactic transformations − a UNIVERSAL SYNTACTIC Δ-GRAMMAR. It is necessary to assume only that the finite vocabulary V of branch-labels is sufficient for the expression of any and all syntactic relationships in any and all languages. Then the set π of all transformations of type 1-3 such that the branch-labels which are employed belong to V will also be a finite set.

A syntactic Δ-grammar which consists of a vocabulary V and a set of rules π has the property that, given any tree with labels which belong to V, every other such tree is derivable from it. In other words, any syntactic transformation (any transformation of trees with labels from V) can be represented as a derivation in this universal grammar.

4.   REGULAR SYNTACTIC Δ-GRAMMARS

It is clear that the universal Δ-grammar proposed above is too strong; while it makes available all the reasonable and useful transformations, it also allows for many superfluous transformations which have no natural interpretation. This is related, in particular, to the fact that the trees used for representing sentence structures of natural languages are not arbitrary, but rather belong to more specialized types which are characterized by restrictions on the nature of branching and on the labeling of branches. For example, let us consider the following restrictions: for every label a_i a number n_i is specified such that not more than n_i branches with the label a_i go down from any node (thus the total number of branches going down from each node is not greater than $n_1 + n_2 + \ldots + n_k$, where k is the total number of different labels). There are also other possible types of restrictions; however, we will have recourse only to the type just mentioned, since, in the system of paraphrasing to which we have been referring, deep syntactic structures are considered in which no more than one branch of each of the types 1, 2, 3, 4, and 6 (= COORD), and no more than a certain fixed number of branches of type 5 (= ATTR) may go down from each node (see Žolkovskij and Mel'čuk 1967b:183).

The indicated restriction can be formulated as follows. Consider the matrix

$$\varphi = \begin{pmatrix} a_1, a_2, \ldots, a_k \\ n_1, n_2, \ldots, n_k \end{pmatrix} \quad ,$$

where $a_1, a_2, \ldots, a_k$ are symbols for labels on branches and $n_1, n_2, \ldots, n_k$ are natural numbers. We will say that a tree whose branches are labeled with symbols from the vocabulary $a_1, a_2, \ldots, a_k$ is φ-REGULAR if, for any $i = 1, 2, \ldots, k$, no more than n_i branches labeled with the symbol a_i go down from any node.

It is apparent that the set of φ-regular trees is better suited than the set of arbitrary trees for representing the sentence structure of natural languages. If syntactic Δ-grammars are to be used for the description of transformations in natural syntax, then it is necessary that these grammars preserve the φ-regularity of the trees which are being processed. To this end, it is natural to require, first of all, that the left-hand and the right-hand parts of elementary transformations be φ-regular trees; we will call such elementary transformations φ-REGULAR TRANSFORMATIONS. By definition, a syntactic Δ-grammar is φ-regular if all of its rules are φ-regular elementary transformations.

A derivation in a φ-regular syntactic Δ-grammar is called a φ-DERIVATION if it consists of φ-regular trees only; correspondingly, φ-DERIVABILITY is defined (cf. p. 160).

Remark 1. The concepts of φ-derivation and φ-derivability are necessary because the φ-regularity of an elementary transformation does not in itself guarantee the preservation of φ-regularity of the trees being processed.

Remark 2. At times we will simply use the word 'regular' instead of 'φ-regular.'

Thus we have introduced a special class of syntactic Δ-grammars: φ-REGULAR SYNTACTIC Δ-GRAMMARS. However, the main point here is not so much the introduction of a new class as the change in our viewpoint: from now on we will not be interested in arbitrary derivations in grammars, but only in φ-derivations.

On p. 163 we explored the topic of the simulation of arbitrary elementary transformations by special (elementary) transformations. It is natural to consider the problem of simulation with respect to φ-regular transformations. However, this requires a certain reformulation of the concept of simulation. Let $m = t_1 \Rightarrow t_2 \mid f$ be a φ-regular elementary transformation and M a set of φ-regular elementary transformations; we will say that the transformation m is φ SIMULATED by the transformations of M if there exists a finite sequence $m_1, m_2, \ldots . m_n \in M$ such that for any φ-regular trees T and T', where T' can be derived from T by the application of m, T' can also be derived from T by the sequential application of $m_1, m_2 \ldots, m_n$, and in such a way that all the intermediate trees are φ-regular.

Now we can formulate a theorem for φ-regular elementary transformations which is analogous to Theorem 1 (p. 163):

THEOREM 1'.

Let φ and φ^1 be, respectively, the matrices

$$\begin{pmatrix} a_1, a_2, \ldots, a_k \\ n_1, n_2, \ldots, n_k \end{pmatrix} \text{ and } \begin{pmatrix} a_1, a_2, \ldots, a_k, o \\ n_1, n_2, \ldots, n_k, 1 \end{pmatrix},$$

where o is a symbol different from all a_i, $1 \leqslant i \leqslant k$. Then any φ-regular elementary transformation can be φ^1-simulated by φ^1-regular special elementary transformations. (Of course, every φ-regular tree is also φ^1-regular.)

The import of Theorem 1' lies in the following. Assume that, in accordance with certain purely linguistic considerations, trees with a certain set of labels on their branches and with some restrictions concerning branching are used in the description of the syntax of a language. If we then add one more label to this set — an artificial syntactic relationship with no linguistic interpretation — special transformations will always suffice for the processing of these trees.

It is natural to ask whether the special transformations will not suffice even without the introduction of a supplementary (artificial) relationship. The following theorem provides the answer to this question.

THEOREM 2.

(a) If $n_1 + \ldots + n_k \geqslant 3$, or $n_1 + \ldots + n_k = 1$, then any $\begin{pmatrix} a_1, \ldots, a_k \\ n_1, \ldots, n_k \end{pmatrix}$ -regular elementary transformation can be simulated by $\begin{pmatrix} a_1, \ldots, a_k \\ n_1, \ldots, n_k \end{pmatrix}$ -regular special elementary transformations;

(b) there exist $\begin{pmatrix} a_1, a_2 \\ 1, 1 \end{pmatrix}$-regular and $\begin{pmatrix} a \\ 2 \end{pmatrix}$-regular elementary

transformations which cannot be $\begin{pmatrix} a_1, a_2 \\ 1, 1 \end{pmatrix}$- or $\begin{pmatrix} a_1 \\ 2 \end{pmatrix}$-simulated

by $\begin{pmatrix} a_1, a_2 \\ 1, 1 \end{pmatrix}$- or $\begin{pmatrix} a_1 \\ 2 \end{pmatrix}$-regular special elementary transformations,
respectively.

Theorem 2 indicates another possible approach to a problem which has been occupying the minds of many linguists for a long time — the problem of constructing a universal syntax as a means of describing, in a general way, all of the syntactic structures which are conceivable in natural languages, as well as their transformations.[13] Thus a calculus of syntactic transformations has been proposed in Saumjan 1965. In view of the fact that the idea of universal syntax is so popular with linguists, it would seem useful to write a simple universal regular Δ-grammar in explicit form.

If the restrictions on branching and the set of syntactic relationships are fixed, it is a simple matter to construct a universal regular Δ-grammar. We will produce such a grammar for the deep syntactic structures which conform to the restrictions indicated on p. 165, i.e., the underlying structures introduced in Žolkovskij and Mel'čuk 1966, 1967a, b. Six types of syntactic relationships are distinguished there: 1, 2, 3, 4, 5, 6; no more than one relationship of each of the types 1−4 and 6 may go down from each node, nor may more than 10 relationships of type 5. Each relationship of types 1−4 is interpreted as a relationship between a predicate and its corresponding argument[14], each relationship of type 5 is interpreted as a relationship between an element modified and its modifier (in the broadest sense of the word 'modifier'), and each relationship of type 6 is interpreted as a relationship between two consecutive coordinated units. The number 10 was chosen as an upper estimate of the number of possible non-conjoined modifiers for a single element being modified. (Later the relationships 5 and 6 have been renamed: ATTR and COORD, respectively; however, this does not change anything in our reasoning below.)

Thus, the universal $\begin{pmatrix} 1, 2, 3, 4, 5, 6 \\ 1, 1, 1, 1, 10, 1 \end{pmatrix}$-regular syntactic Δ-grammar G_u has a vocabulary $V_u = \{1, 2, 3, 4, 5, 6\}$ (the set of deep syntactic relationships), with $\varphi_u(1) = \varphi_u(2) = \varphi_u(3) = \varphi_u(4) = \varphi_u(6) = 1$, $\varphi_u(5) = 10$, and a set of rules R_u, consisting of the following 80 rules:

(1) 12 splitting rules of the form:
  (a) $A \Rightarrow i(B, C) \mid f(A) = B$
  and (b) $A \Rightarrow i(B, C) \mid f(A) = C$ $(i = 1, \ldots, 6)$;

(2)   62 transposing rules of the form:
    (a) $i(A, B) \cdot j(B, C) \Rightarrow i(D, E) \cdot j(D, F)$
and (b) $i(A, B) \cdot j(A, C) \Rightarrow i(D, E) \cdot j(E, F)$; here $i, j = 1, \ldots, 6$, and either
    $i \neq j$, or $i = j = 5$;
(3)   6 merging rules of the form:
    $i(A, B) \Rightarrow C (i = 1, \ldots, 6)$.

These rules encompass all the conceivable syntactic transformations of natural languages. More precisely, it must not be assumed *a priori* that each of the 80 rules has a counterpart in an observable syntactic transformation in a specific natural language; rather, if this means of describing deep syntactic structures (i.e., our 80 rules) is adopted, then no syntactic transformation in any natural language can be discovered which would not be statable in terms of some combination of (consecutively applied) elementary transformations from the set R_u.

It is obvious, however, that the grammar G_u permits us to describe only the purely syntactic aspect of transformations in natural languages. But in linguistic practice (translation, text compression, abstracting, paraphrasing, etc.) a vital role is played by transformations which affect not only the syntactic construction of a text, but also its lexical composition. A richer model is required for the formalization of these transformations.

5.   LEXICAL-SYNTACTIC Δ-GRAMMARS

Let us consider regular trees whose nodes are labeled with symbols from a finite set W — a VOCABULARY OF INDEXED GENERALIZED LEXEMES. We will call such objects FILLED REGULAR TREES. The elements of the vocabulary W — the INDEXED GENERALIZED LEXEMES — are symbols for ordinary words, abstract words, idiomatic phrases and lexical functions (Žolkovskij and Mel'čuk 1967b:186) supplied with subscripts (= indices; hence the term) for those morphological categories which carry semantic information; for example, number (for nouns), tense, aspect and mood (for verbs), degree of comparison (for adjectives). W is the deep lexicon referred to on p. 154.

A filled tree specifies an actual sentence (up to 'superficial' syntactic and lexical differences). Clearly, the description of transformations in all their aspects (taking also lexical transformations into account) depends upon the construction of grammars of still another type — grammars which would deal not with unfilled regular trees, but with filled regular trees. We will call such grammars (REGULAR) LEXICAL-SYNTACTIC Δ-GRAMMARS.

Regular syntactic Δ-grammars may be regarded as a special case of regular lexical-syntactic Δ-grammars, in which the vocabulary of indexed generalized lexemes consists of a single element, so that all tree-nodes are labeled with the same symbol (which is equivalent to being empty).[15]

Formally speaking, a regular lexical-syntactic Δ-grammar is an ordered quadruple $\langle W, V, \varphi, \pi \rangle$, where W and V are finite sets of symbols (W is a vocabulary of node-labels, i.e., of indexed generalized lexemes, and $V = \{a_i, ..., a_k\}$ is a vocabulary of branch-labels, i.e., types of syntactic relationships); φ is a matrix $\begin{pmatrix} a_1, ..., a_k \\ n_1, ..., n_k \end{pmatrix}$, i.e., a mapping of the set V into the set of natural numbers (cf. p. 165); and π is a finite set of elementary transformations, which are defined below.

We will call a tree whose nodes are labeled with symbols from W, and whose branches are labeled with symbols from V, a W/V-TREE. A symbol which is attached to the node a of some W/V-tree is denoted $\lambda(\alpha)$. The composition of a W/V-tree t_0 (with distinguished nodes $a_1, ..., a_n$) and W/V-trees $t_1, t_2, ..., t_n$ is defined in much the same way as in the case of 'unfilled' trees (p. 156), with the following additional requirement: for every $i = 1, 2, ..., n$, the label at the node a_i of the resulting tree coincides with the label at the top node of the tree t_i (and not with the label at the node a_i of t_0). We will continue to use the notation which was introduced on p. 157 for the composition of W/V-trees.

By definition, a W/V-tree is φ-regular if for any $a \in V$ no more than $\varphi(a)$ branches with the label a go down from any one of its nodes.

An ordered triple $\langle t_1, t_2, f \rangle$ (or $t_1 \Rightarrow t_2 \mid f$) will be called an elementary transformation in a given grammar G, where t_1 and t_2 are regular W/V-trees and f is a mapping of the set of nodes of the tree t_1 into the set of nodes of the tree t_2.

Where it seems necessary we will speak of the elementary transformations just defined as $\begin{pmatrix} a_1, a_2, ..., a_k \\ n_1, n_2, ..., n_k \end{pmatrix}$ -regular.

The W/V-tree T' is said to be derived from the regular W/V-tree T by the elementary transformation $t_1 \Rightarrow t_2 \mid f$ if T and T' can be represented as:

$$T = C(T^0; a_0 \mid C(t_1; a_1, a_2, ..., a_n \mid T^1, T^2, ..., T^n))$$

and

$$T' = C(T^0; a_0 \mid C(t_2; f(a_1), f(a_2), ..., f(a_n) \mid T^1, T^2, ..., T^n)),$$

where a_0 is a terminal node of the tree T^0, $a_1, a_2, ..., a_n$ is a repetition-free enumeration of the nodes of the tree t_1, and T' is regular.

Of course, the result of the application of an elementary transformation is defined up to an isomorphism, just as it was for 'unfilled' trees; the definition of isomorphism for W/V-trees can be derived from the definition on p. 156 by adding an additional requirement: if a_2 is the image of the node a_1, then $\lambda(a_1) = \lambda(a_2)$.

φ-derivation and φ-derivability are defined for a regular lexical-syntactic Δ-grammar in exactly the same way as they were for syntactic Δ-grammars; see p. 160.

Within the class of regular lexical-syntactic Δ-grammars (LS grammars), it is possible to distinguish subclasses which are perfectly analogous to the subclasses of syntactic grammars (pp. 160–162); the corresponding definitions are, in essence, the same.

If we wish to preserve the special transformations (pp. 162–163) in LS grammars, it will be useful to introduce a supplementary convention. We will assume that the vocabulary W always contains a special symbol w_0 – an 'empty lexeme'[16] ; then the definitions of the transformations of types 1-3 can be reformulated for W/V-trees in the following way.

(1) Splitting a node: $\overset{A}{\bullet} \overset{B}{\Rightarrow} \overset{a}{\bullet} \overset{C}{\longrightarrow} \overset{}{\bullet}$,

where either (a) $\lambda(A) = \lambda(B)$, $\lambda(C) = w_0$, $f(A) = B$,

or (b) $\lambda(A) = \lambda(C)$, $\lambda(B) = w_0$, $f(A) = C$.

(2) Transposing a node (a branch):

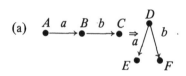

and (b)

where, in both cases, $\lambda(A) = \lambda(D)$, $\lambda(B) = \lambda(E)$, $\lambda(C) = \lambda(F)$, $f(A) = D$, $f(B) = E$, $f(C) = F$.

(3) Merging nodes: $\overset{B}{\bullet} \overset{a}{\longrightarrow} \overset{C}{\bullet} \Rightarrow \overset{A}{\bullet}$,

where either (a) $\lambda(B) = \lambda(A)$, or (b) $\lambda(C) = \lambda(A)$; in both cases $f(B) = f(C) = A$.

Furthermore, still another type of special transformation is necessary for W/V-trees:

(4) Relabeling a node: $\underset{\bullet}{w_i} \Rightarrow \underset{\bullet}{w_j}$, where w_i, $w_j \in W$.

Theorems $1'$ and 2 carry over to LS grammars without change.

A particular manner of writing lexical-syntactic Δ-grammars can be proposed — we will call it the NORMAL FORM — which seems intuitively convenient, at least from the standpoint of eventual applications. More precisely, it is elementary transformations that are written in normal form. The normal form is an ordered pair $\langle \pi, \psi \rangle$, where π is an elementary transformation of trees whose nodes are labeled with natural numbers (these numbers may be repeated) and ψ is the mapping of a finite set of natural numbers into W. The common notation of an elementary transformation is derived from the normal form by filling the nodes in both sides of the transformation in the following way: if the number n of some node belongs to the domain of ψ, then the generalized lexeme $\psi(n)$ is inserted into that node; otherwise, an arbitrary generalized lexeme is inserted in such a way that identical lexemes will appear in nodes which have identical numbers. Thus a single normal form corresponds, in general, to many elementary transformations. In essence, the normal-form notation for an elementary transformation implies the subdivision of this transformation into a syntactic (π) component and a lexical (ψ) component; this corresponds to the division of paraphrase rules into syntactic and lexical rules (Žolkovskij and Mel'čuk 1967b: 189ff). This subdivision increases the explanatory power of a description, since it makes it possible to state the similarities and differences between transformations independently for the syntactic and lexical aspects. Furthermore, the normal-form notation leads to considerable economy. Instead of a list Π of elementary transformations, three lists are used: a list of the first components of the corresponding normal forms (i.e., a list of all π's); a list of the second components (a list of all ψ's); and a list of the correspondences between the numbers of the various π's in the first list, on the one hand, and the numbers of the various ψ's in the second list on the other (i.e., a list of statements indicating which lexical insertions are possible for which syntactic rules, or, equivalently, which syntactic rules are necessary for which lexical substitutions). These three lists should be smaller in total size than the single list Π, since the various π's combine with the various ψ's in many different ways, not to mention the fact that a single normal form can represent many elementary transformations.

This concludes our exposition of the basic formal concepts which relate to Δ-grammars. The linguistic interpretation of these concepts can be found in Gladkij and Mel'čuk 1974, where an illustrative example of a Δ-grammar for Russian is given, which describes the transformations between deep- and surface-syntactic structures of Russian sentences.

APPENDIX
PROOFS OF THE THREE THEOREMS CONCERNING THE SIMULATION OF
ELEMENTARY TRANSFORMATIONS BY SPECIAL TRANSFORMATIONS

Theorem 1 (p. 163).

Any elementary transformation can be simulated by special elementary transformations.

Proof. Assume that $t_1 \Rightarrow t_2 \mid f$ is an arbitrary elementary transformation, and that the tree T' is derived from the tree T by the application of this transformation, i.e.

$$T = C(T^0; \alpha_0 \mid C(t_1; \; \alpha_1, \alpha_2, \ldots, \alpha_n \mid T^1, T^2, \ldots, T^n))$$

and

$$T' = C(T^0; \alpha_0 \mid C(t_2; f(\alpha_1), f(\alpha_2), \ldots, f(\alpha_n) \mid T^1, T^2, \ldots, T^n)),$$

where α_0 is a terminal node of T^0 and $\alpha_1, \alpha_2, \ldots, \alpha_n$ is a repetition-free enumeration of the nodes of t_1.

We will construct a sequence of transformations of types 1-3 which will transform T into T' and which will depend only upon t_1, t_2, and f, such that for any trees T and T', where T' is derived from T by the application of the given transformation, T' will also be derivable from T by this sequence of transformations. This will constitute a proof of the theorem.

The required sequence will be constructed as follows:

(1) Apply a transformation of type 1b to the node $\alpha_0 = A$ of the tree T: $A \Rightarrow a(B, A) \mid f(A) = A$, where a is an arbitrary symbol from the vocabulary (Figs. 1a and b; the tree T before the transformation is represented in 1a, and after the transformation, in 1b).

(2) Applying transformations of type 1a the required number of times, grow a tree isomorphic to t_2 from B as the top node; this tree will henceforth be written simply as t_2 (Figure 1c).

(3) Applying transformations of type 2a the required number of times, transpose (= move) a terminal branch of the tree $\bar{t}_1$ which terminates in the node α_i (obviously, this node belongs to t_1 and is terminal in it) to the node B — moving, of course, together with this branch the full α_i-subtree[17] of T. This subtree coincides with T^i, since there is no branch belonging to t_1 which goes down from α_i.

The remainder of $\bar{t}_1$, i.e., the tree which remains after the branch terminating in α_i has been removed, will be referred to as $\bar{t}_1'$.

The result of step (3) is represented in Figure 1d (assuming $i = 1$).

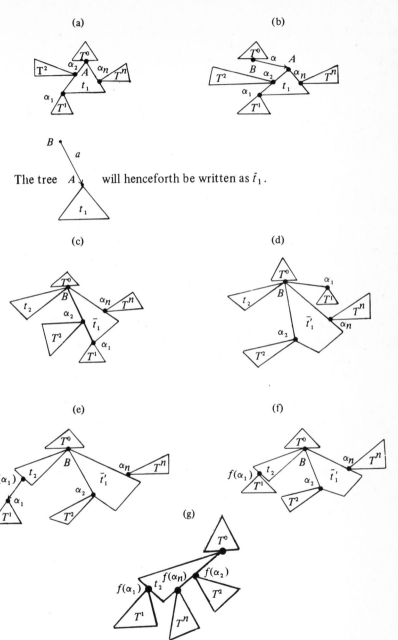

Figure 1

(4) Applying transformations of type 2b the required number of times, transpose the branch which terminates in α_i, together with the tree T^i which hangs from it, to the node $f(\alpha_i)$ of the tree t_2 (Figure 1e). If $f(\alpha_i)$ is the top node of t_2, there is no need of this step.

(5) Applying a transformation of type 3, merge the node α_i with the node $f(\alpha_i)$ (Figure 1f).

(6) Repeat steps (3), (4) and (5) in application to a terminal branch of the tree $\bar{t}_i'$ (this branch need not be necessarily terminal in the tree $\bar{t}_1$). Then, repeat again the same steps in application to one of the terminal branches of the tree which remains now of $\bar{t}_1$, etc., until the tree $\bar{t}_1$ is fully 'dismantled'. The result of all these operations is represented in Figure 1g.

It is clear that the tree which has been derived coincides with T'. It is also obvious that the sequence of transformations which has been constructed is not dependent upon the form of the trees $T^0, T^1, T^2, ..., T^n$. The theorem is, therefore, proved.

Example. Let us consider the elementary transformation π:

$$A \overset{a}{\underset{\bullet \longrightarrow \bullet}{B}} \Rightarrow A \overset{b}{\underset{\bullet \longrightarrow \bullet}{B}}, \text{ where } f(A) = A, f(B) = B \text{ (relabeling a branch).}$$

The sequence of special transformations which replaces the indicated transformation and which is constructed in the manner described in the proof of the theorem, may have the form: (1) $A \Rightarrow c(C, A) \mid f(A) = A$; (2) $C \Rightarrow b(C, D) \mid f(C) = C$; (3) $c(C, A) \cdot a(A, B) \Rightarrow c(C, A) \cdot a(C, B)$; (4) $b(C, D) \cdot a(C, B) \Rightarrow b(C, D) \cdot a(D, B)$; (5) $a(D, B) \Rightarrow D$; (6) $c(C, A) \Rightarrow C$ (here, c is an arbitrary symbol from the vocabulary).

The successive stages of the tree undergoing transformations are represented in Figure 2, a-g.

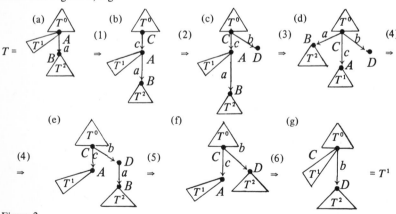

Figure 2

Tree 2g is isomorphic to the tree which can be derived from the tree 2a by the elementary transformation π, and, consequently, can itself be derived from the tree 2a by this transformation.

We chose the sequence of special transformations just presented in order to illustrate the general reasoning used in the proof of the theorem. There is another, simpler way of simulating the relabeling of a branch by special transformations (see p. 163).

Theorem $1'$ (p. 166).
Let φ and φ^1 be, respectively, the matrices

$$\begin{pmatrix} a_1, a_2, \ldots, a_k \\ n_1, n_2, \ldots, n_k \end{pmatrix} \text{ and } \begin{pmatrix} a_1, a_2, \ldots, a_k, o \\ n_1, n_2, \ldots, n_k, 1 \end{pmatrix},$$

where o is a symbol different from all a_i, $1 \leqslant i \leqslant k$. Then any φ-regular elementary transformation can be φ^1-simulated by φ^1-regular special elementary transformations.

Proof. First notice that any $\begin{pmatrix} a_1 \\ 1 \end{pmatrix}$-regular elementary transformation can be simulated even by $\begin{pmatrix} a_1 \\ 1 \end{pmatrix}$-regular special transformations. In fact, $\begin{pmatrix} a_1 \\ 1 \end{pmatrix}$-regular trees are trees without branching and all of their branches are labeled with the same symbol (which is equivalent to the absence of any label). Therefore, any $\begin{pmatrix} a_1 \\ 1 \end{pmatrix}$-regular elementary transformation has the form

$$\begin{array}{ccccccccccc} \bullet \!\longrightarrow\! \bullet \!\longrightarrow\! \bullet & \cdots & \bullet \!\longrightarrow\! \bullet & \!\!\Longrightarrow\!\! & \bullet \!\longrightarrow\! \bullet \!\longrightarrow\! \bullet & \cdots & \bullet \!\longrightarrow\! \bullet & \mid f, \\ A_0 \quad A_1 \quad A_2 & & A_{n\text{-}1} \; A_n & & B_0 \quad B_1 \quad B_2 & & B_{m\text{-}1} \; B_m \end{array}$$

where $f(A_n) = B_m$ (the values of f for the rest of the nodes are immaterial, since nothing can hang from them anyway); obviously, such a transformation can be simulated by $\begin{pmatrix} a_1 \\ 1 \end{pmatrix}$-regular transformations of type 1b (if $n < m$), or type 3 (if $n > m$).

Thus, we can assert that $n_1 + n_2 + \ldots + n_k \geqslant 2$. For this case, the proof of Theorem $1'$ can be derived by the following modification of the proof of Theorem 1. First, after step (1) (the result of which is represented in Figure 1b) we must apply to the node B the transformation $B \Rightarrow b \, (B, C) \mid f(B) = B$, where b is an arbitrary symbol from the vocabulary such that the branches labeled a and b can go down from the same node in a $\begin{pmatrix} a_1, a_2, \ldots, a_k \\ n_1, n_2, \ldots, n_k \end{pmatrix}$-regular

tree. The tree T' (Figure 3) which is derived in this way is
$\begin{pmatrix} a_1, a_2, \ldots, a_k \\ n_1, n_2, \ldots, n_k \end{pmatrix}$-regular, since the node B is terminal in the tree T^0.

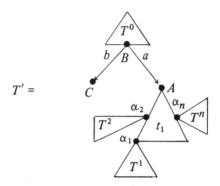

$$T' =$$

Figure 3

Then the steps in the proof of Theorem 1 are repeated, with the following changes:

(a) the tree t_2 is grown from C instead of B;

(b) before each successive branch $c\,(\alpha_j, \alpha_i)$ is moved from the tree t_1 to the tree t_2, it is relabeled, receiving the label o; this is accomplished by means of two transformations of the form $\alpha_j \Rightarrow o\,(\alpha_j, \beta) \mid f\,(\alpha_j) = \beta$, and $c\,(\beta, \alpha_i) \Rightarrow \alpha_i$; consequently, $\begin{pmatrix} a_1, a_2, \ldots, a_k, o \\ n_1, n_2, \ldots, n_k, 1 \end{pmatrix}$-regularity is not disturbed;

(c) after the tree t_1 is 'dismantled', the branch $b(B, C)$ is contracted.

It is clear that if at some step of such a sequence of transformations the tree is not $\begin{pmatrix} a_1, a_2, \ldots, a_k \\ n_1, n_2, \ldots, n_k \end{pmatrix}$-regular, it can be due only to the fact that an 'extra' branch labeled with the symbol o goes down from one of its nodes; and such a tree is $\begin{pmatrix} a_1, a_2, \ldots, a_k, o \\ n_1, n_2, \ldots, n_k, 1 \end{pmatrix}$-regular.

Thus, Theorem 1' is proved.

Theorem 2 (p. 166).

(a) If $n_1 + \ldots + n_k \geqslant 3$ or $n_1 + \ldots + n_k = 1$, then any $\begin{pmatrix} a_1, \ldots, a_k \\ n_1, \ldots, n_k \end{pmatrix}$-regular elementary transformation can be simulated by $\begin{pmatrix} a_1, \ldots, a_k \\ n_1, \ldots, n_k \end{pmatrix}$-regular special elementary transformations;

(b) there exist $\begin{pmatrix} a_1, a_2 \\ 1, \ 1 \end{pmatrix}$ -regular and $\begin{pmatrix} a_1 \\ 2 \end{pmatrix}$ -regular elementary transformations

which cannot be $\begin{pmatrix} a_1, a_2 \\ 1, \ 1 \end{pmatrix}$ - or $\begin{pmatrix} a_1 \\ 2 \end{pmatrix}$ -simulated by $\begin{pmatrix} a_1, a_2 \\ 1, \ 1 \end{pmatrix}$ - or $\begin{pmatrix} a_1 \\ 2 \end{pmatrix}$ -regular

special elementary transformations, respectively.

Proof. (a) For the case of $n_1 + \ldots + n_k = 1$, the theorem has already been proven. Henceforth it will be assumed that $n_1 + \ldots + n_k \geqslant 3$.

Let us begin to transform the tree T, represented in Figure 1a, in the same way as was done in the proof of Theorem $1'$. After the tree has been brought to the form represented in Figure 3 (p. 174), we will transform its subtree t_1 in the following way. Let us take an arbitrary node α_j of this subtree on which the tree T^j hangs; generally speaking, there are several branches of the tree t_1 going down from α_j and terminating in the nodes $\beta_1, \ldots, \beta_p$ (Figure 4a; γ denotes a node which immediately dominates α_j).

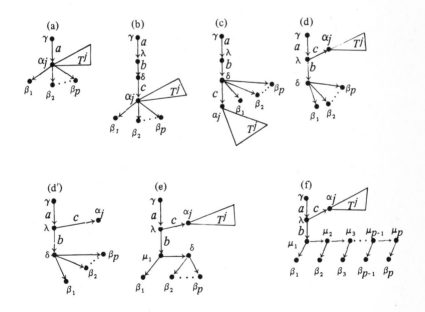

Figure 4

If the node α_j is 'unsaturated' in the tree t_1, i.e., if at least one extra branch can be grown from it without disturbing the regularity of t_1 (the regularity of the entire tree is here not at issue), we can do the following. Applying transformations of type 1b twice, we cause the tree of Figure 4a to appear as in Figure 4b. The symbol c is chosen so as to be compatible with the symbols which label the branches going down from α_j (i.e., so that it is possible to grow from α_j a branch labeled with this symbol without disturbing the regularity of t_1), and symbol b is chosen so as to be compatible with c. Then, using transformations of type 2a, we move all the branches of t_1 which go down from α_j onto δ (Figure 4c) and after this we move the branch c (δ, α_j) onto λ (Figure 4d). The derived tree will be regular due to the choice of the symbols b and c.

If node α_j is 'saturated' in t_1 then, instead of the sequence of transformations just described, the following is done: the transformation $\alpha_j \Rightarrow b(\lambda, \delta) \mid f(\alpha_j) = \delta$ is applied to the node α_j, and then the transformation $\lambda \Rightarrow c(\lambda, \alpha_j) \mid f(\lambda) = \lambda$ is applied to the node λ; as for symbols b and c, it is required only that they be mutually compatible. As a result of this, the tree shown in Figure 4d' will be derived; it coincides, in this case, with the tree represented in Figure 4d, since it follows from the 'saturatedness' of the node α_j in t_1 that $T^j = \mathcal{E}$.

The tree shown in Figure 4d is further transformed into the tree of Figure 4e, the branch (μ_1, δ) being labeled with a symbol which is compatible with the one on the branch (μ_1, β_1). (This is accomplished by means of one transformation of type 1b and one of type 2a; the regularity is, obviously, not disturbed.) Repeating the last step the necessary number of times, we will finally derive the tree represented in Figure 4f.

We shall proceed in this way with all the nodes of t_1. After this, the latter will become t_1^*, in which no more than two branches go down from each node, and trees $T^1, \ldots, T^n$ hang from the terminal branches of the tree t_1^*.

Subsequent transformations proceed as follows. Grow the tree t_2^{**} from the node C (Figure 3) as the top, t_2^{**} being related to t_2 as t_1^* is related to t_1, but with the difference that it does not contain the branches from which the trees $T^1, \ldots, T^n$ hung in the tree t_1^* (so that each 'macrobranch' of t_2^{**} differs from the corresponding 'macrobranch' of t_1^* by the absence of the branch c (λ, α_j) and the tree T^j, which hangs from this branch). Then transpose every T^j, together with the branch of t_1^* from which it hangs, to the corresponding position in t_2^{**} (i.e., to the node of the 'macrobranch' corresponding to the node $f(\alpha_j)$ of t_2, where this 'macrobranch' originates; this node corresponds to the node λ in Figure 4f). The tree which is derived from t_2^{**} as a result of all these transpositions will be denoted t_2^*. After this we will 'dismantle' the remainder of t_1^*, contract branches (B, A) and (B, C) to points and, finally, transform t_2^* into t_2. It is clear that the tree which is derived in this way coincides with T'; it is necessary only to make sure that all of the described transformations can be carried out without disturbing the regularity.

1) Since the tree t_2^{**} is regular, it is clear that when it is grown, regularity will not be disturbed.

2) When a terminal branch of t_1^* is moved into the corresponding position in t_2^{**} (along with the tree T^j which hangs from it), this branch first 'ascends' along a path such that not more than one branch which does not belong to this path goes down from each of its nodes, and then 'descends' by another path which has the same property. It is sufficient to show that just one step of 'ascending' and 'descending' can be carried out without disturbing the regularity. For example, assume that we want to 'raise' the branch $c(B, C)$ from the node B to the node A, and A already has two branches going down from it: $b(A, B)$ and $d(A, D)$ (Figure 5a).

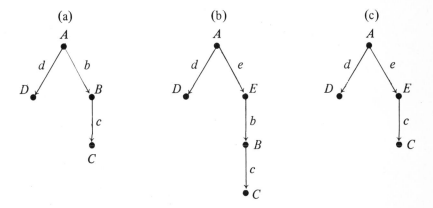

Figure 5

If symbols b, c, and d are mutually compatible, this is accomplished by one transformation of type 2a. Otherwise, at least one of the symbols b, d will be compatible with c[18]; let us assume, in this case, that it is d. Then a symbol e can be found such that c, d, and e are compatible[19]. After the branch $b(A, B)$ has correspondingly been relabeled, as shown in Figure 5b, c (it can clearly be seen that regularity is not disturbed by this), we can 'raise' the branch $c(E, C)$, without loss of regularity, by a transformation of type 2a. We can proceed in the same way, of course, if the branch $d(A, D)$ is absent. The 'descending' of a branch is carried out analogously with the only modification that we must, when necessary, carry out the reverse relabeling of the branches by which the descending branch has 'passed' — because we should not alter the tree t_2^{**}. (It is not necessary to do this in the case of 'raising', since we are not concerned with the preservation of t_1^*; it is destined to be 'dismantled' in any event.)

3) 'Dismantling' the tree which remains of t_1^* is carried out by means of transformations of type 3, applying them always to terminal branches; it is obvious that this cannot disturb regularity.

4) The liquidation of the branch BA is also carried out by means of a transformation of type 3; this branch will be terminal by the time this transformation is applied. Regularity will not be disturbed during the liquidation of the branch BC, due to the fact that node $B = a_0$ is terminal in T^0.

5) Finally, the transformation of t_2^* into t_2 is carried out by means of a procedure which is the exact converse of that which transformed t_1 into t_1^*. Taking into account the fact that the ultimate result of this procedure is a regular tree, it can be concluded that this procedure does not disturb regularity.

This concludes the proof of the assertion (a) of Theorem 2.

(b) Let us consider now the $\binom{a_1}{2}$ -regular elementary transformation

$\pi: t_1 \Rightarrow t_2 \mid f$, where:

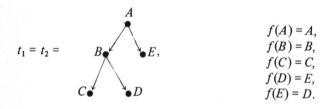

$$t_1 = t_2 = \qquad \begin{matrix} & A & \\ B & & E, \\ C & & D \end{matrix} \qquad \begin{aligned} f(A) &= A, \\ f(B) &= B, \\ f(C) &= C, \\ f(D) &= E, \\ f(E) &= D. \end{aligned}$$

(The labels on the branches are not shown, since they are all identical.) We will show that π cannot be simulated by a $\binom{a_1}{2}$ -regular special transformation.

Let us assume the contrary: assume that there exists a sequence of $\binom{a_1}{2}$ - regular special transformations $\pi_1, \pi_2, \ldots, \pi_n$, which can replace π. This sequence should transform the tree T into the tree T' (Figure 6):

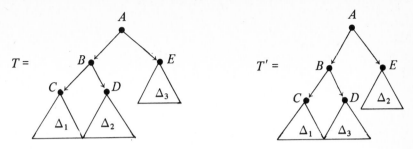

Figure 6

Here Δ_1, Δ_2, Δ_3 are pairwise distinct trees such that there are two branches going down from the top node of each Δ_i. Transformations π_1, ..., π_p cannot affect trees Δ_1, Δ_2, Δ_3 (since the same sequence of transformations must also transform the 'bare' t_1 into itself).

Let us construct two sequences of trees τ_0, τ_1, ..., τ_p and T_0, T_1, ..., T_p, where each τ_i is a subtree of T_i, as follows: $\tau_0 = t_1$; $T_0 = T$; τ_{i+1} is the image of the tree τ_i under an application of the transformation π_{i+1}; T_{i+1} is the image of T_i under the same application of the same transformation. In general, these sequences are constructed non-uniquely (since the possibility is not excluded that the transformation π_{i+1} can apply to τ_i in different ways), but they can be constructed in such a way that τ_p coincides with t_2, and T_p coincides with T'; we will assume that this condition is met. For any node M of τ_i as a subtree of T_i, the set of the numbers of trees Δ_1, Δ_2, Δ_3, which hang in T_i from those nodes of τ_i which are dependent on M, will be called the CHARACTERISTIC of M in T_i (notation: $x(M)$). For example, in the tree $T_0 = T$ (see Figure 6) the node A has the characteristic $\{1, 2, 3\}$, the node B has the characteristic $\{1, 2\}$, and the node C, the characteristic $\{1\}$. We will prove that the characteristic of each node of the tree T_{i+1} either coincides with the characteristic of one of the nodes of the tree T_0, or is equal to $\emptyset$ ($\emptyset$ is the empty set). This will lead us to a contradiction, since the node B in $T_p = T'$ (see Figure 6) has the characteristic $\{1, 3\}$, but none of the nodes of T_0 has this characteristic. It is sufficient to examine how the characteristics of the nodes which are directly affected by the transformation π_{i+1} change; the characteristics of the other nodes obviously remain unchanged.

We will carry out the proof by an analysis of cases which correspond to the possible types of transformations.

(1a) $\overset{M}{\bullet} \overset{P}{\Rightarrow} \overset{P}{\bullet} \longrightarrow \overset{Q}{\bullet}$, $f(M) = P$. Here, obviously, $x(P) = x(M)$, $x(Q) = \emptyset$.

(1b) $\overset{M}{\bullet} \overset{P}{\Rightarrow} \overset{P}{\bullet} \longrightarrow \overset{Q}{\bullet}$, $f(M) = Q$. Here, $x(P) = x(Q) = x(M)$.

(2a) $K \xrightarrow{} L \xrightarrow{} M$ $\Rightarrow$ [tree with top node P branching down to Q and R] , $f(K) = P, f(L) = Q, f(M) = R.$

First, it is clear that $x(R) = x(M)$. It is also obvious that $x(P) = x(K)$. Furthermore, if there are no branches other than (L, M) going down from L, then there are no branches at all going down from Q, so that $x(Q) = \emptyset$. However, if there is one other branch going down from L, say, (L, D), it is impossible for there to be more than one branch going down from L and different from (L, M). Then this branch belongs to τ_i (otherwise L would be the top node of one of the trees $\Delta_1, \Delta_2, \Delta_3$, but in each of these trees there are already two branches going down from the top node); in this case there is precisely one branch going down from Q, i.e. (Q, D), and it belongs to τ_{i+1}, therefore $x(Q) = x(D)$.

(2b) [tree with top node K branching down to L and M] $\Rightarrow$ $P \xrightarrow{} Q \xrightarrow{} R$, $f(K) = P, f(L) = Q, f(M) = R.$

Here, obviously, $x(R) = x(M)$, $x(Q) = x(L) \cup x(M) = x(K)$ (this last equality follows from the fact that there are no branches going down from K other than (K, L) and (K, M)), $x(P) = x(K)$).

(3) $K \xrightarrow{} L \Rightarrow P$, $f(K) = f(L) = P$. Here $x(P) = x(K)$.

Thus we have proved the assertion (b) of Theorem 2 for $\binom{a_1}{2}$ -regular transformations. However, if we place labels a_1 and a_2 on the branches of the trees t_1 and t_2 which we have been considering, in any way which would provide $\binom{a_1, a_2}{1, 1}$ -regularity, and then repeat the subsequent reasoning word-for-word, we will obtain a proof of the assertion (b) for $\binom{a_1, a_2}{1, 1}$ -regular transformations.

NOTES

The original version of this article appeared in Russian in the 1st issue of *Informacionnye voprosy semiotiki, lingvistiki i avtomatičeskogo perevoda* [Informational Problems of Semiotics, Linguistics and Automatic Translation] (Moscow, 1971), 16-41. A preliminary version of it has been published in English as a preprint for the 1969 Concerence on Computational Linguistics, Sånga-Säby, Sweden (Gladkij and Mel'čuk 1969). Reprinted from *Linguistics*, 150, 1975, 47-82.

1. Syntax is to be taken in its broadest sense – as laws, or rules, for building up linguistic units (words, phrases, clauses, sentences) from simpler components.
2. On Meaning ⟺ Text Models see in particular Žolkovskij and Mel'čuk 1966, 1967a,b, Mel'čuk and Žolkovskij 1970; Mel'čuk 1974.
3. In connection with this cf. Worth 1964; and Zaliznjak and Padučeva 1964.
4. Concerning different representations of syntactic structure in natural languages (in particular, about dependency trees) see, for example, Padučeva 1964; Hays 1964; Gladkij 1973: 282-310; Mel'čuk 1979: 3-21.
5. Natural languages typically have such rich means of synonymy at their disposal that a rather complex sentence may have hundreds of thousands or even millions of more or less synonymous paraphrases; see, for example, Žolkovskij and Mel'čuk 1967b: 179-80.
6. It is possible that deriving the DSS's from the input meaning representation is related to the problem of 'extracting' from a graph all of its subtrees which have certain given properties. A solution for such a problem, arising from linguistic considerations, is proposed in Babickij 1965.
7. A node is called TERMINAL if there are no branches going down from it; a branch which enters a terminal node is also called TERMINAL.
8. Note that one of the nodes $a_1, a_2, \ldots, a_n$ coincides with a_0.
9. It should be emphasized that the nodes $a_1, a_2, \ldots, a_n$ are pairwise distinct, while $f(a_1), f(a_2), \ldots, f(a_n)$ are not necessarily pairwise distinct.
10. It is natural to call two Δ-grammars EQUIVALENT, if, for any two trees T and T', the derivability of T' from T in one grammar is equivalent to the derivability of T' from T in the other.
11. In particular, any Δ-grammar in which the difference between the number of nodes in the left- and right-hand part of each rule is greater than one can serve as an example of a Δ-grammar which has no equivalent Δ-grammar with rules of only these types.
12. Operations which combine two sentences into one or split one sentence into two are considered to be transformations of another type.
13. The same is true for Theorems 1 and 1' (cf. pp. 163 and 166). However, Theorem 2 provides a better approach to universal syntax, since Theorem 1' assumes the introduction of an artificial, uninterpreted relationship.
14. Thus, predicates are considered which have no more than four places. This is explained by the interesting fact that words which denote predicates with a greater number of places are encountered only rarely in natural languages. An example of a four-place predicate is the verb *punish*: who (subject), whom (object), for what (motive), and how (nature of the punishment), e.g., *The management punished him for his frequent tardiness by a reduction in pay*. Still, as Ju. D. Apresjan has shown, predicate words with up to six places are possible: e.g., the Russian verb *komandirovat'* 'send in mission': who (subject), whom (object), where (destination), from where (origin), to do what (purpose, goal), for how long (term): *Ego komandirovali iz Moskvy na Kamčatku za ikroj na dva mesjaca* 'They sent him in mission from Moscow to Kamchatka to get some caviar for two months'.

Trying to take care of such cases would raise the number of rules in our universal
Δ-grammar without modifying it essentially.

15. Lexical-syntactic Δ-grammars are the most general of the classes of Δ-grammars
which we consider. Therefore, the name 'Δ-grammars' would be more in keeping with the
generally-accepted method of constructing terminology. However, we have retained the
redundant adjective 'lexical-syntactic' in connection with the use of an analogous term in
the linguistic interpretation we have adopted.

16. The empty lexeme is introduced only for the sake of naturalness; it is possible to do
without it if we decide to accept any indexed generalized lexeme as $\lambda(C)$ in transformations of type 1a and as $\lambda(B)$ in transformations of type 1b. It might be noted that, in
this case, it is not necessary to include the re-labeling of a node among the special
transformations; it can be replaced by one transformation of type 1b and one of type 3a.

17. If a is a node of the tree τ, then we call the subtree τ' which consists of all the nodes
which depend upon a (including a itself) the FULL a-SUBTREE OF THE TREE τ. In
other words, this is a subtree τ' of τ such that τ can be represented in the form
$\tau = C(\tau^0, a \mid \tau')$, given an appropriate τ^0 (the node a is terminal in τ^0).

18. Any two different symbols are mutually compatible, if $b = c = d = a_1$, then $n_1 \geq 2$, so
that any two 'copies' of a_1 are compatible.

19. If $n_1 + \ldots + n_k \geq 3$, then for any two compatible symbols a_{i_1} and a_{i_2} there exists a
symbol a_{i_3} such that all three symbols $a_{i_1}, a_{i_2},$ and a_{i_3} are compatible. In fact, if $k > 2$,
and also if $k = 2$ and $i_1 = i_2$, this is immediately clear; if $k = 2$ and $i_1 = 1, i_2 = 2$, then,
necessarily, either $n_1 > 1$ or $n_2 > 1$, so that, for example, if $n_2 > 1$ the symbol a_2 is
compatible with a_1 and with yet another copy of a_2; if $k = 1$, then any three copies
of a (single) symbol are compatible.

REFERENCES

Arapov, M. V., and V. B. Borščev
 1967   'Sintaksičeskaja model' jazykov s bogatoj flektivnoj sistemoj i svobodnym
     porjadkom slov' [A Syntactic Model for Languages Having a Rich Inflectional
     System| and Free Word Order], *Trudy III Vsesojuznoj konferencii po IPS i
     avtomatizirovannoj obrabotke NTI* [Proceedings of the Third National
     Conference on IR Systems and the Automated Processing of Scientific
     and Technological Information] 2: 16-46. (Moscow).
Arapov, M. V., V. B. Borščev, and Ju.A. Šrejder
 1967   'Jazyk, grammatika, semantika' [Language, Grammar, and Semantics],
     Trudy III Vsesojuznoj konferencii po IPS i avtomatizirovannoj obrabotke NTI
     [Proceedings of the Third National Conference on IR Systems and the
     Automated Processing of Scientific and Technological Information] 2:
     5-15. (Moscow).
Babickij, K. I.
 1965   'O sintaksičeskoj sinonimii predloženij v estestvennyx jazykax' [Syntactic
     Synonymy of Sentences in Natural Languages], *NTI* (6): 29-34.
Baker, B. S.
 1973   'Tree Transductions and Families of Tree Languages' , *ACM Symposium on
     Theory of Computing*, 200-06.
Barbault, M. C., and J. P. Desclés
 1971   'Vers une formalisation des grammaires transformationnelles', *Mathématiques
     et sciences humaines* 34: 27-41.

1972   *Transformations formelles et théories linguistiques* (= *Documents de linguistique quantitative* 11) (Paris).

Beleckij, M. I.
1967   'Beskontekstnye i dominacionnye grammatiki i svjazannye s nimi algoritmičeskie problemy' [Context-free and Dominance Grammars, and Decision Problems Associated with Them], *Kibernetika* 4 : 90-97.

Brainerd, W. S.
1969   'Tree Generating Regular Systems', *Information and Control* 14(2): 217-31.

Chauché, J.
1972   *Arborescences et transformations* (Grenoble).

Chomsky, N.
1965   *Aspects of the Theory of Syntax* (Cambridge, Mass.: M.I.T).

Fitialov, S. Ja.
1968   'Ob èkvivalentnosti grammatik NS i grammatik zavisimostej' [On the Equivalence of PS-grammars and Dependency Grammars], in: *Problemy strukturnoj lingvistiki 1967* [Problems in Structural Linguistics 1967], 71-102. (Moscow: Nauka).

Gavrilova, T. L.
1965   'O strukturnom analize v'etnamskogo teksta i odnom sposobe zapisi ego rezul'tatov' [A Structural Analysis of a Vietnamese Text, and a Representation of the Results], *Problemy kibernetiki* 13: 201-20.

Ginsburg, S., and B. Partee
1969   'A Mathematical Model of Transformational Grammars', *Information and Control* 15(2): 262-334.

Gladkij, A. V.
1973   *Formal'nye grammatiki i jazyki* [Formal Grammars and Languages](Moscow: Nauka).

Gladkij, A. V., and I. A. Mel'čuk
1969   'Tree Grammars (Δ-grammars)', *International Conference on Computational Linguistics* (COLING-69) (Stockholm).
1974   'Grammatiki derev'ev. II. K postroeniju Δ -grammatik dlja russkogo jazyka' [Tree Grammars, II: Towards a Δ-grammar for Russian], *Informacionnye voprosy semiotiki, lingvjstiki i avtomatičeskogo perevoda* [Informational Problems of Semiotics, Linguistics and Automatic Translation] 4: 4-29. (Moscow).

Hays, D.
1964   'Dependency Theory: A Formalism and Some Observations', *Language* 40(4): 511-25.

Hockett, C. F.
1967   *Language, Mathematics, and Linguistics* (The Hague: Mouton).

Katz, J. J., and J. A. Fodor
1963   'The Structure of a Semantic Theory', *Language* 39(1): 170-210.

Katz, J. J., and P. Postal
1964   *An Integrated Theory of Linguistic Descriptions* (Cambridge, Mass.: M.I.T.).

Kolmogorov, A. N., and V. A. Uspenskij
1958   'K opredeleniju algoritma' [Toward a Definition of 'Algorithm'], *Uspexi matematičeskix nauk* [Developments in Mathematical Sciences] 13(4): 3-28.

Kulagina, O. S.
1969   *Nekotorye voprosy preobrazovanij derev'ev zavisimostej* [Certain Questions

Concerning the Transformation of Dependency Trees] (Moscow) (IPM AN SSSR, preprint No. 12); published also in *Problemy kibernetiki* (1971), 24: 161-90.

Lomkovskaja, M. B.
1965   'Isčislenie, poroždajuščee jadernye russkie predloženija' [A Calculus Which Generates Russian Kernel Sentences], *NTI* (7): 33–39; (9): 37–40; (11): 56–65

Mel'čuk, I. A.
1965   'Porjadok slov pri avtomatičeskom sinteze russkogo teksta' [Word Order in Automatic Synthesis of Russian Texts], *NTI* (12): 36–44.
1973   'Towards a Linguistic 'Meaning ⇔ Text' Model', *Trends in Soviet Theoretical Linguistics,* E. Kiefer (ed.) (Dordrecht:D. Reidel), 33-57.
1974   *Opyt teorii lingvističeskix modelej 'Smysl ⇔ Tekst'* [A Theory of Linguistic Models of Meaning ⇔ Text Type] (Moscow:Nauka).
1979   *Studies in Dependency Syntax* (Ann Arbor: Karoma).

Mel'čuk, I.A. and A. K. Žolkovskij
1970   'Towards a Functioning 'Meaning-Text' Model of Language', *Linguistics* 57: 10-47.

Modina, L. S.
1975   'Drevesnye grammatiki i jazyki' [Tree Grammars and Languages], *Kibernetika* 5: 86-93.

Ogden, W., and W. Rounds
1972   'Compositions of *n* Tree Transducers', *Proceedings of the Fourth Annual ACM Symposium on the Theory of Computing,* 198-206.

Padučeva, E. V.
1964   'O sposobax predstavlenija sintaksičeskoj struktury predloženij' [On Representing the Syntactic Structure of Sentences], *Voprosy jazykoznanija* (2): 99-113.

Peters, P. S., and R. W. Ritchie
1973   'On the Generative Power of Transformational Grammars', *Information Sciences* 6(1): 49-83.

Rounds, W. C.
1970   'Mapping and Grammars on Trees", *Mathematical Systems Theory* 4(3): 257-87.

Sgall, P.
1967   *Generativní popis jazyka a česká deklinace* [A Generative Description of Language and the Czech Declension] (Prague).

Šaumjan, S. K.
1965   *Osnovy strukturnoj lingvistiki* [Fundamentals of Structural Linguistics] (Moscow:Nauka).

Tesnière, L.
1959   *Eléments de syntaxe structurale* (Paris:Klincksieck).

Thatcher, J. W.
1970   'Generalized Sequential Machine Maps', *Journal of Computer System Science* 4(4): 339-67.

Varšavskaja, A. I.
1968   'Opyt postroenija grafa, poroždajuščego nekotorye struktury prostogo anglijskogo predloženija' [An Attempt to Construct a Graph Generating Some Simple English Sentence Structures], *NTI*-2 (4): 15-20.

Veillon, G., J. Veyrunes, and B. Vauquois
  1967   'Un métalangage de grammaires transformationnels', in: *2me Conférence internationale sur le traitement automatique des langues* (Grenoble).
Weinreich, U.
  1966   'Explorations in Semantic Theory', in: *Current Trends in Linguistics*, III: *Theoretical Foundations*, 395–477. (London).
Worth, D. S.
  1964   'Ob otobraženii linejnyx otnošenij v poroždajusščix modeljax jazyka' [Representation of Linear Relationships in Generative Models of Language], *Voprosy jazykoznanija* (5): 46-58.
Zaliznjak, A. A., and E. V. Padučeva
  1964   'O svjazi jazyka lingvističeskix opisanij s rodnym jazykom lingvista' [The Relationship Between the Language of Linguistic Descriptions and the Native Language of the Linguist], *Programma i tezisy dokladov v letnej škole po vtoričnym modelirujuščim sistemam* [Program and Abstracts of Lectures in the Summer Institute on Secondary Simulating Systems] 7-9. (Tartu).
Žolkovskij, A. K., and I. A. Mel'čuk
  1966   'O sisteme semantičeskogo sinteza, I: Stroenie slovarja' [A System of Semantic Synthesis, I: The Structure of the Lexicon], *NTI* (11): 48-55.
  1967a   'O sisteme semantičeskogo sinteza, II: Pravila perifrazirovanija' [A System of Semantic Synthesis, II: Paraphrasing Rules], *NTI*-2 (2): 17-27.
  1967b   'O semantičeskom sinteze' [On Semantic Synthesis], *Problemy kibernetiki* 19: 177-238.
  1969   'K postroeniju dejstvujuščej modeli jazyka 'smysl ↔ tekst'' [Towards a Functioning Meaning ⟷ Text Model of Language], *Mašinnyj perevod i prikladnaja lingvistika* 11: 5-35.

ABBREVIATION

NTI –   *Naučno-texničeskaja informacija* [Scientific and Technological Information]

Toward a Formal Definition of Grammatical Case and Gender of Nouns

The development of linguistics has now entered a stage where rigorous logical analysis of its concepts has become possible and necessary. We need not speak of the importance of such an analysis: until the logical structure of a notion is elucidated with sufficient clarity, its use will be impeded in much the same way that reading is made more difficult if the contours of the letters become blurred.

Many researchers have recognized the necessity of making linguistic notions more exact. Occasionally, however, one encounters the erroneous view (perhaps not always fully realized by its proponents) that the transformation of linguistics into an exact science should be connected exclusively with the creation of new concepts, while traditional linguistic notions such as noun, adjective, case, gender, etc. are, in view of their logical inadequacy, to be either ignored or used with no more than a heuristic significance. Such a point of view leads to the conclusion that the introduction of exact concepts and methods into linguistics demands a complete break with tradition. Hence, perhaps, the still rather widely held opinion that 'traditional' and 'structural' linguistics are two distinct disciplines; hence the mistrust which many 'traditional' linguists feel toward exact notions and methods, in which they are inclined to see a destructive factor.

If we are to approach the matter seriously, there can, of course, be no question of ignoring traditional language science and rejecting the concepts which it has developed and which have been used successfully for a very long time. The problem consists first of all in giving JUST THESE NOTIONS a basis which could satisfy today's requirements on the logical structure of scientific concepts. The situation here is to a certain degree analogous to one which at one time occurred in geometry. The fundamental ideas of this science had been used for many centuries without any rigorous logical analysis. Such an analysis was made in the last century, but it did not at all mean that the old categories of geometry were abolished ; these categories merely came to be clearer and more deeply understood. Just thanks to this, however, geometry reached a completely new stage in its development

and made an extremely important advance which otherwise would have
been impossible, and in directions which could not even have been
contemplated earlier. Similarly, the creation of new trends in linguistics
demands logical analysis and the systematization of its traditional concepts.
More specifically, it is necessary to construct a system of linguistic notions
including all of the most important traditional concepts in such a way
that the base of this system is a certain complex of primitive notions.
Such a complex should be logically simple, comparatively 'poor', and easily
surveyable — but at the same time it should be natural; also, we should be
able to obtain all other notions we need from these initial ones in a strictly
formal way,[1] using only logical constructions. A tendency toward this
sort of structure for linguistic theory has existed for some time already;
probably its most vivid manifestation is the renowned book by
L. Hjelmslev (1953). This book, however, was written before methods of
formalization of linguistic notions had been extensively developed, and
it takes as its subject the general principles of linguistic theory, rather than its
actual development. Studies on the formal substantiation of many linguistic
concepts have at the present time advanced rather far, and this creates the
prerequisites for the actual construction of a system of linguistic notions on
the basis of the principles stated above. Nevertheless, the full development
of such a system remains a matter for the future (although perhaps not
the very distant future); the concrete task thus far is to construct certain
partial systems, and it is in the process of solving this problem that we can
hope to establish how a general formalized theory is to be created.

One such partial system is proposed in the present article, which is intended
to define the notions of case and gender of the noun. It is not the first
system to have such a purpose; the definition of both notions has already
been treated several times. To my knowledge the first formal definition of
noun case is contained in the pioneer work of O. S. Kulagina (1958),
marking the beginning of all those studies which have sought to formalize
traditional grammatical notions. A definition of case has been proposed also
by A.N. Kolmogorov and V.A. Uspenskij (see Uspenskij 1957)[2]. Further
variants of formal definitions of case and gender can be found in the works of
S. Marcus (1967a: Ch. IV, 1967b: Ch. VI) and I. I. Revzin (1967: § §40, 45).

All of the works mentioned above (with the exception of Uspenskij 1957,
in which certain semantic elements are found among the basic notions),
use essentially the same system of basic notions — a system whose main
component is the notion of a *grammatically correct sentence.* But this concept
is not simple enough. The set of grammatically correct sentences of a
language is in fact infinite, so any procedure requiring knowledge of this set is
per force infinite and therefore ineffective (strictly speaking, it isn't a

procedure at all). In contrast to this, the present paper proposes a system of basic notions, all of whose components are predicates defined on a finite set and therefore describable by means of finite tables. Using such a system of basic notions should also make it possible to provide for more natural and adequate definitions; in other words, our system makes it possible to come closer to the formalization of the linguistic intuition which underlies 'ordinary', 'non-formal' concepts of case and gender – e.g., the notions of case and gender used in Russian grammatical tradition.

The basic idea of our definitions, which we think coincides with the basic idea of the traditional concepts of case and gender, can be explained as follows: each case is a set of noun forms which are in some sense governed identically by other words, while each gender is a set of nouns which in some sense identically govern forms of other words.

We cannot, of course, expect that our definitions will cover exactly what the grammatical tradition (if there is one) of any given language calls case and gender. On the contrary, the applicability of our definitions to some languages and their inapplicability to others can help elucidate the typological differences between categories which for these languages have traditionally been called by the same name.

1. PRELIMINARY REMARKS

Before presenting our system of basic concepts, it will be useful to make two informal remarks.

Our first remark concerns the general premises behind our approach to grammatical meanings.

We maintain that the lexical and grammatical meanings expressed by the words[3] of a language can be divided into two types.

Meanings of the first type are those which are, so to speak, inherent in the words; that is, those which more or less directly correspond to certain ideas in the consciousness of native speakers and which are easily associated by the speakers with the words in question. All lexical meanings belong here. The plural of the Russian noun, which corresponds to a rather clear idea of 'plurality', serves as an example of a grammatical meaning of this type.

Meanings of the second type are constructs which arise as a result of rather complex abstraction and do not directly correspond to any sort of ideas in the consciousness of the speakers (at any rate not of those who have not studied grammar). We believe that the meanings of cases in modern Russian (except the second genitive and the second prepositional, see below) belong to this type. It is hardly possible, for example, to indicate the definite idea in the consciousness of a native speaker of Russian which is realized by the instrumental case of the noun in each of the phrases (1):

(1) *dovolen synom* '(He is) satisfied with his son', *vygljadit starikom* 'looks like an old man', *rabotajet tokarem* 'works as a lathe operator', *rabotajet lopatoj* 'works with a spade', *vladeet zavodom* 'owns a factory', *zanimaetsja fizikoj* 'is studying physics', *vzvešivaetsja kladovščikom* 'is being weighed by the storekeeper', *idet novoj dorogoj* 'takes the new road', *idet bystrym šagom* 'walks with quick steps', *prenebregajet opasnost'ju* 'ignores danger', *torgujet ryboj* 'trades in fish', *nazvala Ivanom* '(She) called (him) Ivan', *Èto bylo nesčast'jem* 'It was a disaster', *snabžajet toplivom* 'supplies with fuel', *rasstavljaet rjadami* 'arranges in rows', *svistit solov'jem* 'whistles like a nightingale', *boleet grippom* 'is ill with the flu', *vysok rostom* '(He is) tall', *živet pod Moskvoj* 'lives near Moscow', *naxoditsja pod sledstvijem* 'is under investigation', *stoit nad obryvom* 'stands over the precipice', *prjačetsja za derevom* 'hides behind the tree', *bumaga za ego podpis'ju* 'a document with his signature', *spravilsja s protivnikom* '(He) overpowered (his) adversary', *razgovarivaet s drugom* 'is talking with (his/her) friend', *poslal s okaziej* '(He) sent through a person', *buterbrod s syrom* 'cheese sandwich' (lit. 'sandwich with cheese').

Thus the meanings 'nominative case', 'genitive case', etc. of the Russian noun most naturally fit into the second type. We also think it correct to place the meanings 'masculine gender' etc. of the Russian noun in this group.

The meanings of the first type and the grammatical categories which correspond to them will be said to be INTERNAL, and meanings of the second type and their categories will be called EXTERNAL. In all probability, such a division of grammatical categories basically coincides with the usual division into 'semantic' and 'syntactic' categories.

Now we can ask a question as to the place of internal and external meanings and categories in the system of formal language description. Here we can proceed from the point of view according to which language is a working mechanism and any good description of language is a description of how this mechanism works. Ideally, it should allow for reproduction of the operation of the mechanism in all details; i.e., it should be its WORKING MODEL. In such an approach it is reasonable to assume that internal meanings and categories should be organic constituent parts of such a model. Specifically, it seems natural to include internal meanings in the semantic components of 'meaning-text' models, and the rigorous definition of such meanings will be nothing other than an indication of their role in the semantic notation. The external meanings have to be defined on the basis of an analysis of the structure of the language mechanism, or the process of its operation, or the result of this process, that is, speech. We are not obliged here to use all the information we have about language as a mechanism to define each category; on the contrary, it is necessary to limit oneself to the smallest possible body of such information — to only that which is actually necessary. In the first place, this makes the definitions simpler and clearer, and secondly (which is more important), it allows us to show what parts of the language mechanism one or another external category is directly connected with; that is, we can explain its place in the over-all system.

What has been stated thus far makes it possible to clarify the relation between two contemporary approaches to the formal description of language: the 'synthetic' approach, which finds its expression in the construction of so-called 'synthetic models', or 'language models proper' — generative grammars and meaning ⟺ text models; and the 'analytic' approach, which is connected with the construction of 'analytical models', or 'research models', and also with deciphering algorithms. The second approach is more natural for describing external meanings and categories, while the first seems better for all other purposes. Of course, descriptions of an 'analytic', or 'deciphering', nature are also possible for a part of the internal meanings and categories, since the language mechanism need not satisfy any sort of requirements of minimality or independence of constituent parts. These descriptions can have significance in their practical as well as in their purely theoretical aspects; nonetheless, such methods should play a subordinate role for the treatment of internal meanings while they should be considered primary in the study of external meanings.

To sum up: If we wish to understand the nature of one or another external category (or group of external categories) and want to construct its formal definition (and the present study attempts to do just this), then we will have to take as a basis for all our treatments some system of notions which contains maximally explicit information about the structure of the language mechanism, or about the process of its operation, or about speech; specifically, this system can contain certain information about internal meanings and/or categories. It is desirable here to make these basic notions as simple and 'poor' as possible — without destroying the naturalness of their content. We will try to hold to just these principles as we formulate our definitions of case, agreement class, and gender.

The second remark will have a more special character. It has to do with how we refine the notion of 'word'. As is well known, such refinement can result in several different concepts (which are not always sufficiently clearly distinguished in linguistic literature or even in the most recent works on formal language description). A. A. Zaliznjak (1967) lists the following three meanings of the word 'word': 1) 'The word as a unit of the external side of text', that is, in the written form of language, simply a string of letters

between two spaces. A. A. Zaliznjak calls such a unit a SEGMENT. Two
segments are considered identical when and only when they coincide
graphically,[4] independent of their lexical and grammatical meanings; for
example, *luk* in the sense 'onion' and *luk* in the sense 'bow' are identical
segments in the same way as *máčty* 'mast' in the genitive singular and *máčty*
in the nominative plural. 2) 'The word as a two-sided unit of text (i.e.
a unit having both expression and content)'. He calls such an entity a
WORD-FORM. Thus a word-form is a segment taken together with its lexical
and all its grammatical meanings. When any meanings of two word-forms
fail to coincide, these word-forms are considered to be different. E.g.,
máčty in the meaning nom. pl. and *máčty* in the meaning gen. sg. are
different word-forms; *luk* in the meaning 'onion, nom. sg.' is not the same
word-form as *luk* in the meaning 'bow, nom. sg.'3) 'The word as a unit of
the dictionary, that is, as a bilateral extra-textual unit of language which
arises on the basis of an analysis of all the texts of a given language', is a
LEXEME. A lexeme is the set of all word-forms which have the same lexical
meaning (Zaliznjak 1967: § 1.7).

Segments and word-forms can be divided into CONCRETE and ABSTRACT.
A concrete segment is a segment considered together with its position in
the text, in contrast to an abstract segment, which is viewed independently of
its position in the text. Concrete segments which coincide graphically but
differ in the position they occupy in the text are considered to be
REPRESENTATIVES of a single abstract segment (the conditions of segment
identity formulated above thus relate to abstract segments). Concrete and
abstract word-forms are defined in a similar way. (The distinction discussed
here is the same at the well known TYPE-TOKEN distinction.)

These definitions do not, however, exhaust the relevant refinements of the
notion 'word', which might prove to be useful in linguistic theory.
Specifically, the following object which is, in a sense, intermediate between
segment and word-form, seems quite natural: the segment taken together with
its lexical meaning, but without any sort of grammatical meaning. We shall call
such an object a LEXICALLY MEANINGFUL SEGMENT. As was the case with
segments and word-forms, it is necessary to differentiate between concrete
lexically meaningful segments (those considered together with their position
in the text) and abstract ones (those which are treated without reference
to their positions). We will here follow mathematical terminology: an abstract
lexically meaningful segment will simply be called a lexically meaningful
segment, and a concrete lexically meaningful segment will be said to be an
OCCURRENCE of a lexically meaningful segment in a text (for example,
in a sentence). Using this terminology, we can say that two lexically meaningful segments are identical when and only when they coincide graphically

and their lexical meanings coincide. Thus, in the sentence (2):

(2) *Vyveska nad dver'ju čajnoj perekosilas', a v samoj čajnoj ne bylo ni odnoj čajnoj ložki* 'The sign above the door of the tea-house was crooked, and in the tea-house itself there was not a single teaspoon'.

the first two occurrences of the segment *čajnoj* correspond to the same lexically meaningful segment with the meaning 'a type of public house where the customers can drink tea and get simple meals' (S. I. Ožegov, *Slovar' russkogo jazyka*), while the third belongs to a different lexically meaningful segment (with the meaning ≪ adjective from *čaj* 'tea' ≫).

In what follows we will use metonymic phrasing of the type 'the lexically meaningful segment *vodá* 'water'', having in mind 'a lexically meaningful segment the external side of which is the segment *vodá*' (cf. Zaliznjak 1967: 21).

A set of lexically meaningful segments with the same lexical meaning will be called a NEIGHBORHOOD. By the very definition of lexically meaningful segment, neighborhoods should be disjoint sets.

We will now adopt the following terminological convention: since the notion of segment will not be used by us in what follows, we will for the sake of brevity agree to call lexically meaningful segments simply SEGMENTS. It is segments in this sense and neighborhoods which underlie the system of our basic notions.

To conclude this section, let us make the following observation. A definition of AGREEMENT CLASS will precede our definition of gender. The area covered by this concept probably coincides, for a number of languages, with that of the notion 'gender'. In Russian the category which has traditionally borne the name 'gender' differs from the agreement class concept. Since this latter notion is logically clearer and possesses a greater generality than the category of gender as presented in traditional Russian grammar, it seems convenient to treat agreement class as being the simpler, 'more primary' basic category. When the notion of agreement class is defined, we will be able to specify the procedure which builds the concept of 'traditional gender' (see below, Section 5).

The notion of agreement class (like the term 'agreement class' itself) was, I suppose, introduced by A. A. Zaliznjak (1964; cf. also Zaliznjak 1967: §§ 2.14–2.16). It was he who showed that gender and agreement class in Russian do not coincide (Zaliznjak 1964: 26-27; Zaliznjak 1967: 66-67).

2. BASIC NOTIONS

We take as basic the following six undefined notions:
1. The finite set *V* whose elements are interpreted as segments (cf. the

terminological remark above) of some natural language. This set will be called the VOCABULARY, and its elements will be called SEGMENTS.

2. The system of disjoint subsets of set V, which in their aggregate wholly cover this set. These subsets will be said to be NEIGHBORHOODS. Linguistically, each neighborhood is a set of segments having identical lexical meanings — that is, the set of all forms of a single word. Examples of neighborhoods: $\{$ *dom, dóma, dómu, dómom, dóme, domá, domóv, domám, domámi, domáx* $\}$ 'house' (in all number and case forms); $\{$ *nóvyj, nóvoe, nóvaja, nóvogo, nóvoj, nóvomu, nóvuju, nóvym, nóvoju, nóvom, nóvye, nóvyx, nóvymi, nóv, nóva, nóvo, nóvy* $\}$[5] ('new' in all forms); $\{$ *na* $\}$ 'on'; $\{$ *ókolo* $\}$ 'near'; $\{$ *óčen'* $\}$ 'very'.[6]

A neighborhood containing segment x will usually be called a NEIGHBORHOOD OF SEGMENT x.

3. The subset S of set V, interpreted as the set of all nouns of a given language. The set S should be a union of some systems of neighborhoods. (In other words, a neighborhood either is contained in S, or does not intersect with S.)

The segments which belong to S will be called S-SEGMENTS, and the neighborhoods contained in S will be said to be S-NEIGHBORHOODS.

4. The binary relation $\rightarrow$ defined on the vocabulary, which we will call the RELATION OF POTENTIAL SUBORDINATION (the expression $x \rightarrow y$ is read 'x potentially subordinates y').

The expression $x \rightarrow y$ means that there exists a grammatically correct simple sentence of the language in question in which an occurrence of segment x immediately subordinates syntactically an occurrence of segment y. We will assume here that the grammatical subject is always subordinated to the predicate, i.e., to the main verb.

Thus from the grammaticality of sentence (3):

(3) *Žil na svete staričok malen'kogo rosta* 'Once upon a time there lived a short little old man'

with the arrows of subordination arranged as they are, we conclude that the statements *žil* $\rightarrow$ *staričók, žil* $\rightarrow$ *na, na* $\rightarrow$ *svéte, staričók* $\rightarrow$ *rósta, rósta* $\rightarrow$ *málen'kogo* are true. At the same time, the statements *rósta* $\rightarrow$ *málen'koj, na* $\rightarrow$ *svétom, pod* $\rightarrow$ *svéte* are false, since in a grammatical Russian sentence the segment *rósta* cannot subordinate the segment *málen'koj*, the segment *na* — the segment *svétom*, nor the segment *pod* — the segment *svéte*.[7]

Let us make two further remarks concerning the interpretation of the subordination relation in Russian.

(a) In those cases where the choice of direction of the arrow seems disputable (e.g., *dva stola, dvum stolam* 'two tables', *neskol'ko stolov, neskol'kim stolam* 'several tables'), we will not fix the relation of potential subordination in either direction (for example, both of the statements *dva → stola'* and *stola' → dva* will be considered false). Moreover, we will assume that in combinations such as *dva bol'šix stola, dvux bol'šix stolov* 'two large tables', the adjective is subordinated not to the noun, but to the Noun + Numeral phrase as a whole, and on the basis of this assumption we will consider such statements as *stolá → bol'šix, stený → bol'šix* to be false.

(b) We introduce a 'zero copula' which is considered to be the root of the sentence tree in sentences of the type *On učitel'* 'He is a teacher', *Etot čelovek očen' umën* 'This man is very clever', *Vanja sejčas v škole* 'Vanja is at school now'; specifically, these sentences will be analyzed as follows:

(4) *On ∈ učitel', Étot čelovek ∈ očen' umen, Vanja sejčas ∈ v škole*

(∈ designates the zero copula). It is expedient to include the zero copula in the vocabulary *V*. In accordance with what has been just said, we will consider statements such as $\epsilon → on$, $\epsilon → učitel'$, $\epsilon → čelovék$, $\epsilon → umën$, $\epsilon → Vanja$, $\epsilon → v$, $\epsilon → sejčás$ to be true, and statements such as *učitel' → on, umën → čelovék, v → sejčás* to be false.

5. The two subsets of S — say S_1 and S_2 — which satisfy the condition $S_1 \cup S_2 = S$ and which can be interpreted as a set of nouns in the singular and a set of nouns in the plural, respectively. S_1 and S_2 are not necessarily disjoint; the following segments, for example, belong to the intersection $S_1 \cap S_2$: *rýby* 'fish', *téni* 'shadow', *pal'tó* 'overcoat', *sáni* 'sledge' (as regards the last example of Zaliznjak 1967: § 1.12).[8]

6. The two ternary relations $D_1 (x, y, z)$ and $D_2 (x, y, z)$ defined on the vocabulary, which satisfy two conditions: if $D_1 (x, y, z)$, then $y \in S_1$, $x → y$ and $y → z$; if $D_2 (x, y, z)$, then $y \in S_2$, $x → y$ and $y → z$.

The meaning of the expression $D_1 (x, y, z)$ is as follows: there exists a grammatical simple sentence in the given language in which some occurrence of the S-segment y, which has the meaning 'singular', is immediately subordinated syntactically to some occurrence of segment x and immediately subordinates syntactically some occurrence of segment z. The expression $D_2 (x, y, z)$ is interpreted in exactly the same way, by substituting the plural for the singular.

The following statements, for example, are true: D_1 (*staričók, rósta, málen'kogo*), D_1 (*iz, pal'tó, nóvogo*), D_1 (*v, pal'tó, nóvom*) — because in

Russian we have *staričók málen'kogo rósta* 'a short little old man', *iz nóvogo pal'tó* 'from a new overcoat', *v nóvom pal'tó* 'in a new overcoat'. At the same time, D_1 (*v, pal'tó, nóvogo*) is false in spite of the truth of *v → pal'tó* and *pal'tó → nóvogo* (because there is no **V nóvogo pal'tó*). The statement D_1 (*popadájutsja, rýby, krúpnye*) 'are caught, fish, big' is false regardless of the fact that *rýby* $\in S_1$ and there exists grammatical sentence(5):

(5) *V seti popadajutsja krupnye ryby* 'Large fish are (being) caught in the net',

since neither in (5) nor in any other sentence where the segment *rýby* subordinates the segment *krúpnye* does the first of these segments have the meaning 'singular'.

Analogously, the statements D_2 (*iz, pal'tó, nóvyx*), D_2 (*v, pal'tó, nóvyx*) are true, while D_2 (*v, pal'tó, nóvymi*), D_2 (*ot, rýby, krúpnye*) are false.[9]

Thus the basic notions of our system are a set of segments, the subset of S-segments distinguished in it, a system of neighborhoods, the potential subordination relation, the sets S_1 and S_2 and the relations of 'double potential subordination' D_1 and D_2, in which the last two components are not necessary for a definition of case. This means that in order to define the notions of case, agreement class, and gender, we will need the following information about the language in question:

(a) We have to know all the segments of the language.

(b) For each segment we have to know whether it is a noun form.

(c) For each pair of segments we have to know whether they have identical lexical meanings.

(d) For every two segments x, y we have to know whether x can immediately subordinate y in a grammatical simple sentence.[10]

(e) For each S-segment we have to know whether it has the meaning 'singular' and whether it can have the meaning 'plural'.

(f) For every three segments x, y, z where y is an S-segment, we have to know whether it is possible that in some grammatical simple sentence an occurrence of y has the meaning 'singular' (respectively, 'plural'), is immediately subordinated to an occurrence of x, and immediately subordinates an occurrence of z.

No other information is necessary for the definition of case, agreement class, and gender. And (a)–(d) alone suffice for the definition of case.[11]

To conclude this section, it will be helpful to make the following observation. The arsenal of mathematical resources used by us thus far is very poor – it is restricted to the most rudimentary concepts of set theory. Nor will we need a more complex mathematical apparatus below. But since the fundamental notions of set theory are logical rather than mathematical notions, we are justified in saying that our method of defining agreement classes and case does not significantly draw upon mathematical apparatus. This also holds to a significant degree for other definitions of these and similar notions that we know of.

3.   A DEFINITION OF GRAMMATICAL CASE

1. Let O be any neighborhood and y be any segment. We will say that O POTENTIALLY SUBORDINATES y if y is potentially subordinated to at least one segment from O.

For example, the neighborhood of the segment *namereválsja* '(he) intended' potentially subordinates each of the segments *čelovék* 'man', *ljúdi* 'people', *doč'* 'daughter', *ty* 'thou', *čitát'* 'to read' (since the statements *namereváetsja* → *čelovék, namerevájutsja* → *ljúdi, namereválas'* → *doč', namereváeš'sja* → *ty, namereváetsja* → *čitát'* are true). The neighborhood of the segment *obladála* '(she) possessed' potentially subordinates the segments *slon* 'elephant', *slóný, kniga* 'book', *knigi, slonóm, slonámi, knígoj, knigami,* and the (single-element) neighborhood of the segment *za* 'behind, beyond' potentially subordinates the segments *góru* 'mountain', *góry, gorój, gorámi.*

N_O will designate, for any arbitrary neighborhood O, the set of all S-segments which are potentially subordinated to this neighborhood. To simplify our notation we designate N_O as N_x for any segment x which belongs to O. For example, instead of 'N_O where $O = \{$ *stená, stené, ...,* *sténax* 'wall' $\}$ ', we simply write $N_{stená}$, instead of 'N_O where O is the neighbourhood of the segment *sidít* 'sits',' we write $N_{sidít}$, and instead of $N\{za\}$ we write N_{za}.

For example, the set N_{na}(*na* 'on') includes the segments *stolý* 'tables', *stol, stolé, stoláx, stené, ókna* 'windows', etc.; $N_{čérez}$ (*čérez* 'through, across') includes *stolý, stol, ókna,* etc.; N_{pri}(*pri* 'near, at, by') includes *stolé, stoláx, stené,* etc.; $N_{mešála}$ (*mešála* '(she) stirred, bothered, hindered') includes *sup* 'soup', *súpa,*[12] *lóžkoj* 'with a spoon', *lóžkami, otcú* 'to the father', *sestrá* 'sister', *brat* 'brother', etc.; $N_{staráetsja}$ (*staráetsja* 'tries') includes *brat, sestrá, dóžd'* 'rain', *pogóda* 'weather', *putešéstvie* 'trip', etc.; N_{dom} (*dom* 'house') includes *sestrý* 'of the sister', *otcá* 'of the father', *detéj* 'of the children', etc.; $N_{ókolo}$ (*ókolo* 'near') includes *stený, sten, dóma, domóv, okná,* etc.

The sets N_O which correspond to certain O can be empty: e.g. $N_{edvá}$ (*edvá* 'hardly'), $N_{počtí}$(*počtí* 'almost').

2.   It is natural to call the set N_O MINIMAL if it is non-empty and there is no non-empty N_{O_1}, which is its proper subset. Thus, the set N_{na} is not

minimal, since at least $N_{\check{c}\acute{e}rez}$ (and also N_{pri}) is its proper subset. $N_{me\check{s}\acute{a}la}$ is not a minimal set, since $N_{obla\acute{d}aet}$, for example, is its proper subset. At the same time, $N_{\check{c}\acute{e}rez}$, $N_{\acute{o}kolo}$, $N_{star\acute{a}ets\!ja}$, and N_{dom} are minimal.

THE MINIMAL SETS N_0 WILL BE CALLED CASES. If for two different neighborhoods O and O' the sets N_0 and $N_{0'}$ coincide, we will not consider N_0 and $N_{0'}$ to be different cases, but one and the same case.

Thus, $N_{\acute{o}kolo} = N_{dom} = N_{kr\acute{o}me}$ (*króme* 'besides') is the genitive case; $N_{star\acute{a}ets\!ja} = N_{m\acute{o}\check{z}et}$ (*móžet* 'can') is the nominative; $N_{\check{c}\acute{e}rez} = N_{to\check{s}nit}$ (*tošnít* 'nauseates') is the accusative.

3. Obviously, cases do not have to be disjoint sets. The segment *stené*, for example, belongs to N_k (*k* 'to, towards') (the dative case) as well as to N_{pri} (the prepositional case); the segment *stolý* belongs to $N_{m\acute{o}\check{z}et}$ (nominative) as well as to $N_{\check{c}\acute{e}rez}$ (accusative).

The fact that it is possible for certain S-segments to belong to no case is somewhat more unexpected. Thus, the segment *lesú* (*les* 'forest') seemingly belongs to only one set of the form N_0, namely, N_v (*v* 'in'), which is not minimal ($N_{\check{c}\acute{e}rez}$, for example, is its proper subset). The same goes for the segments *godú* 'year', *mostú* 'bridge', and *škafú* 'cupboard'. For this reason, the so-called second prepositional case in Russian (with locative meaning) is not a case according to the above definition.

Neither will the second genitive case (the genitive partitive), which can be equated with the set $N_{nemn\acute{o}go}$ (*nemnógo* 'a little') containing the segments *sáxara* 'sugar', *sáxaru*, *čája* 'tea', *čáju*, *knígi*, *knig*, *skvorcá* (*skvoréc* 'starling'), *skvorčov*, be the case according to the above definition.[13] The set $N_{\acute{o}kolo}$ (the first genitive case) is in fact a proper subset of the set $N_{nemn\acute{o}go}$.

Thus the second prepositional and the second genitive cases occupy a special position in our formal system. This is evidently not a coincidence, since these cases differ from the 'traditional' six cases at least in that they can be viewed as being internal: the second prepositional case always has the meaning 'place', and the second genitive always means 'a part of a whole'. There are two more important differences: first, they have 'independent' forms, which are not homonymous with the forms of the other six cases, for only a small number of nouns; secondly, they do not have independent sets of forms for adjectives which agree with them — the second prepositional case behaves with respect to agreement just like the first; the second genitive behaves exactly like the first genitive. The second prepositional case, however, is typologically closer to the other cases than is the second genitive. The latter contains another case (the first genitive) as its proper subset, and for this reason its use is, so to speak, 'optional': whenever the 'independent' form of the second genitive is used, the form of the first genitive can be used instead (instead of *stakan čaju* 'a glass of tea' it is always possible to say *stakan čaja*);

at the same time, for some (albeit for very few) nouns, the second prepositional has no forms which are homonymous to the forms of other cases — we cannot say * *v lése* instead of *v lesú* 'in the forest'.

This difference between the second genitive and the second prepositional cases is reflected in the following fact : if we modify our definition so that the potential subordination relation is replaced by the relation of double potential subordination then the second prepositional case will be included among the cases (concerning the relation of double potential subordination, see footnote 11; to avoid unnecessary complications we will not explicitly describe such a modification, although it is a natural one); the second genitive, in contrast, will not be a case in this or any other modification of our construction which we could at this point regard as natural.

4.   The following problem arises in view of the possibility of homonymy between case forms (and such homonymy is found in Russian): for a specific occurrence of an *S*-segment in a sentence on which the syntactic subordination relation is given (that is, the sentence is supplied with subordination arrows), determine which case should be assigned to the given occurrence of the segment in the given sentence (a segment can occur in a sentence more than once). Thus for the (single) occurrence of the segment *duše* 'soul' in the sentence (6):

(6)   *Bylo emu mračno i osenne na duše* 'He was in a gloomy autumnal mood'

the problem consists of determining which of the two cases (dative or prepositional) possible for this segment should be actually given to it.

A very simple way of solving this problem (in the case of a simple sentence)[14] consists in the following: let an occurrence of an *S*-segment *x* be fixed in the sentence, and let there be a segment *z* which immediately subordinates this occurrence and which belongs to the neighborhood *O*. The segment *z*, obviously, can be defined in only one way.[15] If $N_{O_1}, ..., N_{O_k}$ are all cases which contain *x* and are contained in N_O, then each of these cases is by definition assigned to the given occurrence of the segment *x* in the given sentence.

In the example given above, if *x* = *duše*, then *z* = *na*. The segment *duše* belongs to two cases (the dative and the prepositional), but only one of them (the prepositional) is contained in the set N_{na} (which also contains the accusative case). Thus the occurrence of the segment *duše* in the given sentence is assigned only one case — the prepositional.

Consider yet another example. Assume that we have to assign cases to the segments *kóška* 'cat' and *lápu* 'paw' in (7):

(7) *Nesčastnaja koška porezala lapu* 'The poor cat cut its paw'.

The immediately subordinating segment for both of these segments is *porézala* 'cut'; there is only one case containing the segment *kóška* 'cat' (the nominative), and it is contained in the set $N_{porézala}$. The segment *lápu* 'paw' also belongs to only one case (the accusative), which is again contained in $N_{porézala}$. Hence, the segment *kóška* is assigned the nominative case, and *lápu* is given the accusative.

5. Two questions now arise:
— Will the procedure we have just presented assign a case to any occurrence of an *S*-segment in a simple sentence (which has been supplied with subordination arrows)?
— Does this procedure guarantee the uniqueness of the case it assigns to an *S*-segment?

We will immediately receive a negative answer to the first question if we remember that there are *S*-segments which do not belong to any case whatsoever. This question can be asked in a somewhat weaker form so that it refers only to those *S*-segments which belong to some case. Even then the answer will be negative. The segment *čáju* 'tea', for example, belongs only to the dative case; but in the sentence *On nalil mne stakan čaju* 'He poured me a glass of tea', this segment is not assigned the dative case, which means that it is not assigned any case at all, since the dative case is not contained in the set $N_{stakán}$. This fact, of course, fully corresponds to our linguistic intuition, since what we have here is the second genitive case, which is not a case in the sense of our definition.

The answer to the second question is also negative. Consider, for example, the sentence

(8) *Oni ne dali plemeni vremeni na razmyšlenie* 'They did not give the tribe time to think it over'.

The segment *plémeni* 'tribe' is assigned two cases, the genitive and the dative, since they both contain this segment and are contained in the set $N_{dáli}$.

At first glance this feature of our procedure might seem to be a shortcoming; but this is only partly true. From the purely syntactic point of view, for example, (8) can be interpreted not only as *Oni ne dali plemeni* [to whom] *vremeni* [what] (i.e. 'The tribe did not receive time'), but also as *Oni ne dali plemeni* [what] *vremeni* [to whom] (i.e. 'Time did not receive the tribe'); the solution of this homonymy is possible only when meaning is taken into consideration.[16]

Let us consider two similar examples. In (9):

(9) *On sel za bjuro* 'He sat down at the desk/behind the desk',

the segment *bjuró* is assigned two cases — the accusative and the instrumental. It seems most natural to understand (9) as *On sel za bjuro* [whither], that is, to interpret *bjuró* as a form of the accusative case. Similarly, in

(10) *On postavil jaščik pod trjumo* 'He put the box under the cheval-glass'

the segment *trjumó* can be interpreted as a form of the accusative case or as a form of the instrumental, and it happens that just these two cases are assigned to this segment by our procedure. (Note that this ambiguity in assigning cases occurs most often with indeclinable nouns.)

Thus in many instances the ambiguity resulting from our procedure corresponds to an ambiguity in the selection of case on syntactic criteria. This is not always so, however. The case of one or another occurrence of an *S*-segment in a sentence usually also depends on other syntactic factors than just what segment this occurrence is subordinated to. Thus, the segment *plémeni* in

(11) *Oni ne dali plemeni zemli* 'They didn't give the tribe any land'

will be assigned, in accordance with our procedure, the genitive and dative cases, and the segment *port'é* 'doorman' in

(12) *On beseduet s port'é* 'He is conversing with the doorman'

is assigned the genitive, accusative and instrumental cases. At the same time, both (11) and (12) are syntactically non-homonymous, and the segment *plémeni* in (11) can only be understood as a form of the dative case, while the segment *port'é* in (12) can only be interpreted to be a form of the instrumental. The exact determination of case in the first instance is based on the fact that the segment *zemli* 'land' is assigned only the genitive case, and the verb *dáli* '(they) gave' cannot have two complements in the genitive case; in the second example we utilize the fact that the verb *beséduet* 'converses' cannot govern a prepositional group consisting of the preposition *s* and a noun in the genitive or accusative case. Thus in both instances we must make use of information beyond the information on potential subordination (which is the basis of our definition of case) and on the subordination actually found in a given sentence (which is the basis of our procedure for assigning a case to an occurrence of a segment in a sentence).

The facts we have just considered suggest that either our definition of case or at least the procedure through which we assign cases must be in some respect inadequate. The following remark can be made. Ambiguities of the type *On beseduet s port'e* would not have arisen if our definition of case had accounted not only for 'immediate' potential subordination, but also for 'indirect' subordination — for example, in the above-mentioned change in the definition where the potential subordination relation was replaced by the relation of double potential subordination. As far as ambiguities of the type *Oni ne dali plemeni zemli* are concerned, to eliminate them we have to draw upon information on the valencies of the words. It seems quite probable that it would be advisable to account for these valencies in some form or other in our definition of case. In general, the definition presented here should be regarded as preliminary; additional work is needed to be able to construct a more adequate definition based on the same idea of 'identical government'. In particular, the question of the inter-relation between this method of defining case and the ideas of R. O. Jakobson's classic work (1936) needs a special treatment.

4.   A DEFINITION OF AGREEMENT CLASS

1. We will need certain auxillary notions in order to define the term *agreement class.*

Given all the primary objects described in Section 2, let k grammatical cases $\Pi_1, \ldots, \Pi_k$ be defined in accordance with the definition in Section 3 (this means ALL the cases thus defined). The numbering of the cases is arbitrary, but will be considered fixed in what follows.

The PARADIGM of an arbitrary S-neighborhood A will be said to be the ordered system of sets $= \langle A^{11}, A^{12}, \ldots, A^{1k}, A^{21}, A^{22}, \ldots, A^{2k} \rangle$, where $A^{11} = A \cap S_1 \cap \Pi_1$, $A^{12} = A \cap S_1 \cap \Pi_2, \ldots, A^{1k} = A \cap S_1 \cap \Pi_k$, $A^{21} = A \cap S_2 \cap \Pi_1, \ldots, A^{2k} = A \cap S_2 \cap \Pi_k$.

Let us consider, for example, the following S-neighborhoods:

$A_1 = \langle$ *dom, dóma, dómu, dómom, dóme, domá, domóv, domám, domámi, domáx* $\rangle$ ('house' in all number and case forms);

$\bar{A}_1 = \langle$ *ded, déda, dédu, dédom, déde, dédy, dédov, dédam, dédami, dédax* $\rangle$ 'grandfather';

$A_2 = \langle$ *reká, rekí, reké, réku, rekój, rekóju, réki, rek, rékam, rékami, rékax* $\rangle$ 'river';

$\bar{A}_2 = \langle$ *rýba, rýby, rýbe, rýbu, rýboj, rýboju, ryb, rýbam, rýbami, rýbax* $\rangle$ 'fish';

$A_3 = \langle$ *seló, selá, selú, selóm, selé, sëla, sël, sëlam, sëlami, sëlax* $\rangle$ 'village';

$\bar{A}_3 = \langle$ *čudóvišče, čudóvišča, čudóviščru, čudóviščem, čudóvišč, čudóviščam,*
    čudóviščami, čudóviščax $\rangle$ 'monster';
$\tilde{A}_3 = \langle$ *pal'tó* $\rangle$ 'overcoat';
$A_4 = \langle$ *sáni, sanéj, sanjám, sanjámi, sanjáx* $\rangle$ 'sledge';
$\bar{A}_4 = \langle$ *roditeli, roditelej, roditeljam, roditeljami, roditeljax* $\rangle$[17] 'parents';
$A_5 = \langle$ *zadira, zadiry, zadire, zadiru, zadiroj, zadiroju, zadir, zadiram,*
    zadirami, zadirax $\rangle$ 'bully'.

We proceed from the assumption that the six usual Russian cases are defined, and we number them in the order commonly used; in other words, Π_1 will designate the nominative case, Π_2 – the genitive, Π_3 – the dative, Π_4 – the accusative, Π_5 – the instrumental, and Π_6 – the prepositional. We then obtain the following paradigms for the above neighborhoods:[18]

$\mathfrak{A}_1 = \langle$ *dom, dóma, dómu, dom, dómom, dóme, domá, domóv, domám, domá,*
    domámi, domáx $\rangle$;
$\bar{\mathfrak{A}}_1 = \langle$ *ded, déda, dédu, déda, dédom, déde, dédy, dédov, dédam, dédov,*
    dédami, dédax $\rangle$;
$\mathfrak{A}_2 = \langle$ *reká, reki, reké, réku, {rekój, rekóju}, reké, réki, rek, rékam, réki,*
    rékami, rékax $\rangle$;
$\bar{\mathfrak{A}}_2 = \langle$ *rýba, rýby, rýbe, rýbu, {rýboj, rýboju}, rýbe, rýby, ryb, rýbam, ryb,*
    rýbami, rýbax $\rangle$;
$\mathfrak{A}_3 = \langle$ *seló, selá, selú, seló, selóm, selé, sёla, sёl, sёlam, sёla, sёlami, sёlax* $\rangle$;
$\bar{\mathfrak{A}}_3 = \langle$ *čudóvišče, čudóvišča, čudóviščru, čudóvišče, čudóviščem, čudóvišče,*
    čudóvišča, čudóvišč, čudóviščam, čudóvišč, čudóviščami, čudóviščax $\rangle$;
$\tilde{\mathfrak{A}}_3 = \langle$ *pal'tó, pal'tó, pal'tó, pal'tó, pal'tó, pal'tó, pal'tó, pal'tó, pal'tó,*
    pal'tó, pal'tó $\rangle$;
$\mathfrak{A}_4 = \langle$ *sáni, sanéj, sanjám, sáni, sanjámi, sanjáx, sáni, sanéj, sanjám, sáni,*
    sanjámi, sanjáx $\rangle$;
$\bar{\mathfrak{A}}_4 = \langle$ *roditeli, roditelej, roditeljam, roditelej, roditeljami, roditeljax, roditeli,*
    roditelej, roditeljam, roditelej, roditeljami, roditeljax $\rangle$;
$\mathfrak{A}_5 = \langle$ *zadira, zadiry, zadire, zadiru, {zadiroj, zadiroju}, zadire, zadiry, zadir,*
    zadiram, zadir, zadirami, zadirax $\rangle$;

2. Let A be an S-neighborhood, $\mathfrak{A}_j = \langle A^{11}, ..., A^{1k}, A^{21}, ..., A^{2k} \rangle$ be its paradigm, and B an arbitrary neighborhood. We will say that the SEGMENT $Z \in B$ AGREES WITH THE SEGMENT $y \in A^{ij}$ FOR THE NUMBER S_i AND THE CASE Π_j ($i = 1, 2; j = 1, 2, ..., k$), if for any neighborhood O for which $N_O = \Pi_j$ there exists a segment $x \in O$ which is such that $D_i(x, y, z)$. For every pair i, j where $i = 1, 2, j = 1, ..., k, B^{ij}$ will designate the set of

the segments from B which agree for the number S_i and the case Π_j with the segments belonging to A^{ij}.

For example, let $\mathfrak{A} = \langle A^{11}, \ldots, A^{16}, A^{21}, \ldots, A^{26} \rangle$ be the paradigm for the neighborhood of the segment *sobáka* 'dog', and let B be the neighborhood of the segment *bol'šój* 'large, big'. Specifically, we have: $A^{11} = \{sobáka\}$, $\Pi_1 = N_{O_1} = N_{O_2} = N_{O_3} = \ldots$, where $O_1, O_2, O_3, \ldots$ are neighborhoods of the segments *uméet* 'can, knows how to', *staráetsja, namerevàetsja*, ..., respectively. There are two segments in the neighborhood O_1 which potentially subordinate the segment *sobáka: uméet, uméla*. The single segment Z, which belongs to B and satisfies at least one of the conditions $D_1(uméet, sobáka, Z)$ or $D_1(uméla, sobáka, Z)$ is *bol'šája*. (This segment actually satisfies both conditions.) It is easy to see that the same holds for O_2, O_3, and in general for any neighborhood O which is such that $N_O = \Pi_1$: if $x \in O$ and $x \to sobáka$; then *bol'šája* will be the only segment Z belonging to B and satisfying the condition $D_1(x, sobáka, Z)$. Thus, *bol'šája* is the only segment that agrees with the segment *sobáka* for number S_1 and case Π_1 (the nominative), so that $B^{11} = \{bol'šája\}$. Analogously, we have, for example, $B^{15} = \{bol'šój, bol'šóju\}$, $B^{21} = \{bo'lšíe\}$

Due to the possibility of homonymy in case forms, we cannot define B^{ij} as simply the set of segments from B which are potentially subordinated to the segments from A^{ij}. We also have to consider the segments which SUB-ORDINATE the segments from A^{ij}, which makes it possible to single out those instances where a segment from A^{ij} is really used in the meaning of a jth case. For example, if we take the neighborhood of the segment *móre* 'sea' as A and the neighborhood of the segment *bol'šój* as B, then the set of segments from B which are potentially subordinated to the segments from A^{11} will include, in addition to the segment *bol'šóe*, the segment *bol'šóm*, which agrees with the segment *móre* for the prepositional but not the nominative case.

Now let A be any S-neighborhood, $\mathfrak{A} = \langle A^{11}, \ldots, A^{1k}, A^{21}, \ldots, A^{2k} \rangle$ its paradigm, and B an arbitrary neighborhood. We define the sets $B^{11}, \ldots, B^{1k}, B^{21}, \ldots, B^{2k}$ in the manner indicated above. If B^{ij} is not empty for any i for which A^{ij} is not empty, then we will call the ordered system of sets $\mathfrak{B} = \langle B^{11}, \ldots, B^{1k}, B^{21}, \ldots, B^{2k} \rangle$ an AGREEMENT SYSTEM (AS) RELATIVE TO NEIGHBORHOOD B WHICH HAS BEEN GENERATED BY PARADIGM $\mathfrak{A}$.

Consider, for example, the neighborhood $B = \{nóvyj, nóvoe, nóvaja, nóvogo, nóvoj, nóvuju, nóvomu, nóvym, nóvoju, nóvom, nóvye, nóvyx, nóvymi, nov, nová, nóvo, nóvy\}$.

The paradigms $\mathfrak{A}_1, \mathfrak{A}_1, \ldots, \mathfrak{A}_5$ treated above generate the following AS's, respectively, for this neighborhood:

$\mathfrak{B}_1$ = ⟨ *nóvyj, nóvogo, nóvomu, nóvyj, nóvym, nóvom, nóvye, nóvyx, nóvym, nóvye, nóvymi, nóvyx* ⟩ ;

$\overline{\mathfrak{B}}_1$ = ⟨ *nóvyj, nóvogo, nóvomu, nóvogo, nóvym, nóvom, nóvye, nóvyx, nóvym, nóvyx, nóvymi, nóvyx* ⟩ ;

$\mathfrak{B}_2$ = ⟨ *nóvaja, nóvoj, nóvoj, nóvuju,* {*nóvoj, nóvoju* }, *nóvoj, nóvye, nóvyx, nóvym, nóvye, nóvymi, nóvyx* ⟩ ;

$\overline{\mathfrak{B}}_2$ = ⟨ *nóvaja, nóvoj, nóvoj, nóvuju, nóvoj, nóvoju , nóvoj, nóvye, nóvyx, nóvym, nóvyx, nóvymi, nóvyx* ⟩ ;

$\mathfrak{B}_3$ = ⟨ *nóvoe, nóvogo, nóvomu, nóvoe, nóvym, nóvom, nóvye, nóvyx, nóvym, nóvye, nóvymi, nóvyx* ⟩ ;

$\overline{\mathfrak{B}}_3$ = ⟨ *nóvoe, nóvogo, nóvomu, nóvoe, nóvym, nóvom, nóvye, nóvyx, nóvym, nóvyx, nóvymi, nóvyx* ⟩ ;

$\overline{\mathfrak{B}}_3 = \mathfrak{B}_3;$

$\mathfrak{B}_4$ = ⟨ *nóvye, nóvyx, nóvym, nóvye, nóvymi, nóvyx, nóvye, nóvyx, nóvym, nóvye, nóvymi, nóvyx* ⟩ ;

$\overline{\mathfrak{B}}_4$ = ⟨ *nóvye, nóvyx, nóvym, nóvyx, nóvymi, nóvyx, nóvye, nóvyx, nóvym, nóvyx, nóvymi, nóvyx* ⟩ ;

$\mathfrak{B}_5$ = ⟨ {*nóvyj, nóvaja*}, {*nóvogo, nóvoj*}, {*nóvomu, nóvoj*}, {*nóvogo, nóvuju* }, {*nóvym, nóvoj, nóvoju*}, {*nóvom, nóvoj*}, *nóvye, nóvyx, nóvym, nóvyx, nóvymi, nóvyx* ⟩ .

As for the neighborhood C = {*mnógie, mnógix, mnógim, mnógimi* 'many'} , none of the above paradigms can generate an agreement system for it; if we define, say, C_1^{ij} for paradigm $\mathfrak{A}_1$ in the same way as we defined B^{ij}, the sets C_1^{11}, C_1^{12}. ..., C_1^{16} will be empty.

Nor will any of the paradigms $\mathfrak{A}_1, \overline{\mathfrak{A}}_1, \ldots, \mathfrak{A}_5$ generate an AS with respect to the one-element neighborhood D = {*čitat'*} 'to read' (we find it convenient to place the infinitive and personal forms of the verb in different neighborhoods), since any segment which belongs to the neighborhoods $A_1, \overline{A}_1, \ldots,$ A_5 cannot potentially subordinate the segment *čitát'* (so that if we define, for example, the sets D_1^{ij} for $\mathfrak{A}_1$ in the same way as we defined B^{ij}, all D_1^{ij} will be empty). However, the paradigm $\mathfrak{A}'$ = ⟨ *staránie, staránija, starániju, staránie, starániem, staránii, staránija, staránij, staránijam, staránija, staránijami, staránijax* ⟩ 'effort' generates with respect to D the agreement system D' = ⟨ *čitát', čitát', čitát', čitát', čitát', čitát', čitát', čitát', čitát', čitát', čitát', čitát'* ⟩ .

With respect to the neighborhood F = {*otéc, otcá, otcú, otcóm, otcé, otcý, otcóv, otcám, otcámi, otcáx*} 'father', each of the paradigms $A_1, \overline{A}_1, \ldots, A_5, A'$ generates one and the same AS $\mathfrak{F}$ = ⟨ {*otcá, otcóv*}, {*otcá, otcóv*}, {*otcá, otcóv*}, {*otcá, otcóv*}, {*otcá, otcóv*}, {*otcá, otcóv*}, {*otcá, otcóv*}, {*otcá, otcóv*}, {*otcá, otcóv*}, {*otcá, otcóv* } .

We will call a neighborhood AGREEABLE if with respect to it the paradigm of each *S*-neighborhood (except 'defective paradigms', which do not contain all cases) generates an AS which contains at least two different sets. Neighborhood *B* in our example is agreeable, while *C*, *D*, and *F* are not.

3. Now let *B* be any agreeable neighborhood, and let $\mathfrak{B} = \langle B^{11}, ..., B^{1k},$ $B^{21}, ..., B^{2k} \rangle$ be some ordered system of subsets of set *B*. $R_{\mathfrak{B}}$ will designate the union of all *S*-neighborhoods whose paradigms generate an agreement system equal to $\mathfrak{B}$ with respect to *B*. (If $\mathfrak{B}$ is not generated as an AS relative to *B* by any paradigms, then $R_{\mathfrak{B}}$ is empty.)

In the example just taken up it is possible to assume that $R_{\mathfrak{B}_1}$, $R_{\mathfrak{B}_2}$ and $R_{\mathfrak{B}_3}$ are sets of inanimate nouns – masculine, feminine, and neuter, respectively; $R_{\overline{\mathfrak{B}}_1}$, $R_{\overline{\mathfrak{B}}_2}$ and $R_{\overline{\mathfrak{B}}_3}$ are animate masculine, feminine and neuter nouns, respectively; $R_{\mathfrak{B}_4}$ and $R_{\overline{\mathfrak{B}}_4}$ are sets of inanimate and animate *pluralia tantum*, respectively; and $R_{\mathfrak{B}_5}$ is a set of nouns of 'common gender'.[19]

The set $R_{\mathfrak{B}}$ will be said to be MINIMAL if it is non-empty and if no non-empty $R_{\mathfrak{C}}$ is a proper subset of $R_{\mathfrak{B}}$. The sets $R_{\mathfrak{B}_1}$, $R_{\overline{\mathfrak{B}}_1}$, ..., $R_{\mathfrak{B}_5}$ treated above seem to be minimal.

We will call the minimal set $R_{\mathfrak{B}}$ the AGREEMENT CLASS (AC) DETERMINED BY SYSTEM $\mathfrak{B}$. If for two different systems $\mathfrak{B}$ and $\mathfrak{C}$ the sets $R_{\mathfrak{B}}$ and $R_{\mathfrak{C}}$ coincide, we shall consider these sets to be not two different AC's, but one and the same AC. For example, $R_{\mathfrak{B}_1}$ coincides with the AC defined by the system $\langle$ *bélyj, bélogo, bélomu, bélyj, bélym, bélom, bélye, bélyx, bélym, bélye, bélymi, bélyx* $\rangle$ 'white'.

Hence, we can assume that there are at least nine AC's in Russian: $R_{\mathfrak{B}_1}$, $R_{\overline{\mathfrak{B}}_1}$, $R_{\mathfrak{B}_2}$, $R_{\overline{\mathfrak{B}}_2}$, $R_{\mathfrak{B}_3}$, $R_{\overline{\mathfrak{B}}_3}$, $R_{\mathfrak{B}_4}$, $R_{\overline{\mathfrak{B}}_4}$, $R_{\mathfrak{B}_5}$. It seems plausible to assume that there are no other AC's [unless we take into account nouns with incomplete paradigms (see below) and words such as *šimpanzé* 'chimpanzee' (see Zaliznjak 1967: p.67)].

4. It seems expedient to introduce some new notions to help us explain the place of 'common gender' (agreement class $R_{\mathfrak{B}_5}$) in our system.

Let *R* be some AC. Δ will designate the set of all ordered systems $\mathfrak{B}$ for which $R = R_{\mathfrak{B}}$. Let $\Delta = \{\mathfrak{B}_1, ..., \mathfrak{B}_t\}$, where for every $l = 1, ..., t$, the system $\mathfrak{B}_l = \langle B_l^{11}, ..., B_l^{2k} \rangle$. Let $B_1^{11} \cup B_2^{11} \cup ... \cup B_t^{11} = \delta^{11}, ..., B_1^{2k} \cup ... \cup B_t^{2k} = \delta^{2k}$. The ordered system $\delta = \langle \delta^{11}, ... \delta^{1k}, \delta^{21}, ..., \delta^{2k} \rangle$ will be called the FULL AGREEMENT SYSTEM (FAS) corresponding to the agreement class *R*.

For example, the full agreement system for the agreement class $R_{\mathfrak{B}_1}$ (see above) will have the form $\langle \delta_1^{11}, ..., \delta_1^{26} \rangle$, where $\delta_1^{11} = \{$ *nóvyj, bol'šój, krásnyj* 'red', ...$\}$, $\delta_1^{12} = \{$ *nóvogo, bol'šógo, krásnogo, ...*$\}$, etc.

We will also say that the AC *R* is a JUNCTURE of the two AC's R' and R'' if the full agreement systems $\mathfrak{B} = \langle B^{11}, ..., B^{2k} \rangle$, $\mathfrak{C} = \langle C^{11}, ..., C^{2k} \rangle$, and $\mathfrak{D} = \langle D^{11}, ..., D^{2k} \rangle$ correspond to the classes R', R'' and R''', respectively, and if two conditions are fulfilled for any $i = 1, 2, j = 1, ..., k$: (1) $D^{ij} = B^{ij} \cup C^{ij}$;

(2) for each element of the set $R_{\mathfrak{D}} \cap S_i \cap \Pi_j$, in B^{ij} as well as in C^{ij} segments can be found which are potentially subordinated to it.[20] The class $R_{\mathfrak{B}_5}$ in our example is the juncture of $R_{\overline{\mathfrak{B}}_1}$ and $R_{\overline{\mathfrak{B}}_2}$.

From the linguistic point of view, the fact that $R_{\mathfrak{D}}$ is the juncture of $R_{\mathfrak{B}}$ and $R_{\mathfrak{C}}$ means that the nouns from $R_{\mathfrak{D}}$ can agree with the words subordinated to them either according to the rules which are operative for $R_{\mathfrak{B}}$, or according to the rules which are operative for $R_{\mathfrak{C}}$.[21]

We will now say that the AC R'' DOMINATES the AC R' if $R' \neq R''$ and R' is the juncture of R'' with some other AC.[22]

The AC $R_{\mathfrak{B}}$ will be said to be PRIMARY if there exists no AC which dominates $R_{\mathfrak{B}}$. In our example, $R_{\overline{\mathfrak{B}}_1}$ and $R_{\overline{\mathfrak{B}}_2}$ dominate $R_{\mathfrak{B}_5}$; all AC's except $R_{\mathfrak{B}_5}$ are primary.

Finally, the union of some primary AC and all the AC's which it dominates will be called a REDUCED AGREEMENT CLASS (RAC).

We obtain eight RAC's in our examples:

(1) $R_{\mathfrak{B}_1}$ ('masculine inanimate gender');
(2) $R_{\overline{\mathfrak{B}}_1} \cup R_{\mathfrak{B}_5}$ ('masculine animate gender');
(3) $R_{\mathfrak{B}_2}$ ('feminine inanimate gender');
(4) $R_{\overline{\mathfrak{B}}_2} \cup R_{\mathfrak{B}_5}$ ('feminine animate gender');
(5) $R_{\mathfrak{B}_3}$ ('neuter inanimate gender');
(6) $R_{\overline{\mathfrak{B}}_3}$ ('neuter animate gender');
(7) $R_{\mathfrak{B}_4}$ ('dual inanimate gender');
(8) $R_{\overline{\mathfrak{B}}_4}$ ('dual animate gender').[23]

5. For the sake of simplicity we have not treated nouns with incomplete paradigms – i.e., those for which there are empty sets among the sets of A^{ij}. If, using the definition of dominance formulated above, we attempt to take such nouns into consideration, they will be classified in special RAC's. In order to obtain a natural interpretation of nouns with incomplete paradigms it seems useful to introduce certain changes into our definitions of dominance and RAC which, however, will not affect these notions in instances where the paradigms of all the nouns are complete.

Let $\delta = \langle \delta^{11}, ..., \delta^{1k}, \delta^{21}, ..., \delta^{2k} \rangle$ and $\bar{\delta} = \langle \bar{\delta}^{11}, ..., \bar{\delta}^{1k}, \bar{\delta}^{21}, ..., \bar{\delta}^{2k} \rangle$ be two full agreement systems. We will say that $\bar{\delta}$ is a CONTRACTION of δ if for any i, j ($i = 1, 2; j = 1, ..., k$) for which $\bar{\delta}^{ij}$ is non-empty, δ^{ij} is also non-empty and the equality $\bar{\delta}^{ij} = \delta^{ij}$ holds.

Now, to change the definition in the preceding section, let us say that the AC R'' DOMINATES the AC R' if $R' \neq R''$ and either R' is a juncture of R'' with some other AC, or the FAS which corresponds to R' is a contraction of the FAS corresponding to R''. For example, the neighborhoods $\{ščec\}$ and $\{drovéc\}$ (diminutive forms from *šči* 'cabbage soup' and *drová* 'firewood' having only the genitive case), as it is easy to see, form an AC. The FAS $\langle \epsilon^{11}, \ldots, \epsilon^{16}, \epsilon^{21}, \ldots, \epsilon^{26} \rangle$ in which $\epsilon^{12} = \epsilon^{22} = \{\| bol'\check{s}\acute{\imath}x, n\acute{o}vyx, kr\acute{a}snyx, \ldots \}$ and the other sets are empty, will correspond to this AC. This FAS will be a contraction for the FAS's which correspond to the agreement classes $R_{\mathfrak{B}_4}$ and $R_{\overline{\mathfrak{B}}_4}$. The AC $\{\check{s}\check{c}ec, drov\acute{e}c\}$ will be contained in the seventh and eighth RAC's.

Furthermore, if we allow for the fact that certain nouns do not have plural forms (cf. note 19), then the FAS which corresponds to such a noun will be a contraction of the FAS corresponding to one of the agreement classes $R_{\mathfrak{B}_1}, R_{\mathfrak{B}_2}, R_{\mathfrak{B}_3}$, so that the *singularia tantum* will be naturally distributed among the first, third and fifth RAC's, respectively. (For example, if we assume that the paradigm of the neighborhood of the segment *molok\acute{o}* 'milk' has the form $\langle$ *molok\acute{o}, molok\acute{a}, molok\acute{u}, molok\acute{o}, molok\acute{o}m, molok\acute{e}*, $\emptyset, \emptyset, \emptyset, \emptyset, \emptyset, \emptyset \rangle$, then this neighborhood, even though it does not occur in the AC $R_{\mathfrak{B}3}$, will still be contained in the fifth RAC.)

Finally, note the following: In our treatment of the nouns which we assigned to the seventh and eighth RAC's, we proceeded from A. A. Zaliznjak's point of view, according to which they have singular forms which are homonymous to the corresponding plural forms. This view seems to us to be far more convincing than the traditional one, which consists in denying the existence of singular forms for these nouns. The applicability of our procedure for distinguishing AC's and RAC's does not, of course, depend on how we look upon the nature of the *pluralia tantum*, although if this view is changed the results of the procedure will also change. Namely, if we accept the traditional viewpoint (according to which, for example, the paradigm of the neighborhood of *s\acute{a}ni* 'sledge' will have the form $\langle \emptyset, \emptyset, \emptyset, \emptyset, \emptyset, \emptyset$, *s\acute{a}ni, san\acute{e}j, sanj\acute{a}m, s\acute{a}ni, sanj\acute{a}mi, sanj\acute{a}x* $\rangle$), the agreement classes $R_{\mathfrak{B}_4}$ and $R_{\overline{\mathfrak{B}}_4}$ will not form separate RAC's, but will be included in others — $R_{\mathfrak{B}4}$ will be contained in the first, third and fifth RAC's (in each of them), and $R_{\overline{\mathfrak{B}}4}$ in the second, fourth and sixth; thus we obtain a system of RAC's which correspond to the traditional Russian gender system.[24]

6. Our definitions do not exclude the possibility of 'gender homonymy', so that we can pose the question of finding a procedure for assigning RAC's to the *S*-segments in a sentence — on the analogy of the procedure described in item 4 of the preceding section. We proceed here from the assumption that the basic information includes not only the relation of syntactic subordination in a sentence, but also an indication of the number — singular or plural — assigned to a particular occurrence of an *S*-segment.

Such a procedure may have the following form. Assume that some occurrence of the *S*-segment *x* is fixed in a simple sentence with a syntactic subordination relation given on it, and let this occurrence be given the meaning either of singular or plural.[25] For simplicity we will limit ourselves to cases where the following two conditions are fulfilled: (i) the S-segment x belongs to some agreement class R, which is the only such class; (ii) the procedure described in item 4 of the preceding section assigns this segment x some case Π_j, which is the only such case. Now let us assume that:

(a) $Q_1, \ldots Q_n$ are all those RAC's which contain R, and $\delta_1 = |\langle \delta_1^{11}, \ldots, \delta_1^{2k} \rangle, \ldots, \delta_s = \langle \delta_j^{11}, \ldots \delta^{2k} \rangle$ are the FAS's corresponding to them (more precisely, the FAS's corresponding to primary AC's, which determine those RAC's);

(b) u is the segment whose occurrence immediately subordinates x;

(c) $u_1, \ldots, u_n$ are all the segments whose occurrences in a given sentence are immediately subordinated to the given occurrence of x and which at the same time agree with x for the number S_i and the case Π_j, where $i = 1$, if the given occurrence of x is assigned the meaning of singular, and $i = 2$, if the given occurrence of x is assigned the meaning of plural. (The segment u is necessarily present — in view of condition (ii); at the same time, the segments $u_1, \ldots, u_n$ may be absent.)

Now we will by definition assign the given occurrence x some of the RAC's from among $Q_1, \ldots, Q_n$ in the following manner: if the segments $u_1, \ldots, u_n$ are absent, then the given occurrence is assigned all the RAC's $Q_1, \ldots, Q_n$; otherwise it is assigned those and only those RAC's Q_e from among $Q_1, \ldots, Q_n$ for which at least one of the segments $u_1, \ldots, u_n$ belongs to δ_e^{ij}.

Assume, for example, that we wish to assign RAC's to the (single) occurrence of the segment $x = zabijáka$ 'bully' in the sentence *Ètot zabijaka postojanno derëtsja* 'This bully is always fighting', where the segment *zabijáka* is assigned the meaning of the singular. The segment *zabijáka* obviously belongs only to the single AC $R_{\mathcal{B}5}$ (see above), and the procedure of item 4 of the preceding sections assigns this segment the only case Π_1 (the nominative), so that conditions (i) and (ii) are fulfilled. We have $u = derëtsja$ 'fights', $n = 1$, $u_1 = ètot$ 'this' (as can easily be checked, the segment *ètot* agrees with the segment *zabijáka* for the singular and for the nominative case). There are two RAC's which contain $R_{\mathcal{B}5}$: the second and the fourth (see above, the end of item 4). If $\delta_2 = \langle \delta_2^{11}, \ldots, \delta_2^{26} \rangle$, $\delta_4 = \langle \delta_4^{11}, \ldots, \delta_4^{26} \rangle$ are the corresponding FAS's, then the segment *ètot* obviously belongs to δ_2^{11} and does not belong to δ_4^{11}. The given occurrence of the segment *zabijáka* is therefore assigned one RAC — the second ('masculine animate gender'). If we consider the sentence *Zabijaka postojanno derëtsja*, where the occurrence of the segment *zabijaka* is also assigned the meaning of the singular, then our procedure will assign this occurrence two RAC's — the second and the fourth (since here the segments $u_1, \ldots, u_n$ are absent).

It is easy to extend the procedure to cover a more general situation, where the segment x occurs in several AC's $R_1, \ldots, R_t$ and the procedure of

item 4 of the preceding section assigns this occurrence several cases:
Π_{i_1}, ..., Π_{i_r}. Then it is natural to proceed as follows: for each pair R_h, Π_{i_g}
($h = 1, ..., t$; $g = 1, ..., r$) apply the procedure described above, and by
definition assign the given occurrence of x all the RAC's obtained by this
procedure for all such pairs.

7. Note that in all of the examples in this section we used the traditional
conception according to which an S-neighborhood includes both singular and
plural forms. If we assume that the singular and plural forms of the noun
belong to different neighborhoods,[26] then the agreement classes for Russian
will, of course, be different. (At the same time, this will not affect the cases!)

5.   A DEFINITION OF GRAMMATICAL GENDER

1. The RAC's we have obtained for Russian are regarded by traditional
grammar as 'secondary' formations produced by combination of the categories
of gender and animacy. It is appropriate here to pose the question of the
place of these categories in our system.

    The category of animacy (in Russian nouns, at any rate) is an internal
category, so that it is hardly advisable to attempt to define it through our basic
notions. As for the category of gender, we will attempt to formulate a
definition for it which seems to adequately reflect its essence, which consists,
roughly speaking, in the following: gender is constructed like an agreement
class, but the role that cases play in the definition of AC's belongs, so to speak,
to the 'formal cases' in a definition of gender; more precisely, if two case-
number forms coincide for a given noun, and if they have the same segments
in agreement with them (for example, the nominative and accusative singular
forms of inanimate masculine and neuter nouns), then these forms should
in a definition of gender, 'fuse' into a single form.[27] Rather than formulate a
definition of gender independently, we think it simpler and more natural
to use the notion of agreement class we have already constructed.

2. Let R be some AC, let $\delta = \langle \delta^{11}, ..., \delta^{2k} \rangle$ be its corresponding FAS and
let A be some neighborhood contained in R. Assume that there exist two
sequences of sets from δ : $\delta^{i_1 j_1}, ..., \delta^{i_n j_n}, \delta^{i'_1 j'_1}, ..., \delta^{i'_n j'_n}$ (it is important to
emphasize that n is the same for both sequences) for which the equalities
$\delta^{i_1 j_1} = \delta^{i'_1 j'_1}, ..., \delta^{i_n j_n} = \delta^{i'_n j'_n}$ hold. We will eliminate all the sets
$\delta^{i'_1 j'_1}, ..., \delta^{i'_n j'_n}$ from the set δ and replace them with asterisks. This operation
will be called a CANCELLATION of the FAS δ, and the set obtained as a
result of the cancellation and consisting of sets and asterisks will be called a
CANCELLED FAS, designated δ'. We will say that neighborhood A is
CONJUGATE with the cancelled FAS δ'.

If, for example, $\delta_1 = \langle\ \delta_1^{11}, ..., \delta_1^{26}\ \rangle$ is the FAS which corresponds to the AC $R_{\mathfrak{B}_1}$ (Section 4, item 3), and A_1 is some neighborhood from the $R_{\mathfrak{B}_1}$, then we will have: $\delta^{11} = \delta^{14}, \delta^{21} = \delta^{24}$; therefore, if we replace δ^{14} and δ^{24} with asterisks, we produce cancellation of the FAS δ_1, and the neighborhood A_1 will be conjugate with the cancelled FAS $\delta_1' = \langle\ \delta_1^{11}, \delta_1^{12}, \delta_1^{13}, *, \delta_1^{15}, \delta_1^{16}, \delta_1^{21}, \delta_1^{22}, \delta_1^{23}, *, \delta_1^{25}, \delta_1^{26}\ \rangle$.

Now, if instead of δ_1 we take the FAS $\bar{\delta}_1 = \langle\ \bar{\delta}_1^{11}, ..., \bar{\delta}_1^{26}\ \rangle$, which corresponds to the AC R^-_1, and if instead of A_1 we take some neighborhood $\bar{A}_1$ from the $R_{\overline{\mathfrak{B}}_1}$, we will obtain a different system of equalities: $\bar{\delta}_1^{12} = \delta_1^{14}, \bar{\delta}_1^{22} = \bar{\delta}_1^{24}$. As a result of the cancellation of the FAS $\bar{\delta}_1$, however, we obtain the same cancelled FAS as in the preceding example.

Of course, different ways of cancellation of any one RAC may be possible (for example, it is possible to eliminate $\delta^{i_1 j_1}$ instead of $\delta^{i'_1 j'_1}$; we should also note that our definition does not contain any requirement of 'maximality' on the sequences $\delta^{i_1 j_1}, ..., \delta^{i'_1 j'_1} ...$; that is, nothing is said of the impossibility of 'further cancellation').

The union of all the neighborhoods which are conjugate with a given cancelled FAS will be called a FORMAL AGREEMENT CLASS (FAC). For the sake of generality, it is convenient to assume that every FAS is also a cancelled FAS and that every AC is accordingly an FAC.

It is clear that all the neighborhoods contained in one AC are conjugate with the same FAS's; therefore, every FAC is a union of some AC's.

Returning to the examples in the foregoing section, we are now able to distinguish for Russian the following FAC's (in addition to those which are AC's):

$R_{\mathfrak{B}_1} \cup R_{\overline{\mathfrak{B}}_1}$ – the FAC corresponding to the following cancelled FAS: $\langle\ |\{nóvyj, krásnyj, ...\}, \{nóvogo, krásnogo, ...\}, \{nóvomu, krásnomu, ...\}, *, \{nóvym, krásnym, ...\}, \{nóvom, krásnom\}, \{nóvye, krásnye, ...\}, \{nóvyx, krásnyx, ...\}, \{nóvym, krásnym, ...\}, *, \{nóvymi, krásnymi, ...\}, \{nóvyx, krásnyx, ...\}\ \rangle$.

$R_{\mathfrak{B}_2} \cup R_{\overline{\mathfrak{B}}_2}$ – the FAC corresponding to the cancelled FAS: $\langle\ |\{nóvaja, krásnaja, ...\}, \{nóvoj, krásnoj, ...\}, \{nóvoj, krásnoj, ...\}, \{nóvuju, krásnuju, ...\}, \{nóvoj, nóvoju, krásnoj, krásnoju, ...\}, \{nóvoj, krásnoj, ...\}, \{nóvye, krásnye, ...\}, \{nóvyx, krásnyx, ...\}, \{nóvym, krásnym ...\}, *, \{|nóvymi, krásnymi, ...\}, \{nóvyx, krásnyx, ...\}\ \rangle$.

$R_{\mathfrak{B}_3} \cup R_{\overline{\mathfrak{B}}_3}, R_{\mathfrak{B}_4} \cup R_{\overline{\mathfrak{B}}_4}$ – FAC's corresponding to cancelled FAS's which the reader can easily construct for himself.

It must be noted that a single FAC can correspond to more than one cancelled FAS. Thus, the FAC $R_{\mathfrak{B}_2} \cup R_{\overline{\mathfrak{B}}_2}$ corresponds, in addition to the cancelled FAS indicated above, to one which is obtained from it by eliminating the set occupying the third (or sixth) position.

3. We will call an FAC a GENDER if it is not contained in any other FAC.

We obtain the following five genders from our example:

(1) $R_{\mathfrak{B}_1} \cup R_{\overline{\mathfrak{B}}_1}$, (2) $R_{\mathfrak{B}_2} \cup R_{\overline{\mathfrak{B}}_2}$, (3) $R_{\mathfrak{B}_3} \cup R_{\overline{\mathfrak{B}}_3}$, (4) $R_{\mathfrak{B}_4} \cup R_{\overline{\mathfrak{B}}_4}$, (5) $R_{\mathfrak{B}_5}$.

Now we will define the juncture of two[28] FAC's as was done for the juncture of two AC's (Section 4, item 4). But instead of the FAS's we will use the corresponding cancelled FAS's if the asterisks in them occupy the same positions; if this condition is not met, we will preliminarily change these cancelled FAS's as follows: Assume, for example, that in the first of the two cancelled FAS's there is the set $\delta^{i'j'}$ in the position with the numbers i', j', and that there is an asterisk in the corresponding position in the second. Then we find i, j such that in the second cancelled FAS the set with which we 'identified' the set with the numbers i',j' during cancellation occupies the position with the numbers i, j (there can generally be several such pairs i, j, in which case we select any one of them). After that, in the first cancelled FAS we take the set δ^{ij} occupying the same position, replace it with the union $\delta^{ij} \cup \delta^{i'j'}$, and replace $\delta^{i'j'}$ with an asterisk. We proceed in this manner for every position which has an asterisk in only one system, whereafter we define the juncture by means of the procedure from item 4 of Section 4. Further, we define the contraction of the FAC's in the same way as in item 5 of Section 4, with the difference that we equate an asterisk to an empty set. Finally, we define the domination for the FAC's as this was done for the AC's in item 5 of Section 4 (and not as in item 4).

A gender which is not dominated by any other gender will be said to be PRIMARY. The set which consists of the union of a primary gender and all of the genders dominated by it will be said to be a REDUCED GENDER.

In our example the genders $R_{\mathfrak{B}_1} \cup R_{\overline{\mathfrak{B}}_1}$ and $R_{\mathfrak{B}_2} \cup R_{\overline{\mathfrak{B}}_2}$ dominate the gender $R_{\mathfrak{B}_5}$, and we have four reduced genders:

$$R_{\mathfrak{B}_1} \cup R_{\overline{\mathfrak{B}}_1} \cup R_{\mathfrak{B}_5} \quad \text{('masculine')}$$
$$R_{\mathfrak{B}_2} \cup R_{\overline{\mathfrak{B}}_2} \cup R_{\mathfrak{B}_5} \quad \text{('feminine')}$$
$$R_{\mathfrak{B}_3} \cup R_{\overline{\mathfrak{B}}_3} \quad \text{('neuter')}$$
$$R_{\mathfrak{B}_4} \cup R_{\overline{\mathfrak{B}}_4} \quad \text{('dual gender')}$$

It is curious that every gender here is a union of just two RAC's, one of which is contained in the class of all inanimate nouns, and the other in the class of all animate nouns.

4. Our definition of grammatical gender, which has been developed to apply mainly to Russian, also seems natural for a number of other languages, including those in which the nouns are not inflected for case (the definitions in Section 3 should give only one case for such a language). For example, for French our definition distinguishes two AC's which consist of masculine and feminine *pluralia tantum*, respectively, together with two more AC's which include nouns of masculine and feminine gender, respectively, with non-homonymous number forms (cf. Zaliznjak 1967: 79). Then an application of the procedures in this section joins both 'masculine' AC's into one gender and both 'feminine' AC's into another. In fact, if we use l_1 and l_2 to designate the sets of all possible masculine singular and plural forms respectively of the French adjective, then the FAS's corresponding to the agreement class R which consists of masculine nouns with non-homonymous number forms, and to $\tilde{R}$ which consists of masculine *pluralia tantum*, will be $L = \langle l_1, l_2 \rangle$ and $\tilde{L} = \langle l_2, l_2 \rangle$ respectively. Obviously, the FAS $\tilde{L}$ can be cancelled to obtain the cancelled FAS $\tilde{L}' = \langle *, l_2 \rangle$, where the FAC corresponding to this cancelled FAS will coincide with $\tilde{R}$. Thus $\tilde{R}$ is a contraction of R, and therefore R dominates $\tilde{R}$. Since each of the sets R and $\tilde{R}$ seems to be a gender, and since R does not dominate any gender other than $\tilde{R}$ and has no gender dominating it, the set $R \cup \tilde{R}$ proves to be a reduced gender. The reasoning for the feminine gender is similar.

ACKNOWLEDGEMENTS

The author became interested in the problem treated in the present paper while reading in manuscript the book Revzin 1967. The author was subsequently able, with great benefit for himself, to discuss the problem with A. A. Zaliznjak and the late I. I. Revzin. A. A. Zaliznjak and I. A. Mel'čuk read one of the first versions of the manuscript; the author has found their criticism to be very helpful. T. I. Šed'ko conducted the preliminary experimental checking of the definitions given here for Russian (see Šed'ko 1971a,b; the cases and genders distinguished in her experiment have largely coincided with the traditional ones) and discovered an inaccuracy in the definition of gender given in the first version. To all these colleagues the author is sincerely grateful.

    The author is also indebted to Johanna Nichols (Univ. of California, Berkeley), who read the English version of this paper, for her numerous remarks and corrections.

NOTES

Originally published in Russian in A.A. Zaliznjak (ed.), *Problemy grammatičeskogo modelirovanija,* Moscow 1973, 24-53. A preliminary version was published earlier (Gladkij 1969). Reprinted with some modifications from: Kiefer, F. (ed.), *Trends in Soviet Theoretical Linguistics,* 1973 (Dordrecht: D. Reidel), 201-230.

1. The word 'formal' here and below means 'rigorously defined, with no logical gaps' (and not 'with no reference to meaning', as the word is often understood in linguistic works). The only time we depart from this definition of the word is when we use it in the term 'formal agreement class' (Section 5).
2. This paper has been a bibliographical rarity for a long time. A somewhat modified presentation of Kolmogorov and Uspenskij's definition can be found in A. A. Zaliznjak's book (1967: §§2.3, 2.4).
3. The vagueness of the term 'word' (see below) does not present any serious obstacles to the present argument.
4. Of course, for the notion 'graphic coincidence' to have an exact meaning, a method of notation would have to be established beforehand.
5. Thus we consider the formation of the comparative degree of the adjective to belong to word formation (cf. Zaliznjak 1967: §2.23). This is, however, unimportant for our discussion.
6. All examples will be Russian. We use an accentuated orthographic notation for the segments in the examples (Zaliznjak 1967: §0.4), but the accent mark is omitted in coherent texts, in one-syllable segments, and over *ë* (cf. *ibid.,* §0.5).
7. Using the notion of a grammatical sentence to interpret potential subordination does not contradict the statement made above that this notion is not included among the basic concepts of our system. We actually need it only for purposes of ELUCIDATION. Besides, a knowledge of the WHOLE SET of grammatical sentences is not required for the practical compilation of a table of potential subordinations.
8. We need the sets S_1 and S_2 only to be able to define agreement class and gender.
9. The relations D_1 and D_2 will be used only to define agreement class and gender.
10. As will be seen from the definitions, this information is in fact needed only for those pairs x, y in which y is an S-segment.
11. Agreement class and gender could (with respect to Russian, in any case) be defined without referring to number, i.e., without using (e), and replacing the two relations D_1 and D_2 in (f) by a single 'relation of double potential subordination' (interpreted in the same way as D_1, but without the requirement that y have the meaning 'singular'). Such a definition, however, would seem less natural.
12. *Mešala → šupa* is true because there is, for example, the grammatical sentence

Ona ne mešala nikakogo supa   'She didn't stir any soup'.

13. Note that allowing phrases such as **nemnogo knigi* (lit. 'a little of book') or **nemnogo skvorca* (lit. 'a little of starling') is to sacrifice precision, but we have to deal with such approximations if we are to differentiate grammatical correctness from semantic normality.
14. We limit ourselves to this case due to the fact that our interpretation of the potential subordination relation (see Section 2) accounts for simple sentences only.

216   Elements of Mathematical Linguistics

15. This assertion follows from the fact that a sentence with the syntactic subordination relation given on it is a tree.

16. Cf. the completely analogous sentence *On ne otdal materi dočeri* 'He did not give back the daughter to the mother/the mother to the daughter', where it is impossible to resolve the syntactic homonymy even by considering meaning (on the basis of just this one sentence). The probability of encountering such a sentence in actual speech, of course, is small, but this fact can be explained by the tendency for speakers to avoid ambiguity.

17. *rodíteli* here is a (lexically meaningful) segment with the meaning 'father and mother' (as in the phrase *moi roditeli* 'my parents') as distinct from the (lexically meaningful) segment *rodíteli* with the meaning 'pl. of *roditel'* 'father or mother' (as in the phrase *vse roditeli, prišedšie na voskresnik – ix bylo desjat'* 'all the parents who came to the Sunday obligatory volunteer work – there were ten of them'). Note that the segment *rodíteli* in the first sense can have both a singular (*moi roditeli* 'my parents') and a plural (*moi i tvoi roditeli* 'my parents and your parents') meaning (cf. *moj i tvoj otcy* 'my and your fathers'). In certain word combinations the segment *rodíteli* can be regarded both as the plural of *roditeli* 'father and mother' and as the plural of *roditel'* 'father or mother'; for example, *roditeli učenikov vtorogo classa* 'the parents of the pupils in the second grade.'

18. In writing the ordered groups of sets of segments, we shall, in order to simplify the notation, identify each one-element set with its single element. i.e., write *dom* instead of $\{dom\}$.

19. We proceed from the assumption here that all nouns have plural forms. If we assume that certain nouns do not have plural forms, the picture changes: the classes $R_{\mathfrak{B}_1}$, $R_{\overline{\mathfrak{B}}_1}$, $R_{\mathfrak{B}_2}$, $R_{\overline{\mathfrak{B}}_2}$, $R_{\mathfrak{B}_3}$, $R_{\overline{\mathfrak{B}}_3}$, will include only nouns which have forms of both numbers, and the *singularia tantum* will constitute separate classes (for example, *singularia tantum* of the neuter gender will make up a class which corresponds to the ordered system of sets ⟨ *nóvoe, nóvogo, nóvomu, nóvoe, nóvym, nóvom*, $\emptyset$, $\emptyset$, $\emptyset$, $\emptyset$, $\emptyset$, $\emptyset$ ⟩, where $\emptyset$ is the empty set.

20. We could by analogy define the juncture of more than two AC's.

21. The notion of juncture is a refinement of A. A. Zaliznjak's notion of 'hybrid agreement class' (Zaliznjak 1967: § 2.15). It would, of course, be possible to 'split' each of the (lexically meaningful) segments of the type *zadira* into two segments having the meanings 'masculine' and 'feminine', respectively (as is done in the second chapter of Zaliznjak 1967), in which case there would be no agreement class $R_{\mathfrak{B}_4}$.

22. In order to obtain greater generality, we should foresee a case where R' would be a juncture of more than two AC's, one of which would be R'' (see footnote 20), but for the sake of simplicity we will limit ourselves to junctures of two AC's.

23. The term 'dual gender' is borrowed from A. A. Zaliznjak (1967: § 2.19). True, Zaliznjak does not distinguish a 'dual animate gender', which seems to us to be a fully natural formation, even though it consists of a very few neighborhoods. Besides the neighborhood of the segment *rodíteli* it includes, for example, the neighborhoods of the segments *suprúgi* 'spouses', *ljubóvniki* 'lovers', *vljublënnye* 'lovers', *narečënnye* 'the betrothed', each of which segments has one or two lexically homonymous segments: for example, besides the segment *suprúgi* 'husband and wife' we have the segment *suprúgi* (pl. of *suprúg* 'husband') and the segment *suprúgi* (pl. of *suprúga* 'wife'), and the neutralization of this homonymy is possible in certain contexts (cf. note 17). As for the neighborhoods of the segments *bélye* 'white' and *čërnye* 'black' as the names of sides in chess, etc. (Zaliznjak 1967: 78), homonymy occurs here, also: in the meaning 'white/black chessmen' these segments fall into the 'dual inanimate gender', but in the meaning 'the player who plays the white/black pieces', they belong to the 'dual animate';

cf. Zaliznjak's examples: *Beri sebe belye, a ja voz'mu černye* 'You take white and I'll take black'; *On vynudil belyx sdat'sja* 'He forced white to surrender'.
24. A.A. Zaliznjak notes (1967:76) that such a gender system is unsatisfactory even with regard to the traditional view of *pluralia tantum*. This, however, is connected with the fact that he refutes one other inexplicit premise in the traditional gender system, which consists in accounting for 'direct' agreement only. We, on the other hand, have retained this premise in our constructions. Accounting for 'indirect' agreement would result in a significant complication of our definitions and at the same time (in contrast to the case system – cf. the end of Section 3), would hardly give us any serious gain in naturalness. (For Russian, it seems that we can note only one instance where some benefit might be derived: the nouns *ščec, drovéc* will not, in the 'non-traditional' interpretation, occur in the seventh and eighth RAC's simultaneously, but will occur only in the seventh, due to constructions such as *Ja videl nekotorye iz tex drovec...* 'I saw some of that firewood . . .' This instance, however, is rather isolated, and the naturalness of such a modification is open to discussion.
25. Here, of course, it is natural to demand that the meaning of singular (plural) be assigned to the given occurrence of *x* only under the condition that *x* belongs to S_1 (respectively S_2).
26. This alternative is discussed in Zaliznjak 1967: §2. 11 and Zaliznjak 1964.
27. The author is indebted for the formulation of this point of view to his discussions with I. A. Mel'čuk.
28. Or more – cf. note 20.

REFERENCES

Gladkij, A. V.
   1969   'K opredeleniju ponjatij padeža i roda suščestvitel'nogo', *Voprosy jazykoznanija* (2): 110–123.
Hjelmslev, L.
   1953   *Prolegomena to a Theory of Language* (Baltimore).
Jakobson, R.
   1936   'Beitrag zur allgemeinen Kasuslehre', *Travaux du Cercle Linguistique de Prague* 6:240-287.
Kulagina, O. S.
   1958   'Ob odnom sposobe opredelenija grammatičeskix ponjatij na baze teorii množestv', *Problemy kibernetiki* 1: 203–214.
Marcus, S.
   1967a   *Introduction mathématique à la linguistique structurale* (Paris).
   1967b   *Algebraic Linguistics: Analytical Models* (N.Y. – London).
Revzin, I. I.
   1967   *Metod modelirovanija i tipologija slavjanskix jazykov* (Moscow: Nauka).
Šed'ko, T. I.
   1971a   'Proverka formal'nogo opredelenija padeža suščestvitel'nogo na materiale russkogo jazyka', *Naučno-texničeskaja informacija*, ser. 2 (5): 28–42.
   1971b   'Proverka formal'nogo opredelenija roda suščestvitel'nogo na materiale russkogo jazyka', *Naučno-texničeskaja informacija*, ser. 2 (7): 29–34.

Uspenskij, V. A.
   1957   'K opredeleniju padeža po A. N. Kolmogorovu', *Bjulleten' ob"jedinenija po problemam mašinnogo perevoda* 5: 11–18.
Zaliznjak, A. A.
   1964   'K voprosu o grammatičeskix kategorijax roda i oduševlennosti v russkom jazyke', *Voprosy jazykoznanija* (4): 25–40.
   1967   *Russkoe imennoe slovoizmenenie* (Moscow:Nauka).

Toward a Linguistic Meaning ⟺ Text Model

SUMMARY

1. The proposed model is a translative, rather than a generative, system; it establishes
correspondences between any given meaning and (ideally) all synonymous texts having
this meaning. I assume here (i) that meaning can formally be described as an invariant
of a set of equisignificant texts, (ii) that analysis of meaning as such lies outside the
model, and (iii) that a Meaning ⟺ Text Model (MTM) is a fragment of the more general
model 'Reality ⟺ (Meaning ⟺ Text) ⟺ Speech'.
2. Five levels of utterance representation are used in our MTM: (I) the semantic level
—a semantic network (semantic atoms – *semes* – connected by semantic relations) plus
indications of topicalization, emphasis, etc.; (II) The syntactic level, with two sub-levels:
(IIa) The deep-syntactic representation of a sentence a deep dependency tree with
universal deep-syntactic relations plus indications of topicalization, anaphoric relations,
and prosody; (IIb) The surface-syntactic representation of the sentence – a surface
dependency tree with the specific syntactic relations of the language in question plus
the same additional information as in (IIa); (III) The morphological level: (IIIa) The
deep-morphological representation of the sentence: a sequence of deep-morphological
representations of word-forms (the name of the corresponding lexeme supplied with a
full morphological description); (IIIb) The surface-morphological representation of the
sentence: a sequence of surface-morphological representations of word-forms (a string
of morphemes and/or morphological operations); (IV) The phonological level; (V) The
phonetic/graphic-orthographic level.
3. The MTM consists of five basic components which establish correspondences
between the representations of the above levels. Examples of the rules of each component
are given.
4. Certain linguistic problems connected with the MTM are mentioned: a new type
of dictionary (two dictionary entries are given); word-derivation and the possible formal-
semantic relations between linguistic signs (*signifié, signifiant,* syntactics – description
of the combinatorial properties of the sign); and a tentative definition of conversion in
English.

This paper proceeds from the following hypothesis: a natural language may
be viewed as a special kind of (logical) device which provides both for
the *comprehension of a given utterance*, i.e., the *perception of its meaning(s)*,
and for the *construction of utterances which express a given meaning*. Then a
language should be a device which provides for correspondences between
meanings and texts, or maps the set of all possible meanings onto the set of
all possible texts – and vice versa.

Hypotheses about such devices can be formulated as functional models, or logical systems, describing the mapping 'Meaning ⟷ Text'. I propose to discuss one such model below.

Here, of course, only a very general description of the model can be given; the exposition will of necessity be sketchy and somewhat dogmatic. The relationship between our Meaning ⟺ Text model and the very closely related linguistic models proposed by the theories of generative grammars and generative semantics will not be touched upon at all. It should be emphasized only that N. Chomsky's theories and their modern development by C. Fillmore, G. Lakoff, J. McCawley, and many others have significantly influenced me. I am in addition particularly indebted to A. K. Žolkovskij, with whom I have worked in close contact for several years. Many of my proposals below have been taken from the joint works of A. K. Žolkovskij and myself (most notably, Žolkovskij and Mel'čuk 1967).

N.B.: Reference will be made exclusively to publications by the authors of the Meaning ⟺ Text model described in this paper.

1.   PROPERTIES OF MEANING ⟺ TEXT MODELS

The main feature of a Meaning ⟺ Text model (MTM) consists in the following: it is not a generative, but a translative system; it does not seek *to generate* grammatically correct (or meaningful, etc.) texts, but merely *to match*, ideally, *any* given meaning with all synonymous texts having this meaning, and conversely, *to match any* given text with all the meanings this text can have. The following three assumptions are made:

(a) We are able to describe the meaning of any utterance in a special semantic language. (Meaning is understood to be an invariant of a set of equi-significant texts and this equisignificance is considered to be intuitely obvious to a native speaker.)

(b) The analysis of meaning itself (the discovery of various semantic anomalies – contradictions, absurdities, trivialities, etc.) goes beyond the MTM as such; a different type of device is needed for this purpose.[1]

(c) Any Meaning ⟺ Text model should be a fragment of the more general model of human (intellectual + linguistic) behaviour: Reality ⟺ Speech, i.e.,

$$\underbrace{\text{Reality} \Leftrightarrow \underbrace{\text{Meaning} \Leftrightarrow \text{Text}}_{\text{II}} \Leftrightarrow \text{Speech}}_{} .$$

| I | II | III |

In my opinion, only fragment II is a legitimate object of linguistics proper; only this fragment is represented in the MTM.

The following five limitations have been observed in my work on MTM:

(i) The MTM is a *purely functional* model. No attempt has been made to relate it experimentally to psychological or neurological reality; for the time being, therefore, the MTM is nothing more than a logical means for describing observable correspondences between meanings and texts.

(ii) The transformation 'meanings ⇔ texts' is described in the MTM only as *a set of correspondences* between the former and the latter. The possible *procedures* for moving from meanings to texts and vice versa are not treated at all. In other words, the MTM in its present state models only speakers' *competence*, and not *performance.*

(iii) Possible 'feedback' between texts and meanings in the process of speaking or understanding (changes in the original semantic message under the influence of an already constructed text, etc.) are not taken into account.

(iv) Functions of natural language other than the communicative one are not considered at all. This entails a view of language as a communication system only, that is, as a Meaning ⇔ Text transformer.

(v) The extremely important question of how language is acquired and perfected will be left completely untouched.

The MTM has been developed primarily on the basis of Russian linguistic data, which will be used as illustrative material in the present paper.

For a general description of the Meaning ⇔ Text model see Mel'čuk 1970 and 1974.

2. UTTERANCE REPRESENTATION LEVELS IN THE
    MEANING ⇔ TEXT MODEL

In view of the fact that homonymy and synonymy, so widespread in natural languages, often obliterate any direct correspondence between meanings and texts, a number of *levels of representation* have been established in the MTM.[2] Five levels for the representation of utterances are distinguished: semantic, syntactic, morphological, phonological, and phonetic/graphic.

(I) *The semantic level:* the utterance is assigned *a semantic representation*; as an example, see (1) — the semantic representation of a set of synonymous Russian utterances exemplified by the sentence

Ivan tvërdo obeščal Petru, čto večerom on primet Mariju samym tëplym obrazom 'John firmly promised Peter that [this] evening he would receive Mary in a most cordial manner'.

(1)

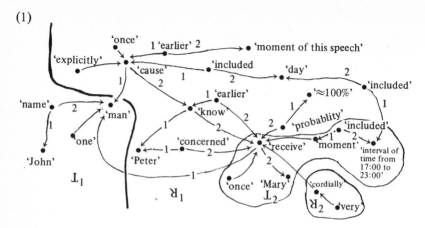

N.B.: This and all subsequent examples do not claim to be semantically precise. They are purely illustrative in nature.

A possible approximate reading: 'A man whose name is John explicitly caused once [past form of verb is represented by 'earlier than the moment of this speech'] (a man whose name is) Peter to know that later he, John, would receive (a woman whose name is) Mary, with which reception Peter is concerned, in a moment included in the time interval from 17:00 to 23:00 in the day of the speech act, and the reception, which has a probability of nearly 100%, would be very cordial'.

The semantic representation consists of the following two components:

1. A *semantic network,* or *semantic structure,* gives the meaning of an utterance without distributing it into sentences or words. (Such linguistic features as the selection of specific words and syntactic constructions are deliberately omitted from the semantic network.) Formally, the network is a connected oriented graph without circuits.[3]

The nodes of the network are *semantic units* (SU) which generally represent 'semantic atoms' – meanings which, within the given description, are considered to be elementary; these meanings are called *semes*. By way of abbreviation, however, we allow 'intermediate' SU's – symbolizing complexes of semes, i.e., whole semantic (sub)networks. Thus, in (1) the SU '*A* ← earlier [than] → *B*' is an abbreviation for 'the time of *A* precedes the time of *B*', and the SU 'know' is an abbreviation of something like 'have true information about'; it is obvious that 'concerned', 'receive', and 'cordially' are all far from elementary. A complete analysis into semes would make the network unreadable.

The arcs of the network are *semantic relations,* i.e., relations between SU's. SU's divide into two classes. One type of SU consists of *names of classes of objects* or *of single objects* – in particular, proper names; semantic relation arcs can only enter them. The other type of SU, conventionally called *predicates*, consists of predicates proper, quantifiers, and logical connectives; arcs can both enter and leave these. (The arrows on the arcs point from predicates to their arguments.)

Elementary predicate semes are never more than two-place; intermediate SU's can have up to five (perhaps more) places. The various arcs leaving a single node are numbered: $A \xleftarrow{1}$ 'cause' $\xrightarrow{2} B$ means that A is the first, and B the second argument of the predicate 'cause' (A is the causer, or the cause; B is the caused, or the result, etc.). Physical distribution on paper of the nodes of a semantic network is obviously of no importance.

2.   The *semantic-communicative structure* of the utterance: topic (L, Fr. *thème*)/comment (Я, Fr. *rhème*), old/new, psychological value of a particular meaning fragment for the speaker, emotional emphasis. This information stands in approximately the same relationship to the semantic network as do prosodic phenomena to the string of phonemes which make up a sentence. (In our simplified examples only the topic-comment division is indicated.)

The division into topic and comment can have successive 'strata'; thus, within the comment of the first stratum in (1), there is a division into L_2 – $Я_2$.

(II) The *syntactic level* is differentiated into two sublevels.

(IIa) *Deep syntax*: the utterance is given as a sequence of sentences; each sentence is assigned a so-called *deep-syntactic representation* (DSR); see (2)–(4) – deep-syntactic representations of synonymous Russian sentences corresponding to semantic network (1):

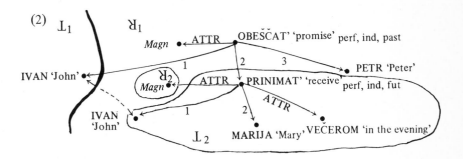

Ivan tvёrdo obeščal Petru, čto večerom on primet Mariju samym tёplym obrazom 'John firmly promised Peter that this evening he would receive Mary in the most cordial manner'.

(3)

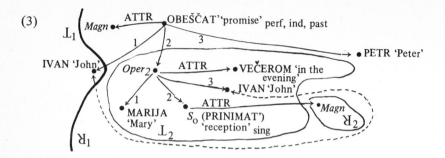

*Ivan tvërdo obeščal Petru, čto večerom Marija najdët u nego samyj tëplyj
〈 radušnyj〉 priëm* 'John firmly promised Peter that this evening Mary
would find a most cordial 〈 hearty 〉 welcome at his home'.

(4)

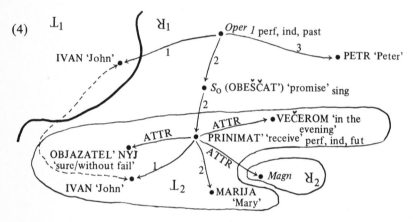

*Ivan dal Petru obeščanie večerom objazatel'no prinjat' Mariju samym
tëplym obrazom* 'John gave Peter his promise that this evening he would
without fail receive Mary in the most cordial manner 〈 most cordially 〉'.

The deep-syntactic representation of a sentence consists of the following
four components:
1.   The *deep-syntactic structure* (DSS) of a sentence is a dependency tree
whose nodes are *generalized lexemes* and whose branches are *deep-syntactic
relations. N.B.*: The linear order of the DSS nodes is not given.
    A generalized lexeme is one of the following four objects:
    Either it is a full lexeme of the language in question (empty words, strongly
governed prepositions and conjunctions, auxiliary verbs in analytical verbal
forms, etc., are not represented in the DSS);

Or it is a fictive lexeme: for example, the symbol for an indefinite personal subject ($\approx$ Fr. *on*, Ger. *man*), which has no expression in an actual Russian text;

Or it is an idiom: e.g., Russ. *s"est' sobaku* 'know something backwards and forwards, know one's stuff', *sinij čulok* 'bluestocking', etc.;

Or it is a symbol for a lexical function (see below).

The symbol of a generalized lexeme can have subscripts for the morphological features which have meaning of their own and are not determined syntactically: number of the noun; aspect, tense, and mood of the verb.

A *lexical function* (LF) **f** is a dependence which connects a key word (or phrase) *W* –the *argument* of LF -- with a set of other words or phrases **f**(*W*) – the *value* of LF – in such a way that for any W^1 and W^2, if only $\mathbf{f}(W^1)$ and $\mathbf{f}(W^2)$ exist, both $\mathbf{f}(W^1)$ and $\mathbf{f}(W^2)$ hold an identical relationship with respect to meaning and syntactic role – to W^1 and W^2, respectively; in the majority of cases $\mathbf{f}(W)$ is also different for different *W*'s, which means that $\mathbf{f}(W)$ is 'phraseologically bound' by *W*. We have arrived at about 50 *standard elementary* LF's – that is, those whose number of possible arguments and number of possible values is sufficiently large. *Complex* LF's, which are composed of elementary LF's, are also possible.

Some examples of LF's:

Syn (*priglašat'* 'invite') = *zvat'* 'ask, call', **Syn** (*xudoj* 'thin') = *toščij* 'skinny' [synonym];

Conv$_{21}$ (*pered* 'in front of') = *szadi* 'in back of', **Conv$_{21}$** (*sledovat'* 'follow') = *predšestvovat'* 'precede' [conversive];

S$_0$ (*polagat'* 'believe') = *mnenie* 'opinion' [nomen actionis] ;

Magn (*priglašenie* 'invitation')= *nastojčivoe* 'urgent, persistent', **Magn** (*bereč'* 'keep, cherish') = *kak zenicu oka* 'like the apple of one's eye'. **Magn** (*xudoj* 'thin') = *kak skelet/ščepka* 'as a skeleton/a lath' [= 'very', i.e. an intensifier] ;

Oper$_1$ (*prikaz* 'order') = *davat'* 'give', **Oper$_1$** (*mnenie* 'opinion') = *imet'*, *priderživat'sja* 'have, hold' [= 'be the subject of''] ;

Oper$_2$ (*priglašenie* 'invitation') = *polučat'* 'receive', **Oper$_2$** (*kontrol'* 'control') = *byt' pod* 'be under' [= 'be the object of'] ;

Real₁ (*obeščanie* 'promise') = *sderžat'* 'keep' [= 'fulfill or perform being the subject of'];

Real₂ (*prikaz* 'order') = *vypolnit'* 'perform, execute' [= 'fulfill or perform being the object of'];

Son (*korova* 'cow') = *myčat'* 'low, moo', **Son** (*stëkla* 'window panes') = *zvenet'*, *drebezžat'* 'jingle, jar' [typical sound]; etc.

LF's play a very important role in synonymous paraphrasing (see below, p. 232 ff.), i.e., on the plane of synonymy reduction. Concerning LF's see Mel'čuk 1967c; Mel'čuk and Žolkovskij 1970: 24-32; Žolkovskij and Mel'čuk 1970: 35-60; Mel'čuk 1974: 78 ff.

A *deep-syntactic relation* is one of the following relations:
— 1, 2, 3, 4, 5 (perhaps 6) are relations which connect a predicate lexeme with its first, second, third, fourth, fifth (or sixth) arguments, respectively:

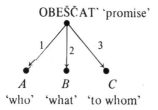

OBEŠČAT' 'promise'

          1   2   3

      A   *B*   *C*
    'who' 'what' 'to whom'

— ATTR is a relation which connects any entity with its attribute, or modifier (in the broadest sense of the term):

TOČKA   ÈTOT
'point' •————ATTR————→• 'this'

PRINIMAT'   VEČEROM
'greet', 'receive' •————ATTR————→• 'in the evening', etc.

— COORD is a relation which connects any two coordinated (grammatically conjoined) entities:

IVAN 'John' PETR 'Peter' I 'and' MARIJA 'Mary',
•————COORD————→•————COORD————→•——2——→•

i.e. 'John, Peter, and Mary'.

— APPEND is a relation which connects the root of the sentence deep-syntactic tree with any so-called 'loose' element (such as a parenthetical expression, interjection, address, etc.):

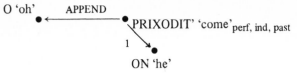

i.e. 'Oh, he came'.

We presume that these relations are sufficient to describe any syntactic construction of any language on the deep level.

2. The *deep-communicative structure* of a sentence includes, specifically, indications of topic and comment, see Ⴑ and Ⴔ in (2)–(4).

3. The *deep-anaphoric structure* of a sentence specifies coreferentiality of particular phrases; in (2)–(4) the coreferential nodes ('the same John') are connected by a dotted arrow.

4. The *deep-prosodic structure* of a sentence presents information about meaningful (i.e. not syntactically conditioned) prosodic phenomena such as intonation contours, pauses, junctures, emphatic stresses, and the like.

(IIb) *Surface syntax*: utterances are given as sequences of sentences; each sentence is assigned a surface-syntactic representation (SSR); see (5), which is the SSR corresponding to DSR (3), and (6) (7), which are the SSR's corresponding to DSR (4):

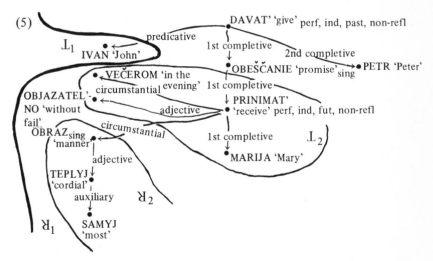

Ivan dal Petru obeščanie večerom objazatel'no prinjat' Mariju samym těplym obrazom 'John gave Peter his promise that this evening he would without fail welcome Mary in a most cordial manner ⟨ most cordially ⟩'.

(6)

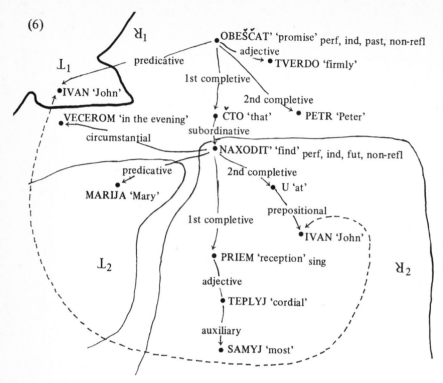

Ivan tvёrdo obeščal Petru, čto večerom Marija najdёt u nego samyj tёplyj priёm 'John firmly promised Peter that this evening Mary would find a most cordial welcome at his home / he would give Mary a most cordial welcome'.

(7)

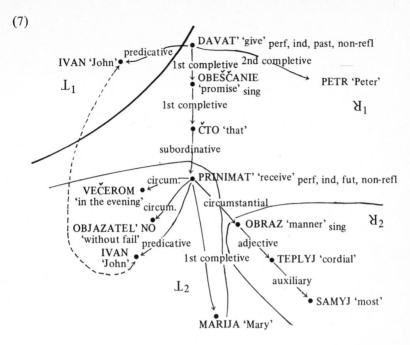

Ivan dal Petru obeščanie, čto večerom on objazatel'no primet Mariju samym tëplym obrazom 'John gave Peter his promise that he would without fail welcome Mary this evening in a most cordial manner ⟨ most cordially ⟩'.

The surface-syntactic representation of a sentence also consists of four components:

1. The *surface-syntactic structure* (SSS) of a sentence is a dependency tree whose nodes are specific *lexemes* (*all* lexemes of the sentence, including the auxiliary, or empty, ones — i.e., function words — as well as zero lexemes such as the zero copula of Russian) and whose branches are *surface-syntactic relations*, or SSR's. About 50 SSR's representing language-specific syntactic constructions can be distinguished, e.g., for Russian. As was the case in the DSS, the nodes of the SSS are not ordered linearly. This is done to keep apart two different types of relations in a sentence: structural, hierarchical relations as such, and those of linear order, which serve as a means (highly important in a language like English) of encoding the former in actual text.

2–4. The *surface-communicative, surface-anaphoric,* and *surface-prosodic structures* of a sentence (analogous to the structures of the deep-syntactic representation).

(III) The *morphological level* also divides into two sub-levels.

(IIIa) *Deep morphology*: utterances are represented as sequences of sentences; each sentence is assigned a sequence of linearly ordered deep-morphological representations (DMR) of word-forms (and indications, which will not be considered here, of prosodic features or punctuation marks); see (8), which corresponds to surface-syntactic representation (6):

(8)   IVAN 'John'$_{sing, nom}$ TVERDO 'firmly'
       OBEŠČAT 'promise'$_{perf, ind, past, non-refl, sing, masc}$
       PETR 'Peter' $_{sing, dat}$ ČTO 'that'   MARIJA 'Mary'$_{sing, nom}$
       NAXODIT' 'find'$_{perf, ind, fut, non-refl, 3sing}$
       U 'at'   ON 'he'$_{masc, sing, gen}$
       VEČEROM 'this evening'
       SAMYJ 'most'$_{masc, sing, acc}$ TEPLYJ 'cordial'$_{masc, sing, acc}$
       PRIEM 'reception'$_{sing, acc}$

A word-form DMR consists of the name of the corresponding lexeme together with the full morphological description needed to specify unambiguously that particular word-form.

(IIIb) *Surface morphology*: utterances are given as sequences of sentences; each sentence is assigned a sequence of morpheme strings and symbols of morphological operations, each of which specifies a word-form; see (9), which corresponds to representation (8):

(9)   {IVAN 'John'} + { SING. NOM }
       {TVERDO 'firmly'}
       {OBEŠČAT' 'promise'} + {PERF} + {PAST } +{MASC}
       {PETR 'Peter'} + { SING. DAT }
       {ČTO 'that'}
       {MARIJA 'Mary'} + {SING. NOM }
       {NAXODIT' 'find'} + {PERF} + {IND. NON-PAST 3 SING}
       {U 'at'}
       {ON 'he'} + {SING. GEN }
       {VEČEROM 'this evening'}
       {SAMYJ 'most'} + {MASC. SING. ACC}
       {TEPLYJ 'cordial' } + {MASC. SING. ACC}
       {PRIEM 'reception'} + {SING. ACC}.

A morpheme is understood to be a class of morphs (= minimal linguistic signs) which have an identical *signifié* and satisfy sufficiently simple distribution rules.

(IV) The *phonological level:* the phonemic transcription of the sentence with all of its prosodemes indicated.

(V) The *phonetic/graphic level:* the phonetic transcription of the sentence showing all prosodic phenomena, or the spelling of the sentence properly punctuated. Levels IV and V are not treated in the present paper.

3. THE DESIGN OF THE MEANING ⇔ TEXT MODEL

Transitions from one level of utterance representation to another are accomplished by the following five basic components of the model.

(I) The *semantic component* establishes correspondences between the semantic representation of an utterance and all alternative (= synonymous) sequences of deep-syntactic representations of the sentences which make up this utterance.

When moving from meaning to text, the semantic component of the model performs the following six operations:

1.   It cuts the semantic network into subnetworks, each of which corresponds to a sentence.

2.   It selects the corresponding words using semantico-lexemic rules of the following type:

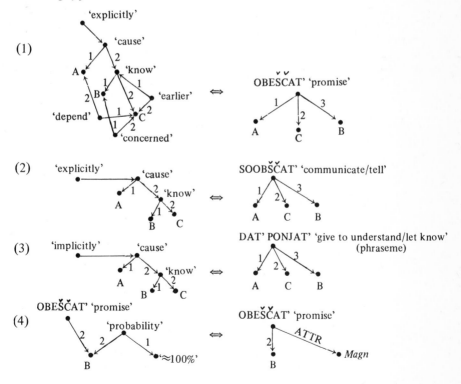

3. It selects the semantic (i.e., syntactically unconditioned) morphological characteristics of the lexical items by means of semantico-morphological rules of the following type:

(5)   'earlier'

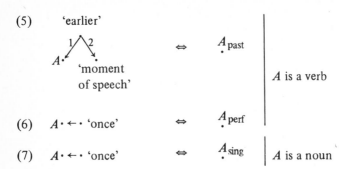

(6) $A \cdot \leftarrow \cdot$ 'once' $\Leftrightarrow$ A perf

(7) $A \cdot \leftarrow \cdot$ 'once' $\Leftrightarrow$ A sing A is a noun

4. It forms the deep-syntactic structure of the sentence.

5. It processes the remaining components of its deep-syntactic representation.

6. It constructs, for each DSS, all its synonymous DSS's such that this synonymy can be described in terms of lexical functions. In other words, it defines an 'algebra' of the transformations over the set of all DSS's which contain LF symbols.

These transformations[4] can be described by two classes of rules:

Lexical rules (of which there are some 60 at present) are either *semantic equivalencies* or *semantic implications*. Examples:

Equivalences:[5]

(8) $\begin{matrix} X & Y \\ C \Leftrightarrow \mathrm{Conv}_{21} & (C) \end{matrix}$

$$C$$
Množestvo A soderžit takže točku x 'The set A also contains the
$$\mathrm{Conv}_{21} \; (C)$$
point x' $\Leftrightarrow$ *Množestvu A prinadležit takže točka x* 'The point x also belong$\mathsf{s}$
to the set A'.

(9) $\begin{matrix} X & Y \\ C \Leftrightarrow \mathrm{Adv}_{1\mathrm{B}} & (C) \end{matrix}$
$\quad\quad C$ $\quad\quad\quad\quad\quad\quad\quad\quad\quad\quad \mathrm{Adv}_{1\mathrm{B}}\,(C)$
On pospešil vyjti 'He hurried to leave' $\Leftrightarrow$ *On pospešno vyšel* 'He hurriedly left'.

$$\overset{X\qquad Y\qquad Z}{(10)\quad C \Leftrightarrow S_0(C) + \mathrm{Oper}_1\,(S_0(C))}$$

$$\overset{C}{}\qquad\qquad \overset{\mathrm{Oper}_1\quad S_0\,(C)}{}$$

On boretsja 'He is struggling' ⟷ *On vedet   bor'bu* 'He is waging
a struggle'.

$$\overset{X\qquad\qquad Y}{(11)\quad \mathrm{Real}_2\,(C) \Leftrightarrow \mathrm{Adv}_{1B}\,(\mathrm{Real}_2\,(C))}$$

$$\overset{\mathrm{Real}_2\qquad C}{}$$

On posledoval ee sovetu uexat' 'He followed her advice to leave'

$$\overset{\mathrm{Adv}_1 _B\qquad C}{}$$

⟷ *On uexal   po   ee sovetu* 'He left on her advice'.

Implications:

(12) $\mathrm{PerfCaus}\,(X) \Rightarrow \mathrm{PerfIncep}\,(X)$

$$\overset{\mathrm{PerfCausFunc}_0\,(C)\quad C}{}\qquad\qquad\qquad \overset{C}{}$$

Petr   zapustil   motor 'Peter started the motor' ⇒ *Motor*

$$\overset{\mathrm{PerfIncepFunc}_0\,(C)}{}$$

zarabotal 'The motor started'.

(13) $\mathrm{PerfIncep}\,(X) \Rightarrow X$

$$\overset{C\quad \mathrm{PerfIncepFunc}_0\,(C)}{}\qquad\qquad\qquad \overset{C\quad \mathrm{Func}_0\,(C)}{}$$

Motor   zarabotal   'The motor started' ⇒ Motor rabotaet

'The motor is running'.

Syntactic rules describe the dependency tree transformations and indicate
what restructuring of the DSS's are necessary when a particular lexical rule
is applied. Thus for the lexical rules (8) – (11) to operate, the following
types of syntactic rules are necessary:

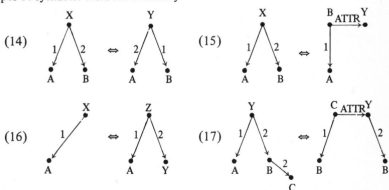

For DSS transformation rules, see Žolkovskij and Mel'čuk 1970: 60-81.

A special formalism has been devised for describing unordered dependency
tree transformations – so called Δ-grammars (Gladkij and Mel'čuk 1969, 1971,
1974; see this volume, pp. 151–187).

(II) The *syntactic component* establishes correspondences between the deep-syntactic representation of a sentence and all the deep-morphological representations which correspond to it. These correspondences are established in two stages.

(IIa) The transition from the deep-syntactic representation of a sentence to all its alternative surface-syntactic representations can be conceived of as two kinds of operations:

1. DSS ⇔ SSS transformations. DSS-to-SSS transformation rules are used when moving from meaning to text and these rules again divide into two classes:

— *Lexical rules* transform the nodes of the trees.

With the help of the lexicon, they 'compute' the values of the lexical functions, e.g.,

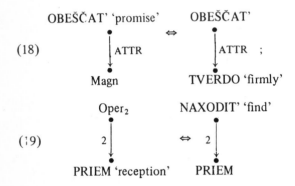

or expand the symbols of the phrasemes into surface-syntactic sub-trees, e.g.,

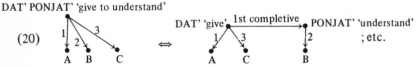

— *Syntactic rules* transform the tree itself, in the following four ways:

(a) The replacement of a deep relation by a surface one:

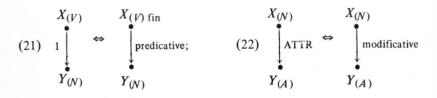

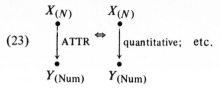

(23)

(*N* stands for a noun, V_{fin} for a finite verb, *A* for an adjective, and Num f‹ r a numeral.)

(b) The replacement of a deep node by a surface relation:

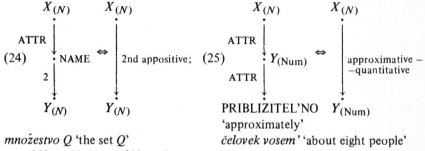

(24) *množestvo Q* 'the set *Q*'
gorod Nansi 'the city of Nancy'

(25) *čelovek vosem'* 'about eight people'

(c) The replacement of a deep relation by a surface node:

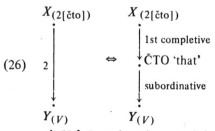

(26)

obeščal, čto primet 'promised that he would receive'

(the notation $X_{(2[\text{čto}])}$ indicates a lexeme whose second deep-syntactic valence slot is filled in the SSS by the conjunction ČTO 'that'; this information is stored in the lexicon).

In addition, the syntactic rules perform the following operation:

(d) The elimination of DSS nodes which occur in deep-anaphoric relations and should not be expressed in the text:

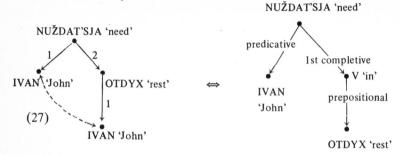

(i.e., *Ivan nuždaetsja v otdyxe* 'John needs rest', but not **Ivan nuždaetsja v svoëm otdyxe* 'John needs his own rest').

2. The transfer of information from components 2–4 of the deep-syntactic representation to the corresponding components of the surface-syntactic representation.

(IIb) The transition from the surface-syntactic representation of a sentence to all alternative linearly ordered sequences of deep-morphological word-form representations. Here the following five operations are performed.

1. 'SSS morphologization', i.e., the determination of all syntactically conditioned morphological features by means of rules such as (28) and (29):

(28)

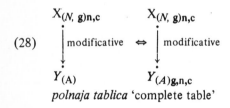

X (a noun) has no numeral depending on it; g, n, c stand for gender, number, and case; A is an adjective, as above.

Table 1   *Pattern of simple noun phrase in Russian*

1	2	3	4	5	6
coord. conjunction	neg. or restr. particle	preposition	quantifier	demonstr. adjective	cardinal numeral
ili 'or'	*ne* 'not'	*iz* 'from'	*nekotoryx* 'some (of)'	*ètix* 'these'	*vos'mi* 'eight'

$$X_{(Pr,2[c])} \qquad X_{(Pr,2[c])}$$

(29) $\Big|$ prepositional ⇔ $\Big|$ prepositional

$$Y_{(N)} \qquad Y_{(N)}\ c$$

v tablice 'in the table'

($X_{(Pr,(2[c])}$ is a preposition governing the case c)

As a result we can obtain deep-morphological representations (DMR's) of word-forms in the SSS nodes.

2. 'SSS linearization', i.e., the determination of the linear order of the word-form DMR's (word order) for subtrees of the SSS corresponding to clauses (within a complex sentence) by means of rules of the following three types (Mel'čuk 1967a):

-- Determination of word order in simple phrases in accordance with patterns of the type shown in Table 1 (bottom of pp. 236−237).

– Determination of the order of simple phrases within derived (full, or compound) phrases.

– Determination of the order of derived phrases within clauses, taking into account topicalization and a number of other intricately interacting factors.

3. Combination of the DMR strings which correspond to clauses into a single DMR string for the whole sentence.

4. Introduction of pronouns into the DMR string (= pronominalization).[6]

5. Obligatory and optional ellipses carried out on the full DMR string.

(*Table 1 continued*)

7	8	9	10	11
possess. adjective	ordinal adjective	adjective	head noun	apposition
našix 'our'	*vtoryx* 'second'	*važnyx* 'important'	*formul* 'formulae'	*Z* 'Z'

(III) The *morphological component* establishes – also in two steps – the correspondence between the deep-morphological representations of a word-form and the word-form itself in phonemic transcription.

(IIIa) The transition from a DMR of a word-form to the SMR of this word-form, i.e., to a string of morphemes and morphological operations; this is done by means of rules such as:

(30) $T_{(N,p)n,c} \Leftrightarrow \{T\}_{(p)} + \{N.C\}$

(T is a stem; n,c represent number and case; p is a set of combinational properties of the stem supplied by the lexicon and called 'syntactics').

An example of the DMR ⟺ SMR transformation according to rule (30):

(31) $\text{PRIEM`reception'}_{(N,p)\text{sing,acc}} \Leftrightarrow \{PRIEM\}_{(p)} + \{SING. ACC\}$

See also two further deep-morphological rules, each with a corresponding example:

(32) $T_{(A,\,p)\text{g,sing,short}} \Leftrightarrow \{T\}_{(p)} + \{SHORT. G. SING\}$

(33)   TVERDYJ 'firm' (A,p) neut, sing, short ⟺ $\{TVERDYJ\} + \{SHORT. NEUT. SING\}$

(34) $T_{(V,\,p)\text{ ind, perf, fut, 3s}} \Leftrightarrow \{T\}_{(p)} + \{PERF\} + \{IND. NON-PAST 3 SING\}$

(35)   NAXODIT' 'find' (V,p) perf, ind, fut, non-refl, 3 sing ⟺ $\{NAXODIT'\} + \{PERF\} + \{IND. NON-PAST 3 SING\}$

(since the perfective future in Russian is formally constructed like the present).

(IIIb) The transition from the SMR of a word-form to its phonemic transcription; this is performed by means of four groups of rules (Mel'čuk 1967b, d, 1968; Es'kova *et al*. 1971):

1. Morphemo-morphic rules of the following type:

(36) $\{PRIEM \text{ 'reception'}\}_{(p_1)} \Leftrightarrow /\text{pr,ijom}/_{(p_1)}$

(37) $\{TVERDYJ \text{ 'firm'}\}_{(p_2)} \Leftrightarrow /\text{tv,ord}/_{(p_2)}$

(38) $\{SING. ACC\} \Leftrightarrow /\emptyset/$ | either decl. II, masc, inanimate (*dom* 'house') or decl. III, masc/fem (*put'* 'way, road', *noč'* 'night')

$\Leftrightarrow /a/$ | either decl. II, animate (*kota* 'cat') or decl. III, neut. (*vremja* 'time')

(39) $\{SHORT. NEUT. SING\} \Leftrightarrow /o/$

(40) $\{NAXODIT' \text{ 'find'}\} + \{PERF\} \Leftrightarrow /\text{najd}/$ | **not** past
$\Leftrightarrow /\text{našed}/$ | past participle
$\Leftrightarrow /\text{našol}/$ | past **and not** participle

(41) {IND. NON-PAST 3 SING} ⇔ /ot/ | conj. I

                        ⇔ /it/ | conj. II

(42) {ON 'he'} + {SING. NOM} ⇔ /on/

(43) {ON 'he'} ⇔ (j) | | **not** after a preposition

         ⇔ /n/ | **not nom** | after a preposition.

2. Accentuation rules perform transformations of the following type:

(44) /pr,ijom + $\emptyset$/ ⇒ /pr,íjom + $\emptyset$/ ⇒ /pr,ijóm + $\emptyset$/

(45) /tv,ord + o/ ⇒ /tv,órd + o/

3. Morphonemic rules perform different kinds of morphologically conditioned phoneme alterations:

(46)   /d/ ⇒ /ž/ (/tv,órd/ – /tv,órže/) | in certain morphs

(47)   /c/ ⇒ /č/ (/pt,ica/ – /pt,íčka/) | only, depending

(48) $\left\{\begin{matrix}/t/\\/d/\end{matrix}\right\} \Rightarrow \Lambda \left(\begin{matrix}/pl,ot + u/ - /pl,ó + 1/\\/v,od + ú/ - /v,ó + 1/\end{matrix}\right)$ | on their syntactics

4. Phonological rules perform morphologically unconditioned phonemic transformations such as the following:

(49)

$$/C_{[\text{voiced}]}\left\{\begin{matrix}C_{[\text{-voiced}]} \,/\\ \#\end{matrix}\right\} \Rightarrow /C_{[\text{-voiced}]}\left\{\begin{matrix}C_{[\text{-voiced}]} \,/\\ \#\end{matrix}\right\}$$

(# stands for the final pause, i.e. the end of a word-form.)

IV. The *phonological component* establishes the correspondence between the phonemic and the phonetic transcription of a word-form.

V. The *graphico-orthographic component* establishes the correspondence between the phonemic transcription of a word-form and its spelling. Its rules have the form:

(50) /Xja/ ⇔ /X/ Я   (/strujá/ *струя*)

(51) /Xju/ ⇔ /X/ Ю   /X/ is not a consonant   (/strujú/ *струю*)

(52) /Xji/ ⇔ /X/ И   (/struji/ *струи*)

(53) /jX/ ⇔ Й /X/ | /X/ is not a vowel   (/kráj/ *край*)

(54) /C,j/ ⇒ /C/ Ь /j/ | /C/ is a consonant   (/sv,in,já/*свинья*)

(55) /C,a/ ⇒ /C/ Я   (/m'áso/ *мясо*)

4. SOME LINGUISTIC IMPLICATIONS OF THE MEANING ⟺ TEXT MODEL

Work on the Meaning ⟺ Text Model has resulted in a number of interesting linguistic problems. I will only mention three of them here (cf. Mel'čuk and Žolkovskij 1970: 40-46).

I

One of the most important components of the MTM is the *lexicon*, which stores all the information (semantic, syntactic, morphological, phonological) about each word necessary for all the components of the model to be able to handle this word correctly. Such a lexicon, or dictionary, known as an *explanatory combinatorial dictionary*, was being developed for Russian for some years: see in particular Apresyan *et al.* 1969. Two entries from this type of dictionary are given below by way of illustration (due to lack of space, without any preliminary explanations: I trust the examples will be sufficiently obvious).

1. *OBEŠČAT'* 'to promise'

OBEŠČÁ|T', *obéščan, ju, eš'*, imperf.

1. *X obeščaet Y Z-u* '*X* promises *Y* to *Z*' = *X* explicitly causes *Z* to know that *Y*, with which *Z* is concerned and which depends on *X*, will occur and that *X* takes upon himself the obligation to cause it.

Cf. GARANTIROVAT' 'guarantee'; UGROŽAT' 'threaten'.

1 = *X*	2 = *Y*	3 = *Z*
who	what	to whom
N_{nom}	(1) N_{acc}	N_{dat}
	(2) V_{inf}	
	(3) *čto* + SENT	

(1) *X* and *Z* are persons.
(2) If *Y* = 2.2, then $M_1(Y) = X$ [$M_1(Y)$ is the first place, or first actant, of *Y*].

Ivan obeščal Petru knigu 'Ivan promised Peter a book'; *Ivan obeščal (Petru) dostat' (emu) knigu* 'Ivan promised (Peter) to get (him) ⟨ he would get (him) ⟩ a book'; *Ivan obeščal, čto kniga budet u Petra zavtra že* 'Ivan promised that Peter would have the book (no later than) tomorrow'.

Syn   : arch. bookish *sulit'* 'promise'; colloq.
                                      obeščat'sja

Syn∩   : *kljast'sja* 'vow'; *zaverjat'* 'assure';
                                      zarekat'sja 'promise not to, renounce';
                                      objazyvat'sja 'pledge oneself'

[Syn∩ stands for an inexact ('semantically intersecting') synonym]

$S_0 = S_2$: *obeščanie* 'a promise'

Sing = Perf   : colloq. *poobeščat'* 'have promised'

$Magn_2^{intens}$: *tvërdo* 'firmly'

$Magn_2^{quant}$ + AntiVer$_2$: *zolotye gory*//colloq. *naobeščat'* [N_{dat}
                                      N_{acc}], *naobeščat's tri koroba* [N_{dat}]
                                      'promise the sun and the stars, make a lot
                                      of (empty) promises' [*X* promises a lot of
                                      Y, but the speaker does not believe that
                                      the probability of *Y* is great]

Promise something in the near
  future ['tomorrow'] without
  fulfilling these promises   : *kormit'* [$N_{acc} = Z$] *zavtrakami* 'feed
                                      someone with (false) hopes'

Promise something instead of
  doing it   : *kormit' obeščanijami* 'feed with hopes'

One cannot rely on the
  fulfillment of that which
  has been promised   : *Obeščannogo (,govorjat,) tri goda ždut*
                                      (proverb), lit. 'You have to wait 3 years
                                      for what you've been promised' = 'Words
                                      are wind'

2. *X obeščaet Y Z-u* '*X* promises *Y* to *Z*' = *X* causes *Z* to conclude that *Y*,
which is connected with *X* by cause-and-effect relations, will occur.

1 = X	2 = Y	3 = Z
who	what	to whom

N_{nom} (1) N_{acc} N_{dat}
             (2) V_{inf} rare
             (3) *čto* + SENT
                 obligatory

(1) X is not a living being, Z is a person.
(2) If Y = 2.2, then $M_1(Y) = X$.
(3) 2.1: N is a predicate.

Begstvo obeščalo nam spasenie 'Flight promised us salvation' *Den' obeščal byt' tëplym* 'The day promised to be warm'.

Syn∩   : *predveščat'* 'portend, foreshadow';
                                predskazyvat' 'foretell, predict'
A_1 (promise a lot of something
good)   : *mnogoobeščajuščij* 'promising hopeful'

2. OBEŠČANIE *'a promise'*

OBEŠČÁNI|E, *ja*, neut. $S_{0,2}$ *(obeščat' 1)* [the fact that something is being promised and also that which is promised].
   Cf. GARANTIJA 'guarantee'; UGROZA 'threat'.

1 = X	2 = Y	3 = Z
whose	what	to whom

(1) N_{gen} (1) N_{gen} N_{dat}
(2) A_{poss} (2) V_{inf} rare
                 (3) *čto* + SENT

(1) X and Z are persons.
(2) If Y = 2.2, then $M_1(Y) = X$.
(3) Y = 2.1, only if O. depends on a
    lexical function verb [*dal obeščanie
    prixoda* 'gave promise of arrival', etc.]
(4) Impossible: 1.1,2 + 2.1.

Obeščanie Petra pridti 'Peter's promise to come'; *moë obeščanie, čto kniga budet zavtra* 'my promise that the book will come tomorrow'; *obeščanie vstreči* 'promise of a meeting'; but **ego obeščanie vstreči* 'his promise of a meeting' is impossible.

Syn   : bookish *posul* '(lavish) promise'
Syn∩   : *kljatva* 'vow'; *zaverenie* 'assurance';
                                slovo 'word'; *objazatel'stvo* 'obligation';
                                obet 'vow'; *zarok* 'pledge'
V_0 : *obeščat' 1* 'to promise'

Magn_1 : *toržestvennoe* 'solemn'

Magn_2 : *tvërdoe* 'firm'

AntiVer_2 : *pustoe* 'empty'; slang *lipovoe* 'false'

$\text{AntiMagn} + \text{AntiVer}_2$: *legkomyslennoe* 'hasty'

$\text{Magn}_2^{\text{quant}} + \text{AntiVer}_2$: *širokoveščatel'nye* 'wide, alluring' | *O.* in plural

Oper_1 : *davat'* $[N_{\text{dat}} \sim e]$ 'give'

$\text{Liqu}_1\text{Oper}_1$: *brat' obratno* ⟨ = *nazad* ⟩ $[(svoë) \sim e]$ 'take back'

$\text{Perm}_3\text{Liqu}_1\text{Oper}_1$: *osvoboždat'* $[N_{\text{acc}} = X \, ot \sim ja]$ 'release from'

Oper_3 : *polučat'* $[ot \, N_{\text{gen}} \sim e]$ 'receive from'

$\text{Oper}_1(\text{Magn}_2^{\text{quant}} + \text{AntiVer}_2$: *davat' kuču* $[\sim j]$ 'give a bunch of, a lot of'

Func_2 : *sostojat'* $[v \, N_{\text{prep}}]$ 'consist in'

Real_1 : *vypolnjat', deržat', sderživat'* $[(svoë) \sim e]$ 'keep one's promise' | M_2 $[O.]$ is an action of X

not Real_1 : *ne vypolnjat', ne deržat', ne sderživat'* $[(svoë) \sim e]$ 'not fulfill, keep one's promise' [not do what one promised], *narušat'* $[(svoë) \sim e]$ 'break one's promise' [do what one had promised not to do] | $M_2 (O.)$ is an action of X

Fact_0 : *sbyvat'sja* 'come true, be realized' | $M_2 (O.)$ is not an action of X

II

Investigating the relations between meaning and text within the framework of our work on MTM — i.e. between *signifiés* and *signifiants* of linguistic units — has made it possible to take a new approach toward problems of word-derivation and treat the latter against the background of the universal scheme of all the relations possible between words with respect to their meaning and form. Since both the *signifiés* (*'A', 'B'*), and the *signifiants* (*A, B*) of two lexemes can (1) coincide (=), (2) be contained one within the other (⊃), (3) intersect (∩) and (4) have no part in common, we have 17 possible formal-semantic relations between words (Mel'čuk 1968).

Both 'classical' facts, i.e., specifically, homonymy (*A = B*, *'A' ∩ 'B' = ∅*), absolute synonymy (*A ∩ B = ∅*, *'A' = 'B'*), 'normal' word-derivation (*A ⊃ B*, *'A' ⊃ 'B'*) etc., and certain little studied phenomena such as 'contrary word-derivation': *A ⊃ B*, but *'A' ⊂ 'B'*, are provided for in the formally derived system. Examples of contrary derivation:

(1) *radovat'sja* 'be glad of' = 'experience emotion X' – *radovat'* 'make glad of' = 'cause to experience emotion X' (and many other similar pairs);

(2) *geolog-ij-a* 'geology' = 'the science of the Earth. . .' – *geolog* 'geologist' = 'a specialist in the science of the Earth...' (and many other pairs);

(3) *A tvёrž-e B* 'A is harder than B' = 'the hardness of A exceeds the hardness of B' – *A tvёrd* 'A is hard' = 'the hardness of A exceeds the norm established for the objects of the class A'. (*N.B.*: 'tvёrže' ≠ 'bolee tvёrdyj', i.e. in Russian there exists a difference between 'harder' and 'more hard' : *A bolee tvёrdyj, čem B* = 'A is hard, and A is harder than B'; but from *A tvёrže B* it does not follow that A is hard: A can be soft, but still harder than B.)

At the same time, such relations as 'moskvič' : 'moskvička' ≠ 'laborant' : 'laborantka' can of course also be easily described – since *moskvič* $\subset$ *moskvič-k-a,* but 'moskvič' $\not\subset$ ˙moskvička' ('moskvič' = 'a male resident of Moscow', 'moskvička' = 'a female resident of Moscow'), while *laborant* $\subset$ *laborant-k-a* and 'laborant' $\subset$ 'laborantka' ('laborant' = 'a technical laboratory worker', 'laborantka' = 'a female technical laboratory worker'),[7] etc.

III

Work on MTM has led me to think of a linguistic sign as a *three-dimensional* entity, or an ordered triple

$$A = \langle A, \text{'}A\text{'}, \Sigma_A \rangle,$$

where A is the *signifiant*, 'A' the *signifié*, and Σ_A is all information about the combinatorial properties of the sign, which in its totality may be spoken of as *syntactics*; cf. above, page 238, rule (30). (Information about part of speech, gender of nouns, lexical functions, etc. belongs to syntactics.) If we consider syntactics an autonomous component of the linguistic sign, on a level with the *signifié* and *signifiant*, we can provide natural enough formal descriptions of phenomena such as English *the cook* – *to cook*, known as *conversion*. I define conversion as a linguistic sign whose *signifiant* is an *operation on the syntactics* of other signs (cf. meaningful alternation: a sign whose *signifiant* is an operation on the *signifiants* of other signs).

Examples of conversion:

$K_1 = \langle V \Rightarrow N^\beta$; 'he who. . .'; $\Sigma_{K_1} \rangle$ (*to cook* – *the cook, to bore* – *the bore*);

$K_2 = \langle N \Rightarrow V$; 'cause to act upon. . .'; $\Sigma_{K_2} \rangle$ (*the bomb* – *to bomb, the machine gun* – *to machine-gun*)

It seems possible to construct a calculus of all conceivable morphological means, or processes, in natural languages.

ACKNOWLEDGMENTS

The first draft of this paper has been read by and discussed with S. Ja. Fitialov, A. Ja. Dikovskij, O. S. Kulagina, N. G. Mixajlova, L. S. Modina, and M. K. Valiev; for helpful comments on the final version I am indebted to Ju. D. Apresjan, L. N. Iordanskaja, N. V. Pertsov, V. J. Rozencvejg, and A. K. Žolkovskij. It is with great pleasure that I acknowledge here their valuable help and sympathetic understanding. Last, but not least, I would like to express my gratitude to Ferenc Kiefer for everything he has done in order to have this paper published in English, and to Johanna Nichols, who has read the English version and made it more readable.

NOTES

Reprinted with some modifications from: F. Kiefer (ed.), *Trends in Soviet Theoretical Linguistics*, 1973 (Dordrecht: D. Reidel), 33-57.

1. Thus we meet here with the essential *asymmetry* of texts and meanings: our model should catch all formal, i.e. linguistic, anomalies of a text, but it does not deal with semantic anomalies.
2. As is widely done: cf. S. Lamb's stratificational grammar, the *Mehrstufiges generatives system* of P. Sgall, and others.
3. The use of a network to represent the semantic content of an utterance is by no means a novelty in linguistic analysis. Suffice it to mention here the pioneer papers Gladkij et al. 1961 and Babickij 1965, as well as Hutchins 1971 (with further references), and many well-known publications in and on inference and question-answering systems (by Quillian, Bobrow, Simmons, Schank, Klein and others).
4. The term 'transformation', as used throughout this paper, is a typical misnomer. What is really meant is CORRESPONDENCE, i.e., a basically static relationship between meanings and the texts carrying them. Under the Meaning-Text approach, static correspondences are strictly separated from all the procedures that actually use them. Only the correspondences are included in our present MTM. Now, in 1983, I consistently avoid employing the term 'transformation' at all.
5. The variables X, Y, Z that appear over elements of rules (8)–(11) correspond to the same variables in syntactic rules (14)–(17) below. When a syntactic rule is applied, its own variables are filled with the corresponding elements of the lexical rule in operation.
6. At present, I think that pronominalization belongs to deep syntax rather than to surface syntax. That is, now I include the introduction of pronouns into the transition from the deep-syntactic representations of a sentence to its surface-syntactic representation (Step IIa), so that the corresponding rules are part of the deep-syntactic component of our model.
7. In Russian, we have both *Ona laborant* and *Ona laborantka,* but not **Ona moskvič.*
8. The direction of the arrow in this and similar cases is determined by the relative semantic complexities of the two words in question.

REFERENCES

Apresyan, Yu. D., Mel'čuk, I.A., and Žolkovsky, A.K.
1969   'Semantics and Lexicography: Towards a New Type of Unilingual Dictionary'.
        In: F. Kiefer, ed., *Studies in Syntax and Semantics*, 1-33 (Dordrecht: D. Reidel).
Babickij, K. I.
1965   'O sintaksičeskoj sinonimii predloženij v estestvennyx jazykax', *Naučno-
        texničeskaja informacija* (6): 29-34.
Es'kova, N.A., Mel'čuk, I.A., and Sannikov, V. Z.
1971   *Formal'naja model' russkoj morfologii. I. Formoobrazovanie suščestvitel'nyx
        i prilagatel'nyx* (Moscow: Russian Language Institute, AN SSSR).
Gladkij, A. V., and Mel'čuk, I. A.
1969   *Tree Grammars* (Stockholm: International Conference on Computational
        Linguistics. Preprint No. 1).
1971   'Grammatiki derev'ev. I. Opyt formalizacii preobrazovanij sintaksičeskix
        struktur estestvennogo jazyka', *Informacionnye voprosy semiotiki,
        lingvistiki i avtomatičeskogo perevoda* 1: 16-41 (Moscow: All-Union Institute
        of Scientific and Technological Information, AN SSR).
1974   'Grammatiki derev'ev. II. K postroeniju Δ-grammatik dlja russkogo jazyka',
        Informacionnye voprosy semiotiki, lingvistiki i avtomatičeskogo perevoda
        4: 4-29 (Moscow: All-Union Institute of Scientific and Technological Information,
        AN SSSR).
Gladkij, A.V., M.V. Rybakova, and T.I. Šed'ko
1961   *Sxema semantičeskogo jazyka-posrednika dlja zapisi matematičeskix tekstov*
        (Moscow: All-Union Institute of Scientific and Technological Information,
        AN SSSR).
Hutchins, W. J.
1971   *The Generation of Syntactic Structures from a Semantic Base* (Amsterdam,
        London: North-Holland).
Mel'čuk, I. A.
1967a   'Ordre des mots en synthèse automatique des textes russes', *TA
        Informations* (2): 65-84.
1967b   'Model' sprjaženija v ispanskom jazyke', *Mašinnyj perevod i prikladnaja
        lingvistika* 10: 21-53; also in: *Soviet Papers in Formal Linguistics*, ed. by
        V. Ju Rozensveig, 1973, Vol. I (Frankfurt: Athenäum).
1967c   'K voprosu o 'vnešnix različitel'nyx èlementax': semantičeskie parametry i
        opisanie leksičeskoj sočetaemosti', *To Honor Roman Jakobson . . .* ,
        1340-1361 (The Hague: Mouton).
1967d   'Model' sklonenija vengerskix suščestvitel'nyx', *Problemy strukturnoj
        lingvisticki*, 344-373 (Moscow: Nauka).
1968   'Stroenie jazykovyx znakov i vozmožnye formal'no-smyslovye otnošenija
        meždu nimi,' *Izvestija AN SSSR*, Serija jazyka i literatury 27 (5): 426-438.
1970   'Towards a Functioning Model of Language'. In: M. Bierwisch and K. E.
        Heidolph, eds., *Progress in Linguistics*, 198-207 (The Hague: Mouton).
1974   *Opyt teorii lingvističeskix modelej Smysl ⟺ Tekst'* (Moscow: Nauka).
Mel'čuk, I. A., and Zolkovskij, A. K.
1970   'Towards a Functioning 'Meaning-Text' Model of Language', *Linguistics*
        57: 10-47.

Žolkovskij, A. K., and Mel'čuk, I. A.
1967   'O semantičeskom sinteze', *Problemy kibernetiki* 19: 177-238.
1970   'Sur la synthèse sémantique', *TA Informations* (2): 1-85 (translation of the preceding article).

László Desző
Studies on Syntactic Typology and Contrastive Grammar

1982. 15 x 23 cm. 307 pages.
Hardback. DM 84,−; US $38.25 ISBN 90 279 3108 9
(Janua Linguarum, Series Maior 89)

At present, typology is one of the most rapidly developing branches of general linguistics. Linguistics describing or comparing various languages recognize the necessity of applying its results. Many linguists, however, know only the past stages because of the lack of a comprehensive book on present-day typology. On its part, this volume of studies introduces the reader to some major fields of grammatical typology: sentence structure and its expression with different types of case systems, ordering sentence constituents, etc.

The author presents the results of the general typology of the subsystems and demonstrates their application to the description and comparison of various languages. When dealing with theoretical and methodological questions, he comments on such fundamental issues as theory, method, metalanguage, laws, research program from the point of view of a typologist. He studies the various approaches to the integration of the results of present-day typology required by the development of both typology and contrastive linguistics. The optimum form of its application to descriptive and contrastive or comparative studies is typological characterization and the comparison of the characterized individual languages.

Bohumil Trnka
Selected Papers in Structural Linguistics

Contributions to English and General Linguistics Written in the Years 1928−1978
Edited by Vilém Fried

1982. 15 x 23 cm. XII, 392 pages.
Hardback. DM 126,−; US $57.50 ISBN 90 279 3148 8
(Janua Linguarum, Series Maior 88)

Collection of fifty-one papers by Bohumil Trnka, the cofounder and first secretary of the Cercle linguistique de Prague. Some of the papers were originally published in Czech and appear here for the first time in English translation. As a consistent follower of the structural and functional approach characteristic of the Prague School, the author has applied this method of analysis both to the diachronic and synchronic phenomena of language.

The papers are grouped into five sections − General Linguistics; Synchronic Phonology; Statistical Linguistics: Historical Linguistics: Diachronic Phonology and Morphology; and Synchronic Morphology, Syntax and Style. An Afterword by Roman Jakobson follows.

Prices are subject to change without notice

mouton publishers
Berlin · New York · Amsterdam

George Horn

Lexical-Functional Grammar

1983. 15 x 23 cm. IX, 394 pages.
Hardback. DM 140,−; US $63.75 ISBN 90 279 3169 0
(Trends in Linguistics, Studies and Monographs 21)

The analysis outlined in this monograph is formulated in the context of the major developments in linguistic theory over the past decade stemming from the proposal of the so-called Lexicalist Hypothesis of Chomsky. The most significant product of linguistic research during this period has been the development and expansion of the lexical component and consequent reorganization and reformulation of the rules of the transformational-generative model, in which this component has been assigned many of the tasks formerly associated with the syntactic component.

More recently, various counterproposals to Chomsky's analysis have been suggested. Perhaps the most important of these was developed by Bresnan, the key feature of which is the virtually complete reduction of the syntactic component.

The present work is an attempt to extend and reformulate certain of Bresnan's and Chomsky's ideas, combining the basic organization of Chomsky's model, in which lexical and non-lexical operations are clearly distinguished, with a non-syntactic account of bound anaphora, control, and NP movement phenomena. The proposed model provides a framework in which universal generalizations can be captured, and language variation can be accounted for without the complex machinery of Chomsky's current analysis, at the same time maintaining distinctions that are obscured in Bresnan's purely lexical analysis.

Prices are subject to change without notice

mouton publishers
Berlin · New York · Amsterdam